FIRST
FAMILY

Also by
CASSANDRA A. GOOD

Founding Friendships

gton's Heirs and

the Making of America

FIRST FAMILY

CASSANDRA A. GOOD

HANOVER
SQUARE
PRESS

HANOVER
SQUARE
PRESS™

Recycling programs
for this product may
not exist in your area.

ISBN-13: 978-1-335-44951-1

First Family

Copyright © 2023 by Cassandra Good

Hanover Square Press
22 Adelaide St. West, 41st Floor
Toronto, Ontario M5H 4E3, Canada
HanoverSqPress.com
BookClubbish.com

Printed in U.S.A.

Table of Contents

Note on Terminology

In this book, I use first names for the members of the Washington and Custis families and last names for others with whom they interacted. Note that Elizabeth Parke Custis went by "Betsey" as a young woman but "Eliza" after her marriage in 1796.

When discussing slavery, I have chosen my wording according to still-evolving standards in the historical profession at the time of publication. Rather than "owners" or "masters," I use the term "enslavers," and rather than slaves, "enslaved people." This shift in language recognizes the humanity of individuals held in bondage and the inability of any one person to truly "own" another. To avoid repetition, I occasionally use the term "bondspeople" in lieu of "enslaved people."

There are two terms for which historians are still debating the best substitutes: "runaway"/"running away" and "plantation." For the former, I describe enslaved people who fled bondage as having freed themselves; while some scholars currently use the phrase "self-emancipated," this term may obscure reality because it implies a legal process of emancipation. Finally, while I recognize the unduly positive connotations of "plantation," I find the current substitutes ("slave labor camp" or "forced labor camp") problematic in myriad other ways. Therefore, I have used "plantation" in this book, and I believe it will be clear to readers that these were not the romantic places of popular imagination.

Family Trees

NOTE: These family trees are not comprehensive; rather, they cover all relevant people who are mentioned in this book and some who are not mentioned here but appear in the Custis grandchildren's correspondence. They are drawn from numerous sources, including family trees compiled by Mount Vernon Historian Emeritus Mary Thompson, Tudor Place staff, and the Martha Washington Papers; Alice Torbert's *Eleanor Calvert and Her Circle*; family bibles and correspondence; newspaper obituaries; will and probate documents; and gravestones.

The children of Custis men and enslaved women are shown on page 18 and the men's names are marked with an asterisk (★). These were sexually exploitative relationships and were not openly acknowledged or documented during the men's lifetimes. Study in this area is ongoing and subject to change. These sections of the tree are based on careful research, documentation, and collaboration with scholars at Mount Vernon and Arlington House as well as the descendant community.

FAMILY TREE OF GEORGE WASHINGTON

Augustine Washington (1694-1743)

m **Jane Butler** (1699-1729)

— **Lawrence Washington** (c1718-1752)

— **Augustine Washington II** (1720-1762) *m* **Anne Aylett** (d. 1773)

  └── William Augustine Washington (1757-1810)

m **Mary Ball** (1708-1789)

— **GEORGE WASHINGTON** (1732-1799) *m* **MARTHA DANDRIDGE CUSTIS** (1731-1802)

— **Elizabeth "Betty" Washington** (1733-1797) *m* **Fielding Lewis** (1725-1781)

— Fielding Lewis Jr (1751-1803) *m* Ann Alexander (1756-1809)

— John Lewis (1785-1814)

— Charles Lewis (1775-1829)

— 5 other children

— George Lewis (1757-1821)

— Betty Lewis (1765-1830) *m* Charles Carter (1765-1829)

— Lawrence Lewis (1767-1839) *m* Eleanor Parke Custis (1779-1852)—*see* Custis tree

— Robert Lewis (1769-1829)

— Howell Lewis (1771-1822)

— **Samuel Washington** (1734-1781) *m* **Anne Steptoe** (1739-1777)

— George Steptoe Washington (1771-1809)

— Lawrence Augustine Washington (1774-1824)

— Harriot Washington (1776-1822)

— **John Augustine Washington I** (1736-1787) *m* **Hannah Bushrod** (1738-1801)

— Mary

— Jane Washington (1759-1791) *m* William Augustine Washington

— 6 children

— Bushrod Washington (1762-1829) *m* Julia Ann Blackburn (1768-1829)

— Corbin Washington (c1765-c1799) *m* Hannah Lee (1766-c1801)

— John Augustine Washington II (1792-1832) *m* Jane Charlotte Blackburn (1786-1855)

— John Augustine Washington III (1821-1861)

— 6 other children

— 5 other children

— **Charles Washington** (1738-1799) *m* **Mildred Thornton** (c1737-1804)

— George Augustine Washington (c1758-1793) *m* Frances "Fanny" Bassett (1767-1796)

[niece of Martha Washington]

— 3 more children

— **Mildred Washington** (1739-1740)

CUSTIS FAMILY TREE

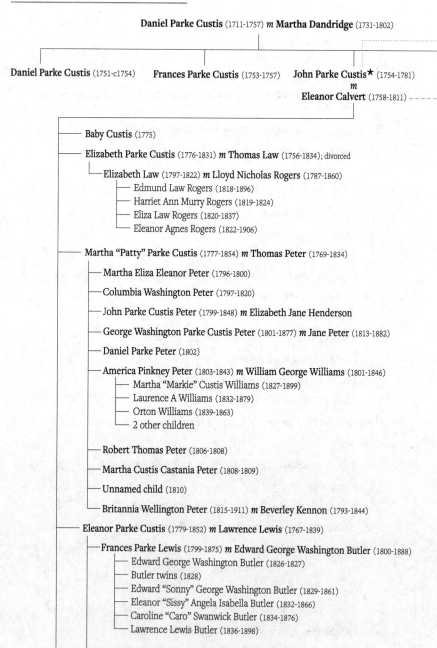

Daniel Parke Custis (1711-1757) *m* Martha Dandridge (1731-1802)

Daniel Parke Custis (1751-c1754) Frances Parke Custis (1753-1757) John Parke Custis★ (1754-1781)
m
Eleanor Calvert (1758-1811)

- Baby Custis (1775)
- Elizabeth Parke Custis (1776-1831) *m* Thomas Law (1756-1834); divorced
  - Elizabeth Law (1797-1822) *m* Lloyd Nicholas Rogers (1787-1860)
    - Edmund Law Rogers (1818-1896)
    - Harriet Ann Murry Rogers (1819-1824)
    - Eliza Law Rogers (1820-1837)
    - Eleanor Agnes Rogers (1822-1906)
- Martha "Patty" Parke Custis (1777-1854) *m* Thomas Peter (1769-1834)
  - Martha Eliza Eleanor Peter (1796-1800)
  - Columbia Washington Peter (1797-1820)
  - John Parke Custis Peter (1799-1848) *m* Elizabeth Jane Henderson
  - George Washington Parke Custis Peter (1801-1877) *m* Jane Peter (1813-1882)
  - Daniel Parke Peter (1802)
  - America Pinkney Peter (1803-1843) *m* William George Williams (1801-1846)
    - Martha "Markie" Custis Williams (1827-1899)
    - Laurence A Williams (1832-1879)
    - Orton Williams (1839-1863)
    - 2 other children
  - Robert Thomas Peter (1806-1808)
  - Martha Custis Castania Peter (1808-1809)
  - Unnamed child (1810)
  - Britannia Wellington Peter (1815-1911) *m* Beverley Kennon (1793-1844)
- Eleanor Parke Custis (1779-1852) *m* Lawrence Lewis (1767-1839)
  - Frances Parke Lewis (1799-1875) *m* Edward George Washington Butler (1800-1888)
    - Edward George Washington Butler (1826-1827)
    - Butler twins (1828)
    - Edward "Sonny" George Washington Butler (1829-1861)
    - Eleanor "Sissy" Angela Isabella Butler (1832-1866)
    - Caroline "Caro" Swanwick Butler (1834-1876)
    - Lawrence Lewis Butler (1836-1898)

(child by enslaved woman: see next page)

Martha "Patsy" Parke Custis (1756-1773)

(children from second marriage: see next page)

— Martha Betty Lewis (1801-1802)

— Lawrence Fielding Lewis (1802)

— Lorenzo Lewis (1803-1847) *m* Esther Maria Coxe (1804-1855)
  — George Washington Lewis (1829-1885)
  — John Redman Coxe Lewis (1834-1898)
  — Lawrence Fielding Lewis (1834-1857)
  — Edward Parke Custis Lewis (1837-1892)
  — Charles Conrad Lewis (1839-1859)
  — Henry Llewellyn Daingerfield Lewis (1843-1893)

— Eleanor Agnes Freire Lewis (1805-1820)

— Fielding Augustine Lewis (1807-1809)

— George Washington Custis Lewis (1810-1811)

— Mary Eliza Angela (1813-1839) *m.* Charles Magill Conrad (1804-1878)
  — Angela Lewis Conrad (1836-1837)
  — Charles Angelo Conrad (1837-1892)
  — Lawrence Lewis Conrad (1839-1883)

— Custis twins (1780)   *(children by enslaved women: see next page)*

— George Washington Parke Custis★ (1781-1857) *m* Mary Lee Fitzhugh (1788-1853)

— Baby Custis (1805)

— Martha Elizabeth Ann Custis (1806-1807)

— Mary Anna Randolph Custis (1807-1873) *m* Robert E. Lee (1807-1870)
  — George Washington Custis Lee (1832-1913)
  — Mary Custis Lee (1835-1918)
  — William Henry Fitzhugh Lee (1837-1891)
  — Ann Carter Lee (1839-1862)
  — Eleanor Agnes Lee (1841-1873)
  — Robert E. Lee Jr. (1843-1914)
  — Mildred Childe Lee (1846-1905)

— Edwa Hill Carter Custis (1809-1810)

Eleanor Calvert *m* **David Stuart** (1753-1814)

- **Ann Calvert Stuart** (1784-1823) *m* **William Robinson** (1782-1857)
- **Sarah "Sally" Stuart** (1786-1870) *m* **Obediah Waite** (d. 1842)
- **Arianna Calvert Stuart** (1789-1855)
- **William Shalto/Sholto Stuart** (1792-1820)
- **Charles Calvert Stuart** (1794-1846) *m* **Cornelia Lee Tuberville**
- **Eleanor Calvert Stuart** (1796-1875)
- **Rosalie Eugenia Stuart** (1801-1886) *m* **William G. Webster** (1801-1869); divorced
- *Plus 7 children who died in infancy*

John Parke Custis ★ *by* **Ann/Nancy Costin Holmes**

- **William Costin** (1780-1842) *m* **Philadelphia Judge** (1779-1831)
  - Louisa Parke Costin (c1804-1831)
  - Ann Parke Costin (1807-?)
  - Charlotte Parke Costin (c1808-1880)
  - William Custis Parke Costin (c1813-c1888)
  - Harriet Parke Costin (1820-?)
  - George Calvert Parke Costin
  - Frances "Fanny" Parke Costin

George Washington Parke Custis ★ *by* [**Arianna?**] **Carter** (?)

- **Maria Carter** (1803-1886) *m* **Charles Syphax** (c1791-1867)

George Washington Parke Custis ★ *by* **Caroline Branham** (1764-1843)

- **Lucy Branham** (1806-?) *m?* **Harrison**
  - Robert H. Robinson (1824-1909)
  - Eugenia (1830-1897)
  - Sarah (1832-?)
  - Charles (c1843)

Prologue

ON A COLD DAY IN NEW YORK CITY IN THE
winter of 1789, a family prepared to sit for their portrait. This
was no ordinary family: it was President George Washington's.
They were America's very first "first family." They stood frozen in their poses before the artist in a rented house with luxurious mahogany furniture, rich carpets, and newly painted walls.
Through the windows, they could watch white-sailed ships make
their way down the East River. In the finished painting, it is the
Potomac River that curves gently through the background. In
the forefront, George and Martha sit across from each other at
a table with a map of the new District of Columbia unfurled.
George rests his arm on the shoulder of a young boy in a coral
suit standing at his side, while a girl in a white gown stands behind the table and next to Martha. Visible in the shadows of the
painting, an enslaved man stands behind the white family. When
the portrait was finally completed nearly a decade later, the artist,
Edward Savage, reproduced *The Washington Family* in thousands
of prints that made their way into homes across the country.[1]

In the late eighteenth and nineteenth centuries, everyone in
the new United States would have recognized these children.
But as far as most Americans in the twenty-first century know,

George Washington never had any children. Some may have read the words of George Washington's most famous eulogist: "AMERICANS! he had no child—BUT YOU,—and HE WAS ALL YOUR OWN."[2] Who, then, are these children; who was Washington's family? It was a question I started asking over a decade ago, when I first came across Washington family members in historic records. Clearly, I thought, what I needed was a family tree. As it turned out, this was no simple task.

There were no comprehensive family trees online. With further digging, I located a Washington descendant who had compiled just what I was looking for: a massive family tree that showed all the descendants of George Washington's father.[3] It arrived in the mail in a tall poster tube, and the document I opened stretched five feet long and two feet wide. The tree mapped out ten children (by two wives), forty grandchildren, one hundred thirty great-grandchildren, and around three hundred great-great-grandchildren. Sprawled out on the floor, I leaned down over the long document to read through the names. The children from the family portrait—who I had learned were Eleanor (Nelly) and George Washington (Wash) Parke Custis— weren't there.

The Custis children's names were absent for good reason: they were not blood-related to George Washington at all. They would only appear on a separate family tree for the Custis family, into which their grandmother (and future first lady) Martha had first married. Martha Dandridge had entered one of Virginia's wealthiest families when she wed Daniel Parke Custis in 1750. The pair had four children, but only the two youngest, John "Jacky" Parke Custis and Martha "Patsy" Parke Custis, survived past toddlerhood. When Daniel died suddenly in 1757, Martha became the wealthiest widow in the colony—a prime catch for a young man on the make like George Washington.

George and Martha married in 1759, when George was almost twenty-seven and Martha nearly twenty-eight. George's marriage to Martha propelled him into Virginia's upper gentry. Bringing his wife, her children, some of the eighty-four enslaved people she inherited, and her wealth to Mount Vernon, George expanded the house (inherited from his brother Lawrence, who died young) and profited off the labor of bondspeople to make his estate productive.[4] Martha maintained her role as the primary parent, with the often-absent George as a stern but loving stepfather to Jacky and Patsy Custis. Jacky was, his stepfather said, "a boy of good genius," but he was a lazy student who George lamented was more interested in "Dogs Horses & Guns" than learning. Jacky dropped out of one school after another. His sister Patsy had to stay close to home because she suffered from seizures, which her parents did everything they could to treat. Nonetheless, their "Sweet Innocent girl" (as George called her) died after a fit in 1773 at only seventeen.[5]

Soon after, Jacky married—against his stepfather's advice, who felt the twenty-year-old Jacky was too immature and irresponsible—a young Maryland woman named Eleanor Calvert. Eleanor and Jacky had seven children, four of whom survived, before Jacky died suddenly in 1781. Elizabeth (Eliza), Martha (Patty), Nelly, and Wash Parke Custis, then, were in today's parlance George Washington's stepgrandchildren. While Americans in the eighteenth and early nineteenth centuries did not use the language of "stepfamilies," such blended families were quite common due to high death and remarriage rates.[6]

With four children aged five or under on her hands, Eleanor Calvert Custis might well have been overwhelmed. Martha, missing having children in the house, offered to take Nelly and Wash and raise them at Mount Vernon with George. This would not have been unusual at the time, and Eleanor and her elder daughters lived close by and visited regularly. There was as of yet no legal form of adoption, but people referred to Nelly and Wash as George's "adopted" children. Nonetheless, this was also a time when blood relationships were central to legal definitions of family and inheritance. Thus George Washington could essentially adopt two children and raise them as his own, but "have" no children.[7]

Indeed, while never having any biological children of their

own, George and Martha raised and supported other children beyond the Custis grandchildren. They took in a bevy of nieces and nephews over the course of their decades together. Both George and Martha had numerous siblings and, in George's case, half siblings. A rotating cast of orphaned nieces and nephews, or those whose parents had too many children at home to support, made temporary homes with the Washingtons. Others received considerable financial support and advice. It was Bushrod Washington, the eldest son of George's late eldest full brother, who inherited the famous Washington estate of Mount Vernon.[8]

Is Edward Savage's family portrait really *the* Washington family, then? It turned out that the answer to my question—who was George Washington's family?—was far more complicated than I imagined. Over more than a decade, I have searched through images, objects, houses, financial records, letters, and diaries scattered over museums and archives from Boston to New Orleans. I read nineteenth-century newspaper and magazine articles, spoke to living descendants, and conferred with archivists and fellow historians. I spent months researching at Mount Vernon, working through papers in its library vault and talking with curators and librarians there. As the pieces fell into place, I found that there was no single definition of George Washington's family or who counted as his descendants. But one thing was clear: for Americans from the Revolution to the Civil War, the Custis grandchildren were George Washington's family.

This was no accident: it was the result of choices that George, Martha, the Custises, and the Washington nieces and nephews all made.[9] While George supported many of his nephews and nieces, his closest emotional bonds were with Martha's grandchildren. They, especially Nelly and Wash, spent the most time living with him, hearing his stories, and experiencing life as the nation's first "first family." Martha prioritized keeping the family together, bringing the children with them as the capital city moved from New York to Philadelphia. The public visibility all four siblings gained during the presidency cemented their role as George's family early on in their lives. None of George's blood-related family members ever had this kind of close access and public recognition.

After George Washington's death, the Custises and the Washington nieces and nephews continued on diverging paths. While a Washington nephew inherited Mount Vernon, the house was an empty shell when he moved in; all the Washington furniture, china, clothing, and other household objects that quickly attained the status of relics ended up in the Custis grandchildren's hands. The grandchildren, then, had both the family stories and belongings that could keep George's memory and legacy alive. They chose to use those strategically at every step, while the Washington nieces and nephews lived largely in obscurity as small Virginia planters. When Bushrod Washington, inheritor of Mount Vernon, died in 1829, his obituary did not even mention his relationship to his famous uncle. His nephew and grandnephew who next owned Mount Vernon, John Augustine Washington II and III, similarly preferred to stay out of the limelight.[10]

It was the Custis grandchildren, then, who took center stage as George Washington's family. They nurtured their celebrity as the first family, contributing to political discussions, inviting visitors to their homes to share stories and display relics, and serving as representatives of George Washington's Revolutionary legacy at social and political events. None of them had any particular talents or accomplishments in their own right; their fame came from who they were and how they shaped their public personas, not what they had done. It is hard to overstate just how famous George Washington was in the late eighteenth century: one writer has called him "America's first celebrity in chief."[11] The Custises simply needed to grasp onto and perpetuate that celebrity by presenting themselves as his surrogates and keepers of his legacy. It didn't hurt Nelly and Wash that the Savage family portrait remained ubiquitous in America until the Civil War, copied by young women in needlework and printed as lithographs in versions that subtly changed with the times. Many Americans had some version of this image in their homes, and those who did not surely recognized it.

Interestingly, the shadowy figure of the enslaved man in the background of the painting disappeared from several versions of the image in the antebellum era. Americans preferred not to see the first president as an enslaver.[12] Bondspeople had not disappeared from the Custises' lives, however. Most of the enslaved at Mount Vernon had been owned by the Custis estate, not George Washington himself, and they remained in bondage to the Custises after George and Martha died. All four grandchildren lived with and depended upon enslaved people and their children who had come from Mount Vernon, although few records of these bondspeople survive. The Custises also had Black relatives born into slavery through the sexual violation of enslaved women. The latest research points to the probability that their father Jacky had a son, William Costin, with an enslaved woman, and Wash Custis had numerous children with bondswomen as well. While Costin and several of Wash's mixed-race children gained their freedom, the Custises excluded them all from the siblings' quest to remain known as George Washington's family. In that sense, they were truly erased.

The fact that Americans today know little to nothing about the white members of the Custis family is not an act of deliberate erasure, but rather a subtler process of forgetting. Who were these celebrated siblings, and how did they handle being the first "first family"? How would they use the fame and power that came from their ties to George Washington; how could they live up to the Revolutionary legacy? What did it mean to be part of a political family in a democracy, particularly for women? This book reveals the forgotten story of a family that Americans two hundred years ago knew quite well: Eliza, Patty, Nelly, and Wash Custis.[13] It is a story of four proud but profoundly flawed people that has much to reveal about how we understand both our country and our families.

CHAPTER 1

Washington's Children

IT HAD BEEN HUMID AND RAINING, DAY after day, for ten days straight at Eleanor Calvert Custis's family home of Mount Airy in Maryland. But in the early morning of August 21, 1776, the weather began to clear. Eleanor had gone into labor with her second child while it was still dark, at 3:00 a.m., and as the sky began to lighten, she gave birth to a chubby newborn girl. Eleanor's first baby had died, but this child was hardy. Her husband Jacky wrote to his mother soon after to announce the news, gleefully describing the infant as a "strapping Huzze" with a double chin that made her resemble the family's longtime doctor as well as "fine black Hair, & Eyes." Jacky hoped that his mother and stepfather would be godparents for his daughter, later christened Elizabeth Parke Custis, and announced he would be writing his stepfather to make the request. But at the moment, as Jacky knew, his stepfather was rather preoccupied: George Washington, commanding general of the Continental Army, was stationed in Manhattan preparing for the invasion of General Howe's thirty thousand British troops.[1]

The ink had barely dried on the Declaration of Independence. George Washington was running the army from a borrowed house in Richmond Hill, on the outskirts of New York City, releasing daily orders to punish wayward troops in the ragtag colonial army and appointing new officers to commands. Only the day before his stepgranddaughter's birth, he had ominously reported that "the Army may expect an attack as soon as the wind and tide shall prove favourable."[2] Martha Washington had left New York as the danger heightened and was staying in Philadelphia; surely the news of the birth of a healthy granddaughter brought her joy in that anxious time.[3]

This baby, unlike the first, would survive. Jacky's choice of words about his daughter—calling her a "strapping Huzze"—were in some ways prescient. A hussy was a brazen woman, a jezebel, a flouter of the polite norms of society, and Elizabeth would grow up to be tarred with similar insults. But for now, she was the family's "little Bet," who by November 1777 had "grown fat as a pigg," according to Martha. Soon after, as George Washington hunkered down with his men for an uncomfortable winter at Valley Forge in Pennsylvania, back home at Mount Vernon, Eleanor had another daughter, Martha Parke Custis. Her grandmother and namesake reported that the child was "a fine girl," and Jacky said his "little Pat" was "the most Good natured Quiet little Creature in the World." The sturdy Bet, not yet two, was "very saucy and entertaining," and she was already starting to talk—although, as Jacky joked, she could not yet say "Washington."[4]

Jacky, now just twenty-three but the father of a growing family, seems to have decided it was time to take on more adult responsibilities. He and Eleanor had no permanent home; they had largely traveled between her father's home of Mount Airy in Maryland and Mount Vernon, and he also owned his father's extensive properties in Tidewater Virginia. As a Virginia gentleman, he knew most of his time would be devoted to supervising the extensive Custis lands and extracting value from the hundreds of people he enslaved but rarely if ever mentioned in writing.[5] During the American Revolution, however, he wanted to serve his fledgling country in some form, especially as General Washington's stepson. He would not join the army; although this is never discussed in any surviving writings, surely Martha could not have supported her one surviving child risking his life, and Jacky was probably already feeling overwhelmed with the amount of time and attention his family estates required. His young wife didn't want him to leave, either.[6]

In the spring of 1778, Jacky Custis took two important steps. He needed to establish a home for his growing family, and he wanted to live near George and Martha in Fairfax, Virginia. He decided around this time to sell some of his southern properties and purchase two tracts of land amounting to about two thousand acres on the Potomac River ten miles north of Mount Vernon. The northern property, around the river's bend as it snaked northwest, cost him £12,100 and would later be named Arlington. The southern tract, Abingdon (where Reagan National Airport is now located), came at a far higher price: Jacky agreed to buy it on a mortgage with compound interest to be paid off over twenty-four years at a staggering final cost of £48,000. George, busy with running the daily affairs of the army and readying for a summer of fighting, still spared time to advise his headstrong stepson against this imprudent financial arrangement. But Jacky was determined to plunge ahead, and the final deeds were signed that December.[7] Now that he owned homes in multiple places, he made another big move: he ran for the Virginia House of Delegates from both New Kent and Fairfax counties (which was possible because representation in Britain and the colonies was rooted in land ownership rather than residency) and was elected from Fairfax.[8] This would mean he would be spending part of his time in the Virginia capital of Williamsburg, where he owned a town house and would be closer to the Custis plantations. Still, he would spend most of his time farther north in Fairfax.

That winter, the Custises moved into the 1740s brick house at Abingdon. It was a typical one-and-one-half-story house with a center door, two windows on either side, and dormers above. From its perch on a hill, there was an expansive view across the Potomac River. The Custises furnished the house amply, and it became a gathering place for the gentlemen of Alexandria. The walls were hung with prints and family portraits, and the shelves groaned with a large collection of books, some inherited and some recently purchased from England (although Jacky was no great reader). Guests would have been seated on mahogany chairs at a table set with glass candlesticks and fine ceramic plates. Little Bet joined the guests, likely perched on her father's lap, and he and his friends taught the precocious girl their favorite bawdy songs, which Bet memorized with ease. Jacky would place Bet on the table, and she paced its length, head held high, singing for a table of men who almost fell out of their chairs laughing. Even the enslaved people would watch from the hall and enjoy a rare moment of laughter with their enslavers. Eleanor Custis protested that it was inappropriate for a three-year-old to sing such songs, but Jacky's response must have stung his wife: he didn't have a son, so his daughter "must make fun for him, untill he had."[9]

That fun was what Jacky needed to distract him from other troubles. In March of 1779, Eleanor Custis had given birth to another daughter and a namesake, Eleanor "Nelly" Parke Custis, but both Eleanor and her baby were unwell after her birth. Eleanor sent Nelly to be nursed by a woman on one of George Washington's plantations, while at Abingdon she relied upon enslaved women like "Mammy Molly" (a Custis bondswoman from Mount Vernon) to care for her elder daughters.[10] She grew well enough to swiftly become pregnant again (not nursing would have made this easier, too), giving birth to twins a year later who died within a few weeks.[11] Meanwhile, Jacky was attempting to make Abingdon profitable, "struggling with every Inconvenience that a Person can meet with." He was trying to drain a peat-filled swamp—not with his own labor, but commanding that of the people he enslaved—to create good farmland. He was so busy at home that, while he was reelected in 1779 and 1780 to the House of Delegates, he was never appointed to key committees because he always arrived late. Jacky could be a serious and stern disciplinarian with his daughters, though; when Bet made the mistake of getting a cotton seed stuck in her nose, he removed it and then whipped her for her foolishness. He didn't know quite how to handle his headstrong and tempestuous daughter and worried that her "uncontroulable" emotions would bring her suffering.[12]

Jacky himself was no model of probity. He had been financially reckless in the purchase of his Fairfax lands (especially with the mortgage) and was struggling to turn a profit. It is also likely that as his wife recovered from the birth of their daughter, Jacky fathered a child by an enslaved woman on the Custis estates named Ann (also known as Nancy). Ann was twenty years old and may have been enslaved on the Custises' lands on Virginia's eastern shore. She gave birth to a fair-skinned son named William in 1780. While no written records from William's lifetime survive that identify him as Jacky's son, it is entirely possible people at the time thought or knew he was.[13] If the white Custises and William knew each other as children, there is no documentation of it.

Jacky would soon have one final child: in April 1781, Eleanor Custis gave birth to the couple's seventh child, and Jacky must have been overjoyed that it was a boy. Named after his stepgrandfather, George Washington (Wash) Parke Custis had a difficult start in life. Soon after his birth, an illness that his father called "a kind of bloody Flux" passed through the family, and Jacky feared that his long-awaited (white) son would not survive. Despite the summer heat and humidity, Wash recovered. With a male heir finally safely in place and his plantation taking shape, Jacky decided he could sit out the Revolutionary War no longer. His stepfather's forces were en route to Yorktown, near the mouth of the York River southeast of Williamsburg, and Jacky headed south to join them as a civilian aide. On his way, he could also do something George Washington had no time for: try to track down some of the seventeen enslaved people who had fled Mount Vernon for the promise of freedom behind British lines, often on ships anchored off the Virginia shores. Jacky determined that most had died, as "the Mortality that has taken place among the wretches is really incredible."[14]

The enslaved people fleeing bondage were not the only ones to suffer at Yorktown. Relatively few soldiers were killed and wounded in the battle that marked the end of major conflict in the war. However, disease was rife in the crowded camps of soldiers and enslaved people who had escaped bondage as they hunkered down in the woods and mosquito-infested wetlands of Tidewater Virginia. Smallpox, malaria, and camp fever (typhus) spread rapidly, and sick soldiers filled the hospitals in Williamsburg. Jacky, who had been unwell before he left Abingdon, fell gravely ill. He was taken upriver thirty miles to his uncle Burwell Bassett's home at Eltham, and somebody (likely George Washington himself) wrote to Jacky's wife and mother that he was dangerously ill. Fortunately, Martha and Eleanor, bringing five-year-old Bet with them, were not far away; they had traveled south to Williamsburg a few weeks earlier.[15] The carriage ride to Eltham must have seemed excruciatingly slow as they were anxious to reach Jacky. When they finally arrived, Eleanor sat on the bed beside him and would not budge. Bet barely recognized her father's face, drawn thin and pale by illness, and she was mostly kept out of the sickroom.

Not long after night fell on November 5, the twenty-seven-year-old Jacky died. Years later, Bet recalled that upon hearing of her father's death, she demanded to see him, and when taken into the room, she "called upon him to return to me."[16] Witnessing the loss of a parent at such a young age was not uncommon in the eighteenth century, but it must have left an indelible mark nonetheless. Her grandmother Martha had lost the last of her children, and Eleanor Custis was left a widow at only twenty-three. Her young children had lost their father. Jacky's death would change all of their lives irreparably, in ways they could not yet imagine on that dark November night.

Soon after Jacky's death, the Washingtons and Eleanor Custis decided that Eleanor could not care for four children alone at Abingdon—even when "alone" meant with the help of over seventy enslaved people. Martha loved children, and now she had none; why not send the two youngest Custises to live with her and George at Mount Vernon once the Washingtons had moved back permanently? Such an arrangement was not uncommon; even in families with two living parents, sometimes one or more children might be sent to live with relatives.[17] As Nelly explained (using adoption loosely here, as it was not formalized): "G.W.P. Custis (then only six months old) and self were adopted by general and Mrs. Washington. and ever treated as their children."[18] George Washington would receive a yearly annuity from the Custis estate to pay for the children's needs, and they would be cared for by "Mammy Molly," who would return from Abingdon to Mount Vernon. The elder girls had become attached to Molly, who may have tended to their own needs more closely than the girls' mother, but for Molly, the return to Mount Vernon may well have been a chance to reunite with family and friends.[19]

George and Martha would raise Nelly and Wash, but the Washingtons were not the children's legal guardians; still at the helm of the Continental Army, George had far too much to do to manage their complicated finances. He had spent years managing the Custis estate for Jacky until his stepson reached the age of majority, and he had neither the time nor the inclination to get involved in those affairs again; he was not even home at Mount Vernon, but hundreds of miles away at Newburgh, New York. In early 1782, George Washington and Martha's brother

Bartholomew Dandridge exchanged letters in which each pressed the other to take up the task. "Such aid however, as it ever may be with me to give to the Children—especially the boy—I will afford with all my heart, & with all my Soul," George told his brother-in-law, but he would not be their legal guardian, and he didn't know who else but Bartholomew could do it.[20]

As it turned out, there was soon somebody else who could. Eleanor Custis was still young and beautiful—not to mention rich—and she was not content to remain in seclusion at Abingdon. She rode through the countryside on horseback and began attending dances in Alexandria, drawing admiring glances in both settings. She wrote playfully to a male friend in January 1783 that "I will not trust Myself, but hope & expect to baffle all the sly attempts of Cupid & remain E Custis," but by the end of the summer she was engaged to Dr. David Stuart. Stuart, the son and grandson of Virginia clergymen, had been educated in medicine in Paris and Edinburgh; in 1783, he had just returned to America and begun practicing in Alexandria. While he was not wealthy, he was far better educated than most of his fellow Virginians, and perhaps he dazzled Eleanor with stories of his time abroad. While he eventually became what one of his step-daughters called a "gloomy Mortal," as a younger man on the make, he had some charm.[21] The new Mrs. Stuart could have chosen to remain a wealthy widow, but she was still young—and she needed a legal guardian for her children. Serious and straightforward, Stuart was the right man for this task, and George Washington soon found in him a trusted friend and advisor.

Nearby at Mount Vernon, by early 1784, the newly constituted family was settling in. George had officially resigned his commission in December 1783 in Annapolis and rushed home for Christmas. After the constant stress of war, he and Martha delighted in having young Nelly and Wash living with them. When the Marquis de Lafayette visited that summer, he reported that George "loves them with great tenderness." Wash had become so plump—"fat and saucy," as his adoptive father said—that the family began calling him "Tub," and he was a happy child who delighted in playing with the many visitors to Mount Vernon. One French visitor was so charmed by watching Wash ride his blue toy horse that he sent the boy another one in red, which George reported "he begins now to ride with a degree of boldness which will soon do honor to his horsemanship."[22] Little Nelly was not so plump as her brother, but she too saw her every whim and wish catered to by her anxious and loving grandmother.

Despite George's retirement, life at Mount Vernon was far from quiet. In addition to Nelly and Wash, over the next several years the household continued to grow. Martha's niece Fanny Bassett, who had lost her mother in 1777, moved permanently to Mount Vernon in late 1784, and George's nephew George Augustine Washington joined them later in 1785 (and promptly fell in love with and married Fanny). Another Washington niece, Harriot, arrived in 1787. There were constant visitors from across the country and abroad, so much so that George described the house as "a well resorted tavern." But visitors enjoyed seeing a more private side of the war hero; one visitor called it "one of the highest privileges" to observe the venerable general "kind and benignant in the domestic circle, revered and beloved by all around him."[23]

The true "domestic circle" went far beyond the white family; there were over two hundred enslaved people on the estate, in addition to white servants. With the enslaved people, George and Martha were not benevolent parental figures but demanding enslavers; it was the hard labor of the enslaved, inside the house and out, that enabled the Washingtons to graciously receive a steady stream of guests and provide the best for their adopted children. Enslaved people cared for the family and their guests, from George's valet William Lee to a fair-skinned and freckled young girl named Ona Judge, who served as Martha's maid. William's brother Frank and Ona's half brother Austin were waiters, while Caroline Branham and Sal kept the house clean by, among other tasks, dusting, changing bed linens, and emptying chamber pots. Molly, likely with help from Ona, cared for Nelly and Wash, while seamstresses Betty (Ona's mother), Alice, and Charlotte sewed under Martha's demanding eye.[24] For all that George described the retirement of life at home as a cloistered retreat, Mount Vernon was a workplace where hundreds of enslaved people labored.

There was also a small army of craftsmen renovating the house and grounds. After an absence of eight years, George saw much to be done to both repair and improve Mount Vernon. The piazza facing the Potomac River got a new ceiling, scaffolding went up to repair the mansion's shingle roof, trees were planted, and the serpentine walks at the west front of the house were laid. The large, unfinished north or new room was fitted out in extravagant style with new lathing on the walls, the addition of cove ceilings, stucco on the walls and ceilings, and decorative plaster ornaments added above windows and doors. Several other rooms in the house had ceilings repaired.[25] The family was living in a construction zone.

Nonetheless, Nelly and Wash needed order and education. George began searching for a man to serve as tutor for the children and a secretary for himself in 1785, and he finally found the right person: Harvard-educated New Hampshire native Tobias Lear. It was not unusual for college-educated New Englanders to serve as tutors in the South, where they taught subjects including classical languages, grammar, religion, math, and geography. Parents expected tutors to discipline the children, and this was especially necessary for the Custis children: the exuberant Wash was, George said, "as full of spirits as an egg shell is of meat," but he was also "the pet of the family" and in need of some boundaries.[26] Lear arrived in May 1786 and swiftly became a valued part of the household. The following year, one of George's former Revolutionary War aides, David Humphreys, came to Mount

Vernon to help George organize his papers, and he too spent time with the children. Nelly, who had always loved poetry, sat on his lap every day memorizing verses with him, and into her old age she still remembered speeches from Homer's *Iliad* that Humphreys taught her. Nelly also took dancing lessons with her elder sisters and Harriot Washington, taught by a dance master who came to Mount Vernon.[27]

Dance lessons were one of many excuses for the Stuart family to visit the Washingtons. The elder Custis girls—now called Betsey and Patty—also had their own tutor at Abingdon. The tutor soon found the precocious Betsey to be an exemplary student. "That was an extraordinary child," the tutor told David Stuart, "& would if a Boy, make a Brilliant figure." Overhearing this, Betsey jumped in and asked that they teach her just what a boy would learn and claimed that it was unfair that she wasn't taught classical languages. "They laughed & said women ought not to know those things," Betsey later recalled, and "mending, writing, Arithmetic, & Music was all I could be permitted to acquire." It was not the last time she would feel frustration and regret at being treated differently because of her gender. She was also unhappy with the changes in life at home. In August 1784, Eleanor Stuart gave birth to Ann, her first child with David Stuart, and another daughter, Sally, was born just under two years later. There was no more singing and dancing on the dining table; with her mother's attention diverted, her enslaved nurse Molly gone, and a new, strict stepfather, Betsey relished her visits to Mount Vernon. Whenever the carriage left to bring the family back to Abingdon, she craned her neck to gaze at the house for as long as it remained in view and cried. She adored her grandmother, and she seems to have made it clear to her mother that she'd prefer to live at Mount Vernon.[28]

Life at Mount Vernon was starting to change in the spring of 1787. Political leaders were convinced that the new nation's governing document, the Articles of Confederation, was too weak and needed rethinking; Shays' Rebellion, a violent uprising in Massachusetts the previous year, had brought the situation to a crisis point. In February, the Confederation Congress voted to form a convention with delegates from each state to review the Articles, and George was under pressure to attend. He had retired; should he go back? Martha was too happily settled with the children to go with George to Philadelphia, where the convention would be held. Reluctantly, he agreed to participate and left Mount Vernon in early May.[29] Martha must have looked on with growing concern over the following year as it became clear that George was going to be returning to public life for the near future.

Throughout the convention, the framers imagined George Washington as the obvious choice to be the first president. He had served as president of the Constitutional Convention, and his endorsement of the new governing document helped it gain support for ratification. George had just returned to Mount Vernon after four and a half months away when newspapers began reporting that he would be president. In his writings, at least, George expressed that he was not enthusiastic about the prospect; it was expected in the new nation to reject ambition and serve in government as a duty, but George's reluctance has a ring of truth.[30]

A key factor in favor of George Washington's election as the first president was that he had no direct descendants. George could be a father figure to nephews, nieces, stepgrandchildren, and even adopted children, but none of them stood directly in line to inherit either his political position or his estate. The British had a fixation on full-blooded, or direct, descent, around which their ideas about family and laws of inheritance turned. John Adams could breathe a sigh of relief that George had no direct blood-related son or daughter to be married off to European royalty. As full ratification of the Constitution came closer

in the spring of 1788, numerous newspapers trumpeted George
Washington as the obvious choice for president and listed reasons in his favor. Among them: "As having no son—and therefore not exposing us to the danger of an hereditary successor."[31]

George's adopted son, Wash, was just seven years old as these
great developments unfolded. Under Tobias Lear's tutelage, he
was learning both penmanship and gentlemanly conduct; his
first surviving piece of writing is a thank-you note to George
and Martha's good friend Elizabeth Powel, who had sent him a
book as a gift. A few wobbles and his large, careful handwriting betray his young age, but his spelling and sentiments have
clearly been coached; an energetic boy just shy of seven was unlikely to come up with "I will endeavour to imitate the good
characters which I find described in the book." Perhaps Wash
and Nelly, along with Betsey and Patty at Abingdon, heard the
echo of cannons firing on June 28, 1788, as the city of Alexandria celebrated Virginia's ratification of the Constitution, which
(along with New Hampshire) meant enough states had ratified
to make the Constitution the country's new law of the land.[32]

That winter, their stepfather David Stuart (now a member of
the state legislature) was chosen as one of the electors who would
select the president. Less than two weeks after his wife gave birth
to another daughter (Arianna), he traveled to the state convention
to vote for George Washington for president.[33] The electors' bal-
lots would not be counted in Congress until April, however, so
the families at Mount Vernon and Abingdon waited anxiously for
the official word. George and Martha must have already decided
that she and the children would go with him to the nation's current capital in New York; this would be too long a separation for
Martha from George, and Martha could not bear to leave Nelly
and Wash. George told his friend Henry Knox that waiting for
the final news made him feel like "a culprit, who is going to the
place of his execution; so unwilling am I" to leave the comforts

of home.[34] The family waited for Secretary of Congress Charles Thomson to deliver the official word of his election.

When Thomson arrived in person around noon on April 14, 1789, weary from riding on rutted roads through storms for a week, Nelly and Wash probably knew just who this visitor was and why he was there. Thomson read a formal address announcing George's unanimous election as president and stating that Thomson would accompany him to New York to begin his duties. George was prepared with a written reply, crafted with the help of David Humphreys, which he almost certainly read aloud in response. He announced that he would leave with Thomson in just two days. He had had plenty of time to prepare himself and the estate, which would be managed in his absence by his nephew George Augustine Washington. At ten in the morning on April 16, George left home with Charles Thomson. He recorded in his diary: "I bade adieu to Mount Vernon, to private life, and to domestic felicity; and with a mind oppressed with more anxious and painful sensations than I have words to express, set out for New York."[35]

Martha and the children would not join him for another month. They all needed time to prepare, both practically and for the emotional separation from Eleanor, Betsey, and Patty. As difficult as this change was for the household at Mount Vernon, it was even worse for those left behind at Abingdon. Betsey recalled that George's election caused the family "much affliction" and "sorrow."[36] She and her sister went to Mount Vernon to spend time with their younger siblings and grandmother before they departed. Eleanor, who had given up Nelly and Wash with the expectation of living close to them, tried to convince Martha to leave at least Nelly at Abingdon. She was worried about her young daughter being exposed to the social whirl of New York and the attention that would come with being in the president's family, and she knew that Martha would not give either of the children the discipline and boundaries they needed.

She could not tell Martha this, of course, so she argued that it would be unfair for Nelly to get social and educational advantages her elder sisters would not. But Martha would not part with Nelly now. Eleanor agreed, reluctantly, knowing that Tobias Lear, whom she had befriended, would be accompanying them and could help to keep the children in line.[37]

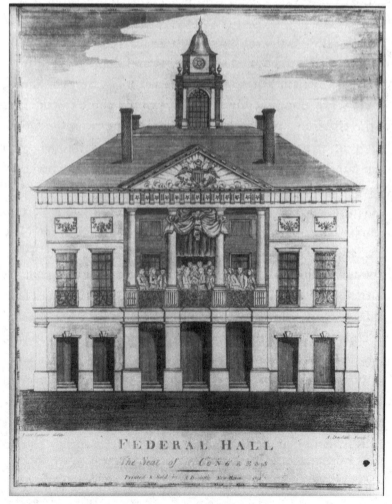

FEDERAL HALL
The Seat of Congress

While George Washington was inaugurated before large crowds and fanfare in New York, Martha and the children were not present.

Amos Doolittle, *Inauguration of George Washington at Federal Hall, New York*, 1790. Washington, Library of Congress.

Challenging as it was, the Washingtons at least had a choice about their movements and how to arrange their family; for the enslaved people who would accompany them to New York, the separation from their families was forced. Seven enslaved people left Virginia to go to New York and serve the Washingtons, along with a heavy and constant stream of guests. Ona Judge and her half brother Austin would have each other, but had to leave the rest of their family behind to continue their household roles in New York. George's manservant William Lee, along with postilions (men who rode and steered the horses pulling a carriage) Giles and Paris, and house servant Christopher Sheels, would serve alongside them.[38] Molly would come to take care of the children. Unlike the Washingtons and even the Custis children, these men and women could not stay in touch with their families by letter, and they had no control over when they next saw each other again.

George's nephew Robert Lewis came up to Mount Vernon from his home in Fredericksburg to accompany the party to New York and stay on as a secretary for his uncle. From the diary he kept during this time, we get a clear picture of every stage of the journey. When he arrived on May 14, he found the household in disarray as enslaved people finished packing for Martha and the children. With stuffed trunks loaded onto carriages, they finally departed at three in the afternoon on May 16. A number of enslaved people gathered to see them off, and Robert recorded that they were "greatly agitated" and "much affected." To Robert, this seemed to be because they were "tak[ing] leave of their mistress," and that may have been cause for worry; they had no way of knowing how George Augustine and his wife Fanny would run the estate or how they would be treated. But worse was parting with their own family members traveling to New York against their will. As the carriage rode away, they called out, "God bless you all."

The worst leave-taking for the white family was yet to come. The party went first just a short trip north to Abingdon to take Betsey and Patty home. They stayed at Abingdon that night and the following one, preparing for an early morning departure on the 18th. Even with the horses hitched and bags loaded, it was hard to make their final departure as everyone was in tears, "the children abawling."

"So pathetic and affecting a scene," Robert Lewis wrote, "I never wish to be again witness to." Twenty years later, Betsey wrote that remembering the "agonies" of that morning still pained her.

The journey was not an easy one. They suffered through treacherous river crossings and finally made it to Baltimore, where they were feted by the gentlemen and women of the city.[39] Similar festivities greeted them in Philadelphia. Finally, they approached New York. On Wednesday the 27th, the same decorated barge that had carried the president into the city with fanfare the previous month now carried his wife and children across the river into the temporary capital. They were welcomed into New York City with a celebratory parade, and an amazed Wash "seemed to be lost in a mase."[40] For the first time in their lives, Nelly and Wash were sharing in their stepgrandfather's fame.

The burgeoning, bustling city of New York was an exciting change for Nelly and Wash. The city was just recovering from what a visitor in 1787 had called "prostration and decay" due to a large fire during the British occupation in the Revolutionary War. By 1789, there were 4,200 houses in the city (rebuilt in brick rather than wood), their tiled roofs spreading across the southern end of Manhattan Island. Federal Hall, where George Washington had been inaugurated on April 30 (Wash's eighth birthday), was still under construction.[41] Congress had rented a house for the family at the northeast edge of town, at what were then Pearl and Cherry streets (near the on-ramps to the Brooklyn Bridge today). The house was not in a fashionable neighborhood, and it was far too small for the extensive household, which included seven enslaved people, fourteen white servants, and five secretaries.[42] The house also held entertaining spaces and George's official office space, offering the family little privacy.

Nonetheless, the children enjoyed the hustle and bustle. Nelly sat by the front windows, entranced by watching the carriages and people pass by; Martha remarked that the ten-year-old was "a little Wild creature," and she could not get her to focus. The children turned the attic of the house into a playroom, and Wash and his friends even put on a production of *Julius Caesar*, with Wash as the treacherous Cassius.[43] Music teacher Alexander Reinagle came to give Nelly music lessons, while the artist William Dunlap taught her drawing, and the children worked with other private tutors before enrolling in small private schools that fall.[44]

Aside from the hush that came over the household in June when George fell seriously ill from a fever and tumor in his leg—even the street was roped off to keep the noise of carriages from disturbing him—Nelly and Wash had every opportunity to relish the delights of the city. They visited a museum of "natural curiosities," went to the theater to see a comic opera, and even visited a wax museum, where their stepgrandfather came face to face with his likeness in wax, dressed in military uniform.[45] While New York was busy and crowded, it was still small; Wash often slipped away to run and play in the fields that adjoined the growing city.[46] Some days, George, Martha, and the children took a carriage ride on a fourteen-mile loop around Manhattan Island. While they took in the fresh air, their ornate carriage emblazoned with the Washington family crest, pulled by six horses driven by enslaved servants Giles and Paris dressed in resplendent liveries, surely drew the eyes of everyone they passed.[47]

While Wash and Nelly enjoyed themselves, it was a stressful time for George and Martha as they adjusted to their highly public roles and reestablished a smoothly run household. Martha was busy finding teachers for the children, paying visits, and holding receptions; in all this she had Ona Judge and Robert Lewis helping her. George worried about his every move as president, knowing that whatever he did would set a precedent. He was particularly careful to signal that the new nation would not be governed by his family, but by those with the best qualifications. When his nephew Bushrod Washington wrote requesting an appointment as district attorney, George refused and explained, "the eyes of Argus are upon me, and no slip will pass unnoticed that can be improved into a supposed partiality for friends or relations."[48] He also had family troubles to handle; his mother, who had long suffered from breast cancer, passed away in late August. Soon after, David Stuart wrote to inform him that he could not keep up with the disastrous mortgage Jacky had taken on Abingdon, and a legal judgment against them would mean "the whole family would be ruined." George and Martha agreed that Stuart should negotiate with the previous owners of Abingdon to return the land, although the Stuarts would hold on to the unmortgaged and less developed northern tract.[49]

Hearing of the pleasures and advantages that Nelly and Wash were enjoying in New York was painful for Eleanor and her elder daughters back home. Tobias Lear kept Eleanor updated on the children's activity and behavior, and Eleanor was relieved that Martha "has at least seen the nesessity of making the D[ea]r Children respect as well as love her, for that they never wou'd have done had she continued her former improper indulgence to them." Still, she missed them deeply and regretted that Betsey and Patty could not share these opportunities; Abingdon was too remote to have top-notch tutors come in, or to go to the theater. "I often lament My D[ea]r Bett & Patt cannot have the same advantages," she told Lear; they had learned to play the harpsichord, "but they take no pleasure in playing to chairs, & Tables." However, she insisted, "if they are not accomplish'd Women, nothing shall be left undone by Me to make them good Women." For their part, the girls were "chearfully submiting to the retired life" at Abingdon, at least in their mother's hearing.[50]

Beyond the educational and cultural advantages Nelly and Wash had in New York, they also had far more public exposure than their sisters. It is unsurprising, then, that only they appear in Edward Savage's famous family portrait painted at this time, with no sign of Betsey and Patty. Nelly and Wash occasionally attended public functions, and because their house was in effect the headquarters of the executive branch, they met all of the key figures in the new government.[51] Indeed, Martha and the children were always in the public eye, and they had responsibilities as the president's family. There was not yet an official term for the president's family or even his wife; "first lady" and "first family" were not in common use for another one hundred years.[52] It was clear, however, that like the royal family when the colonies were ruled by the king, the president's family would have a public, ceremonial role. Before Independence, the colonists had looked on King George III's family with respect and affection, offering prayers and blessings on the family's behalf and tracking the birth dates of princes and princesses in their almanacs.[53] The presidency and George Washington himself were not entirely divorced from the traditions of royalty; one journalist even called George the "Monarch of Mount Vernon." George III had been the "Father of his People"; George Washington was the "Father of his Country." The citizens of the United States did not want the president's family to fill the same role now that power was to be elected rather than inherited, but they still seemed to crave a family that served as a model of and symbol for the nation.[54]

While almanac pages of royal family birth dates were replaced with a listing of top government officials, the president's family lived under the public's watchful gaze. To the press the family was, in one historian's words, "nothing more than an extension of the man who was at its head."[55] When there were large public events, Martha often accompanied George, and sometimes the children were involved as well. When George was ill during the Fourth of July celebrations in 1789, Martha attended with the children in his place. Wash also played another role: he marched in the day's procession, dressed in a miniature copy of George's buff-and-blue military garb, along with sons of other leading politicians.[56] Now Wash wasn't just wandering through the crowds in a daze; he was on parade himself.

While Wash couldn't yet shape his own public image, George and Martha knew what they were doing. As John Adams remarked years later, "if he [George] was not the greatest President he was the best Actor of the Presidency We have ever had." George was not simply the disinterested, aloof but admirable statesman; he cultivated that image with what Adams called "Shakespearean... Excellence in Dramatic Exhibition." His purpose in doing so was as much or more about embodying legitimacy for the new nation rather than personal pride; the Custis children seem to have soaked up the strategy rather than the motivation.[57]

In late February, the family moved to a much larger house owned by the fashionable French minister on Broadway Street in the heart of the city, with a center hall flanked by large public reception rooms and a rear balcony overlooking the Hudson River. Their neighbors included the French and Spanish ambassadors and the Secretary of War, Henry Knox. They were quite near Federal Hall, where Congress met, and Bowling Green Park, where locals took walks while adorned in the latest fashions. Perhaps the children spotted the empty foundation where the statue of King George III once stood and heard stories about how General George Washington had defeated his armies.[58]

Nelly, now nearly eleven, was swept up in the city's social life, much to her mother's dismay. Eleanor worried that she would become "an affected, trifling Miss of the Ton" courted as the president's adopted daughter by "every Fop." Wash, at least, did not attend these social gatherings, but Eleanor believed that Martha was "too much pleased with the attentions paid to Nelly to judge of their impropriety."[59] Already, Nelly was playing the pianoforte and singing for her grandparents' prominent guests while her brother steered clear of company. Visiting ladies also admired Nelly's paintings and commissioned works from her, and the attention sometimes embarrassed her. When the protofeminist writer Judith Sargent Murray was visiting, Nelly seems to have sensed a kindred spirit and clung to her to get away from the other ladies' requests for her artwork. Murray was kind to Nelly and found her to be a "little charmer," although Murray learned from George and Martha that Nelly "was not sufficiently industrious." Apparently, Nelly had told them that "if they will but allow her frivolity, until she hath completed her twelfth year, she will yield the rest of her life to their direction."[60] It was a tough balancing act for Nelly, paraded out to entertain the nation's elite and with every entertainment available to her, but at the same time expected to apply herself to her studies.

The family would not stay in New York for long, however. While the government met there for the first year of the new nation's existence, it was intended to be a temporary location. In the First Federal Congress, there had been ugly fights over the location of the new nation's capital city; various locations had their local boosters, and one observer said that the issue of where to place the capital "has already nearly broken up the confederation." George's stepson-in-law David Stuart, among others who had invested in the Potomac Navigation Company to boost commerce on that river, was arguing for placing the capital at the popular center of the country, near the meeting of the Potomac and Anacostia rivers. George himself had been president of that company until 1789, and members of Congress knew he, too, favored that site. The choice of a location ultimately became wrapped up in larger regional conflicts and emerging partisan struggles over the economy. The compromise deal struck in Congress in 1790 stipulated that the government would move to Philadelphia for ten years while a new capital in the District of Columbia was constructed.[61]

SECOND STREET. North from Market S.! & CHRIST CHURCH.
PHILADELPHIA.

Just three blocks from the President's House,
this would have been a familiar scene for Wash and Nelly.

William Birch, *Second Street North from Market St. with Christ Church–Philadelphia*, 1800.
Washington, Library of Congress.

When the family arrived in Philadelphia in 1790, it was the largest city in the country, with 7,000 houses and 45,000 people, counting the outlying parts of the city. Most of the houses were brick, many with stone bases and staircases leading up from smooth pavements to white doors. It was the cultural center of the country, with several theaters, a circus, and the nation's first

museum, opened by Charles Willson Peale. A French visitor
commented, surely with some exaggeration, that the shops were
"as well furnished as those of Paris or London." Foreign visitors
admired Philadelphia and called it "the pleasantest place of residence" and "the finest city" in the country. Yet it was still a work
in progress; the planned grid of streets stretched approximately
two miles west from the waterfront of the Delaware across to
the Schuylkill, but the city barely made it halfway across this
expanse. The rest remained countryside, and in the summer,
the noise of frogs filled the air. While William Penn's plan included a large central square and four surrounding squares, they
had not yet been made into parks; in fact, Centre Square was
an execution site.[62]

Philadelphia may have been a welcome change for the enslaved people in the household, albeit in different ways than for
the white family. The same group of bondspeople (minus William Lee, who had been sent home due to poor health) served
the first family, with the addition of enslaved cook Hercules
Posey and his son Richmond. Philadelphia was fast becoming the center of Black intellectual life and antislavery activism, and there were some two thousand free Black people in
the city (double the number in New York).[63] When Hercules
and Richmond went to the central market to shop for cooking supplies, they entered "the great curiosity of the city"—a
half-mile-long covered space down the center of Market (also
called High) Street with gaps for cross streets and crowds of
people of all ages, races, and classes.[64] Hercules also sold kitchen
scraps and was permitted to keep the money, with which he
purchased fine clothes and a gold-headed cane to display on
evening outings. Ona Judge, who accompanied Martha when
she paid calls or took the children out to plays or the circus,
would also have been well-dressed, but her role required her
to remain silent.[65] Serving the president's family meant being

on display along with them, which Hercules seemed to relish but others may have simply endured.

Life in Philadelphia brought other changes for the enslaved people in the household. Pennsylvania law stipulated that enslaved people brought into the state would automatically become free after residing there for six months, and the Washingtons devised a plan to circumvent the law: every six months, George Washington sent the enslaved home to Mount Vernon for a short visit, resetting the clock. While this at least meant that they would have the chance to see their families, the Washingtons were skirting the law in order to maintain ownership of human property. The bondspeople also needed to adjust to working alongside a new staff of fifteen white servants. As in New York, the Washingtons' new house in Philadelphia was packed, nowhere more than the attic where enslaved people and servants slept, divided among six cramped rooms.[66]

The Washingtons, of course, lived in what George called "the best *single House* in the city," owned by his friend Robert Morris. The house sat on Market Street between Fifth and Sixth streets, quite close to the State House where Congress met. It didn't look much different from other large brick houses in the city; intricate adornments were reserved for the interiors of homes. The layout of the house offered little separation between public spaces and intimate family quarters. Visitors entered a long passage with green carpet lit by a tall window at the back of the house. To the left of the passage sat a grand staircase, to the right a family dining room facing the street and a state dining room at the rear, where the enormous dining table could seat more than thirty. The state drawing room sat immediately above, decorated primarily in green and lit by an eight-armed glass chandelier. An ell extending behind the house was purely service space on the first floor, with a kitchen, washhouse, and servants' quarters, while on the second floor was space for the family: George's private study (a mix of office and dressing room), his and Martha's bedchamber, and two small bedrooms for the children. The third floor had three small bedchambers for George's secretaries, conveniently located on the same floor as George's presidential office. However, this location for the precursor to the Oval Office meant that whenever George had meetings, his guests had to climb up three flights of stairs, passing by whatever other activity was going on in the house.[67] Alexander Hamilton must have greeted Wash, his own son's schoolmate, on his way to meetings; perhaps Nelly asked Thomas Jefferson about his daughter, her friend Maria.[68]

Residence of Washington in High Street, Philad.

The Washington family lived in this rented home on
Philadelphia's Market (or High) Street from 1791 to 1797.

William Breton, *Residence of Washington in High Street, Philad[elphia]*,
from Watson's *Annals of Philadelphia*, 1830. Washington, Library of Congress.

Nelly and Wash could not have escaped the press of politics in their daily lives or even within their own home. In addition to cabinet meetings in George's presidential office, George held levees (receptions) for male guests on Tuesdays from three to four, and Martha had less formal drawing rooms for men and women on Fridays from eight to ten at night. On Thursdays,

George and Martha hosted dinners for politicians and their families.[69] While Wash does not seem to have attended these events, Nelly did, and both children witnessed a constant influx of elite visitors. When there was political tumult, they must have sensed the tension and overheard heated conversations. The stress and constant scrutiny of the presidency wore on both George and Martha, and the children were not immune; Nelly noted that the family was "surrounded by censorious, envious, busy people ready to catch every word and action, and to construe them improperly."[70]

Visitors to the President's House would have also seen, but likely not acknowledged, enslaved people, including Nelly and Wash's caretakers Molly and Ona. Unlike other enslaved people who slept in the attic or back slave quarters, Molly and Ona slept on the floor of Nelly's and Wash's small bedrooms on the second floor in the ell over the kitchen.[71] Molly was old enough to be their grandmother, Ona young enough to be their elder sister, and yet Nelly and Wash could command them as their mistress and master. The children would have learned from observing their grandparents that as whites, they were fundamentally different from African Americans and that (for Martha if no longer for George, as we'll see) holding African Americans in bondage was the natural order of things. This was precisely the sort of power that white Northerners were worried would corrupt the morals of the children of enslavers, and indeed, Tobias Lear saw the negative impact it had upon Wash. In addition to his grandmother's pampering, "the servile respect which the Servants are obliged to pay to him" was already making him conceited. Tobias confided to David Humphreys that these two factors "will form his character in such a manner as to render him extremely disgusting."[72]

While Martha might indulge her grandson and overlook his faults, his mother and stepgrandfather saw that he required discipline. At the time, parents were supposed to use both affection and authority in raising children, and boys needed to learn a careful balance between autonomy and self-restraint.[73] The other adults in the Washington household were deeply concerned that Martha's parenting was too tender and overindulgent. When Martha and the children visited Mount Vernon in late September 1790, Eleanor and her other children joined them there, and Eleanor reported on her own observations of Wash to Tobias Lear. Martha mentioned to Eleanor that she had been trying to get Wash to write Lear himself and he hadn't, so Eleanor sat him down beside her and had him write the overdue letter. Getting Wash to do as he was told wasn't difficult; "any thing I request altho in the mildest manner he does."

"Is it not cruel," she asked, "to spoil such a child"? Even George watched his wife's handling of Wash "with pain," but according to Lear, "he is unwilling to take such measures as might reclaim him, knowing that any rigidity used towards him would perhaps be productive of serious effects on her."[74]

How much was Martha's parenting responsible for Wash's conceit and lack of focus? His father had been little different; was it her fault that both her son and grandson were unruly, spoiled, and inattentive? It is possible that the criticism built on existing beliefs that grandmothers were too affectionate and spoiled their grandchildren. Besides, Jacky and Wash were little different from many other young men in the South; many, including the sons of other founders, grasped onto the autonomy their parents had fostered without learning obedience and restraint.[75] But in the household's view, at least, the responsibility for Wash's failings largely fell upon Martha. She did seem to take some of the criticism to heart and start to require Wash to write his mother every Sunday afternoon, telling her he had been to church that morning and "heard an excellent sermon." Wash ultimately blamed that one piece of routine for his "distaste for church & for letter-writing."[76]

George tried to see that Wash received the best education

possible, but he must have been frustrated to already see early echoes of Jacky's poor study habits. Based on Tobias Lear's favorable report on the College of Philadelphia (later University of Pennsylvania, but then a school for both boys and young men), George sent Wash there at age ten. But when Lear quizzed Wash the following spring to check his progress, he found that Wash was falling behind in reading, writing, and math (we can only hope he was exaggerating when he said Wash "cannot tell 100 from 1000"). George, perceptively, said he had suspected Wash wasn't learning there because he enjoyed attending too much. The fault, they thought, was with the school and not the pupil; other leaders whose sons attended with him were also doing poorly. George himself talked to the head of the school to be sure there would be better discipline. But George was not solely a disciplinarian; when Wash was seriously ill in the summer of 1790, George sat at his bedside.[77]

Nelly, too, could be unruly, but she kept busy with school as well as dance, music, art, French, and guitar lessons. Her grandparents still called upon her to entertain their guests with her growing musical repertoire, although as Nelly joked, the venerable guests "do not know one note from another." She befriended daughters of leading men in the city, including Maria Jefferson, Maria Morris, and Elizabeth Beale Bordley. At fourteen, she stayed up until 2:00 a.m. working on an epistolary novel with Maria Morris, with Maria writing the sentimental letters and Nelly the witty ones.[78]

The children were likely both a distraction and a balm for George Washington as he dealt with the stresses of politics. It was not only the Custis children that he was looking after; he was also guiding the education of his late brother Samuel's two sons and providing a home and financial support for Samuel's daughter Harriot at Mount Vernon. Then there were his sister Betty's children, whom he had taken in at various points; Robert, in his early twenties, was still living with him as a secretary.[79]

Family matters could not keep George from grappling with the ongoing foreign policy challenges, fighting with Native peoples to dispossess them of their lands, and growing partisan tensions, both in the country and in his own cabinet. The struggle over the location of the nation's capital and Hamilton's financial plan had created a growing rift between cabinet secretaries Thomas Jefferson and Alexander Hamilton and the nascent factions they headed, Democratic-Republicans and Federalists. These early versions of political parties coalesced during the 1790s, with the Democratic-Republicans favoring a small central government, an agricultural economy, and alliance with France, and Federalists supporting a stronger role for federal leadership, a commercial economy with banks and manufacturing, and stronger ties with England.[80]

There was one political project that George relished, and it was the one that happened to be most closely intertwined with the interests of his family: the building of the new capital city on the Potomac River. While Congress had decided on the general location of the ten-square-mile capital, they tasked George with choosing the exact location—and his choice was telling. George moved the boundaries of the new federal city further south than he was initially authorized, pushing the city as close to Mount Vernon as possible and encompassing lands that he and the Custises owned in what is now Arlington and Alexandria. He had high hopes that land in the new federal city would increase in value, so it is difficult to see this decision as purely disinterested (although, to be fair, local landowners whom Jefferson consulted on his behalf also recommended stretching south to Alexandria). George chose Eleanor Stuart's husband David as one of the federal district's first three commissioners; while David was qualified for the post, this gave George a family member and confidant in a position to shape the future of the city. With his background as a surveyor and his hopes for the economic promise of the Potomac, it is unsurprising that at times he was far more interested in the future of the new capital than the rough and tumble of politics in the present one.[81]

Still, the country seemed stable enough to George that he could retire; he began discussing his plans in the spring and asked James Madison to help him to write a farewell statement that May. But many friends and advisors urged him to stay on, and by that fall, nobody had even floated the idea of running against him.[82] He talked it over with his close friend Elizabeth Powel, who wrote a strongly worded letter insisting that he must run again for the good of the country. What must the discussions have been like with Martha, who had once compared her life as the president's wife to that of a prisoner?[83] Did Nelly and Wash ask about his plans?

Whatever the final deciding factor, George chose to stay on, and he was officially declared the winner of the second presidential election on February 13, 1793. He was inaugurated for the second time on March 4 at noon in a very brief ceremony in the Senate Chamber of Congress Hall, before a small audience of both men and women. His inaugural address was a concise 135 words, beginning simply, "I am again called upon, by the voice of my country, to execute the functions of its Chief Magistrate."[84] In the coming years, the voice of his country would become increasingly splintered, and the partisan attacks began to target George. The next four years would not be easy for George and Martha as they weathered both public life and their grandchildren's awkward years of young adulthood. The first family was maturing in the glare of the public eye, and growing pains were inevitable.

CHAPTER 2

The First Family Grows Up

LIFE ON THE PUBLIC STAGE, NELLY CUSTIS concluded at the end of her stepgrandfather's presidency, was wretched. "The most exalted situations are generally those of most misery," she wrote, and it is no wonder she thought so after experiencing George Washington's second term in office.[1] While he had been reluctant to return to public service for his first term, at least then he had widespread public support. But from the start of his second term, partisan strife and diplomatic controversies pushed him slightly off his pedestal; the adored father of the country was now, like other prominent politicians, subject to ugly attacks. He was deeply wounded by the criticism and kept busy putting out fire after fire to keep the country at peace. For all his legendary control of his emotions, at times his temper got the better of him.[2]

It's hard to imagine that the whole household could do anything but feel this tension and strife. Political conflict didn't just hit close to home; the president's office was immediately upstairs from his, Martha's, and his adopted children's bedrooms. His secretaries lived and worked in the house. Nelly and Wash were entering their young adulthood just as the country was experiencing an awkward stage in its own growth. The novelty of life in the nation's capital was wearing off, and for all the excitement of Philadelphia, there was also the stress of living at the center of the partisan storm.

There was the added challenge for the Custis family that Nelly and Wash's elder sisters, Betsey and Patty, were living over one hundred miles away in rural Northern Virginia. Two years earlier, the family had moved even deeper into the country-side when they gave up Abingdon, unable to pay the expensive mortgage Jacky Custis had entered, and retreated to David Stu-art's house, Hope Park, near Falls Church. They were so isolated and in such financial straits that they didn't even have a car-riage good enough to go out and pay social calls. Eleanor was often too indisposed to travel anyway; since her remarriage in late 1783, she had already had four children (as her friend Tobias Lear joked, "Mrs. Stuart goes on in the usual way—producing a new inhabitant to the United States every year").[3]

For all that their mother Eleanor worried that the elder two were missing out on key opportunities in the city, they were also protected. Betsey and Patty could live privately in a home that was not also a public office, with parents who were not pre-occupied with the presidency and who could provide structure and boundaries to their children (perhaps, in Betsey's eyes, too much so). Eleanor and Lear also still thought there was real risk for the younger children in being raised by Martha; as Lear told David Humphreys in 1793, "very much do I fear that [Martha] will experience many sorrowful hours on their accounts when the effects of her blind indulgence of them comes to display itself more fully—every day produces sad proofs of the evil tendency."[4]

Proper guidance was particularly important for the older girls, now seventeen and fifteen, as they neared marriage; while choice of a spouse was up to the young woman, her parents were there to make sure she met "suitable" men and chose well.[5] Indeed, Ferdinando Fairfax, one of George's godsons, had been trekking to Hope Park to court Betsey. The close family connection, his good nature, and his "handsome fortune" made the family hopeful his courtship would be successful, but Betsey was not interested. There is no sign her family pressured her to change her mind (nor, given her personality, does it seem likely they could have prevailed). And while Patty was a bit young for courting, she was supposedly the prettiest of the eligible Custis sisters.[6]

The second term of George's presidency was a time of upheaval and unpleasant growing pains for the nation and the first family. Whether in Philadelphia or Virginia, the Custises saw their celebrated stepgrandfather subjected to vicious partisan attacks while they were in the tenuous transition from childhood to adulthood.[7] In the four long years of George's second term, from 1793 to 1797, the girls took firm steps into adulthood while Wash seems to have remained rather carefree. Nelly more than any of them, often at her grandmother's side at social events in the capital city, would have been deeper in the mire of partisan warfare than her other siblings. By the time George retired in March 1797, he and the family were indelibly changed.

In the spring of 1793, news from France shook Philadelphia: King Louis XVI of France had been executed, and war had broken out in Europe. This posed a challenge for the Washington administration: the United States government had signed a treaty of alliance with France under its king, but did the treaty still stand? Was America obligated to join France in its war against Great Britain? There was a tense cabinet meeting on the morning of April 19, with Jefferson and Hamilton sparring on opposite sides; could Nelly and Wash hear their raised voices carrying through the house?[8] The president sided with Hamilton and issued a Proclamation of Neutrality on April 22. Perhaps in a bid to maintain normalcy for the children as tensions escalated in the city, George took Nelly and Wash to the circus with his friends the Powels two nights later.[9] But as the weather warmed, so did the controversy over France.[10]

It was not a pleasant summer in the Washington household. Thomas Jefferson reported to James Madison that George was worn down by "little lingering fevers"; it would be unsurprising for the health of anyone, much less a man in his sixties, to suffer under the stress. The newspaper attacks hit George harder, indeed "more than any person I ever met with," Thomas wrote. The new French ambassador was only making things worse; Edmund Charles Genet, bolstered by support from some in the American public, was commissioning privateers to attack English ships and wanted American military aid. The criticisms of the president, first fueled by his elaborate social functions that some found redolent of monarchy and now bolstered by his unwillingness to support the budding French republic, reached an ugly apex. One broadside, titled *The Funeral Dirge of George Washington and James Wilson, King and Judge*, imagined George's beheading. When Secretary of War Henry Knox shared this in an early August cabinet meeting held to discuss what to do about Genet, George lost his cool and "got into one of those passions when he cannot command himself," as Jefferson put it.[11] Perhaps his angry words carried beyond his office and made those who overheard wary around him. It's not surprising that Nelly decided to leave and visit her mother's family in Maryland that summer.[12]

It was a summer shaken by losses for George and indeed the city of Philadelphia. George's nephew and manager at Mount Vernon, George Augustine Washington, had died that spring of tuberculosis at age thirty-five, and his replacement, Anthony Whiting, passed away soon after. Tobias Lear also decided to leave the household to start a business venture, and not long after, his young wife Mary also died.[13] Such frequent losses were painful but common; white Americans who survived past age ten could only expect to live to around fifty-five, and many died much younger, but they still lived longer lives than their British counterparts.[14] Beyond the Washington household, yellow fever began to take hold in Philadelphia, becoming an epidemic by the end of the summer. Some 10 percent of the city's population died within the span of several months. Those that could afford to flee to the countryside did so; the Washingtons left later than most, in the second week of September.[15]

It must have been a relief to get away from the pestilence of both disease and partisan politics to the seclusion of Mount Vernon. George was still hard at work, but he took a day away from his correspondence to march as a master Mason with the local Masons for a ceremony to lay the cornerstone of the Capitol Building in the District of Columbia.[16] The Stuarts took the rare journey from Hope Park with Betsey and Patty to the site of the future Capitol, where they met up with George and likely Martha, Nelly, and Wash. After several speeches, the crowd gathered to eat barbecued ox, but the children hung back. George stepped away from the bustling table and brought them to join the celebration and fill their stomachs before the trip back home. The occasion etched itself into Patty's memory, and she would tell her children of the day years later.[17]

George kept close tabs on the situation in Philadelphia, where he reported in mid-October that "the disorder was raging more violently than ever"; soon, the government was going to have to meet somewhere, whether in Philadelphia or elsewhere.[18] Perhaps he also considered his family, recognizing the emotional and physical toll of the previous few months; Nelly had gotten sick during her visit to Maryland and was still looking unwell, and all of the family had had to deal with the political tensions.[19] Perhaps it was to raise Nelly's spirits, and in turn raise all of theirs with her playing, that he ordered a large and sophisticated harpsichord from London for her in late September.[20]

The unexpected trip home also gave the elder Custis girls a chance to visit their siblings and grandparents. One visitor reported stopping at Mount Vernon in October and finding a quiet family scene—George, Martha, Bartholomew Dandridge, Fanny

Bassett Washington, and the Custis children. George's other secretaries had not accompanied him, so the family had more privacy than usual. The visitor found all of the girls "handsome and agreeable" and enjoyed hearing them play and sing; it was a rare opportunity for Betsey and Patty to have an audience.[21] Perhaps Nelly had brought home the English guitar with her initials carved in an ivory rosette over the sound hole, which George had given her as a gift. Any of the girls could have played a borrowed spinet, and they might have sung from Nelly's book *Original Scottish Airs* or music her sisters had copied into a manuscript music book, including "General Washington's March."[22]

By November, it was safe to return to the North, and the Custis siblings broke up again. They returned to a changed city; everyone in Philadelphia had lost friends, family, or both, and many people wore black mourning clothes. It was still not deemed safe to have concerts or balls, so the evenings were quieter than usual.[23] The trauma of the fever seems to have calmed the political climate some; George's main problem that winter was finding a replacement for Thomas Jefferson, who resigned as Secretary of State at the end of the year. When George's birthday came in late February, the chastened population celebrated, and for George the celebration had double cause—it was the final day of the troublemaker Genet's term as French ambassador.[24]

By March, there was new hope in the air. The weather the whole month was, in George's words, "extreame fine," and while Nelly and Wash had been unwell all winter, they were getting healthy again. Nelly's harpsichord had arrived, and she was hard at work practicing for hours under Martha's watchful eye, adjusting her fingers to the wide double keyboards and pausing her playing to cry in fatigue and frustration. The sophisticated features of the instrument allowed Nelly to manipulate the sound, from emulating the gentle pluckings of harp strings to swelling the sound in a crescendo. As health returned to the family and the city, Nelly could play ever more skillfully for their guests up-stairs in the yellow sitting room as they sipped their tea.[25]

George Washington purchased this double manual harpsichord with
mahogany-veneered case from London for Nelly in 1793.
Nelly was a skilled musician and often played for guests
at the President's House and later Mount Vernon.

Harpsichord, made by Thomas Culliford & Company, 1793.
Courtesy of Mount Vernon Ladies' Association.

There was more good news in the family back in Virginia. Their mother had had another baby, a son named Charles Calvert, the previous month. And, Martha learned, it looked like Patty had attracted the attention of the son of a wealthy Georgetown businessman and landowner; Robert Peter's son Thomas, eight years Patty's senior, had asked the Stuarts for permission to court her. Martha was delighted at the idea of Patty being "settled with a prospect of being happy" and had heard that Thomas was intelligent. Judging by his large collection of books, he was at least an avid reader, and his hobbies including playing the flute and attending horse races. At six feet tall and with dark brown hair and blue eyes, he was also handsome.[26]

Nelly, too, was now drawing admirers. She turned fifteen in March, and her friend Elizabeth Allen's eighteen-year-old brother Andrew wrote her a love poem. Andrew's father had represented Pennsylvania in the Continental Congress but could not agree with the push for independence, and he resigned his seat. As a loyalist, he lost his estate and fled to England, returning in 1792 after he was pardoned. He still identified as British, and came back to Philadelphia as British consul. Andrew, then, did not come from a family well-suited to marry the president's adopted daughter. Nelly was unconcerned by this but did not take Andrew very seriously; she later recalled that she was "too happy & too gay" to fall in love with him. Had she been more serious, she thought, she could have; as an old woman, she remembered "how handsome how healthy, how witty & how agreeable he was, more so than any one I ever knew."[27]

He expressed himself fulsomely (if not originally) in his poetic tribute. "To thee Fair Maid, let love his homage pay," the poem opened. Her cheeks were "blushing as the dawn," her "beauteous lips" formed "smiles angelic," and she had a voice "which listening angels might with rapture hear." The poet knew his suit was hopeless, but he pledged to remain steady to her. Was this effusive rhapsody just his own version of the popular poetry of the day, or were his feelings genuine? Nelly thought he probably wrote with more passion than he felt. While she didn't have serious feelings for Andrew, she valued the poem, saving it until burning it just before her marriage. She didn't need the paper copy; she had memorized it, and as an old woman she committed it to paper again.[28]

She may not have been ready to fall in love yet, but Nelly was growing up. By that fall, Martha reported that "Nelly is a woman in size" (Wash, however, was just becoming "a sturdy Boy"). Nelly still had a youthful cheerfulness and high spirits, which in turn charmed and frustrated George and Martha. "No one laughed more heartily" than George when Nelly told stories of her misadventures and pranks, and he enjoyed Nelly's "joyous and extravagant spirits."[29] But Martha fretted that Nelly needed "a little more Gravatie" to grow out of her current "half crasey" state. Nelly was perpetually a bit disheveled and windblown; her grandparents' friend Elizabeth Powel told her, "You look as if your clothes were thrown on with the Pitchfork." Martha knew Nelly received enough praise as it was, and was careful to point out her granddaughter's faults. But Nelly needed only to look into her eyes to know she was truly and deeply loved.[30]

In the fall of 1794, the family escaped Philadelphia in case yellow fever broke out again, staying at a rented country house north of the city in Germantown. There Nelly spent her time visiting her friend Maria Morris at Morris's family's country house, teaching her pet green parrot to sing a duet of a song from a popular comic opera, and learning to ride horseback. She told her best friend Elizabeth Bordley that she was "harum scarum sans soucie"—scatterbrained and carefree.[31] Martha had another way of putting it—Nelly refused to guard her health carefully enough and was "a pore thoughtless child."[32]

However, George Washington was not in the least relaxed. The family had gone to Germantown rather than Mount Vernon because George needed to stay in Pennsylvania to deal with a growing insurgency in the western part of Pennsylvania. Farmers there had been protesting the federal tax on whiskey, passed as part of Hamilton's financial plan in 1791, because the tax especially burdened small farmers of wheat. Protestors responded to taxes they felt were unjustified in the same way they had during the Revolution: petitioning for relief, then tarring and feathering tax collectors, and then laying siege to the home of the federal tax collector. By early August, the president had proclaimed that the militia would be called out if the protestors didn't disperse by the end of the month. This struggle was about more than a tax, just as the American Revolution had been: it was about the power of the federal government, something the Washington administration was determined to keep a grasp on and even enlarge.[33]

When the rebels didn't relent, the Washington administration charged forward with overwhelming force: nearly thirteen thousand men would rendezvous in Carlisle, Pennsylvania. These included several of George's own nephews—one son each of his brothers Samuel and Charles, and his sister Betty's sons George, Howell, and Lawrence.[34] George himself rode out to inspect and organize the troops, leaving the children with Martha, who remarked gloomily, "god knows when he will return again." Fortunately for Martha, as George traveled and spoke with military leaders, he felt confident that the troops would have no trouble restoring order. It was a serious uprising, but his confidence was well-placed; George headed home three weeks later, and troops quelled the so-called Whiskey Rebellion.[35]

By the time he returned, the family had already gone back to the President's House in Philadelphia.[36] George had reached a breaking point with the partisan attacks, and his annual address the following month was perhaps the most partisan speech he ever gave. He spoke longer than usual, chronicling the Whiskey Rebellion and briefly blaming the unrest on the Democratic Societies (clubs supporting the positions of the Democratic-Republic faction).[37] It would be the first and only time he publicly lashed out at his opponents, although he certainly did so in private—both in letters and at home, where Nelly in particular was imbibing a fierce Federalist loyalty.

In the midst of the tumult that summer and fall, George was also thinking about his role as a father figure to the three Custis girls, particularly as Patty neared marriage. Looking forward to her own entry into adulthood as a married woman, Patty wrote to her stepgrandfather to request a miniature of him. Miniatures could be just as expensive as full-size portraits, and George sent her one by the artist Walter Robertson. Soon after, Betsey wrote asking for one of her own, "as *I* have *no other wish* nearer my *heart* than that of possessing your likeness." She wanted to be able to see an image of the face of the man she "look[ed] up to with greateful affection as a parent to myself and family."[38] Despite the formality of her request, George's response showed that they shared a tender relationship and he wanted to guide her as a father.

Rather than simply replying that Betsey could have a miniature of him, he questioned whether an image of her grandfather was really "the *only* wish of your heart." She had just turned eighteen; wasn't she starting to think of romantic love? Certainly she must be, and he had some advice on finding the right kind of husband. He was sober and down-to-earth, although his advice was very much in keeping with the ideals of the time; she must not "look for perfect felicity" or deep passion. "Love is a mighty pretty thing," he wrote, "but like all other delicious things, it is cloying...[and] too dainty a food to live upon *alone*." If not love, what should she seek in a mate? A sensible man whom she could respect and esteem, and who could support her financially. He told Betsey he was giving her different advice than that he had shared with Patty, advice "more applicable to yourself," and clearly he was concerned that this headstrong and passionate girl would follow her heart rather than her head.[39]

In one of the only surviving letters from George Washington to one of his stepgranddaughters, he offers Eliza (then called Betsey) courtship advice.

Letter, George Washington to Eliza Parke Custis, 1794 September 14.
Courtesy of Mount Vernon Ladies' Association.

Betsey surely valued this letter from her stepgrandfather, which she saved and passed down in her family.[40] But she may have wondered in frustration where she was to meet any man to marry, much less an ideal mate. She and Patty were still stranded much of the time at Hope Park; it's a mystery how Patty managed to meet Thomas Peter. Perhaps they occasionally traveled to Alexandria to go to a ball and stay with friends, and Patty had charmed Thomas over the course of several dances. Patty at least would be getting away; after she married Thomas Peter at Hope Park on January 6 (the Washingtons' own anniversary), she and Thomas moved into a large row home on K Street in George-town. It was a happy escape; the two were well-matched, and years later, Patty would admit that "my home seems bereft of its best half when he is absent." They also traveled to see family for their honeymoon, as was customary, and Betsey accompa-nied them to Philadelphia at the end of the month.[41]

Betsey and Patty perhaps brought with them to Philadelphia enslaved women of David Stuart's, Moll and Nancy Butcher, who had been helping them dress and otherwise tending to them for the past four years (but not at Stuart's expense; he paid himself for their hire to the Custis children from their father's estate).[42] There they would have found five enslaved people they knew from visits to Mount Vernon—Molly, Ona, Hercules, Rich-mond, and Joe.[43] Their futures, at least, were more secure than the sixty-eight enslaved people owned by the Custis estate whom Patty received as her dowry. These men and women were almost certainly drawn from the Custis estates southeast of Richmond, separated from their families and communities. The Peters had no use for so many people, although they did have farms north of the city in Maryland; David Stuart rented many of them to work at Hope Park, while Thomas Peter sold over twenty of them the following year. Thomas, unlike George Washington, seems not to have worried about separating families; he sold enslaved couple Michael and Molly's two eldest daughters, ages eleven and eight, away from their parents.[44]

As enslaved families on the Custis estates waited to learn their fates, Patty and Betsey were enjoying themselves in Philadelphia and even took a short trip to New York to explore and see a play. They spent six weeks at the President's House, with Martha proudly introducing her elder granddaughters to their promi-nent friends in the city. John Adams thought them "fine girls" and thought one of them (probably Patty) was "a fine bloom-ing, rosy Girl," in contrast to Nelly, whom he thought weak "for want of exercise." Both countryside and city agreed with easygoing Patty, who probably delighted in being introduced as a married woman and seeing the capital city with her new husband. Philadelphia got quieter in early March as Congress adjourned and representatives traveled home, and Thomas and Patty left soon after. The prospect of returning to Hope Park without Patty must have seemed bleak, so Betsey decided to stay on in Philadelphia.[45]

Even with Congress in recess, there were plenty of people to entertain in the city. In early April, George and Martha gave a dinner to the English, Spanish, Portuguese, and Dutch ambassa-dors and their wives. Betsey and Nelly might have joined them and likely played music after the meal. One visitor to a dinner at the President's House reported meeting Nelly's "elderly sister" (likely an unfortunate slip of the tongue for "elder") whom he found less pretty than Nelly but "very agreeable."[46] Her grand-mother, on the other hand, found Betsey far from agreeable.

Betsey wasn't outgoing like Nelly, in part because of having lived in such isolation. The ever-sociable Martha thought Betsey was "very grave" and had hoped that "being in the gay world would have a good effect on her." Yet all Betsey wanted was to stay at home and be by herself; she refused to accompany Mar-tha and Nelly on social visits or to the dancing assembly. Even going to church was too tiring. Ill health was not the problem; although Betsey "often complains of not being well," she looked quite healthy to Martha. While initially the change to city liv-ing had been exciting, perhaps the reality of her younger sis-ter's marrying before her and a future helping her mother raise a brood of half siblings in the countryside drew her into depres-sion. Here in Philadelphia was her chance to meet a husband, her one escape route, but she seemed determined not to take it; Martha concluded Betsey was determined "to be alone," although whether this meant in the house or in life is unclear.[47]

It wasn't that Betsey was spending her time reading, sewing, or practicing music; both she and Nelly had become listless and would stand by the tall windows looking down at the busy street, watching carriages and overhearing snips of conversations as people walked by. Sometimes Betsey took walks with her grandfather around the city, and she began accompanying him to the studio of the artist Gilbert Stuart, where he was sitting for a portrait. She stood behind Stuart, watching as he layered stroke after stroke of paint, which gradually came to life as George Washington's face.[48] The artist needed to get to know his subjects to capture them on canvas, and he had trouble getting George to relax enough to get at the man beneath the stern visage. Perhaps having Betsey there, joining in their chats, helped George to open up.

One day, supposedly, she wandered into the studio during a walk, wearing a simple greenish-brown dress, a shawl made by her grandmother drawn over her shoulders and her straw sun hat with red ribbons in her hand, and stood with her arms crossed, watching the artist at work. Stuart turned and saw her, and was determined to paint her just as she looked then.[49] Whether or not this is precisely how he was inspired to paint Betsey, he soon began work on her portrait.[50] He depicted Betsey in simple country attire with a wooded backdrop and the hint of a stream in the distance. But unlike most portraits of women, including others by Gilbert Stuart, Betsey is not demurely posed with her gaze off into the distance or resting gently on us. Arms crossed, eyebrows raised, and the corner of her lips turned up in a hint of a smile, she looks the viewer in the eyes with confidence and self-command. Her stare is arresting, even demanding, and it is clear that this is no ordinary young woman.[51]

This was not the sort of woman who was to everyone's taste, and perhaps part of why she refused to go out is that she felt she could never quite fit in with other young men and women. But Betsey had made enough friends at the beginning of her visit and at events at the President's House that people started to come see her; indeed, Martha said "she had had a great many visits."[52] It seems likely that one of those visitors was a man who may have come to the house initially to see her stepgrandfather. He was a former British official some twenty years Betsey's senior who had recently moved to America, and his name was Thomas Law.

Thomas Law had spent nearly twenty years in India, where he had worked his way up from clerk to provincial judge and built a fortune of £50,000 at a time when only perhaps 1 percent of British families had incomes over £500 per year. He arrived in America aiming to invest not simply in land but in the success of the new nation.[53] Thomas had purchased some five hundred lots in the new federal city at a high price, and as George kept closely involved in the development of the city, Thomas needed to work with him.[54] Thomas was splitting his time between Philadelphia and the District of Columbia, and he met with George in Georgetown in April 1795 when the president took a short trip south.[55] Had the two met before, and had Thomas met Betsey yet? All we know is that Thomas later recalled that he "caught [her] fancy on my first arrival in america. She was a beautiful young woman with a fine person, & nearly related to Genl washington." That close relationship was quite likely the primary draw for Thomas as he started investing in the city George Washington was helping to design. Whenever they initially met, they began writing to one another, making Betsey's life more bearable when she returned to Hope Park that summer.[56]

George Washington and his family left Philadelphia for Mount Vernon early on the morning of July 15, 1795, George riding separately in a phaeton with his family in a coach-and-four and two enslaved men accompanying them on horseback. He was probably relieved to get away, because he had yet another controversy on his hands. A year earlier, he had appointed John Jay to go to Great Britain to negotiate a treaty to deal with British trade restrictions, impressment of American sailors, and occupation of northern forts in America. In March, he received a copy of the treaty and, seeing how little the United States gained from it, planned to keep it confidential at first. But the public learned of it, and the backlash was swift; the treaty still did not establish America's economic independence from Britain, and it ignored impressment. Americans around the country met in committees to write petitions against the treaty, and Democratic-Republican newspapers fumed against it. George, influenced by Alexander Hamilton, decided the treaty would help maintain peace, and the majority of senators agreed with him, ratifying it in late June. The full text of the treaty was published on July 1, and several days later, on the Fourth of July, a mob burned an effigy of John Jay on the outskirts of Philadelphia, an act of protest soon copied in other cities. The anger was about more than just the treaty or Jay; many people were furious that the president and his administration were not paying attention to the will of the people.[57]

In other words, it was a good time to get out of the city. But they weren't home long when George received a letter from his Secretary of State, Timothy Pickering, urgently summoning him back to town. It wasn't only to deal with the treaty; Pickering and Treasury Secretary Oliver Wolcott had documents implying that Attorney General Edmund Randolph, a long-time Washington ally, had been conspiring with the French. George left Mount Vernon on August 9 and, soon after his return, took two decisive steps: he signed the Jay Treaty and he interrogated Edmund Randolph, who immediately resigned in fury. But the criticism in the press would only get worse. In October, his harshest critic, Benjamin Franklin Bache (Benjamin Franklin's grandson), published a story in his *Aurora General Advertiser* saying that the president had been taking more money than he was supposed to from the government (technically he was, but with Congress's approval).[58] Then Edmund Randolph got his revenge, publishing a pamphlet defending his own conduct, criticizing George Washington, and revealing the president's hesitations about the Jay Treaty.[59]

Perhaps it was to spare Nelly from this drama, or to keep Betsey company, that Martha decided that Nelly needed to stay at Hope Park for the winter. Martha claimed that it would be good for Nelly to spend more time with her mother, but this had never been a concern for her before; there were likely other reasons. Besides keeping Nelly away from the partisan vitriol or providing companionship for Betsey, Nelly would also be able to help Patty when she had her first child that winter. Perhaps she would also meet a husband who lived closer to home. Martha left for Philadelphia with Wash (who was likely oblivious to the political turmoil) in mid-October, and the parting with Nelly must have been painful for them both. "To part from Grandmama is all I dread," Nelly wrote her friend Elizabeth the day before Martha departed. "I have lived with her so long—& she has been more than a Mother to me." She had never been away from Martha for more than a short period since she was two, and being away from her grandmother was "the greatest trial, I have ever experienced."[60] She was far closer to Martha than her mother, and she was unaccustomed to living in the seclusion of Hope Park.

But even with Nelly there as a confidante, Betsey seems to have kept her courtship with Thomas a secret. Nineteen-year-old Betsey seems not to have wanted to turn to anybody at Hope Park for advice, and she wrote a cryptic letter in early January to George Washington asking him for advice—but on what? He would advise her "as if you were my own daughter," but he wasn't sure what topic she wanted advice on. "Am I to wait your explanation, or am I to guess at your meaning?" he asked her in reply. He took a guess that for "a girl of nineteen," it must be about love. Did Martha know about Thomas and give George a hint? If so, the advice he gave her on the type of man to marry was a subtle rebuke of Thomas as a mate; if not, George might have later been embarrassed by his words when he learned of the match.

George was more specific and blunt than he had been in his letter over a year earlier. Yes, marriage should be based on friendship rather than just passion, but there was much more. The ideal mate was a person of the same age ("for you and old age, no more than winter & Summer, can be assimilated"); Thomas was twenty years older. The man should be an American; Thomas was British. His wealth should not be based "upon adventitious or fortuitous matters"; Thomas had invested a massive amount of money gambling that he could profit off the new federal city. Avoid the "satirical person, [who] ridicules & exposes the foibles—the persons—& dress of every one"; Thomas clearly delighted in poking fun at others. Another piece of advice would provide prescient: "congeniality of temper, is essential."[61] Had George known that her potential mate had illegitimate sons, not so much younger than Betsey, whose mother was a South Asian woman—a fact Betsey knew and apparently accepted—he might also have counseled against marrying a man with children.[62]

What must Betsey have made of this letter, reading it quietly away from her family to prevent them from prodding into its contents? Things were quite far along with Thomas; did her stepgrandfather's advice mortify her? Force her to consider cutting off the relationship? Soon after she received this letter, she, Nelly, and their mother traveled to Georgetown to stay with the Peters and help Patty with the birth of her first child. It is possible she slipped out to see Thomas while she was there, and not long after she arrived in the city, they announced their engagement. Her mother and stepfather were surprised; while women were supposed to choose their own spouse, it was generally with their family's knowledge and advice. But Betsey, her stepfather told George, "made entirely her own bargain in a Husband." Eleanor and David were concerned about the age difference, but David was reassured after meeting with Thomas that he was "a man of very superior understanding" and large wealth. Thomas had even shared with his prospective stepfather-in-law "the most honourable testimonials of his conduct when in the service of the East India Company." In short, David saw in him an ideal investor in the new federal city—what that meant as a husband was unclear. He would have preferred that Betsey at least not be saddled with mixed-race stepchildren, but Thomas refused to give up his sons.[63]

Betsey wrote George to share the news of her engagement, emphasizing that she had considered things carefully (likely including his own concerns) and asked for his approval after Thomas wrote seeking his blessing as well. George was not thrilled, but he was not going to interfere with Betsey's wishes. Writing to Betsey's stepfather, he admitted that Thomas—"so far as I have obtained any knowledge of his character"—had a decent reputation, but he was a foreigner. Could he be an agent for the British government or its business interests? Might he move back to England against Betsey's wishes?[64] Thomas's own writings give some credence to the idea that he was at least thinking of setting up a trading relationship with the British-government-supported East India Company; he wrote a friend back in England in January 1796 that he intended "to set up an Agency for India at Washington City." Marrying Betsey was one piece of his larger scheme; in the very sentence prior to this, he said, "I hope to obtain the heart of Miss Custis the President's grand daughter." Marrying into the president's family was a strategic move. There was clearly affection involved in this match, but like all good marriages from Thomas's upper-crust British background, it was also economically savvy.[65]

If Betsey was going to marry Thomas, George argued, they needed a prenuptial agreement that preserved Betsey's wealth at the very least. To Betsey, his response was essentially this: if you're *sure* he's the man you want to marry, I approve. He chided her for keeping this matter a secret from him; she could at least tell him now when they planned to marry. "You know how much I love you," he reassured her, and after the preceding words, that assurance must have been welcome. He also wrote Thomas, frankly sharing that the engagement was "a matter of Surprize" and giving his approval. However, he made clear that he expected a prenuptial agreement and that Thomas had better plan to be in America permanently, "for it would be a heart rending circumstance" to take Betsey away from her family.[66] Coming from the president—and a key force in Thomas's investment plans in DC—surely he could do nothing but consent.

Nelly, too, was shocked by the engagement when Betsey finally told her, but it was part of a larger shift in how Nelly thought about herself. She wrote a chatty letter to her friend Elizabeth Bordley back in Philadelphia with news "which I think will surprise you a *little*." It was *"Strange most passing strange,"* she continued, "quite unaccountable (you will cry!) 'tis strange my Dear but nevertheless quite true beleive me." With her elder sisters both married, she would now officially be Miss Custis, rather than Miss Nelly Custis—a customary change in title that signaled in part her eligibility for marriage. Yet she imagined herself and her friend to be spinsters "& so likely to remain to the end of time" (rather comical when Nelly was not quite seventeen). But she was feeling older and more responsible now that she was an aunt and "two or three inches taller upon the strength of it." When she wrote Elizabeth, her mother and sister had just left her behind to help Patty and the baby, christened Martha Eliza Eleanor Peter. ("Thus all the names of its nearest relations are taken in at once without giving offence to any. I approve very much of this way of getting quit of all the family names at once.") She declared herself at once "manager, Nurse, & housekeeper" and was kept so busy she had barely left the house.[67] Yet she was not doing this alone; there was a household of enslaved people cooking, cleaning, and stepping in to care for Patty or the baby whenever needed.

At the time, enslaved people were very much on George's mind. In fact, before he had addressed Betsey's engagement in his letter to David Stuart, he had written at length about his plans for his lands and bondspeople. A week earlier, he had advertised some of the outlying farms at Mount Vernon for lease (his house was located on what he called the "Mansion Farm," but there were also four other adjacent farms). He had become convinced that running a large farm with hundreds of enslaved people could never be as profitable as he had hoped or achieve his vision of English-style agricultural improvement. However, if some of the land was taken off his hands, he could also do without as many bondspeople and hire out the Custis enslaved, then make extra money by selling western lands he owned.

George was willing to take some financial loss to extricate himself from the institution of slavery; the cleanest financial solution would have been to sell enslaved people, but he did not want to separate families. His letter on the plan, as well as David's response, are a bit hard to follow; clearly the men had been having private conversations on the matter for some time. George may have discussed the possibility of freeing his own enslaved people, but they were both concerned with the Custis enslaved. Not only were the Custis bondspeople at Mount Vernon intermarried with George's own, but both George's plantation and David's were farmed by them.[68] George and his stepson-in-law were thus weighing both ethical and financial concerns as they planned for the future of both the enslaved community and the Custis children.

Surely the enslaved people themselves, having only recently experienced wrenching separations when Patty married, braced for the future. Betsey, too, would probably inherit over sixty people at the time of her marriage just as Patty did. As Thomas was not especially comfortable with slavery, he told Betsey's stepfather David Stuart that it was up to her what to do with them.[69] Not long after they married, he mentioned a plan to set them up on a farm in Virginia and allow them "to work out their freedom," but nothing ever came of it.[70] It may also have been Thomas who suggested that Betsey's possible half brother William Costin plus William's mother and half siblings be part of her dowry so that he could free them.[71]

The Laws had little need for labor beyond a few enslaved house servants; they would hire out some people to David Stuart and some to Wash, while others might be lucky enough to stay where they were and experience a change only on paper. It appears that only William Costin and his relatives would later be freed, however.[72] Martha apparently also promised Betsey that she would inherit Martha's valued maidservant after Martha's death. Ona, who knew Betsey to be temperamental and difficult, "was determined never to be her slave."[73] As the family's return to Virginia approached, Ona realized that her best chance to make good on this determination was in the coming months in Philadelphia.

In the meantime, Philadelphia was abuzz with both the president's birthday celebrations and the news that his eldest stepgranddaughter would be marrying "the English East India Nabob." On February 22, bells pealed just after midnight, cannons fired later in the day, and there were a supper and ball in the evening with five hundred people in attendance.[74] But not everyone was eager to wish George a happy birthday; the Democratic-Republicans went so far as to vote down a measure to adjourn the House of Representatives for thirty minutes in his honor.[75] Perhaps even this insult did not lessen Martha's excitement about Betsey's marriage to Thomas Law; soon before this, she had been "as gay as a Girl" in sharing the news with John Adams and recounted the tale of the engagement "in a very humerous style." John and Abigail—perhaps reflective of the sentiment of other friends of the Washingtons—looked on the match less favorably. Abigail thought Thomas would "Do for a Virginia girl" who was accustomed to out-of-wedlock mixed-race children. While she passed along her congratulations to Martha through John, she noted that "when I was young I liked a young Man much better for a companion than an old one."[76]

Thomas married his young bride on March 21, 1796, at Hope Park in a small private ceremony. There was "no dancing or parties of any kind," Nelly said, because her sister didn't want them.[77] She was an unconventional bride in a more important way as well: at her stepgrandfather's insistence, the pair later signed a marriage settlement that gave Betsey control over her own property "for her own entire separate use & possession." It was an arrangement occasionally used by wealthy families to escape the total loss of women's legal control and property ownership called coverture that normally came with marriage in this period. It also protected women and their future children from husbands who might squander their fortunes (which was likely George's concern here). Such agreements weren't particularly common in the early United States, although they were more prevalent among wealthy Virginia families. They also didn't necessarily give women more power; usually these settlements placed financial control in the hands of a trustee rather than the woman herself, and this was the case with the Laws' agreement.[78]

Still, it was the beginning of a new chapter for her, signified by an entire change in her name: besides her new last name, it seems that Thomas called her Eliza, and so she shifted to the more mature nickname. When George and Martha wrote Thomas to congratulate the couple, they now referred to her as Eliza.[79] The Laws moved into a large three-story brick home facing the Potomac River in the southwest quadrant of the District of Columbia as they waited for their permanent home closer to Capitol Hill to be completed. Looking out of the tall windows

over the wide, languid river, the couple must have imagined the
future of the federal city.[80] Mrs. Eliza Custis Law would now
be one of the leading figures of the fledgling society; the Laws
already surveilled the burgeoning capital from a carriage that
one observer thought was unlike any other in America. "She
has every chance for happiness," her sister Nelly concluded.[81]

Nelly herself reaffirmed her determination to remain single,
including in a letter to George recounting her time in Georgetown. She had attended a ball there, but took no interest in the
young men she met there and felt nothing for any of them. Here
George, having already written to her sisters on the subject, decided to reply with advice to his youngest stepgranddaughter
on love and marriage. He wrote on the day he knew the Laws
were marrying, and Nelly must have been thinking of her own
future. First, she should not imagine that she had such control
over her emotions as to choose whether or not to be attracted
to the men she met; attraction was natural and inevitable, and
she must not "boast too soon, nor too strongly, of your insen-
sibility to, or resistance of its powers." Yet as he had told Eliza,
the passions of love "ought to be under the guidance of reason."
When she met a man she was attracted to, she should use her
reason to ask herself what she knew of the man, his background,
his character, and his fortune. She must not give her heart "until
she had secured [her] game." He dismissed her claim to "remain
Eleanor Custis, Spinster," ending his letter with "every blessing,
among which a good husband when you want & deserve one."[82]

What Nelly most wanted at that moment was to be with her
grandmother, not a husband. By May 1796, they had been apart
for seven months, and "I wish more & more every day to see
her."[84] The household in Philadelphia was at that time astir with
preparations for the future. Martha was packing for their return
to Mount Vernon, and she now had two more people to prepare:
Lafayette's sixteen-year-old son George Washington Lafayette,
fleeing the French Revolution as his family members were im-

prisoned, had joined the president's household along with his tutor the previous month. George himself was thinking further ahead, knowing he absolutely would not run for president again. He needed to address the American people with an official farewell that expressed his hopes for the future, and he took up an earlier draft from 1792 (he surely regretted now not retiring then) and began to work on a new version with Alexander Hamilton's help.[85] It was as the family was distracted that Martha's maidservant Ona Judge secretly packed her belongings and, as the family ate dinner in the late afternoon of May 21, slipped out of the house in the first step of her journey to freedom.[86]

Despite the distractions of preparing to leave town, the Washingtons sprang into action. They placed runaway ads in two local newspapers, describing Ona's appearance so that anybody who spotted her would recognize her and know to alert the Washingtons—who offered a reward for tips. George was not going to give up on finding and retrieving her, but he had other matters to attend to.[87] The Washington household left Philadelphia in mid-June with their French guests and without Ona. Throughout the summer, diplomats—including a group of a dozen Catawba people on an informal visit to pay respects and perhaps make small requests—came to Mount Vernon to meet with the president. He also kept up a correspondence with his advisors about what to do with his ambassador to France, James Monroe, who he felt was not following instructions and was being overly friendly to the French.[88] He left Martha and the children at Mount Vernon in mid-August and returned to Philadelphia, and Eleanor Stuart, Patty, and Eliza came in his stead. Nelly was "as happy as a mortal can wish to be," home with her grandmother, mother, and sisters. They played and sang, took walks and horseback rides, and Nelly practiced her French, likely with the help of their French guests.[89]

When the family returned to Philadelphia soon after, the mood there had changed. George's presidency was nearing its end, and on September 19, he published the farewell address he had labored on for so long. For the rest of her life, Nelly remembered watching him at work on drafts of the speech, on one occasion in the summer of 1796 bringing him silk thread to sew the sheaf of pages together.[90] The address set out his advice for the country as it moved forward in a precarious position, with its main allies in Europe at war abroad and partisan factions at war at home. His vision for the country was in many ways a response to the rising partisan strife, but it also built on his years of experience in public service.[91] This speech marked his metaphorical passing of the torch, and as attention turned to the presidential election, the attacks on George Washington subsided.

Late that fall, George focused on getting Wash settled at Princeton, hoping that the fifteen-year-old (college education began earlier then) would finally apply himself to his studies. From childhood, Wash had demonstrated what George called "an almost unconquerable disposition to indolence in every thing that did not tend to his amusements." George had tried urging him gently to spend his time wisely, but now that Wash was nearing adulthood, he would take a firmer tone.[92] Evidently, George felt comfortable giving Wash the kind of stern advice and guidance that Martha never really had; George wrote him lengthy letters urging him to study hard, form good habits, and choose suitable friends, all in preparation to be "a useful member of Society."[93] His letters to Wash are far more formal than those to his stepgranddaughters, in part to impress upon his charge the importance of his education—if George could help it, Wash would not follow in Jacky's footsteps.

Nelly, returning to live in Philadelphia for the last time, would have enjoyed the whirl of social activities as her stepgrandfather's presidency came to a close. In mid-January, she became an aunt for the second time when Eliza gave birth to a daughter also named Eliza (Eleanor Stuart, too, had had another baby—named Eleanor—about ten days earlier).[94] Nelly Custis was now a beautiful young woman just shy of eighteen; one visitor had recently written that she had "more perfection of form, of expression, of color, of softness, of firmness of mind than I have ever seen before or conceived consistent with mortality." With Wash out of the house, she had a chance to practice her French and bond with George Washington Lafayette, who was the same age as Nelly and treated as part of the family. She could also now attend her grandmother's drawing rooms with less shyness, including chatting with young gentlemen. At one such event, the senior Lafayette's friend the Chevalier de La Colombe engaged Nelly for some time in private conversation, although when pressed as to whether it meant anything, Nelly retorted in a way that must not have surprised George—"if there was [anything to it] the Gentleman alone was acquainted with it."[95] Nelly was clearly the most eligible young woman in the capital city; when she left Philadelphia, there would be a gap waiting to be filled for the new "Miss Custis of the place."[96]

The whole family must also have attended the huge celebration of George's birthday on February 22, when some 1,200 people attended a ball at Ricketts' Amphitheatre. As a member of the first family, Nelly could not have wanted for partners. As she danced in the candlelight, George surveyed the scene cheerfully, his face finally looking more healthy than haggard after the years of stress. But with the end of his presidency less than two weeks away, he was also filled with a mix of emotions so strong that they showed on his usually stony countenance. One observer noted that he was so overcome by emotion that "he could sometimes scarcely speak."[97]

There was one last levee, one last drawing room, and then George Washington's presidency officially ended on the day of John Adams's inauguration, March 4, 1797. The day dawned cloudy, but the skies cleared and the air was brisk. The family accompanied George on the short walk to Congress Hall at Sixth and Chestnut streets. Nelly took a seat towards the back and next to a family friend because she could not bear to be seated just before George as his successor was inaugurated. George walked to the front of the room, dressed in a black suit, to thunderous applause. He sat to the left of the Speaker's chair, which John Adams soon occupied, on a raised dais. During the short ceremony, occasionally a short sob broke from the crowd, and John Adams himself wept. George kept his habitual composure, but as John closed his inaugural address, George took in the tears on the faces of his audience, and several tears fell from his own eyes.[98]

That night, as the family returned to Ricketts' Amphitheatre for a farewell dinner with several hundred people, the organizers unveiled a transparent painting, lit from behind by candles, of George Washington with Mount Vernon in the distance. Finally, after decades of public service, the Washingtons were returning home for good. Their enslaved house servants could return to their families, although leaving behind whatever ties they had formed in Philadelphia's Black community. The family packed up their belongings in the President's House for the last time and left Philadelphia five days later.[99] George Washington had left the presidency, but the power and fame of the presidency had not left him, and it wouldn't leave his stepgrandchildren, either.

CHAPTER 3

The Ruling Family of Washington

AMID THE BUMPING AND SWAYING OF THE carriage on the rutted dirt roads through Maryland, Nelly Custis felt mixed emotions. The journey from Philadelphia was tiring and boring; on the weeklong trip home to Mount Vernon, shut in a carriage and layered in warm clothes against the cold March weather, she had plenty of time to consider what she was leaving behind and what was ahead. In her six years in Philadelphia, she had formed close and lifelong friendships, as well as having had access to the best theater, museums, education, and society in the new country. It hardly seemed real that "Grand-papa is no longer in office" and she and her grandparents were moving permanently back to Mount Vernon.[1]

Perhaps it was not until Nelly awoke to a beautiful, sunny March morning several days after they returned that she realized how glad she was to be home. After several wet and cool days, it was looking like spring; flowers were opening, the grass was turning from its winter brown to a lush green as it sloped down to the Potomac River behind the house, and a chorus of birds kept up a steady song. "When I look at this noble river, & all the beautifull prospects around," she reflected, "I pity all those who are in Cities, for surely a country life, is the most rational

& the most happy of any." The view from the back portico of Mount Vernon out across the river and the wooded shores of Maryland was, one European visitor wrote, "perhaps the most beautiful view in the world."[2]

Away from the noise, smells, and bustle of Philadelphia, there were other pleasures as well. Her mother, half siblings, sisters, and young nieces were close by, and George Washington had left behind the stresses of the presidency and "already turned Farmer again." Nelly would learn to garden and help Martha run the household (both benign-sounding tasks, except that they really meant directing the labor of enslaved people), and in her leisure time she would play the harpsichord and sing duets with her sisters.[3] Her brother Wash was still away at college at Princeton, but she had a surrogate brother in George Washington Lafayette, who, with his tutor, was staying on with the family as he awaited news that it was safe to return to France.

Those first days back at Mount Vernon were a sort of honeymoon for Nelly and her grandparents, but George and Martha in particular soon had to face reality. First, the house and grounds: having not lived there for more than a few months at a time for eight years, George found everything "to be exceedingly out of Repair." The furniture in the rooms was sagging and worn, and much of it would need to be replaced with the better pieces from Philadelphia. George immediately hired workers to spruce up the house and outbuildings, and soon the house was noisy and dusty with the renovation work. "We are all on litter & dirt," George noted.[4] It could not have made Martha's job getting the household back in order easier, and Nelly, too, must have felt the inconvenience. It surely increased the strain and work for the enslaved house servants, newly adjusting to having the family back in residence and now having to cook and clean in the middle of a renovation. Most troubling for Martha was finding a new cook; their enslaved chef Hercules Posey had left Mount Vernon to find freedom on George's birthday a month earlier.[5]

There was another, more lasting reality: the family had left the presidency behind, but they could not get away from either politics or celebrity. Nor, perhaps, did they want to. George Washington was not just the first to serve as president, but also the first to *leave* the office; to what extent he would still have a role to play had yet to be determined. George asked his Secretary of War, James McHenry, kept on by President John Adams, to update him on what was happening in the government; he could not trust the newspapers alone and wanted inside information.[6] He had no plans to make his views public, but he would keep up correspondence with those in power and was not shy about sharing his views.

The artist and engraver of this print capitalized on the success of the popular print of Edward Savage's "The Washington Family" with a different composition. Unlike Savage, Paul has included three rather than two of the siblings; it is unclear which sister is omitted. The print was popular in the nineteenth century.

Edward Bell after Jeremiah Paul, *The Washington Family*, 1800. Fletcher Fund, transferred from the American Wing. New York, Metropolitan Museum of Art.

As for his and indeed the family's celebrity, he still met with veneration wherever he went—and it often came to him. On his ride home from Philadelphia, mounted troops escorted him, and the firing of cannons and a sixteen-gun salute welcomed him into his namesake capital city. Mount Vernon was once again hosting a constant stream of visitors from America and abroad. Everyone from a Polish nobleman to congressmen to the future king of France came to see the former president. George and Martha regularly presided over large dinners with a mix of family and strangers; in addition to unrelated visitors, the elder Custis girls Eliza and Patty, their husbands, and their young children were regular guests.[7]

Day after day, the large table in the dining room had to be set with silver and china, with porcelain dishes laden with meats, vegetables, and puddings set out symmetrically in the middle of the table and the mahogany chairs arranged just so. Dinner was served around three, after which the men stayed around the table drinking Madeira and chatting. George then spent several hours reading newspapers and answering letters before everybody gathered again for tea at sunset and several hours of conversation.[8] Within a few months of this, George and Martha were so worn down that George had invited another of his nephews to come help entertain guests.[9] There would be no rest, however, for the enslaved cooks, waiters, and housemaids like Frank Lee, Christopher Sheels, and Caroline Branham, who were doing the truly hard labor.

Even though the Custis grandchildren were no longer living together, their lives after the presidency followed a similar path: they entered adulthood as celebrities ready to take their place in society as leading figures in or near the new capital city. Eliza and Patty, long distant from the presidential family, now became part of the extended household and delighted in serving as representatives of George in the city. Nelly did not seem to mind sharing the limelight with her sisters and was well on her way from flighty lightheartedness to a more sedate adulthood (for good or ill). Wash gave his adoptive parents the most trouble, but even he began to find his footing as a public figure. They all expected many happy years with George and Martha at Mount Vernon and in the growing federal city.

When it came to sixteen-year-old Wash Custis, George Washington was determined to push him—even drag him—into a future different from Wash's father's. Jacky Custis had, to his stepfather's frustration, spent more time socializing than he had studying with his private tutor in Annapolis, and he lasted less than six months at King's College in New York.[10] Ensuring that their children were well-educated was a priority for George and his fellow founders; they were convinced that the new nation needed well-educated men to maintain the young republic. As George told Wash again and again, education was necessary for him to become "a useful member of society" and serve his country. Although he did not write it directly to Wash, he hoped Wash could someday serve "in the Council of his Country"—in other words, in elected or appointed office in the government. The founders had unrealistically high expectations for the next generation, demanding virtuous behavior, genteel manners, and studious attention to subjects ranging from math to classical languages. In keeping with their larger ideals of self-government, they also wanted their sons to *choose* to dutifully do all of this rather than be coerced into it. No wonder that so many of them beyond Jacky and Wash failed.[11]

The good-natured Wash was, as ever, eager to please his step-grandfather. There is no sign he had any ambition to serve in government—imagine trying to live up to George Washington's example!—and he knew he stood to inherit vast plantations and enslaved laborers. He may well have felt that a college education was unnecessary, but he revered George and would do as he was told. He reported in late March 1797 that he was progressing in his studies of Roman history, French, philosophy, and geography, although he still struggled with math. George responded with praise for Wash's improved writing, both in his hand and style, and used the favored tactic of late eighteenth-century fathers to coerce their sons: conditional love. If Wash kept up his studies, he would be "a welcome guest at all times at Mount Vernon"; the reverse, of course, was that his adopted father did not want to see him if Wash slacked off.[12] When Wash stopped to visit the Washingtons' friends, the Morrises, on his way home soon after, both Robert Morris and his wife wrote George praising Wash's progress; Wash "is astonishingly improved and is a manly fine Fellow." George must have shared this letter with Martha and Nelly, because soon after, Nelly wrote a friend offering the same praise—Wash was "astonishingly improved."[13]

Yet soon after Wash returned to Princeton the following month, he wrote home to George that he wanted to leave college. The letter does not survive, so it's unclear why; perhaps the visit home to Mount Vernon, where the rest of his family was finally reestablished, had made it hard to return to student life and rules. George was at his wit's end; "I could say nothing to him now, by way of admonition—encouragement—or advice, that has not been repeated over & over again," George sighed to Princeton's president, Samuel Stanhope Smith. This time he would try making Wash feel guilty for defying his family's wishes—and it worked. "My very soul tortured with the sting of conscience at length called reason to its aid and happy for me triumphed," Wash wrote to George. It was an uphill struggle. He was determined to show that he had turned a corner, skipping a Fourth of July ball so as not to distract from his studies (unnecessary, George replied) and reporting dutifully on exactly with whom he was corresponding. George had little patience with any of this; when Wash said it had been a stifling 110 degrees at Princeton, George retorted that that was impossible because it hadn't gone above 91 at Mount Vernon.[14] No matter what he did, it seemed, Wash could not please George.

Perhaps it was because he felt he could never live up to

George's standards that Wash just could not keep up the strict behavior and obedience required of him at college. He was not alone; young men in colleges regularly broke the rules and even started riots in this period. Particularly for Southern white men, who had grown up with enslaved people at their command, living under a college's rules chafed at their independence. In their eyes, submission to authority was for the enslaved, not for young white gentlemen.[15] By September, Smith was reporting to George of Wash's poor behavior, and Wash was suspended and sent home for "various acts of meaness & irregularity" as well as "having endeavoured in various ways to lessen the authority & influence of the faculty."[16] Wash returned to Mount Vernon in early October and would never return to Princeton (whether this was his, George's, or Smith's decision is unclear).

George was not ready to give up on Wash's education, but if Wash was going to study on his own, he would need a routine. George provided him with a model daily schedule, which "*if really applied to it*, instead of running up & down stairs, & wasted in conversation with any one who will talk with you," should work. George himself followed a strict daily schedule, rising at 5:00 a.m. and riding out early to survey his farms; Wash, at seventeen, simply did not have this kind of discipline. Granted, his was not an overly taxing schedule; Wash was to study between breakfast and an hour before dinner (from around eight to two), and if he had any work to finish up, again from around eight at night until he went to bed. In the afternoons and early evenings, he could do what he pleased. Wash knew he was under surveillance, though; when George was in the house, he kept an eye on Wash to make sure that he stayed in his room. With Wash's bountiful energy and lack of focus, however, self-directed study was just not going to work.[17]

It was a frustrating situation for the whole family. George saw Wash off on a visit to his mother and stepfather at Hope Park and sent along a letter asking the Stuarts what they thought should be done; "what is best to be done with him, I know not," George admitted. While there were several other colleges Wash could go to, George didn't think it was worth it if Wash was opposed to the idea—and yet Wash was so deferential and afraid of disappointing his stepgrandfather, he wouldn't say anything. Maybe he would be more open with his mother? The Stuarts weren't sure what to do with him either; never an optimist, David Stuart dourly concluded that "His habits and inclinations are so averse to all labour and patient investigation, that I must freely declare it as my opinion that not much is to be expected from any plan." Wash seemed to agree; he didn't want to go to Princeton or any other college, because "he found his habits of indolence and inattention so unconquerable, that he did not expect to derive any benefit from the plans pursued in them." He seems to have absorbed the constant criticism from his adopted father, stepfather, and likely his teachers. David Stuart rode over to Mount Vernon to confer with George, and George ultimately concluded that the best plan was to send Wash to St. John's College at Annapolis because that's where George thought there would be "less of that class of people which are baneful to youth."[18] Wash himself had no say in the matter.

Despite Wash's own belief that he could not succeed in college, off he went to Annapolis in March 1798. He found it "a very pleasant place" and took a room in the three-story brick house of "a Mrs. Brice a remarkable clever woman."[19] A room in a town house could not have been as comfortable as life at Mount Vernon, but he seemed determined to make the best of it. Wash was flattered by the welcome he received from the people in Annapolis; surely the city's residents knew who he—and his grandparents—were. Nonetheless, his new professor John McDowell had the same assessment of him as all his previous teachers had: he wasn't a bad kid, but he simply could not do math or focus on his studies, and he could learn something one day and forget it the next.[20]

Still struggling at yet another school, Wash found pleasure where he could, entering Annapolis society and making new friends—as well as falling for a young woman named Miss Jennings. The Jenningses were a prominent family in Annapolis, but it's unclear precisely which young Jennings this was; it may well have been Elizabeth, daughter of the recently deceased Thomas Jennings.[21] Wash knew that at just barely seventeen, he was too young to marry, and he told Miss Jennings that he could not even become engaged unless his family approved. Somehow, George found out and was horrified. For George, it was another repeat of Wash's father: it had been while studying in Annapolis that Jacky had met Eleanor Calvert, and against George's wishes, Jacky ultimately left college to marry her when he was just twenty and she seventeen.[22] George wrote Wash a letter that must have struck Wash, struggling into manhood, to the core. George remonstrated that "a *boy* your age" was too young to form "a serious attachment." His mother, too, wrote him in distress. Wash admitted to both that he had been courting Miss Jennings with the aim of formally proposing to her in the future, a plan the young woman wisely refused.[23] An open admission of affection was not, among elite men and women of this era, strictly an engagement, but it was not something women did unless they were sure a man intended to marry them.[24] Miss Jennings was not going to gamble and wait.[25]

The next month, as he packed to come home for a break at the end of the term, Wash wondered whether he was coming home for good. He knew his studies were falling short, and it would not have been surprising if his family wanted to keep him away from Miss Jennings. Wash wrote George asking about how to pack; for a trip home or a permanent return? This sparked George's formidable temper. "The question, 'I would thank you to inform me whether I leave it entirely, or not, so that I may pack up accordingly,' really astonishes me!" George fumed in reply, "for it would seem as if *nothing* I could say to you made more than a *momentary* impression." Hadn't he told Wash that the goal was to finish his education? Wash returned home in a sullen mood, likely embarrassed at having been so chastised by George and knowing that, despite failure after failure, he was going to have to continue in college.[26]

George was annoyed to find Wash hiding away from guests and wandering the house "moped & Stupid." His stepfather saw little point in sending Wash back to Annapolis, and his mother feared he would rekindle his relationship with Miss Jennings (perhaps ruing her own early marriage and wishing otherwise for her son). But George was firm; Wash *would* go back to college. Early September and the start of the fall term came, and while Wash said he was willing to go back to St. John's, his body language showed the opposite. Perhaps Martha pleaded his case, or George gave in because he was pressed by greater concerns. Wash would stay at Mount Vernon and receive private tutoring from Tobias Lear, who had recently returned to the household.[27]

The long and frustrating quest to educate Wash Custis had essentially reached its end. Had Wash—and his father Jacky—failed, or had George and Martha failed them? Clearly neither of the Custis young men were great students, with their good humor far outpacing their self-discipline. Martha had fretted over and spoiled both of them, and many educators blamed lax parenting as the source of the young men's failures.[28] But Jacky's and Wash's poor educational careers were rather typical, caused by some alchemy of parenting, societal mores, educational techniques, and individual skills and temperament. If Wash could not please George Washington by succeeding in school, he would find some other way to bring honor to his famous stepgrandfather.

Nelly's life post-presidency was off to a much more pleasant start than her brother's. When she returned home in 1797, she was eighteen, beautiful, charming, and rich, not to mention being a member of the former first family: in short, she was one of the most eligible women in America. Her two elder sisters had married well, and now it was her turn to find a suitable spouse.

John Adams and perhaps George himself had hoped Nelly and John Quincy Adams might make a match, uniting the two leading Federalist families.[29] But this was not dynastic Europe; Nelly would make her own choice, however loaded it was in the public eye. With her granddaughter's formal education over, Martha was now focused on teaching her the skills necessary to be a genteel housewife and effective manager of enslaved people. Still, Nelly had few required tasks and plenty of leisure time. "I am not very industrious," she admitted to a friend, "but I work a little, read, play on the Harpsichord, write, & walk, & find my time fully taken up with these several employments."[30] While Nelly demurred that she had rarely left home ever since her return to Virginia, she had regularly attended teas and balls both for amusement and in search of a husband.

An eligible young woman like Nelly could not enter society without being closely observed and becoming the subject of gossip and rumors. In mid-April she attended a ball at the newly built Union Tavern in Georgetown, where she must have drawn attention by dancing six dances with a wealthy, handsome Marylander named Charles Carroll. With his blond hair, blue eyes, and experience traveling in Europe—not to mention his well-regarded family background—he made an attractive choice for Nelly. People had sung his praises to her, but apparently directly to the young man as well; Nelly found him to be full of himself. So she assured her friend Elizabeth Bordley, whose suspicions were raised when she heard about the six dances with Charles. That was no cause for drawing conclusions, Nelly explained; women usually stayed with the same partner for an entire ball in Maryland and Virginia.[31]

But those six dances seem to have stuck in local gossipmongers' memory, because after Charles made a short visit to Mount Vernon an entire year later, rumors reached Wash in Annapolis that he was there to propose to Nelly. Wash, perhaps trying to prove his maturity to George, wrote him reporting the rumor and conveying his approval in terms that sound straight out of a Jane Austen novel. He had heard that Carroll was:

> a young man of the strictest probity and morals discreet without closeness, temperate without excess and modest without vanity—possesed of those amiable qualities of benevolence and friendship which are so commendable in any one, and with as few vices as the age will admit of.

Be that as it may, Nelly had no intention of marrying him, and he never asked her. George denied the rumor to Wash, while Nelly responded heatedly to her friend Elizabeth Bordley when the gossip reached Philadelphia. Had Nelly been keeping her engagement a secret from her best friend, Bordley probed? "*Report* has often informed me that he was attached to a certain Eleanor Parke Custis, an *oddity* of these parts," Nelly wrote, "but as *he* has never told it to *her* by *tongue*, or *pen*, therefore she is yet in the *dark* as to the *truth* of the surmise & consequently she is not, nor has been engaged to said Charles Carroll."[32]

Carroll wasn't the only man that rumors linked with Nelly. The gossipmongers, she sighed, needed to "allow her to *marry who* she *pleases*, & *when she pleases* without perpetually *engaging her to those whom she never had a chance of marrying*, & *never wished to be united to.*" Being a celebrity on the marriage market, even in the late eighteenth century, was a harrowing experience. In the summer of 1797, word spread that she would marry George Washington Lafayette, who had been staying with her family. But the young Lafayette was a brother and friend to Nelly; "as to being *in love with him* it is entirely out of the question," she told Elizabeth Bordley emphatically. She had yet to meet the man whom she loved *"with all my Heart"*—a love based not in romance, she explained, but esteem (a notion wholly in keeping with George's advice). It was possible she would never meet such a man, she admitted; "if so—then I remain *E P Custis Spinster for life*."[33]

Barely ten days after Nelly penned these words, another single young man joined the household at Mount Vernon. Lawrence Lewis was a tall widower of thirty-one whose figure was slimmer than his uncle George Washington's but whose face was very like George's.[34] This mature, serious nephew doesn't seem to have attracted much of Nelly's notice; he had come to help his uncle in any way possible, although he admitted that he was "un-tutored in almost every branch of business." Lawrence's father Fielding had lost his fortune during the American Revolution and died in 1781, when Lawrence was just fourteen. As one of a dozen children in a financially strapped family in Fredericksburg, Virginia, Lawrence had never had the kind of educational opportunities available to the Custises. As when George had hired Lawrence's elder brothers as secretaries during the presidency, George employed Lawrence as much for his nephew's benefit as for his own. Lawrence was not destitute, though; he had inherited about a dozen enslaved people from his father and had a small plantation northwest of Fairfax in the foothills of the Shenandoahs.[35] To Nelly, he was probably just another in a long line of secretaries serving her stepgrandfather.

Besides, Nelly was too busy enjoying her carefree round of entertainments to focus on any one man for long. She rode into Alexandria with her brother "full gallop" through the pouring rain, soaking her fine dress and beaver hat; attended parties that went until five in the morning; and critiqued theater performances that did not live up to those she had seen in Philadelphia. She mocked one suitor who had "a pug nose, ugly mouth," a lisp, and glasses, of questionable intelligence since he had only spoken to her of "*little Cupids* by wholesale, with *Hearts, darts, hopes, fears, heartachs,* & all the etcetera superfluous, of the *tender passion*." She played with Patty's and Eliza's young daughters and helped Patty come up with the name for her second daughter—Columbia, "after the *City*, & district of Columbia." In her cheerfulness, she found even the icy barrenness of the winter landscape "so bleak & sublimely horrifying that I am quite delighted" and a perfect backdrop to read the popular gothic novel *The Mysteries of Udolpho*.[36] She could be flighty and knew that others thought so; "it being a received opinion that I am a rattle brain, cracked pated inconsistent oddity," she recorded in a short autobiography written for a friend. She was not wife material, she admitted, but "I am a good sort of a good for nothing somebody."[37] Nelly's playful assessment did hit on a key truth: in some sense, she would always be a "somebody" because of her relationship to George Washington, whether she was good for anything or not.

Nelly downplayed her accomplishments, however. She had real musical and artistic talent; one smitten visitor to Mount Vernon declared, "She plays the harpsichord, sings, draws better than any woman in America or even in Europe."[38] She was also far more engaged with the world around her than she sometimes let on. Nelly began to see herself as an adult with real responsibilities, particularly those that came with the great wealth she already held and was due to inherit. This recognition is evident in one small act: her designation of George Washington as a proxy to vote for her in the election for the board of directors of the Bank of Alexandria. George had bought her four shares in October 1797, and all adult stockholders, male or female, technically had a right to vote in such elections (although many didn't bother, and at eighteen Nelly might not yet qualify as an adult). Her stepgrandfather was also a shareholder, and it seems likely she would have deferred to his choice of candidates; nonetheless, here Nelly was acting as an independent woman of means.[39]

Nelly had strong political opinions, clearly shaped by George Washington's own but expressed with less delicacy and moderation. "Although I am no politician I can assure you," Nelly wrote Bordley, using a typical female disclaimer, "yet I cannot avoid expressing my opinion of the *French*."[40] In the same dramatic and humorous manner in which she described balls and suitors, she decried the French and their government as tensions heated up between America and France during what historians call the Quasi War in 1798. The French, now at war with the British, were angry that Americans continued to trade with Great Britain. They seized over three hundred American merchant ships and essentially refused to negotiate with the Americans absent significant bribes. Understandably, many Americans were insulted, and the Federalist-led government began preparing for war. Other than for a brief period in the summer of 1798, there was little expectation that the French would actually invade; the "war" turned out to be largely the US Navy protecting American ships as they crossed the Atlantic.[41]

As tensions heated up in late 1797 and early 1798, though, Nelly saw real danger ahead from France. She wouldn't "trust the life of a *Cat* in the hands of a sett of people who hardly know religion, humanity or Justice." While "some frenchmen I esteem highly—but those barbarous *democratic murderers*, or rather *Demons*, I shall ever abominate." Soon she was ready to declare herself "an outrageous politician" and a Federalist partisan. Even her musical choices were political; she regularly sang a tune that expressed *"strong patriotic feelings."* She imagined forming a regiment of women soldiers in black dresses and black leather helmets with plumes of black feathers to fight the French; "how glorious, to be celebrated as the *preservers* of our *Friends & Country*," she exclaimed.[42]

Around this time, according to John Adams's recollection around twenty-five years later, Nelly did something nearly as bold: she rode to the county courthouse on election day and "demanded her right to vote as a free holder."[43] Virginia law permitted adult white males who owned twenty-five acres of land with a house or fifty acres of unsettled land ("freeholders") to vote, and according to Adams, by that time Nelly met the land ownership requirement (Adams was mistaken). She had not yet

reached the minimum voting age of twenty-one, and of course
she was not male, but unqualified voters regularly turned up and
tried to vote—just not women.[44] Nelly would almost certainly
have known that at this time, single women property owners in
New Jersey could vote. But in her correspondence, Nelly never
mentioned women's right to vote or even engaged with the nascent women's rights literature, which focused on women's rights
as wives and to an education.[45] Given that there is no other account of this tale among the voluminous Custis papers or the
writings of those who knew her, it may have as much truth as
the rumors about the men she was engaged to marry. Nonetheless, such a story could only spread—and remain in someone's
memory for decades—if it sounded like something the impetuous, spirited, and highly political Nelly would have done.

Nelly did take firm action to support her political commitments. She announced that she would reject any (male) family
member who declined to fight the French if they invaded. This
hit close to home; when she expressed that sentiment, Congress
was in the process of naming George Washington as commander
in chief of the provisional army being raised in case of just such
an invasion. At the time, the president and commander in chief
were not synonymous, and President John Adams wanted the
experienced and popular general to lead the military effort.
George agreed on the condition that he serve as the organi-
zational head rather than actually going out in the field unless
absolutely necessary.[46]

When Secretary of War James McHenry came personally to
Mount Vernon to deliver George's commission in July 1798,
Nelly took the opportunity to ask for his help getting a standard (flag) made for a local company of volunteer dragoons.
Following up in writing (despite what she admitted was the irregularity of a lady opening a correspondence, especially with a
cabinet secretary), she asked that the standard be decorated with
the figure of America (often depicted as a woman) presenting a
flag with "my favorite Motto—Conquer or Die" to a member

of the dragoons. She would not have her own female regiment, but she was adopting this company and wanted "*My* Standard to be the handsomest ever seen in America." He had the standard made for her, and she was finally able to present it to the captain of the Alexandria Independent Dragoons in December 1798. Her letter accompanying it and the captain's reply (lauding the "fair Daughters of Columbia" who had "overcome the timidity natural to the sex" and expressed opposition to the French) were printed in newspapers across the country.[47] George Washington was back in command—indeed, when these letters were published, he was in Philadelphia coordinating the raising of the army—and Nelly was entering the national stage in a new way.[48]

Nelly was hardly thinking of marriage until the specter of war opened her eyes to what—or rather *whom*—she stood to lose. George's nephew Lawrence had been quietly pursuing Nelly, unbeknownst to George, and Nelly had refused him. She had sworn never to marry a widower or a relative of George Washington, and Lawrence was both.[49] However, when Lawrence asked his uncle for a commission in the new army and was appointed captain in a regiment of light dragoons, the prospect of losing him shook Nelly.[50] "Cupid," she explained, "took me by surprise." She resisted it, but finally she had to admit to herself that she was in love with Lawrence.[51] Cupid certainly was surprising; Lawrence was no match for Nelly's beauty, wit, or charm and could not have kept up with her intellectually. Perhaps she saw the older Washington nephew as a steadying force, and he was certainly a ticket to keeping her in close contact with George and Martha. With George away in Philadelphia but Martha surely aware of the proceedings, Nelly and Lawrence agreed to marry on George's birthday that coming February. When George returned in mid-December, he seems to have been pleased by the engagement; he told several friends in language rather playful for him that before Lawrence "enters the Camp of Mars" he was first "to engage in that of Venus."[52]

As it turned out, Nelly was not willing to let Lawrence risk going to war, despite her strident martial claims months earlier. Just before their marriage, Lawrence wrote Secretary of War James McHenry declining his commission; it was enclosed in a letter from George, explaining Lawrence's choice. It is hard to imagine that George agreed with this decision, but Nelly had a formidable will, and he left the decision to the couple. Nelly further cemented her power in the relationship by deciding where they would live. Initially they had planned to move to Lawrence's farm in the Shenandoah Mountains, but not long after the marriage, she concluded that "I prefer'd a *room* in my Beloved Grandmama's house, to a Palace away from her." We do not know how Lawrence felt about these decisions; as a young man in straitened financial circumstances marrying a wealthy, beautiful young woman, he may have simply relished his luck. Nelly was, as he told a friend, a wife in "every way calculated to make the Matrimonial state desirable, and a Heven on Earth."[53]

There was good reason for both George and Martha to be pleased with the match; Nelly was marrying a young man of related pedigree—and even a family resemblance—to George, tying the Washington and Custis lines even closer together. George took a real interest in the love affair, and Nelly shared her love letters from Lawrence with him.[54] She wanted George to procure her marriage license as her legal guardian, but since he had never officially taken on that role, in her last days as a single woman he became her guardian. On George's sixty-seventh birthday, he dressed in his buff-and-blue Continental Army uniform and watched his nephew and stepgranddaughter wed at Mount Vernon just as night fell on the cold, clear day. Nelly wore a white gown and white plume in her hair, her grandmother donned a flowered satin gown, and the bridegroom was probably in his uniform from his earlier military service. Decades later, an enslaved house servant remembered watching the ceremony (likely from the back of the room or the doorway) and partaking of the huge spread of food; it was a joyous day for the entire household, particularly since it seemed that none of the enslaved would be forced to leave with the newly married couple.[55] Americans celebrated the marriage as far away as Boston, where John and Abigail's son Thomas (whom his parents had hoped might marry Nelly himself after John Quincy had wed) toasted Nelly at a birthday ball for George Washington. *"Miss Nelly Custis,"* he declared, raising his glass high, "may her nuptials, on this day, lay the foundation for a numerous race of heroes & of patriots." The crowd applauded loudly, both for the celebrity first daughter and the notion that George Washington's family line would continue through her.[56]

The future of the dynasty had a somewhat inauspicious beginning. After an exhausting round of parties in the couple's honor, both at Mount Vernon and beyond, the Lewises traveled for the entire spring and summer visiting Lawrence's relatives around Virginia. At his brother George's home in Fredericksburg, one of Lawrence's eyes became so inflamed that he had to be shut in a dark room for an entire month; Nelly was beside herself with anxiety. Then she fell dangerously ill for a month herself.[57] But by the time the couple returned to Mount Vernon, Nelly was visibly pregnant, and the pair were healthy again. They would not, however, be leaving anytime soon; George gratified Nelly's wish to stay close to her grandparents by promising the couple a two-thousand-acre parcel of his estate that included his "best, & most productive" farm, Dogue Run.[58]

War had not come to America's shores after all, as the newly expanded American naval power successfully protected American shipping and tensions with the French diminished.[59] The whole Washington family was probably relieved, and there was greater ease at Mount Vernon. Nelly settled back in at Mount Vernon with her grandparents, brother, and husband, "now a sedate matron" and "exalted & converted into a rational being" by her marriage and impending motherhood.[60] Wash, pleased by having received a commission in what would have been Lawrence's regiment (at least, George thought, it would "divert his attention from a Matrimonial pursuit...to which his constitution seems to be too prone"), had had the honor of a military appointment without actually having to go to war. George had even given him a sword on the day Wash was awarded his commission, purportedly telling him, "This sword, sir, you are never to draw but in a just cause, or in defence of your country." Wash had in fact left home and served briefly at the arsenal at Harpers Ferry, but he never had to raise his sword.[61]

As the threat of war faded, George eased back into his retirement while Martha, still recovering from a serious bout of illness, sewed clothes for her expected great-grandchild and directed her enslaved seamstresses in the production of clothing for the estate's enslaved people. The only excitement for some time came when Wash tramped into the house after a successful hunting trip announcing a "Valient Deer" he had snagged for dinner. That is, until Nelly went into labor on November 27 and gave birth to a healthy baby girl whom she named Frances Parke (called Parke). Soon after Parke's birth, a visitor at Mount Vernon remarked upon "the tranquil happiness that reigns throughout the house." Martha was enjoying "the pretty little stranger," and she and George were also delighted that Nelly's sister Patty had given birth to a son two weeks earlier.[62]

While Nelly was weak and still confined to her bed (a period of "lying in," or bed rest, was common after childbirth), the household was settled enough that the new father Lawrence set off with his brother-in-law Wash for a short trip to check up on Wash's estates in New Kent County, Virginia.[63] They departed on horseback on "a bright frosty morning" on December 9, and George saw them off after his morning ride. As the young men departed, one remarked to the other, "I never saw the Genl. look as well in my life." After surveilling the land and the large population of people working it for several days—the people whose labor made Wash's carefree lifestyle possible—the pair turned back to ride home to Mount Vernon. Some distance from home, Lawrence spotted an enslaved man in the Washington livery riding towards them on horseback and noted it with concern; something must be wrong for the man to be so far afield. Lawrence was afraid to voice his fears, and perhaps his hand trembled slightly as the enslaved servant handed him a letter with a black wax seal. He tore it open, and there on the road, he and Wash learned that George Washington was dead.[64]

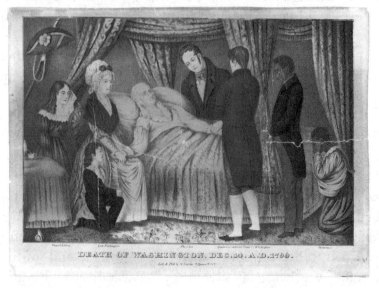

In this image of Washington's death created several decades later, the artist portrays Washington as a father with grieving children (presumably Nelly and Wash) at his bedside. Neither was in the room or as young as portrayed here, but their inclusion in this later print shows the continuing public awareness of them as Washington's children long into the 19th century.

Nathaniel Currier, *Death of Washington, Dec. 14. A.D. 1799* [between 1835 and 1856]. Washington, Library of Congress.

Lawrence and Wash returned as mourners to Mount Vernon, where they learned that the man who had seemed so healthy days before had fallen ill after riding in a mix of rain, hail, and snow driven by a brisk wind on December 12. It had seemed like an ordinary cold at first, but by the afternoon of December 14, his breathing was labored, and he knew he was dying.

Martha, Tobias Lear, three doctors, and enslaved servants Caroline Branham, the children's former nursemaid Molly, seamstress Charlotte, and George's valet Christopher Sheels crowded into the bedroom around George's white canopied bed. George wondered when Lawrence and Wash would be back, and must have been pained to learn it might not be for another week. Lear wrote to Thomas Law and Thomas Peter, summoning them, Eliza, and Patty to come as soon as possible. But it was too late: George Washington died peacefully between ten and eleven that night. The room fell silent as Dr. James Craik shut his eyes and Martha declared firmly, "All is now over, I shall soon follow him!"[65]

But Martha still had something to live for: her grandchildren and a growing brood of great-grandchildren. In the days and weeks after, as the country sank into mourning, Martha kept a "solemn composure" that somehow shook Thomas Law more than tears could have. Her deep religious faith had taught her, in Nelly's words, a "pious resignation to the dispensations of Providence" and "devout submission to his Divine Will." Still, she could not bear to go back into the room where George had died, and she moved upstairs to a small garret bedchamber. Nelly, already weak, struggled more with the loss and remained confined to her bed into January; her growing and smiling daughter was her greatest comfort.[66] Wash diverted his grief into writing an address to American youth honoring George Washington, which he circulated to his friends—the beginning of a long career of tributes he would give to his famous adoptive father.[67]

Some newspapers reported that the Custis grandchildren stood to inherit the Washington fortune. It was a logical assumption, as all four were nationally known as his family, while the blood-related Washington nieces and nephews remained fairly obscure. In fact, George directed that the money earned from the sale of his extensive landholdings be divided into twenty-three parcels among various nieces and nephews plus the Custises. Wash and

Nelly were singled out because, as George noted, he and Martha had "reared them from their earliest infancy." George formally gave Nelly and Lawrence the Dogue Run farm he had promised them (where the cash inherited from his estate could finance building a house), while Wash received George's 1,200 acres of land along a creek called Four Mile Run near Alexandria and one square of land for future development in the District of Columbia. No one would inherit ownership of George's enslaved people; his will stipulated that they be freed upon Martha's death (an act of benevolence that had limited financial repercussions for his main heirs because they already owned or would inherit many other enslaved people). The biggest blow to the Custises—although they probably knew this was coming— was that George's nephew Bushrod Washington, a justice of the still relatively powerless Supreme Court, would inherit Mount Vernon after Martha's death. But for the time being, little changed in the daily routine of the household.[68]

The focus of the family shifted to the new young generation. By late March, the weather had warmed, and everyone was well enough for a large party to gather at Mount Vernon for the baptism of Parke and the Peters' infant son John. But in an age when infancy and childhood were precarious and mortality was high, the return to normal could not last long. In late August 1800, both Parke and Nelly fell dangerously ill, and Eleanor Stuart rushed to Mount Vernon to help nurse them both. To Eleanor's relief, both mother and daughter began to recover, but no sooner had this happened than an express letter arrived from Georgetown announcing the death of Patty's four-and-a-half-year-old daughter Eleanor. The family was stunned; Eleanor Stuart had just come from the city and had seen her granddaughter in good health. The illness was swift, and the young Eleanor was old enough to know she was dying, telling her parents "she was going to God." Patty bore the loss with the sort of religious resignation Martha had modeled, and devoted her attention to keeping up with her chubby son John as he crawled busily around the house.[69] Martha had still more great-grandchildren to come: the next year, Nelly had another daughter whom she named after her, and Patty had a son named after George. Even Eleanor Stuart added another child to her brood of six with David Stuart, a girl named Rosalie for Eleanor's sister-in-law.[70]

A few hours' ride north of Mount Vernon and across the Potomac River, Washington City was growing swiftly in the years after George's retirement, with the elder Custis granddaughters and their husbands firmly entrenched as leaders in its burgeoning society. The federal government would be moving to the new capital in mid-1800, and the late 1790s were a time of busy but frustrating construction. The area set aside as the District of Columbia included the existing ports of Georgetown and Alexandria, but the federal government would be housed in new buildings constructed on rural land purchased from local proprietors. That area of development would be called Washington City. It was far from even a village; the land that would become the capital city was still a wooded area with a smattering of houses. Investors—including Thomas Peter and, more significantly, Thomas Law—were buying land and putting up houses on speculation, but the homes were scattered and as yet empty. "To be under the necessity of going through a deep wood for one or two miles, perhaps, in order to see a next door neighbour, and in the same city," a British traveler remarked, "is a curious, and, I believe, a novel circumstance." It was still an untamed spot, filled with chirping birds high in the trees and scores of wild ducks flapping in formation above the Potomac River.[71] The white stone Capitol Building rose atop a central hill with the President's House on another. But there was a dark side to the wooded beauty and fresh construction: it was enslaved people who cleared trees and constructed the public buildings. Most families, including the Peters and Laws, had small numbers of enslaved people living and working in their households and more laboring or hired out to other households or on outlying farms.[72]

Thomas and Eliza Law were key boosters of the capital to come, ignoring the slow progress and dependence on enslaved labor. George Washington had kept a close eye on his namesake city's progress, and Law was quick to remind city commissioners of his family ties to the first president. Thomas was busy investing in the construction of houses, and he and Eliza relocated several times in the eastern part of Washington City as they offered a succession of homes for rent. His fellow investors were often frustrated with what one called "this strange inconstant unsteady man," and at one point Thomas himself was ready to give up and return to England (what Eliza thought of this, or if she even knew, is unclear).[73] Thomas must also have had some tense conversations with his brother-in-law Thomas Peter. Peter, his father, and his uncle were major landowners but were based in Georgetown, whose residents Thomas Law thought were trying to stymie the development of Washington City and divert it to Georgetown.[74]

As important visitors from around the new country and abroad came to see the growing city, the Laws were their hosts. George Washington, of course, stayed with the Laws as well as the Peters when he traveled up to the city, enjoying the chance to see his stepgranddaughters and their children. George's frequent visits to them could only have increased their standing in local society. When Prince Louis-Philippe of France arrived in 1797, he stayed at the Laws' home, and Thomas showed him around the city; Polish writer Julian Ursyn Niemcewicz also made an extended stay with them. Niemcewicz found Eliza "most beautiful and accomplished," the family well-situated, and yet Thomas seemed unhappy; he did not have enough to occupy his restless intellect and drive.[75] He was constantly popping in on his neighbors, even if it meant walking or riding miles around the city, and he was known as an eccentric who occasionally forgot his name—and on one occasion when visiting the baths at Berkeley Springs, he supposedly even forgot his clothes and entered a party nude.[76]

The Laws and Peters spent their days in a round of social visits and inspections of the construction of new buildings. In their circle—*the* circle in the city around 1800—were William Thornton, architect of the Capitol, and wife Anna Maria; Samuel Harrison Smith, editor of Washington City's first newspaper, and wife Margaret; naval commander Thomas Tingey and wife Margaret; General Uriah Forrest and son Richard, who both took up posts as government clerks; and investor James Barry and wife Joanna. Nelly and Lawrence often joined this group on visits to the city while still living at Mount Vernon, and after the government fully relocated, a new cast of diplomats, cabinet secretaries, and congressmen joined the locals. So intimate was this initial circle that when the Peters and Thorntons tried calling on the Laws at their new house on a warm January day in 1800 and found no one at home, they climbed in through an open window and explored on their own.[77]

Eliza thrived in the convivial atmosphere and enjoyed welcoming newcomers. When Margaret Bayard Smith first moved to the city and rented a house from the Laws, she stopped by for an informal visit to Eliza and immediately felt at home. Eliza showed her the new, modern range (which had only started replacing open hearth cooking in wealthy households) in the kitchen, then brought her upstairs to hang curtains, where they "chatted like old acquaintance."[78] Every new member of Congress and government official came to call on "The celebrated Mrs. Law"; she reported that "every day & all day some person is coming in," one of her favorites being the new Vice President Aaron Burr. Samuel Mitchill, a New York intellectual and member of Congress, found her "indeed a superior Woman." She was "lively, active, quick of perception and full of self-possession and confidence"; long gone was the sullen young woman who had lurked around the President's House several years earlier.[79] Her uncle George Calvert's new wife Rosalie, who had recently moved to America from Belgium, called her "the most charming woman I have met in this country" and found the Laws' home delightfully full of dignitaries and government officials.[80]

Nelly and Patty neither wanted to nor could be such central figures in the city's society. While Eliza had become a staunch Democratic-Republican, sharing her husband's views, her sisters remained committed Federalists. The Federalists' hold on the city was vanishingly brief; John and Abigail Adams did not move into the President's House* until November 1800, only months before John would leave office and Democratic-Republicans captured Congress. Nelly made sure to send a letter of welcome to Abigail, on her own and her grandmother's behalf, in a formal letter signifying the ties between two first families rather than an enduring friendship. Wash, generally disconnected from society as he was nineteen and more interested in hunting than visiting, contributed venison as a welcome gift to the Adamses along with Nelly's letter. While Martha Washington had been friends with Abigail, the Custis women were never close with the Adamses. In fact, a few years earlier, Abigail's cousin had noted that they were "very jealous of any praise bestowed upon the present President, as tending in some measure to detract from the merits of his Predecessor." Patty in particular had been in a huff when John Adams decided to skip the Washington birthday ball one year and was not shy about sharing her feelings.[81]

Nelly and Patty didn't like John Adams, but in their eyes he was far better than his successor, Democratic-Republican Thomas Jefferson. It is little wonder that Nelly abhorred him, given her grandmother's feelings. According to a later and per-

---

* The president's residence was generally called the Executive Mansion or President's House in this period, although the term "White House" began in the 1820s. The latter became the official name in 1901 (William Seale, *The President's House: A History* [Washington DC: White House Historical Association with the cooperation of the National Geographic Society, 1986], 1: 123, 2: 654).

haps exaggerated account, after the incoming president visited Mount Vernon in early 1801, Martha declared it "the most painful occurrence of her life" besides her husband's death. She was certain that Jefferson had known that a visit would be offensive given how he had worked against the Federalists and George Washington.[82] Nelly reflected after Jefferson's inauguration that the country was "completely degraded." She attended a ball the night before he was sworn in wearing a white plume on her head, a gift from Federalist vice presidential candidate Thomas Pinckney, as a "badge of Federalism," clearly broadcasting her political allegiance. Nelly had lost her taste for visiting the city now that the Democratic-Republicans had taken the presidency and Congress; she declared in early 1802 that she avoided the city because "there are too great a number of Democrats there, for [my] person to be comfortable, who has a natural antipathy to those animals."[83] Patty, living in a rented row house on the edge of Georgetown on K Street, planned to stick to the still-Federalist port city and await the return of the Federalists to Washington.[84] They left Eliza to reign as one of the queens of Washington City society.

Back in Virginia, their brother Wash had just turned twenty-one and decided to try entering politics himself. Perhaps his dislike of Jefferson was part of the impetus; he ran for state delegate from Fairfax County on a conservative Federalist platform. He particularly opposed the expansion of the right to vote in many states (albeit not Virginia) that had helped Jefferson come to power. Giving any more people the right to vote could "terminate in universal suffrage, which is one of the greatest evils that can afflict us," he said. While these ideas were not unusual among the property-owning white men voting in Fairfax County, the two candidates elected were both Democratic-Republicans. Wash came in third, followed only by one other candidate, a "Stuart" who may well have been his stepfather David. At least in his letter to the local newspaper,

Wash handled the loss philosophically, expressing his honor at being supported by men he respected and hoping that the voters would soon realize the "absurdity" of Democratic-Republican views.[85] Nonetheless, it would be the last time Wash Custis ever ran for elected office.

Throughout this political tumult, Martha Washington had refused to leave Mount Vernon. When George was buried, she had told Tobias Lear to leave the vault open because she would be joining her husband there soon.[86] But she was only in her late sixties; there was no reason to believe she would not survive her husband for many years, as a white woman who reached seventy at the time could expect to live an average of another seven years.[87] To Martha, though, life had stopped; she lived in a sort of frozen reality at Mount Vernon, served by enslaved people on the same daily schedule. George's nephew Bushrod had advised her to get "clear of her negroes & plantation cares & troubles," but it appears she was not ready to act immediately. Doing so would have meant splitting up the families of George's enslaved people intermarried with the Custis enslaved, which troubled Martha. Whether she eventually simply took Bushrod's advice or, as Abigail Adams reported, came to fear that it was not a safe situation—after all, some of the people feeding her and with free rein of her house had much to gain from her death—she freed George's bondspeople in January 1801.[88] While this was not a major disruption in her daily life, it must have rippled through the enslaved communities on the five farms of Mount Vernon like small earthquakes, as husbands and wives left their cabins to find new homes and work as free people.

The stasis at Mount Vernon was not destined to last long. By March of 1802, a visitor there noted that "the poor old Lady looks badly." She had simply lost the will to live; after George's death, she said, "Life was no longer desirable."[89] By early May, she was gravely ill and knew it would be her final illness. She summoned her grandchildren and their spouses to Mount Vernon, giving them parting wisdom, asking that her correspondence with George be destroyed, and perhaps sharing the plans for her estate.[90] She was lucid and at peace, even pointing out the white gown she wanted to wear when buried. At noon on May 22, 1802, she passed away in the small garret bedroom in a house filled with her grandchildren and great-grandchildren.

Eliza's daughter, little Eliza Law, paced the floors in silent tears as her mother, aunts, and uncles began to come to terms with a new reality. With both George and Martha gone, the years of happy retirement at Mount Vernon came to an abrupt end for the whole extended family. Who were they without their illustrious grandparents? Perhaps the wax figure that appeared of Nelly alongside George and Martha in Boston's Columbian Museum in July 1802 offers a metaphor.[91] All of the Custis siblings and Nelly in particular were celebrities both known and admired across America. But like wax, their celebrity was solid yet impermanent; it needed climate and care to last. Maintaining that celebrity would be their task, their career, even their calling, for decades to come.

CHAPTER 4

Washington City's First Family

ON A HOT DAY IN MID-JULY 1802, GEORGE Washington's heirs opened Mount Vernon to visitors to auction off the personal belongings of the most beloved man in America. It was a painful day for the Custises; the home they had lived in (Nelly and Wash still lived there) and loved was going to be emptied of its contents so that its new owner, George's nephew Bushrod Washington, could move in. While the Custises knew Bushrod, they saw him as an interloper in their home, and a rumor spread in Washington City that Wash Custis refused to give Bushrod a room to stay in or even food at the family table. The families fought over which objects were part of the house. For instance, was the key to the Bastille, a gift from Lafayette and now nailed to the wall, an object to be auctioned or a permanent fixture? Apparently Wash won that fight, and Bushrod had to pay to keep it.[1]

George had left most of the contents of the house to Martha after his death, and in her will, she stipulated that most of the objects be auctioned off to raise money for her orphaned nephews' education. She was sure to leave her grandchildren, particularly the sole male Custis heir Wash, important family heirlooms like the silver plate, china, and family pictures in her will. Nelly also received some furniture and china, while her sisters, already established in their own houses, each received one piece of furniture and one work of art. That still left plenty to be sold to raise money for Martha's nephews; the local newspaper in Alexandria had advertised that on July 20, household items "of almost every description" would be sold for cash to the highest bidder.[2]

However, that is not what happened. When the visitors arrived, they discovered that the family had already purchased almost everything for themselves. Several of George and Martha's nephews were there, but it was the Custis grandchildren, particularly Wash, who had snapped up most of the goods. He was about to set up housekeeping for himself for the first time, and his sisters, too, had growing households, so some of their purchases (like the bedpan Patty and her husband bought) were practical. But Wash and his sisters also knew that George Washington's possessions were relics with an almost sacred patriotic power. Like religious relics tied to specific saints, the objects associated with George had a spiritual power and authority that allowed those viewing or interacting with them to feel closer to the late president.[3] If the Custises could not keep Mount Vernon, they could at least fill their own homes with powerful relics that brought forth the memory of Washington.

After the few items left over to auction to the public were sold—a fish kettle, some stone pots, a few prints and lesser paintings—the guests watched in shock as the family heirs retreated into another room to divvy up George Washington's clothes. They divided the clothes into lots and drew straws to see who got each dress coat, pair of breeches, and waistcoat. Eliza and Thomas Law were lucky enough to get his buff-and-blue uniform as well as a pair of velvet breeches that Eliza would snip patches from to give as gifts over the coming years.[4]

It was not so far removed from how the Custis grandchildren had split up the 150 enslaved people they had inherited. Across four pages, one for each grandchild, they scrawled lists of names and dollar values in ink, some scratched out and others added in, with the values tallied up to ensure a relatively equal division. The Custises saw the enslaved people, like the clothes and furniture, as one more lot of relics of Mount Vernon to help build their wealth and power.[5]

This page comes from a set of four lists dividing the Custis estate's enslaved people at Mount Vernon among the four grandchildren, with bondspeoples' names and dollar values.

Division of Dower Slaves relating to Martha Washington's estate, 1802.
Courtesy of Mount Vernon Ladies' Association.

When the family emerged from that room, one can imagine that the Custises held their heads just a little bit higher than everyone else. They were coming away with everything they needed—

both the personal memories and the material goods—to assert themselves as the standard-bearers of George Washington's legacy. They would refuse to fade into obscurity in the absence of their famous grandparents. Unlike the royal family, which had permanent celebrity status by heredity, the late president's family would have to continue to cultivate their place in the public eye. For continued fame, the Custises would have to strategically craft a visible place at center stage. Using the connections and skills they had built growing up in the Washington household, they would build their lives as independent, powerful actors in the new capital city. Thomas Jefferson might be president, but the Custises were determined to be the city's first family.

None of this is to suggest that Martha's grandchildren had an easy transition to their new lives after her death. They were left alone to figure out what it meant to be George Washington's family in the absence of George, Martha, and Mount Vernon. They had mourned at a private funeral on May 25, 1802, three days after Martha's death, watching her be laid to rest alongside her husband in the family vault. No one was as stricken as twenty-three-year-old Nelly Custis Lewis, the youngest of the Custis sisters. The night of her grandmother's death, both of Nelly's daughters fell seriously ill with measles. Nelly herself was heavily pregnant and seems to have been stunned into silence by her loss and grief. After the funeral, she took to her bed with a fever and rash, and a visiting cousin was afraid Nelly would succumb to grief and illness.[6] But her suffering would only increase through the summer.

Nelly had lost the most important person in her life, and she would never have the same kind of bond with anybody else again. It unmoored her. "I shall never know happiness again," she declared several years later. Martha was "the source from whence I derived every earthly feeling, my love and gratitude were unbounded, and never can I cease to feel deeply for her irreparable loss."[7] The playfulness of her younger years disappeared, replaced by both mundane domestic concerns and a certain bitterness. Nelly also had to adjust to a much quieter life after years of celebrity and a whirlwind of entertaining the leading figures in the nation. She and Lawrence moved to a tiny wing of a partially built home until the complete house could be constructed. In many ways her suffering, and that of many others that summer, had only just begun.

The Custises and their enslaved people did not leave Mount Vernon immediately. There was much to be settled before its new owner, Bushrod Washington, could move in. Nelly and Wash were not eager to leave their home behind—as the story of Wash's lack of hospitality for Bushrod suggests—and Wash may have even tried to buy the estate. Supposedly Wash had approached Bushrod about purchasing Mount Vernon, but Bushrod's wife Julia did not want to sell.[8] If Wash did make the offer, it was out of sentimental attachment to the estate rather than need. He stood to inherit a Potomac River estate about fifteen miles north of Mount Vernon and his father's extensive Custis plantations further south. Then again, Bushrod did not much need the house either. He and his wife had never been close with George Washington or spent much time at Mount Vernon. Both Wash and Bushrod were perennially short of cash; perhaps the twenty-one-year-old Wash hoped to liquidate other holdings to pay for Mount Vernon. Whatever his plan, it was not to be; the Custis family would have to carry on George Washington's legacy without Mount Vernon. They may have lost the estate, but at least Bushrod had no interest in being his uncle's standard-bearer, which left the field open for the Custis grandchildren.

The Lewises stayed at Mount Vernon through June, as both Nelly and her younger daughter remained unwell. By June 10, the ten-month-old Martha Betty Lewis was so ill that her parents held a rushed baptism for her. If they could not save her body, they could at least take care of her soul. Little Martha, named after Nelly's beloved grandmother, had been a happy and healthy child until catching the measles in late May. She was "the most engaging and beautiful Child I have ever seen," Nelly recalled. On June 19, she died.[9] She would join her great-grandmother in the family vault.

It was only a month later that the auction had taken place, sending ripples of rumor through elite circles in Washington about the Custises' zealous possessiveness. After the sales, both the material artifacts of George Washington's legacy and the family itself dispersed. Less than a week later, Eliza's husband Thomas Law departed for England on business. Patty and the Peters returned to Georgetown. Wash was adrift; he moved to Alexandria to stay temporarily with family friend James Craik.[10] The Lewises left for the cooler air of their plantation in north-western Virginia, and Nelly must have endured an uncomfort-able carriage ride as she approached the birth of her third child. She liked the quiet countryside nestled beneath the Shenandoah Mountains, but it, too, would become a place of loss. While vis-iting her husband Lawrence's sister Betty Lewis Carter at her home Western View in August, Nelly gave birth to a son chris-tened after his father and paternal grandfather, Lawrence Field-ing Lewis, but he died the same day.[11]

In less than three months, Nelly had lost her grandmother and two children, not to mention her childhood home. It was probably small comfort to move to the Lewises' estate at Wood-lawn, within view of Mount Vernon; indeed, Nelly found it "a continual source of uneasiness." Perhaps this was why she and her husband traveled to Boston and told friends that they might move to New England.[12] Nelly continued in the years ahead to wish she could move north, but Lawrence never wanted to. After all, they had two houses and plantations in Virginia, and this was their livelihood. When they first arrived at Woodlawn in 1802, they likely moved into a small side wing. Living with a growing family in a small space could not have been ideal; Nelly was perhaps charitable when she described it as "rather inconvenient." Lawrence did not even contract with a builder to construct the central wing of the house until three years later.[13] For Nelly as well as Patty and Wash, who would also live in cramped side wings of houses as the central buildings were constructed, building both their houses and their family image was a long, arduous process.

Nelly and the Lewises had not come to Woodlawn alone, though; they had a number of familiar bondspeople they had inherited from Martha Washington. Serving them in the house were Mima, Eve, and Delia; Dolcey did spinning and washing. David Gray, former overseer at Muddy Hole Farm, perhaps superintended planting at Woodlawn, while a carpenter named Sims could have been put to work building their house. These enslaved people provided the Lewises the comfort of familiar faces and tangible links to Mount Vernon, at the expense of the comfort and family ties of the enslaved themselves.[14]

Many of the enslaved had been forced to endure more than just leaving the only homes they ever knew; as the Custis grandchildren each took their share of dower slaves, they split up perhaps two-thirds of all families. Besides the problem that many dower slaves were married to now-freed Washington slaves, the Custises occasionally even separated families that were entirely part of the dower estate. For instance, house servant Mima's husband Godfrey went to Tudor Place with the Peters, while the Custises sent their children with Mima to the Lewises. The Peters sent most of the enslaved people they claimed the farthest from Mount Vernon, to the Peters' farm Oakland in Seneca, Maryland, although some were also sent to Effingham, a plantation they owned north of Washington City near what is now Howard University.[15] Family stories and the ability to shape the future for the next generation were lost in these family separations; it is rare that historians can find glimpses of the enslaved people as individuals, and if they capitalized on their association with George Washington, almost no record of that exists.

The enslaved people at Mount Vernon thus suffered a different sort of grief from that of the Custises. As for myriad enslaved people elsewhere in early America, the death of an enslaver meant displacement, loss of home, and being torn apart from family and friends.[16] George Washington had known this would happen. Had he given Mount Vernon to the Lewises or Wash, far more stability could have been preserved. But in giving the estate to Bushrod, he knew that the entire enslaved community would be dispersed and a new set of enslaved people settled on the estate. If the Custises were at all concerned about the impact of their division of the dower enslaved people, they left no trace of it. They also expressed no interest in freeing any of the dower bondspeople, so many of whose family members George Washington had owned and now freed. As they shaped Washington's legacy, they baldly rejected his tentative moves towards antislavery.

There was one notable exception, however. Only days after the sales at Mount Vernon, Thomas Law stood before a District of Columbia judge and manumitted four people: Nancy Holmes, Paul, Jenny, and William. It is unclear who Paul and Jenny were, but William was almost certainly William Costin, Nancy Holmes's son and probably the Custises' half sibling. While Thomas was the one to sign the manumission papers, these were almost certainly people Eliza had inherited as her dowry in 1796. Why not free them immediately? The fact that the Laws waited until after Martha's death suggests that perhaps Martha would not have supported the emancipation. William Costin and his mother settled in Washington City as free people, but they stayed close to the Laws. It was likely in their household that William met Delphy Judge (Ona's sister), whom Eliza inherited after Martha's death and who married William. Five years later, Thomas would free one Delphy Costin and her two young daughters, along with the rest of Nancy Holmes's children.[17]

★ ★ ★

Twenty-one-year-old Wash Custis, now the owner of thirty-six enslaved people from Mount Vernon (in addition to over one hundred fifty bondspeople on the Custis properties farther south and many more people rented from his mother) as well as a massive collection of Mount Vernon objects, could not delay setting up housekeeping. In early August, he made an agreement with his mother to buy out a piece of property his father had purchased from Gerard Alexander and which was now her dower land.[18] This land, adjacent to the Abingdon estate, fronted the Potomac River across from Washington City. It stretched up a large hill and back to Four Mile Run, where Wash had inherited a tract of land from George Washington, and he initially named the property Mount Washington. In August, Wash moved into a tiny four-room brick cottage near the river, squeezing in alongside what he called his "Washington Treasury" of objects purchased at the sale after Martha's death.

The property was mostly wooded and had only a thin strip of fertile land along the river, although the hillside sloping down to the river made good pasture land. He directed the enslaved people to clear and farm that plot with wheat, corn, and a garden with fruits and vegetables to sell at local markets; establish a fishery for shad and herring on the river; raise livestock; and sell timber from the woods up the hill and on his Four Mile Run tract.[19] Many of the enslaved people put to this work had probably been rented from Wash's mother and were already living on the land; he needed experienced farm laborers because the people coming from Mount Vernon were almost entirely house servants. Ultimately, though, he had far more enslaved people than he needed at Mount Washington.

Most of his income would come from his other Custis lands southeast of Richmond. Overall, one scholar estimates, he had inherited some 18,000 acres of land. The plantations on the Pamunkey River had been the main source of income, producing wheat and corn. Wash appointed James Anderson, former farm manager at Mount Vernon, to manage those properties. To establish his new plantation at Mount Washington, Wash hired the former gardener from Mount Vernon and a farm manager to direct the growing of corn and wheat there as well; he was ideally positioned on the Potomac River, below the treacherous falls, to ship those crops to Europe. He stocked his farm with equipment and livestock he had purchased at the Mount Vernon sales earlier that summer.[20]

The most pressing issue for Wash was to build a house on his estate so that he could move out of the damp cottage crammed full of his Mount Vernon purchases. While he left no record of his choice of architect, it was most likely a recent British arrival named George Hadfield. Hadfield had studied classical temples, which clearly influenced the design he created for Custis's grand house.[21] The home, built at the crest of a hill overlooking the river and the new capital, would have a wide frontage accented by a portico with eight large columns. Wash could look down on the growing city, perhaps spotting the roof of the President's House or the small initial wing of the Capitol Building perched on the bare hilltop of Capitol Hill. From the portico he would survey his stepgrandfather's namesake city, presiding over it from a respectable distance.

Residents of Washington City, in turn, would eventually be able to spot the home resembling a Greek temple atop the highest point on what came to be called Arlington Estate and recognize it as the home of George Washington's adopted son. The central building and two low wings added up to a 140-foot-wide frontage that, from its hilltop perch, would be easily visible from a distance. Enslaved workers cleared the land, dug the foundations, and made the bricks from nearby clay deposits.[22] As was customary, the house began with the building of one of the small wings. By the time the north wing was finished at the end of 1803, his aunt Rosalie Stier Calvert declared that the house "will be very handsome and will be seen from all points of Washington."[23] This would not simply be a house, but a visual statement of Wash's prominent place in his stepgrandfather's namesake city.

As a new year began, Wash began thinking more seriously of other steps he could take besides the building of his home to assert his place as a gentleman farmer and carrier of George Washington's legacy.[24] In late January, he gave a portrait of George to the Alexandria Academy. Combining two paying school programs and a free school for poor children, the Academy had been a regular beneficiary of financial gifts from the first president. Wash addressed a letter to the academy's trustees lauding the virtues of "America's favorite son." It was the first of many occasions on which Wash would use his ownership of Washington objects and connection to the founding father as entrées to making public statements and speeches (the letter and the reply, as he either expected or requested, were published in the local newspaper). In response, the president of the trustees wrote a reply that expressed precisely what would have pleased Wash most: the trustees' "ardent wishes, that, treading the steps of your venerable kinsman, you may prove useful to your Country, and at a far distant period, leave a name which shall be illustrious."[25]

Soon after, Wash launched a scheme that he hoped would enable him to help his country: the creation of an American breed of sheep to lessen America's dependence on imported textiles. Wash's stepgrandfather had presided over the breeding of American donkeys (a tradition Wash would continue), and Wash was venturing into a new species—a project that later earned him the sneering nickname "little ram." There were already sheep in America, of course, but their wool was spun into coarse cloth, in contrast to the finer, softer cloth produced in English factories from merino wool. Merino sheep were difficult to import from France and impossible to get from Spain, which entirely banned their export. Since the 1780s, many of the nation's leading figures (including both Washington and Jefferson) supported the import of merinos to jump-start the domestic textile industry.[26] The desire for a domestic sheep industry was a rare point of bipartisan agreement: while Democratic-Republicans were no fans of manufacturing, they did support lessening dependence on British imports, especially clothing. Indeed, soon after Wash placed an advertisement offering a cash prize for the best American-bred ram lamb (with two years lead time), "Democraticus" wrote a letter to the newspaper praising Federalist Wash's patriotic plan.[27] Wash might not want to run for office (nor could he, as a resident of the Arlington portion of the District of Columbia), but he had found a way to insert himself in the national conversation, carrying forward a small part of his stepgrandfather's patriotic vision.

Eliza, meanwhile, lived on the other side of the city and the political divide from her siblings, accruing power in Democratic-Republican circles. As her siblings settled into homes outside of the heart of the new capital city, Eliza returned to her role as a socialite from her base in the Laws' home on New Jersey Avenue, one of the diagonal streets stretching out from Capitol Hill. The house was located near the future south wing of the Capitol, an ornate sandstone building designed by the family's friend William Thornton that would later be paired with a north wing and a central domed hall.[28] The city's ungraded dirt roads flooded in the rains, and the five thousand residents were spread out, anchored by the ports of Alexandria and Georgetown but with only small clusters of houses and government buildings in what is now the heart of the city. There were shantytowns of construction workers and poor people who had moved to the city in hopes of finding work. For all the great hopes of George Washington and real estate speculators like Thomas Law, Washington City was far from flourishing; one congressman called it "both melancholy and ludicrous," while architect Benjamin Henry Latrobe thought it "an enormous baby of a town."[29]

Only the North Wing of the U.S. Capitol building had been built when the government moved to D.C. in 1800. The building would not be completed, with two wings and a domed center connecting them, until 1826.

William Birch, *A view of the Capitol of Washington before it was burnt down by the British*, ca. 1800. Washington, Library of Congress.

Thomas Law had other hopes in which he was disappointed: his marriage with Eliza had not brought either of them the happiness the pair expected. Both opinionated and strong-willed, the Laws struggled to live together peacefully. Neither wanted to disturb Martha Washington by separating, but after Martha's death, Thomas quickly prepared to leave for England, supposedly to raise money for another development project.[30] Frustrated at Thomas's refusal to allow her and their daughter to accompany him, Eliza focused her energy on Thomas's real estate business. She (or likely an enslaved worker under her command) dug up dirt from one of Thomas's empty lots to fill an unsightly trench across the street in front of buildings they hoped to rent. Thomas's mixed-race son from India, John Law, reported that this would make the homes easier to rent, not to mention sprucing up the streetscape. John had come home on a visit from Harvard, and he had an enjoyable vacation with Eliza and her daughter. "Little Eliza," as he called his half sister, greatly missed her father but had also "improved in beauty & understanding" since he last saw her. After he returned to Boston, his seven-year-old half sister sent him "a thousand kisses" through her mother.[31]

Eliza was not just active in business matters; her real passion remained politics. As Washington's stepgranddaughter, she felt empowered to express her many strong opinions. At this particular moment in 1802, the latest diplomatic crisis was that the Spanish had blocked navigation of the Mississippi River at New Orleans while they briefly controlled Louisiana before returning it to the French in 1803. Americans, including Eliza, were furious. Congress had taken no action, but Eliza knew what she would do if she were the president: "I would make short work & march at the Head of ten thousand Men, take possession of the Spanish territories, & liberate them from the state of degradation into which they are sunk." They would have to do that sooner or later, she thought, so why not go ahead now? "We have spirit enough to strike the first blow," she concluded.[32]

President Jefferson opted to send James Monroe to negotiate with the French for the purchase of New Orleans rather than leading troops into battle, but Eliza remained militant—in style if not in action. She was often spotted riding through the city on horseback and wearing colorful clothes, including a buff-and-blue habit evoking the Revolutionary Army. William Thornton reported the following summer (after the Louisiana Purchase and concerns of war had abated) that "Mrs: Law has dashed in a very high military Stile lately, & I suppose will beat up for Amazonian Volunteers." He imagined her "on Horseback to be *taken off* by the Ladies, although attended by seven Officers." Another neighbor saw Eliza on horseback with a tall feather on her cap (like those worn by soldiers), practicing her archery skills.[33] Eliza also went riding in more civilian apparel, traveling regularly to Riversdale to ride with her aunt Rosalie Calvert, who was in fact two years Eliza's junior. They were accompanied not by officers but by gentleman friends, "our beaux," as well as two enslaved people in English-style livery. Even Rosalie thought Eliza was unusual, though she saw her more positively than Thornton; Eliza was "truly a woman who has no equal."[34]

Eliza continued to socialize with the city's elite, keeping active in politics by hosting politicians in her home as so many other women did, but the lengthy visits of her mother's large family cramped her style.[35] "All the members came to visit me," she told Thomas in February, but with the house full of her half sisters, the congressmen had not come again. She grew closer to Aaron Burr, whom she saw frequently and hoped would soon "triumph over all his enemies." Her friendship with politicians gave her insight into the latest political news, particularly that which might affect Thomas's business interests. She let Thomas know that while there had been a proposal in Congress to split up and retrocede the District of Columbia back to Maryland and Virginia, it had been defeated (residents of the new federal district already disliked losing the right to vote in national elections, while some in Congress had never liked the idea of federal jurisdiction anyway). Both supporters and opponents of this plan saw it as a backdoor way to move the capital out of DC, which would have greatly injured Thomas's investments. Nonetheless, Eliza felt the "plague and anxiety" his investments there had already caused wasn't worth it and advised him to sell some of his property.[36]

Thomas's absence soon started to wear on Eliza, even if living together had been challenging. On the back of her February letter to her husband, she scribbled a fond note: "soon may we embrace you again my Love—never will I be separated from you again." As the months stretched on, she received fewer letters from him and became frustrated. She expected him back that spring, then over the summer at the anniversary of Martha's death. By the end of September 1803, she was ill and staying home "in the daily hope" of Thomas's return.[37] October passed, and still Thomas had not arrived. By the time of the yearly Washington Jockey Club horse races in mid-November, Eliza had thrown herself back into social life.[38] Each day the house was full with visitors, or they spent the entire day visiting friends. It was also an exciting time in the family, as Patty had given birth to a daughter, America, in October, and Nelly had a healthy baby boy, Lorenzo, just after the races. Eleanor Stuart also had another child soon after Nelly, her twenty-first and last; as Rosalie joked, "these women are making certain that the country not become depopulated" (sadly, the child did not survive).[39]

All the activity must have been a welcome distraction for Eliza, but the house emptied of visitors and was quiet again after the races. It was then, finally, that Thomas came home. Whether she greeted her prodigal husband on his return with anger or happiness, she presented it to Washington society as a cause for celebration. She hurriedly organized a massive ball at their home, spanning three large rooms "all crowded with the best company of the place," according to her friend Margaret Bayard Smith. Eighty people were there, and it would have been more had not Madame Pichon, the young and accomplished wife of the French ambassador, been holding a party the same night. One room was for games like chess, another for dancing to "delightful" music, and the third was set for "a handsome & excellent supper" served at 11:00 p.m. The party lasted until one in the morning, and presumably guests left with the impression that the reunited couple would now return to their life together.[40]

It seems, though, that Thomas's return brought all their struggles back to the surface. Eliza's annoyance at Thomas's long absence likely clouded their relations on his return. Thomas also did not come back to Washington alone. Eliza had learned that he had a third Anglo-Indian son, John's brother Edmund, living in England. Eliza must have been surprised, as she only knew of the two sons he brought to America originally, John and George (who had died in 1796). However, she urged Thomas to bring Edmund back to the United States.[41] Perhaps the fact that her husband had kept the existence of another child secret from her for years wore at her. Thomas appears to have also brought home someone far more problematic: a French mistress.[42] Eliza knew Thomas had had a female companion or "bibi" in India, but that was before they were married; beyond the infidelity (which was frowned upon in America but not grounds for separation or divorce), it would have been a blow to her considerable pride. Thomas bemoaned that he had "indulged in dreams of bliss which have vanished, life is dull & unprofitable without loving & being beloved." Eliza's "mind is totally alienated from me," he told a friend.[43] By the spring of 1804, it was clear that the marriage had fallen apart. They simply could not live together anymore.

Eliza's family concluded that the separation was caused by conflicting personalities. Her aunt Rosalie lamented that the Laws had parted "without good reason." They had "separated amicably"; their personalities were mismatched, and they simply had not been able to handle living together. It made no sense to Rosalie, who herself had had to accept a husband who fathered another family by an enslaved woman and who was quite the independent, capable woman in her own right. She had a personality just as strong as Eliza's, and yet she had made a happy life as a wife and mother. "Never was anything stranger," she thought, "because they only reproach each other about their manners and dispositions."[44] Similarly, Nelly attributed the separation to "difference of disposition," something that she increasingly experienced in her own marriage.[45] Perhaps George's words from nearly ten years earlier came back to haunt Eliza: what, after all, had he advised her to marry for? Love was not enough; "good dispositions" were a key requirement.

Nearly twenty years later, Thomas wrote a lengthy poem on the demise of his marriage with the ironically cheerful title "A Family Picture." The poem detailed Eliza's mercurial temper, with pouts, sighs, frowns, and tears. No matter what he did, he recalled in verse, "In vain I endeavoured to banish her gloom." Finally, Thomas lost his patience:

> I address'd her "my dear" I have tried every way
> To render you happy, yet all is in vain
> The more I endeavour the more you complain…
> Since we cannot live happy, we'd much better part
> You are right, she exclaimed, 'tis the wish of my heart

He had hoped the separation would be only temporary, but "shame, pride, and ill humour"—whether his, hers, or both is unclear—had kept them apart.[46]

A failed marriage was scandalous enough, but the failure of *this* marriage—a leading city investor and a member of Washington's family—made irresistible fodder for gossip. Louisa Catherine Adams wrote her husband of the rumor that the Laws would separate, and Dolley Madison told her sister that Eliza "expects soon to be fixed on a Farm by herself & the observations are terribly against her."[47] The story of Eliza's wish for a farm of her own was true; Thomas complained to his son John that Eliza "demands land for a new house."[48] By mid-May, Louisa Adams confirmed that the couple had actually done it—they had separated. Eliza "had made a Vow never to live with him," and while they lived in the same house for what must have been an uncomfortable several months, they were devising plans for a legal separation.[49]

In the wake of the American Revolution, divorce was becoming more common, but it was still undesirable and quite difficult. In Maryland and Virginia, the old English model requiring an act of the legislature for a divorce persisted. Even states that allowed divorce only granted it in cases where the marriage promise had been broken, such as through adultery, desertion, or extreme cruelty. Separation agreements devised by third parties had long served as a feasible substitute when divorce was unavailable or difficult to obtain. If the Laws had tried to divorce in Virginia, where they had married, they had little chance of success; they did not meet the strict criteria and Virginia had only granted its first divorce in 1803. Eliza could stay out of the public eye and effectively end her marriage privately, while maintaining claims to Thomas's financial support (which divorce often did not grant).[50] While she would not be able to marry again, at this stage she seemed to have little desire to do so: she craved an independence unavailable to married women. In a society that privileged married women over unmarried and often shunned the separated or divorced, Eliza was making a bold and risky decision.

Eliza's wish to leave her husband and live on her own, perhaps combined with stress that may have made her emotionally unstable, led many in Washington society to describe her as crazy. This appears to have been Thomas's public explanation. He wrote to a friend that "Mrs. Law is deprived of sensibility by her sickness" and was even more explicit in a letter to his son: Eliza's "mind was affected" and "I fear her mental derangement is hereditary."[51] Her aunt Rosalie said "he has always been a little crazy, and I think she is too."[52] It was not surprising that the Washington City gossips judged Eliza harshly. Thomas later told his son that he had fought "the calumny of her enemies & the censorious who wished to injure her character," and he noted that even her family opposed her and spoke ill of her. "I alone felt for her," he said.[53]

Was Eliza mad, or merely exercising the independent and stubborn spirit she had always possessed? Thomas criticized his wife's "haughty spirit of independence." A friend in her circle wrote of the separation between Thomas and "his Amazonian wife," conjuring images of a militant and masculine woman out of step with the proper wifely role.[54] Her aunt Rosalie also raised the specter of unwomanly behavior: "In her tastes and pastimes she is more man than woman and regrets that she can't wear pants."[55] The "insanity" and independence were not two separate explanations; they were, in great part, one and the same. In this era, women who sought independence and authority, particularly outside of marriage, were often described as manly, self-absorbed, and strange.[56]

In August, Eliza packed her dresses, filled George Washington's old trunks with family relics, and prepared to leave her husband's home and her status as a leading figure in Washington society forever. She traveled out of the city on rough dirt roads for the nearly ten-mile ride to the Calverts' home, Riversdale. She likely brought several enslaved house servants with her, but she did not bring her eight-year-old daughter.[57] Thomas almost certainly had legal custody of the girl, although Eliza maintained some control. It appears that they agreed that it would be best to place their daughter in a boarding school in DC while they regrouped. Custody of children had automatically gone to fathers for centuries in English law, and while mothers might gain custody of their children by the early nineteenth century, formal legal guardianship usually stayed with men (if not the husband, other male relatives could step in).[58]

As Eliza made the move, Thomas, Eliza's uncle George Calvert, and her brother-in-law Thomas Peter drew up two legal documents specifying the terms of the separation. Eliza, as a feme covert, could not sign for herself; married women's legal identities were subsumed under those of their husbands. Perhaps Eliza was in the room for the discussion of the agreement, but more likely she had made her wishes clear to the male relatives acting on her behalf. Thus on August 9, 1804, Thomas and Eliza's relatives signed a document declaring that the couple had "mutually agreed to live in future separate and apart from each other." It was accompanied by two indentures establishing the financial transfers from Thomas to Eliza's representatives, including an annual payment of $1,500.[59] There were no formal terms for the guardianship of their daughter, which was not unusual for such agreements.

Eliza likely missed being in the thick of society in Washington City as she got settled in her temporary home at Riversdale. Without a home of her own, she had no stage to display her Washington relics and play hostess and perhaps even kingmaker for the city's political elite. Yet she could not complain about her new accommodations. Riversdale was a light-filled Georgian house with spacious rooms. Eliza may have stayed in the best guest room upstairs, with tall windows through which she could have gazed southward back towards Washington City.[60] Eliza and Rosalie had been close friends, but within several months of living together, Rosalie had soured on her niece. Eliza's presence had become grating, and Rosalie no longer found her congenial: "like all American women she has no sensitivity and her tastes and propensities are completely different from mine."[61] While Eliza was a polite houseguest, Rosalie was also tired of having what felt like a third wheel in her marriage.[62] Neither her friendship with her aunt nor her marriage would ever be repaired. Eliza continued to hold on to the dream of real independence: land and a home owned by herself alone. It was a dream better suited to a man, but Eliza knew she had the determination, family connections, and wealth to make it reality. With a home of her own again, she might reclaim her political fortunes.

The siblings continued to build homes and families worthy of the Washington legacy amid the constant thrum of new political developments. Beyond Eliza's drama, it was a busy winter in Washington. In late January 1804, there were celebrations heralding the Louisiana Purchase, and there were balls every Tuesday alternating between Georgetown and Capitol Hill. The Peters gave a large ball in early February that many of Washington's leading figures attended, including Wash and likely Eliza. Perhaps they spotted John Quincy Adams and James Madison huddled over a table playing chess rather than joining the dancing.[63] But the Peters largely remained aloof from formal political circles; as a friend of hers said, Patty sat above the city in Georgetown and "looked down upon the democratic administrations of Jefferson and his successors in a spirit of scornful protest." She eagerly awaited the election of another Federalist president, "in whose court she might conscientiously assume the commanding place to which descent and talents entitled her."[64]

Meanwhile, just as Eliza's marriage had been splintering in 1804, Wash was in the thick of courting Mary Lee Fitzhugh, known by her nickname Molly. He had known Molly since childhood, because she was the daughter of George Washington's friend William Fitzhugh. In the 1790s, the Fitzhughs moved back and forth between their country house, Chatham (near Fredericksburg, Virginia), and their town house on Oronoco Street in Alexandria. Wash had surely visited the elegant Georgian townhome, which took up half of a city block, with his grandparents.[65] He was seven years older than Molly, so for much of his life, she had probably meant little to him. But now in her teens, she was serious, pious, and well-read, although no beauty. She was in many ways a perfect complement to the warm, cheerful, and somewhat impetuous Wash, and the two fell in love. It was an excellent match, combining complementary personalities and the sort of genteel Virginia ties that Wash needed to maintain his social status.

The one love letter by Molly surviving from their courtship is written in a neat but inelegant hand, and much of her character and interests that appear there persisted throughout her life. The letter begins with her concern for an ill enslaved person, which launched her into a page-long discourse on Christian duty and preparation for death. Molly's religious faith was central to her identity and called her in particular to work to improve conditions for enslaved people. But Molly knew that Wash "loves to see me gay and happy," for while he was religious, he never looked to his faith (or most other matters) with Molly's seriousness. She shifted to quote poetry from Alexander Pope and expressed her sorrow about being separated from him. While the letter is undated, they were engaged by this time (perhaps the spring of 1804), for Molly called Wash her "lover" and "my dear George."[66]

One letter from Wash to Molly also survives from the period of their engagement. His letter, too, is representative of his interests: he writes mostly of farming and working on the house. The weather was "too dull for writing or reading," so he had spent time plowing instead. He planned to start making more bricks (or rather, have his enslaved people do so) to make progress on "our Castle." Perhaps at Molly's suggestion, he had done some serious reading the night before: he reported that he had read Gibbon's *Decline and Fall of the Roman Empire* before bed.[67]

Like his stepgrandfather, though, Wash's focus was on practical concerns for the present rather than studying the past. He needed to establish a financially successful estate where he could bring his future bride. Wash continued to plot new moneymaking schemes, even writing his family's enemy Thomas Jefferson to suggest that the government build a bridge across the Potomac to connect Washington City to his Mount Washington estate. Jefferson's response was neither encouraging nor friendly, whether out of dislike for the idea or the family, so Wash seems to have dropped it.[68] He remained hard at work, however. When his cousins came to visit him in April, they found him busy caulking a boat. Leaving his work, he offered them wine and showed them around the one completed wing of the house. While his cousin Cornelia thought the house would eventually be "a very showy handsome building," the room they saw did not impress her.[69]

Wash had his hands full between establishing a new plantation and supervising the rest of his lands. A lengthy letter to his farm manager at his White House plantation in New Kent County covered a range of plans and suggests he was struggling with the weight of his responsibilities; he did not have George Washington's meticulous and focused approach to management. He wanted to build a mill and a distillery, visit his eastern shore lands and try to sell some of them, grow purple straw wheat, and have plaster of paris laid down to enrich the soil. He was concerned to hear of "Night Balls" in the slave quarters (a small respite for people forced to do hard labor) and wanted to avoid the expense of paying an overseer. The manager also reported that his bondspeople didn't have enough clothing, which Wash was surprised to hear because his stepfather had assured him they had plenty.[70] At only twenty-three and with no father to guide him, Wash appeared unsure about how to manage his extensive holdings in land and human beings.

In July 1804, however, Wash had reason to feel he had truly achieved adulthood and independence, as well as carrying forth George Washington's legacy in a public venue. On the Fourth of July, he gave his first public oration in a voice that was "full, rich, and melodious." Alexandria's Washington Society (a Federalist group of which he was a member) had invited him to address them at the Episcopal Church at noon on Independence Day. Wash's speech was a passionate cry for patriotism and against partisan fighting. It also, like all of the many orations he would give over the years, praised his famous stepgrandfather. He used the occasion to decry the lack of a formal monument to mark Washington's grave, gesturing pointedly towards the Capitol (where there had been plans to move the tomb). Wash was proud of his maiden speech and asked the *Washington Federalist* to publish it, which it did—the oration took up nearly an entire page of newsprint.[71]

Three days later, he was again at the center of a celebration when he married Molly Fitzhugh. It was a hot day, reaching ninety degrees, and a large crowd of friends and family gathered at the Fitzhughs' Alexandria home. Reverend Davis, who had married Nelly and Lawrence, officiated. Nelly was pleased with the match, calling Molly "in every respect amiable and much beloved."[72] There was one point of awkwardness, however: Thomas Law had not been invited. The legal documents arranging the Laws' separation had not yet been signed, and the couple was still living in the same house. Wash had visited Thomas several days before the wedding and gave him no indication of any displeasure; why had he even come to call on him if not to explain the lack of an invitation? Thomas was upset and offended.[73]

Thomas could not have stewed over the matter for long, though, because two days later, the Laws' friend Aaron Burr shot and killed Alexander Hamilton in a duel in New Jersey. Both men wrote the customary letters to their closest kin the day before the duel just in case they were killed. Burr's letter from July 10, 1804, gave his daughter Theodosia instructions on handling his estate, and while the main body of the letter ended with affectionate words for her, the lengthy postscript sent his greetings to somebody else: Eliza Custis Law. It closed simply: "Assure Mrs. Law of my latest recollection. Adieu. Adieu. A. Burr."[74]

What did this mention of Eliza, as the final thought in one of the last letters he might ever write, mean? He and Eliza had become particularly close during Thomas's time in England, and in the months before the duel, Eliza was in the process of separating from her husband. Burr had left Washington in March to go home to New York and campaign for governor, so he and Eliza had not seen each other for months. If they corresponded in that time, the letters do not survive.[75] Eliza knew Theodosia, so sending a greeting through her is not entirely surprising. Still, for Burr to have mentioned Eliza in this context suggests their friendship was a very close one. It was a natural pairing; Burr particularly liked and respected independent women.[76] It also meant that Eliza shared a close bond with a man her siblings would have loathed.

While none of the siblings recorded their responses to Hamilton's death, their reactions probably differed. Eliza, the only Democratic-Republican in the family and already a Burr supporter, likely sided with him. Martha, Nelly, and Wash would have joined the Federalist outcry against Burr (the public response to the duel was quite partisan; one Federalist senator noted in the fall that when Burr returned to the city, Jefferson and his fellow Republicans treated him with more friendliness than ever before).[77] It was perhaps inevitable that none of the siblings would be friendly with Jefferson, either; even Eliza never mentioned him. As Nelly told a friend, in acid tones, "I have not the honor to be in that *great mans* good graces, nor can one who knew so well the *first President*, ever wish to be noticed by the present chief magistrate."[78] The Custises could push forward in their political reign without him.

Nelly was far more focused on domestic rather than political life at this time. With several young children and a plantation to help manage, as well as living farther from the capital city than her siblings, she was somewhat removed from public life. At eighteen miles away, she rarely ventured into Washington City. "We live very retired," she explained, "and my life is devoted to my darling children....I have determined to give up every thing which would prevent my devoting myself entirely to their wellfare." She was no longer the "lively Giddy Girl" of the past, but rather "a sedate Grave Matron." Indeed, when artist Gilbert Stuart painted Nelly in 1804, he depicted her reclining pensively in a chair with sad brown eyes gazing into the distance. "I look back with sorrow," she wrote, "& to the future without hope."[79]

Nelly's daily life fell into a routine that had more order and stability than she had experienced in the preceding years. Her nephew (but near contemporary) Gabriel Lewis came to stay with the family and helped with all of her tasks running the household, including caring for Nelly's toddlers Parke and Lorenzo and managing enslaved people. The pair got along well, and Nelly wrote him a playful letter after he left for Kentucky, sharing that the family had "mourned your absence in sackcloth and ashes."[80] Nelly also had another healthy child, a daughter whom she named after both herself and an old school friend: Eleanor Agnes Freire Lewis. The "fine fat girl," as Nelly described her, had the most beautiful eyes and eyelashes Nelly had ever seen. She sewed for the children and had begun to teach Parke to read, and she planned to hire tutors so that Parke could receive the finest education possible. Yet she was not happy; she was constantly anxious about the children's health. Even when they were healthy, she admitted she was afraid they would fall ill again.[81]

Her home life was not entirely without its pleasures, however. The Lewises' home at Woodlawn, designed by William Thornton, was finally nearing completion; the original wing the family had squeezed into was now connected to the central building and another wing on the opposite side, all brick-clad. The structure is still graceful and impressive today: the wide central building is of a standard Federal-style design, with a central hall and rooms on either side, but it is ornamented with an elegant elliptical curving staircase with a sumptuous walnut banister. The parlor or music room's large windows overlook Mount Vernon and the Potomac River, and the room has particularly high ceilings suited to acoustics for playing music. Woodlawn would be home to numerous Washington relics that allowed the Lewises to remind visitors of their famous family connections.[82]

Both of her sisters began to plan similar five-part houses to stage their own vast collections of Washington relics just as Woodlawn neared completion, and they too would have prominence of place on hilltops visible from far below. In July 1805, Eliza finally got what she had longed for: a farm of her own. She purchased just over one hundred acres in Alexandria from Francis Peyton for $5,000 and named the estate Mount Washington (borrowing the name from her brother, perhaps). It was "a pretty piece of land," Rosalie reported, though she worried that Eliza was too depressed to enjoy it.[83] Eliza planned a central house connected to wings like Woodlawn, but it would only be one room deep rather than two. It sat on a hill overlooking Washington City, Alexandria, and the Potomac River. She could survey even more of George Washington's domain than her siblings.

The house had a drawing room and dining room which, although not large, had intricate woodwork, including pastoral scenes above the windows. Upstairs were three small rooms, and atop the house was a cupola overlooking what Eliza described as "a delightful, variegated landscape." The house was surrounded by a cedar hedge and garden, while the acreage was mostly cultivated and had over two thousand fruit trees. Eliza moved into the house while it was in progress, bringing with her several horses and at least six enslaved people.[84] She finally had her full independence, and in naming the estate for her illustrious grandparents, she hitched her newfound identity to the Washington name.

Her sister Patty Peter's house would be far grander. Patty and her husband purchased a small estate above the port town of Georgetown, part of the new District of Columbia. This eight-and-a-half-acre plot would not be a farm; the Peters had land in Maryland for that. Rather, it would be the site of a mansion atop a hill overlooking Georgetown and beyond to the Potomac River and Wash's house. When the Peters bought the property in the summer of 1805, it had two small buildings the former owner had constructed. They hired their friend William Thornton to design a main house connecting the existing buildings and moved into the smaller wings that fall. The grand Federal building with its half-round portico supported by Doric columns would not be complete for more than a decade.[85] Like her brother, Patty stuffed the hundreds of objects she and her husband had purchased at Mount Vernon into the small structures and awaited a grander stage.

Meanwhile, Wash was busy settling into married life at his renamed Arlington estate. It is unclear precisely when and why he switched the name from Mount Washington, but he made the change soon after his marriage. Arlington was the name of the family's original estate on Virginia's eastern shore, and perhaps he wanted to pay tribute to his Custis roots. His new home, like Nelly's, was staffed by familiar faces, as many of the enslaved people he took from Mount Vernon had worked among the family in the mansion house. Caroline Branham, the Washingtons' housemaid, probably led the cleaning and sewing duties, as well as emptying chamber pots and lighting the fire each morning as Wash and Molly awakened. Christopher Sheels, who had been Washington's valet, likely took on that role for Wash at Arlington House. Christopher's sister Judy, along with Betty Davis and Charlotte, did the sewing for the household.[86] While these longtime members of Wash's household may have been a soothing presence for Wash and his new wife, that comfort came at the expense of people who had no choice but to be there. Molly nonetheless found the duties of being the wife of a plantation owner and enslaver burdensome, and she fretted in particular about the difficulty of making good Christians of "the most depraved family of slaves that I have ever known."[87]

Wash seems to have been more focused on agricultural ventures than the well-being of his bondspeople. On April 30, 1805, he held his first annual sheep shearing event at his estate. This was the event he had advertised two years earlier, offering a prize for the best American-bred sheep. But this was far more than an agricultural event: the date Wash chose was both his birthday and, more importantly, a Federalist holiday commemorating George Washington's first inauguration. The large crowd in attendance were primarily Federalists, including a number of Wash's neighboring gentleman farmers—although only one had brought a ram to exhibit. As he would do every subsequent year, Wash hosted a meal for his guests under the shade of one of George Washington's Revolutionary War tents that he had purchased at the estate sale several years earlier. This was no small camping tent—the large "banqueting tent" could seat up to fifty people. Wash decorated it with laurels and hung a portrait of George Washington at one end, and each year he gave a speech and toasts invoking the general's memory. It was a showy but effective display—as one reporter described it, "none could enter it without reverence, none behold it without respect."[88] Wash basked in the reflected glory of his stepgrandfather.

His growing stature, however, did not mean that Wash was leading a life of ease. He was in debt to the Mount Vernon estate for his many purchases—including that of the tent—and his farms were not as productive as he had hoped. Newspaper ads from 1805 attest to a number of ventures he hoped would raise funds—a development on his Four Mile Run tract, the sale of firewood from his forested estate, and making his "noble animal" the jack (male donkey) Columbus available for breeding. In each case, he invoked a Washington connection to lure buyers—the development of homes would be called "Mount Vernon"; the firewood was from the "Forest of Washington"; and the jack was descended from two famous (as far as donkeys went!) animals owned by George Washington himself.[89] None of these plans, much less his earlier ones, solved his financial problems: in his aunt Rosalie's opinion, "with all his fanciful schemes of industry he spends a lot of money to no gain and neglects his affairs and the supervision of his properties."[90]

Personally he struggled as well: two years in a row, just weeks after the sheep shearing event, Molly had baby girls who did not survive. Her daughter born in 1805 died the same day, and the next daughter—Martha Elizabeth Ann Custis—died at only ten months old.[91] It would not be until 1807 that Molly and Wash had a child who survived. However, by this time he had fathered at least one child with an enslaved woman on his estate. The child we know most about is Maria Carter, born in 1803 or 1804 to an enslaved woman possibly named Airy or Arianna Carter, and at some stage (it's unclear when), Wash decisively recognized her as his daughter.[92] What must Molly, having lost two children, have thought of the healthy babies with Wash's looks about them living in the slave quarters? The situation was common in the South, including within her extended family; Wash's uncle George Calvert had a large family with an enslaved woman at Riversdale, and his father Jacky had probably fathered William Costin and perhaps other mixed-race children.[93]

Women like Molly—or Rosalie, or Eleanor Stuart—had few options in the face of their husbands' sexual abuse of the women they enslaved. One Southern woman later bemoaned the "monstrous system" in which "our men live all in one house with their wives and their concubines, the Mulattoes one sees in every family exactly resemble the white children."[94] But most women recorded little or no response to the situation, as speaking out could bring shame on them, their marriages, and their families. However, some white women demanded the enslaved women their husbands had sexually exploited be sold, while others even violently attacked the women.[95] Molly Custis, though she would become an antislavery activist in the coming years and often expressed her sympathy for the enslaved, was unlikely to have taken such bold steps. As a woman in a slave society, she and her sisters-in-law entered careers as wives and mothers—as well as owners of dozens of human beings, some of whom were their own or their husbands' blood relations.

The years after Martha's death were formative ones for all four grandchildren. All of them built homes within a day's ride of Mount Vernon on hilltops with vast vistas, signaling their prominent places in a new nation without George and Martha Washington. They took advantage of every opportunity to retain and reinforce their Washington connections. Meanwhile, George's nephew Bushrod Washington moved into an empty Mount Vernon estate, bringing his own enslaved people and struggling to balance traveling to Washington City and riding to circuit courts as a Supreme Court justice with bringing Mount Vernon back to life. He was forced to borrow over $3,000 (around the cost of building an entirely new home at the time) for furniture and farm implements alone, and he wrote with some embarrassment to his and his uncle's friend Elizabeth Powel to request help repaying the loan.[96] Unlike Eliza and Patty, he was never very engaged in the new capital's social life; and unlike Wash, he neither gave public speeches about his illustrious uncle nor made efforts to remind the public about his family connection. He had no desire for the celebrity status the Custises apparently craved; he was content to be known for his own deeds.

The Custises eagerly seized the stage Bushrod had ceded and quickly carved out public and highly partisan identities. While they suffered the joys and sorrows attending having children in an era of high infant mortality, all but Nelly remained engaged in public life. Eliza would take a hiatus while building her home at Mount Washington outside of the city, but it proved short-lived. As conflict with England and France heated up at the end of the first decade of the nineteenth century, neither she nor her siblings could resist entering the fray. The bases they had established in the first years of the new century launched them all into the thick of a fight that would come closer to home than any of them could have imagined.

CHAPTER 5

A Country and Family Split

BY 1807, THE CUSTIS SIBLINGS HAD BEEN IN so much turmoil that their uncle George Calvert had had enough. They had turned to him as "chief advisor," especially during Eliza's separation from Thomas, but also "whenever one of them behaves badly."

"He often sends them all to the devil," his wife Rosalie reported, "saying he wishes he didn't have 'a relation in America.'"[1] The Custises were all now married parents of young children living in their own homes, but they still seemed a bit lost without George and Martha Washington to turn to for guidance. It didn't help that the siblings had diverging political views as tensions both abroad and at home came close to a boiling point.

America was teetering on the brink of war with both Great Britain and France, stoking partisan divisions between the pro-British Federalists and pro-French Democratic-Republicans. Eliza was the family's sole Democratic-Republican, and like her fellow partisans, she felt that the British were exploiting the United States and decisive action was needed. If some in her party leaned in favor of Napoleon's French forces against Great Britain in the ongoing Napoleonic Wars, Eliza went to the extreme. Most Americans saw Napoleon as a threat to republican values, but Eliza admired him. Federalists, on the other hand, felt that Napoleon posed such a threat to Great Britain and representative governments as a whole that the British needed American support. All of this was complicated by the way both Great Britain and France used naval power on the high seas to try to restrict America's international trade.[2]

The Custises and the United States were of the same age, around thirty. The siblings and the nation had achieved independence, but there were still constraints that chafed on both. With expressions of strong positions came blowback; with growing responsibility came stress. Autonomy and turmoil were intertwined. As George Washington's heirs, the Custises felt that they had a duty—and a right—to play a role in the new nation's struggles. As they became bolder in their political speech, their status as celebrities did not insulate them from criticism. Eliza had already had a bitter taste of this in her separation from her husband. As it turned out, that would just be the beginning. The years leading up to the War of 1812 were a tumultuous time in which passions and sorrows ran high, especially in the homes of the Custis grandchildren.

The United States government found itself in a nearly impossible position in these years. The Napoleonic Wars had begun in 1803, and the repercussions rippled out across the Atlantic. The British and French both sought favored trade status with the United States, and the two European powers saw each other as an existential threat. The British saw American trade with France as support for their enemy, and the French felt the same about America's trade with Great Britain. Thus both powers began using their navies to intercept American merchant ships carrying goods to each other. Americans could not afford to cut off their two key trade partners, nor could they afford to take a side. They also struggled with how to stop the British from impressing (essentially kidnapping) sailors from American ships, which happened with increasing frequency as the Royal Navy needed as many sailors as it could get. From around 1805, American shipping suffered constant attacks, and the government struggled to find policy solutions.[3]

While it was obvious that Eliza would support American action against Britain, her brother Wash and brother-in-law Lawrence were also concerned with protecting American interests from British attacks. In June 1807, the British warship *Leopard* stopped the American warship *Chesapeake* off the Virginia coast in order to recover British sailors who had supposedly deserted the Royal Navy. When the *Chesapeake*'s captain refused, the British fired and ultimately killed three American sailors.[4] The incident caused widespread indignation across the country, including in the Custis family. Lawrence Lewis saw this as nearly an act of war; "the Sword is drawn, never to be sheathed, untill we can appease the shades of our murdered countrymen. I am no advocate for War," he said, but he preferred "War rather than a disgraceful peace."[5]

Eliza felt similarly. Despite illness and distance from Washington City, she managed to stay engaged with the latest political developments. She was happy to learn in late July 1807 that the government was building a new fort at Warburton, slipping in a reminder of her famous stepgrandfather with the comment that "Genrl W[ashingto]n always said it was the spot from which the Potomac must be defended." But she was still frustrated that the government wasn't pursuing a more aggressive response to the attack on the *Chesapeake*. "Why are not all the frigates getting ready[?]," she asked. Her martial spirit was raised: "the day of Retribution is at hand & they will mourn in blood, the unprovoked insult they have given us."[6] As an heir of the first president, she had to continue his legacy of protecting the nation's honor.

President Thomas Jefferson did not believe he had the authority to begin a war—that was up to members of Congress, and they would not be in session again until October. In early July, he issued a proclamation commanding armed British vessels to leave American waters.[7] This was a good first step, Eliza believed, although not enough. She would have called Congress back sooner and sent out all of America's frigates to protect American sailors. "Let England beware," Eliza said, "she may think this Country unable to Cope with her—but our Eagle may be roused, & maintain the Combat with her lion." The United States could also take more peaceful action, she thought, by building financial independence with government support for manufacturing.[8]

This was not an orthodox position in her party, but it was one she shared with her brother Wash. Federalists were more likely to be pro-industry while Democratic-Republicans sided with agrarian interests, and Wash brought the two together in his sheep schemes. In late 1807, Congress had passed an embargo on international trade, making increased domestic production vital. Wash took advantage of the opportunity, sending President Jefferson a waistcoat woven from Arlington wool and publishing a pamphlet titled *An Address to the People of the U. States on the Importance of Encouraging Agriculture & Domestic Manufactures* in the spring of 1808. He prefaced his pamphlet with a reflection on how he saw his role in politics:

> In the war of politics which has long unhappily raged among us, I have ever beheld the scene without a desire to participate any further than necessity, or a sense of duty, might warrant. But in the humble walks of rural life, in the promotion of agriculture and Domestic œconomy, I have endeavoured to take as active a part as my situation, and means of knowledge would admit. Convinced that agriculture is the great basis of all national prosperity, the key-stone that centers the arch of government, and the great impetus that moves the machine of national wealth and individual industry, I have been a laborer in its cause.[9]

In other words, he had no interest in partisan politics; he was simply a humble farmer doing his part, and it was a similar part to that George Washington had hoped to play as an agricultural reformer.[10] Wash knew better: agriculture and domestic manufacturing had been pitted against each other in partisan warfare going back to the 1790s.

Just over a year after publishing his pamphlet, he wrote an article for the *Alexandria Gazette* venting his frustration that partisanship was blocking progress on his pet issue. "The subject of domestic manufactures has unfortunately been made a party question... But is there a party within our country, which can oppose the policy tending to promote her industry and preserve her honor?" He recalled the glorious history of the Revolution and called on his fellow Americans to unite in support of economic independence—hardly an inspiring rallying cry, but he wrote passionately. His writings were published and circulated nationally, and an article in the *Boston Patriot* named him one of "the most distinguished patrons of American Agriculture."[11] Nonetheless, his Arlington Improved sheep never achieved the popularity of Spanish merinos, which had become much cheaper to import to America.[12]

Wash's fame as a promoter of agriculture and manufacturing also came with frequent public criticisms, none so sustained and vitriolic as a series of letters published in the Washington newspaper *Spirit of '76* in 1810. The letters were signed by "Cornplanter," whom Wash probably did not know was John Mercer Garnett, a conservative Democratic-Republican congressman from Virginia. Garnett worried that government support of domestic manufacturing would make people dependent (in contrast to self-sufficient farmers), so he opposed Wash's ideas on political grounds. Although the two men were strangers, Garnett also made things personal. His opening salvo questioned how both Wash and his fellow sheep enthusiast Robert Livingston could be praised as patriots "merely for doing that which is to benefit themselves an hundred fold as much as it does any body else." Breeding sheep made them richer, not national heroes.[13]

This began a monthslong public dialogue in the newspaper between Cornplanter and Wash. Wash called Cornplanter's allegation "slander" and suggested that the proper targets for criticism were the Democratic-Republican "demagogues" pushing for war. He also doubled down on his self-image as a modest farmer, writing that his hands were "hardened by labour, and industry," not the soft gloved hands of a gentleman profiting off of his sheep. Cornplanter's reply called Wash "that irascible little gentleman" and zeroed in on the root of Wash's fame: not his own accomplishments, but his family ties. "If Mr. C. shines at all," Cornplanter sneered, "it must be, like the moon, with borrowed lustre. He must illumine society, by reflected light; by associating with others."[14] His "lustre," of course, was "borrowed" from George Washington.

Cornplanter's critique was not a casual remark; it seems to have been the basis of his animosity towards Wash. When a defender of Wash calling himself "Virginian" entered the conversation and noted that Wash "has been bred in the school and under the eye of Washington," Cornplanter pounced. He pointed out that Washington "was nothing more than his [Wash's] grandfather, and that by marriage only." He went on to note sarcastically that the government was taking advantage "of the inestimable services of this gentleman" with an appointment as justice of the peace for Alexandria. This was a federal appointment, but an exceedingly minor one. If Wash really wanted to help his country in this moment of international peril, Cornplanter argued, he should get himself an appointment to go negotiate with the French.[15] This was certainly not going to happen—Wash had neither the background nor the skills, much less any interest, in taking on a national role. The local work of being a justice of the peace, and an appointment in the summer of 1810 as the

captain of the Alexandria Light Dragoons (from which he resigned before the war began), were enough for him.

Wash's friend "Virginian" responded to Cornplanter's attacks
with some sarcasm of his own. "What will your ingenious correspondent say," he asked the newspaper's editor, "when informed that this very same G.W.P. Custis has actually had the
hardihood to become 'Captain of the Alexandria cavalry'?" He
then responded with further sarcasm to the charges that Wash
was simply basking in the glow of his family ties to Washington,
although what he said actually addressed far broader concerns:

> What possible object can he have in view, but to hold himself
> up as the lineal descendant of Washington and lawful heir
> to the crown of America—to preach up new constitutional
> doctrines—and finally to enforce them, with the sword and
> pistol! But fear not, my countrymen! while Cornplanter lives,
> you have nothing to apprehend...

Cornplanter had never expressed concerns that Wash was trying to capitalize on his relationship to Washington to seize political power; rather, Cornplanter suggested Wash wasn't doing
enough. Wash's openly avowed lack of political ambition had
largely forestalled public concern that he would see himself as
"lawful heir to the crown of America." The image Virginian
painted of Wash leading a military coup was ridiculous precisely
because nobody, even in private conversation, would have accused him of being ambitious for political office. The dispute
with Cornplanter dragged on for several more months before
petering out, but it signaled the scrutiny ahead as Wash took on
more political causes.[16]

Eliza took a more aggressive stance than her brother, and she
bemoaned that she could not go into the field herself with the
military. "What a pity it is, that I am not commander in Chief
of a great Army," she told John Law. "I would take you for my

Aid de Camp & together we should do wonders." Typical of
Eliza, she did not see herself as the aide, but the leader. Surely
she knew this was impossible, but the erstwhile "Amazonian
wife" was not entirely joking. In the same letter she asked John,
who still lived in Washington, to tell the Secretary of the Navy
"with whom I have often conversed on military & Naval affairs" that the government should build towers to protect the
harbors. She even had recommendations for the local cavalries'
uniforms.[17] She made no apologies for making these remarks as
a woman, as so many other women talking about politics did;
she made her pronouncements with the directness and confidence of a white man.

Nelly and Lawrence Lewis were less interested in being drawn
into the diplomatic turmoil of this era, but they could not avoid
it because of their place in the Washington family. Two sons of
Lawrence's brother Fielding (named after their father, the husband of George Washington's sister Betty Washington Lewis)
had been impressed by the British Navy. Impressment was not a
new problem for Americans, and it had accelerated as the British
desperately needed men for naval ships in the Napoleonic Wars.
The British were not supposed to impress foreigners; they were
ostensibly seeking British subjects who had deserted. This included British-born men who had immigrated to America and
become American citizens, a change in nationality that the British refused to recognize. British naval ships would stop American merchant ships, and officers would remove any sailors they
claimed were British subjects. It was nearly impossible to tell the
difference between British and American sailors, and the Royal
Navy ultimately impressed around 10,000 sailors from American ships between 1793 and 1812 (the vast majority of whom
were US citizens). While this is not a particularly large number over twenty years, many Americans saw it as a humiliating
practice that denied their newfound sovereignty and independence. Perhaps no single case of impressed sailors represented

that more so than that of Charles and John Lewis, Lawrence and Nelly's nephews.[18]

Charles and John had not had easy lives even before they were impressed by the British. Their father had lost his fortune and had been held in debtors' prison in 1790, and the family later moved to Fairfax County not far from Mount Vernon. They were in such financial straits that Betty Lewis had told her brother George Washington that her grandchildren might "go naked if it was not for the assistance I give" to them. While their father had occasionally dined with the Washingtons at Mount Vernon, there is no indication that Charles or John ever even met their great-uncle.[19] Both had to make their own living at a young age and found work as sailors on merchant ships.

It was an unhappy coincidence that the brothers were both captured by the British and impressed into the Royal Navy. Charles, forced to fight for a country against whom his great-uncle had helped his homeland win independence, proclaimed his relationship with George Washington on his very body. He had the initials of numerous family members tattooed onto his arms and breast, gunpowder staining the punctures etched into his skin, but the two that stood out were GW and MW for George and Martha Washington. How better to assert his nationality than with such permanent marks, marks that may well have antagonized the British sailors he was forced to serve with. His younger brother John took a more strategic course and began writing the only person he knew who might have the connections to free him: his uncle Lawrence.

Lawrence hadn't heard from John in years and had no idea where he was, so he must have been surprised to receive a packet from the American consul in Liverpool in 1810 with letters from John. The first letter was from March 1809 and reported "my Unhappy State of life in the British Service On board of the Sloop of War *Rose*." He begged his uncle to write to the consul and send whatever money was needed to free him. He made a more specific request in his 1810 letter: Lawrence needed to send evidence of his "Birth & Parentage" to prove he was American. He also asked Lawrence to ask Congress to address the British Admiralty on his behalf, "being as I am a citizen of America & a native of Virginia; & Particular as my Dear Father being a Distant Relation of General George Washington."[20] Like Charles, he knew that the relationship to the first president was worth more than proving his citizenship; it testified to his powerful connections and drew on Americans' attachment to Washington.

Despite John's pleas, it took Lawrence nearly two years to file formal paperwork to try to secure his nephews' release. He did notify William Lyman, the American agent stationed in Britain working to free American sailors, of his nephews' impressment soon after receiving the packet from Liverpool. But he did not gather official documents attesting to the men's identities until January 1812. Lawrence, his brother Robert, and their cousin Bushrod Washington all signed statements attesting to Charles's and John's identities. Both Lawrence and Robert noted that the men's father was George Washington's nephew. Lawrence then sent the materials to Daniel Brent, a clerk in the State Department who had apparently raised the issue with Secretary of State James Monroe.[21] Soon after, Monroe took on the cause, writing to the British ambassador to ask him "to contribute all in your power" to free "the Great-Nephews of the late General Washington." As it turned out, Lyman's efforts eventually bore fruit, and it appears that both John and Charles were freed before Lawrence's evidence or the ambassador's intervention reached England.[22] Lawrence and his nephews had been forcibly dragged into the conflict between America and England, and their story would fuel the fires of war several times in the coming years.

Was Nelly, too, involved in this struggle? She could not have engaged in official correspondence on these matters, but these were her nephews, and Lawrence must have shared these letters with her. John specifically sent "my kind and affectionate love to Aunt Lewis," so she probably knew him.[23] It was impossible to stay neutral as the diplomatic struggle hit so close to home. Having been raised as an ardent Federalist, perhaps she was torn as Great Britain and America were at loggerheads. Her fiery political passions, though, may well have been roused by this brazen act of the British against her nephews.

As the Custises dealt with international affairs, they were also touched by some happiness and even more misery at home. From 1807 to 1811, the four siblings and their spouses had seven babies, only one of whom survived; this was far worse than the 15 to 25 percent mortality rate for babies before the age of one in America at the time. Patty Peter's losses were staggering: she gave birth to and lost four children over this period.[24] It is hardly surprising, then, that she appears to be the only sibling who was not politically engaged in this period. When she did leave home, she insisted on bringing all of her children with her to pay social calls, and the children's poor behavior hardly endeared her to her hosts.[25]

Wash and Molly also struggled with the losses of babies, but Wash somehow seems to have stayed upbeat. When they lost a ten-month-old girl in March 1807, Molly had probably only recently realized she was pregnant again. On a visit to the Annefield estate in the Shenandoah Valley, their daughter Mary Anna Randolph Custis was born on October 1, 1807. Molly could "scarcely believe" her good fortune in being the mother of this small, smiling infant. Only feeling "her *weight* when in my arms" proved that this child was real and alive.[26] She reveled in her newborn daughter's smiles ("for she smiles already strange as it may appear") and, as a deeply religious woman, surely prayed that this baby would survive.

Mary Anna would live, but the couple's final child would not. Molly had one more daughter, Edwa, in August 1809, but she died just over a year later. Molly wrote to friends in deep sadness, and they replied with letters urging her to take comfort in her faith. "He gives objects of attachment, links the heart by closest ties, and then calls the precious magnet to his own Bosom," one friend wrote. "You have even at this time the great comfort of thinking that your darling Angel has been removed from you to a region of pure and everlasting joy," another said, "reunited for ever in heavenly love to your Parents Sisters Children, which had gone before ready to receive her." Both reminded her that she still had "precious Mary."[27] Mary would remain Molly and Wash's lone surviving child, and her parents lavished her with attention and care.

Nelly and Lawrence had similar struggles. While her daughters Parke and Agnes and son Lorenzo had survived, she lost two sons, Fielding Augustine and George Washington Custis Lewis, just short of their second birthdays. George "was uncommonly large and apparently very healthy" as well as "most beautiful and engaging," but she lost him to "a virulent attack of the croup" in December 1811. He was, as she noted, the fourth child she had lost. Illnesses regularly wracked the family, and on one visit, Eliza thought that five-year-old Agnes "looks like a spectre." When the family was healthy, Nelly focused her energies on educating her children, especially Parke. While Lorenzo was "mischievous, rather indolent, and not so quick in learning as his Sister," Parke "has fine talents, is docile, dutiful, & pious, a very retentive memory and very ambitious to excel in every thing she undertakes." Nelly taught her music, drawing, and French as well as basic subjects like reading and writing, drawing on her own fine training in Philadelphia.[28]

She and the children rarely saw friends or family or even left home, so their visit to Mount Vernon with a heavily pregnant Patty and her children in August of 1810 must have been a special treat. Patty wanted her children to see "the place where I had spent the happiest years of my life." She had talked of Mount

Vernon so often and so fulsomely that her daughter America "thought it must be something more than trees and house and land, and it did not answer her expectations." Of course, Mount Vernon was "more than trees and house and land" to the Custises; at every turn they felt, as Nelly said, "many pleasing and some very painful recollections."[29] Pleasure at happy memories with their grandparents was tinged with pain at their loss, and the family's loss of Mount Vernon.

The grandchildren's mother Eleanor Stuart would soon be lost as well. In the summer of 1811, Eleanor was quite ill, possibly with consumption (tuberculosis). Around that time, she wrote Nelly in a shaky hand reporting that she "coughed a good deal today" and that she had "suffered much with my blister," which a doctor had likely caused in the belief that it would draw out toxins. Eleanor knew she was dying, and worried for her family; beyond her grown children, she still had six children with her second husband at home, the youngest of whom was only nine. "Perhaps the Father of Mercy in pity will spare Me a little longer to My helpless family," she sighed.[30] She was not spared much longer. In mid-September, she moved to Tudor Place so that Patty and probably local doctors in Georgetown could care for her. She died two weeks later. Patty was comforted by "being with her in her last moments," but Eliza was stunned; she had been sure her mother would recover.[31] Another vital link tying the siblings together had broken.

Eliza also had other troubles at home in this period. Such a character was not suited for living in a farmhouse several miles from town, especially given the political drama unfolding so close by. In the spring of 1808, John Law reported to his father that Eliza had "become completely tired of her farm & is now solicitous of selling it, as might have been expected." John said that this was because "her disposition fits her for nothing but a round of society," showing little sympathy for Eliza's social and political isolation at Mount Washington. She decided that she would prefer to be in Georgetown, where her daughter was then in school.[32]

In March 1809, she finally gave up on the farm and put it up for sale. Perhaps she would have preferred to live in the city and maintain a country estate, but she couldn't afford to. She still had not paid the previous owner the full $5,000 she owed for it, and he was now suing her guarantors—Thomas Peter and her uncle George Calvert. In John Law's estimation, she had also spent "at least $3000" renovating and improving the property. Even if she had been happy there, she probably could not have stayed. Her financial situation was so dire that John worried that "there is such little prospect of her living with any kind of respectability in Georgetown."[33] It seems that there were no buyers interested in the estate; finally, in November 1809, her half sister Ann Stuart Robinson's husband William Robinson purchased it at the inflated price of $10,000. Robinson was probably doing this to help his sister-in-law, as he never seems to have done anything with the estate and finally sold it in 1835 for $3,000. Buying and selling property as a separated but still married woman was messy, and the deed of sale had to explain that she was "duly authorized and privileged to act for herself as a single woman" and still included Thomas Law as a party to the deed.[34]

That legal impediment would soon be out of the way, though: only months after Eliza advertised Mount Washington for sale, Thomas Law asked her to formalize their separation with a divorce.[35] It is not clear why, after five years of living separately, he now decided to pursue this course; he told his son that he did so "in conformity to the advice of mutual friends" and "to confirm our separation."[36] He told her brother-in-law Lawrence Lewis that he wanted "to release Mrs Law from all restraints" and that he felt he was "an impediment to her happiness."[37] If he was hinting at some desire on Eliza's part to remarry, certainly none existed at this time, and Eliza was infuriated at the request. It seems far more likely that it was Thomas who wanted to remarry.

There is no written evidence surviving in Eliza's own words of her anger at the request for a divorce, but this is not what she wanted. She may have had any number of reasonable concerns: losing her allowance payments from Thomas, losing control and access to her daughter, and public notoriety. Thomas, however, could not understand why she would be opposed to a divorce, writing a lengthy letter to John venting about her. "Sensible impartial men" had urged her it was the right thing to do; why would she not listen to them? He had been more than fair to Eliza, he insisted, and he worried that his only alternative might be to return to England with his daughter. He didn't want to threaten Eliza with this possibility, but he didn't know what else to do.[38] He had moved to Vermont, where the laws made divorce easier to obtain.[39] Eliza did not have to go there; she just had to agree to the divorce in writing, and apparently she eventually did. Thomas also had to obtain depositions from people who knew them demonstrating Eliza's "refusal to cohabit as a wife" and her "desertion & living in a state of separation from bed & board with a total neglect of all duties as a wife" in order to provide legal grounds for the divorce. Given that this was a mutual separation, it's easy to imagine Eliza's being incensed at the accusation of desertion and neglect of wifely duties.[40]

In January 1811, she was further mortified to find that "all the City" knew that the divorce between George Washington's stepgranddaughter and her ex-husband was finalized even before she did. A friend called on her to tell her that she had heard about it "in a large company," although her stepson John also came to let her know. "The divorce was an act in which I never had any concern," she told John, and "the final termination of the proceedings can affect me but little in any way— it cannot cause sorrow, for I hope it will bring peace to me at least on this subject—it cannot cause joy, for I expect no good to myself or those I love." She tried to be magnanimous towards Thomas, telling John of "my sincere wishes for *his* happiness," but followed this with "my prayer that he will not let any persons excite him again, to *destroy mine*." This made it a bit hard to swallow her claim that "I forgive all that ever past which I deem'd injurious to me." Eliza evidently did not want to carry Thomas's name any longer, announcing that she would now go by "Mrs. Custis" ("Mrs" was often used by older women, whether married or single). She assured John that she still saw him and Edmund as part of her family and still signed herself "your mother & friend."[41]

It took very little time for relations between the Laws and the entire Custis clan to sour. In March, against Eliza's wishes, Thomas removed young Eliza from school in Georgetown and took her to Philadelphia to complete her education. Now that they were officially divorced, he would take full custody of their daughter. In the letter he wrote her about the arrangements, Thomas addressed his ex-wife as "Mrs. Law" and wrote entirely in the third person, stifling his annoyance in honeyed language. Nelly and Lawrence decided to step in to see if Thomas would send Eliza junior to Woodlawn so she could stay close to her mother, but Thomas stood firm: they had agreed at the time of the separation that he had custody of the girl. He replied to Lawrence's suggestion with a polite but slightly awkward letter in which he refused to be dissuaded. The whole family was upset, and Patty thought Eliza "look[ed] very badly" because of the emotional strain.[42] As it turned out, this was not the only reason relations between Thomas and the Custis clan were souring.

After Thomas's arrival in Philadelphia to take his daughter to school, he learned that Nelly had written Elizabeth Bordley to warn her of rumors that Thomas had divorced in order to marry Bordley. Nelly accused Thomas's sons of spreading this rumor, and Thomas did not think this was altogether impossible. When he heard the rumor from his friend John Mifflin, he explained that his sons "may have conjectured whom I was likely to chuse" based on the fact that he "esteem'd" Bordley. He reported this to John, assuring him that "You know full well…that I never intimated any attachment between us."[43] He must have written Edmund as well, who replied that the notion that he spread this rumor was a "wilful falsehood." But there was truth to the underlying story: Edmund assured him that "after you imparted to me your wishes on this subject the name of Miss Bordley on no occasion to the best of any recollection has ever escaped my lips."[44] How long had Thomas been interested in Nelly's old friend? Was she in fact the impetus behind the divorce?

Even if there was truth to the rumor, Thomas was deeply upset at "how it must wound the feelings of Miss Bordley" and averred that "in all my life I have never been so severely gall'd." His sons were even angrier; John wrote with fury of Nelly's "calumny," and Edmund told his father, "The malignity & fiend like spirit of persecution of Mrs Law's relations ought not to give you the least uneasiness, except to excite your pity for them. Despised by all & unhappy themselves, they wish to render every one equally so." Edmund was ready to cut Eliza off entirely: "Her character is completely developed, & I am desirous of dropping the intimacy," he said. It was not just that he now disliked her; he had heard that Eliza had been using her continued good relations with Thomas's sons as evidence that Thomas was treating Eliza poorly. John apparently suggested that his father investigate a libel charge, but Thomas demurred that the rumor "has failed to injure me" and taking legal action would only make things worse. By August, John, who seems to have once been genuinely close with Eliza, was done with her forever.[45]

Thankfully, despite all the pain and struggle over these years, there were happy times as well. Wash always seemed to be the happiest of the siblings. He remained deeply in love with his wife, writing her in the fall of 1811 that "You are all my happiness & pride & without you I should have no object to live for." He conveyed a kiss with an asterisk at the bottom of the letter labeled "a kiss for you" and also asked that she "kiss precious Old Mary over & over for me." Molly and Mary were staying with friends or family in healthier climes, likely closer to the mountains, while Wash supervised the enslaved people he forced to labor at Arlington as they worked through the rain and mud of a warm September. As in his earlier writings about farm work, he claimed to be working a plow himself and said he was out with his men until nine at night. He urged her not to come back until October when the air had improved, assuring her that they were making progress on the house and gardens.[46]

They were still living in the two small side wings of the house, crammed in with the Washington relics, but served by more enslaved people than he had employment for. Molly had inherited sixteen enslaved people upon her father's death in 1809, and Wash was responsible for running his father-in-law's Ravensworth estate with even more bondspeople until Molly's brother reached the age of majority.[47] In December 1811, Wash advertised some thirty-seven enslaved people for sale. It is unclear who these people were; perhaps they were part of his inheritance from his mother after her death. His ad in the *Alexandria Gazette* expressed his hope that local farmers would buy all of them, presumably to preserve the families, but he was selling them first and foremost to raise money.[48] The husband and father who sent his wife kisses and adored his daughter Mary was the very same man who sold human beings, in part to provide for the interests of his white family. The seemingly private world of home and affection was intimately tied to larger forces at work in the nation, including the growing domestic slave trade.

There was no better example of these close links between home and the wider world than Eliza's romantic adventures in the wake of her divorce. By the summer of 1811, Eliza had shed her connections with the Laws and had reentered the Washington City social and political scene. She moved back into town and supposedly made her name change known by being introduced as "Mrs. Custis" at a crowded levee at the President's House.[49] She became close with Dolley Madison, visiting her regularly and even serving her as a nurse when Dolley was seriously ill.[50] Her aunt Rosalie was displeased with this friendship, complaining, "She behaves very imprudently and is quite intimate with Mrs. Madison and the party we call in derision, 'the Court.'"[51] It was probably not only Eliza's intimacy with Dolley Madison that Rosalie thought imprudent; Eliza was by this time receiving regular visits from the new French ambassador, Louis Serurier. He was the same age as Eliza and already a seasoned diplomat for a country that Eliza adored. Her love for France and desire for greater diplomatic ties between France and the United States were deeply personal; *"I would marry a frenchman as soon as any other,"* she declared.[52]

She was just as strident in declaring her allegiance to the French. The relations between America and France had become increasingly strained as the French escalated their economic warfare against America between 1810 and 1812.[53] Yet Eliza's support for the French and animosity towards the British were both unflagging and vociferous. She admired "the Great Napoleon," while even most pro-French Americans would not praise the military leader and dictator ("he has had faults, but so have other mortals," she demurred). At a party in the spring of 1812, she censured another guest as a "British Partisan." It was no wonder, then, that she reported to a friend, "I am the friend of the French and incur the enmity of their foes, who abuse me terribly."[54] It was not solely her political friendship for the French that brought her abuse; it was her ties to specific Frenchmen like Serurier.

In late July 1811, Eliza wrote to her friend David Bailie Warden about her budding relationship with the French ambassador. Warden was an Irish-born intellectual and diplomat, and it is unclear when he and Eliza first met and became friends; the first surviving letter between them is an unfinished autobiography that Eliza wrote for him in 1808. Warden had been stationed in France with minor diplomatic appointments from 1804 until 1810, when he quarreled with American ambassador General John Armstrong.[55] He traveled to Washington to lobby for a new appointment in France, and as he waited in Annapolis to sail back to France, he received the first of many long, confessional letters from Eliza. She signed this letter as his "Sister" and, in these years when she did not get along well with her own brother and sisters, clearly saw him as a surrogate brother.[56]

Her letter, and the many that followed, revealed more of her romantic hopes and trials than most letters between siblings, especially a brother and sister, normally would. She began her discussion of Serurier rather coyly, saying that he "must marry one of our Ladies who can win his heart, & who has influence in our country." If he married an American, Eliza thought, "it would unite our people to him." Who better to do this than a powerful woman sincerely attached to both French and American interests—in other words, Eliza herself? Her friend Ruth Barlow, who was soon to leave for France herself with her husband Joel (the newly appointed ambassador), advised Eliza to stop receiving Serurier's visits. "She constantly warns me against the danger of loving S—," Eliza confided, but she had no intention of heeding this advice. She told Ruth that she would still welcome Serurier's visits; "I already admired & esteem'd him, & should pray to Cupid not to wound me too deeply—or to pierce his heart with the same dart." She admitted to Warden that she didn't have any expectation that Serurier would propose to her; even if they were only friends, she intended to maintain the relationship and "do him all the service in my power."[57]

It is not entirely clear why Ruth Barlow was concerned about Eliza's relationship with Serurier, but it provoked Eliza's defiance and propelled her to continue her efforts to find a French husband to further her political aims. She told Warden that in the face of opposition to her relationship with Serurier, "*I am as firm as* Mt Atlas... I am not subject to any mortals controul." It was this independence that she had sought in her separation from Law, and now that she was divorced, she fully embraced it.[58] She also wrote Joel Barlow in praise of Serurier and "his wish to conciliate the good will of our people." Her purpose was not simply to curry favor for Serurier, but to encourage American diplomats in France to support French interests as tensions between the two nations grew. "My thoughts are all filled with the wish and anxiety to serve the cause of France," she told Warden. She also raged against the British, and said she intended to "talk to the members of Congress."[59]

As a famous figure in the capital city, Eliza's flirtations with Serurier continued to attract attention; perhaps that was her aim in the end. British ambassador Sir Augustus John Foster recorded the rumor that Serurier had proposed to Eliza in his diary in mid-November, while a gossipy letter from a Washington woman a month later conveyed that "the French Minister 'tis said is courting Mrs Custis, alias Law, I dont say tis a fact—he certainly admires her much, and visits her often."[60] Another letter offered an even nastier account:

> Mrs Custis swears no one shall take the Frenchman from her with impunity—tho' some are trying notwithstanding her threats—indeed it is as good as a farce when they all meet—such watching—peeping and snarling they remind one of two or three dogs, with a bone to contend for.[61]

Apparently Eliza was not the only woman interested in Serurier.

As 1812 dawned, though, the attention of Eliza and other Washingtonians turned to new French arrivals. In January, a man calling himself the Count de Crillon arrived in Washington; he was actually Paul Émile Soubiran, a Frenchman who was on the run from European authorities for a variety of petty crimes. Crillon (along with a man named John Henry) had come to Washington to push a scheme to sell intelligence on the British to the American government, but few trusted Crillon. Serurier certainly didn't, and Foster notes that at an evening party at Eliza's on January 26, all of the guests "agreed Crillon was an Imposter." President Madison and Secretary of State James Monroe, in their eagerness to make the case for war with England, took the bait and ultimately paid Crillon and Henry a massive sum for their ultimately unrevealing documents.[62] Crillon soon fled with his money, and in his place came yet another dubious Frenchman, the Chevalier de Greffe.

Francois Denis de Greffe was born in Bayonne in 1778 and served in the army from the age of thirteen until he was jailed for cheating at cards with his fellow soldiers in 1809. De Greffe insisted that the charges against him were "false" and "ridiculous," and claimed he was acquitted but forced to leave France. He sailed to North America later that year, possibly to prepare to serve as a French agent in Havana or Mexico; he complained that he was forced to retreat among "the savages of North America." Tall and blond, he spoke English well and clearly charmed Eliza when he arrived in Washington in 1812. He told Eliza and others who would listen that he had been wronged, but in the wake of Crillon's visit, many doubted his sincerity. When Eliza introduced de Greffe to the British ambassador, Foster noted in his diary that "it is strongly believed that he is a Swindler."[63]

Eliza vouched for both de Greffe and another new arrival named Ballastero, whose motives were also dubious. Foster later wrote about two foreign visitors, likely de Greffe and Ballastero, who offered to break into Serurier's desk and share his dispatches (surely for a fee). He noted that these men "were very generally admitted into society, having been introduced by an elderly lady of great family connection, the highest indeed in the states, to whom if one of them did not get married it was his own fault."[64] While Eliza was far from elderly at this point, it seems quite likely that Foster was referring to Eliza. In Eliza's zeal for the French, she was staking her reputation—and, ultimately, her heart—on de Greffe in particular. She admired "the dignity, & modesty of his appearance, & his elegant manners," and she was drawn to his role as "a gallant officer."[65]

While de Greffe may have been "admitted into society," several of Eliza's friends in both Washington and Paris were concerned. Eliza wrote Ruth Barlow in August 1812 asking her to have her husband Joel "make enquiries about Col de Greffe & write me everything you hear."[66] But it turned out that she did not want to hear what the Barlows found out. Ruth's sister Clara Baldwin Bomford, then in Paris with her sister and brother-in-law, wrote Anna Maria Thornton a lengthy letter reporting on de Greffe's treachery that fall. In France, "his conduct was such that he was shunned by all classes of people." She then told the story of de Greffe swindling a young man from New Orleans, Hugues de la Vergne, whom he met in New York, out of $10,000, and sending la Vergne to France with bad bank notes. When la Vergne tried to draw on the notes, French authorities put him in jail, where he remained until Joel Barlow took up his case and was able, with the help of the Marquis de Lafayette, to free la Vergne and send him back home. David Bailie Warden had heard the same story. "I hope Mrs. Custis has been deceived for the last time by strangers unworthy of her acquaintance," Clara wrote. "Her heart is too good & her feelings too ardent for her own happiness."[67]

Eliza was infuriated by these accounts against de Greffe. When Anna Maria Thornton received the letter from Clara, rather than share it with Eliza, she "read the letter to all her visitors." Eliza called on Anna Maria, who she said *"has always been my enemy"* and insisted upon seeing the letter—as well as warning her that de Greffe could sue her. Eliza believed de Greffe's account of his interaction with Hugues de la Vergne, which she conveyed to Warden. Over and over again, she defended de Greffe and asked Warden to help her long-suffering friend. Her admiration for him seemingly knew no bounds: "he is the only man I ever knew, calculated to preserve my affection. He has modesty & dignity blended, as they were in the Immortal Washington."[68] As usual for Eliza, the reference to her stepgrandfather was a shorthand that signaled her family ties and made her claims difficult to challenge.

With war on the horizon, the residents of the nation's capital celebrated the birthday of the country's greatest war hero, George Washington, in February 1812. There were two balls in the District, one in Georgetown and another in Washington City. The Georgetown ball, at the Union Tavern, was held the day before Washington's birthday, and many prominent figures in Eliza's orbit attended—Serurier, the spurious Count de Crillon, British ambassador Augustus Foster, and Anna Maria Thornton. Eliza was there, as was Patty Peter. A visitor to the city named Phoebe Morris reported to her sister that the decorations had been "arranged by Mrs Custis, one of the nearest relations of Genl Washington" (whom Phoebe declared to be "certainly very ecentric [sic] & I think a little crazy"). The ballroom was decorated in a martial spirit, with muskets, pistols, and regimental colors covering the walls. A rather poorly painted image of George Washington was on display in front of the musicians. But anybody searching for a better likeness of the general could have found several—displayed on Eliza's and Patty's bodies.

"Mrs Custis was decorated with miniature pictures of her Illustrious relative, some round her neck, & others round her arms," Morris reported, "while her sister, Mrs Peter, wore *two* as large as *warming pans*, one representing the General, which rested upon her bosom, & the other his Lady, which dangled below her waist."[69] Morris was likely exaggerating; while Patty

Peter owned images of her grandparents that were larger than standard miniatures, they were nowhere near the ten- to twelve-inch diameter of a warming pan. Nonetheless, the sisters had both visibly broadcast their ties to the Washingtons. It is possible that this was a competitive rather than concerted effort, as Patty and Eliza stood on opposing sides of the political divide. Both Federalists and Democratic-Republicans wanted to claim George Washington as a symbol and to justify their policy positions (although the Federalists did this more often and successfully).[70] Patty and Eliza may have been trying to stake a visual, political claim to George Washington's legacy in a particularly fraught political moment.

In early 1812, the United States teetered on the brink of war with both Great Britain and France. Democratic-Republicans in Congress spoke of war as the only way forward, and popular anger about British attacks on American commerce was growing. Were threats of war just a ploy to pressure the British, or was there a real chance of rupture?[71] For the Custises, this was no distant international struggle: it was personal. While Nelly remained out of the public eye, Eliza, Wash, and Patty were all increasingly vocal in their political positions. The country's coming crisis was a moment of opportunity for the family, a chance to deploy the power from their connection to George Washington to make their voices heard in ways they never had before.

CHAPTER 6

The Custises at War

ON APRIL 30, 1812, WASH CUSTIS WELCOMED
guests to his eighth annual sheep shearing at his Arlington estate. It was an unusually warm day as several local gentlemen,
including Wash's brothers-in-law Lawrence Lewis and Thomas
Peter, presented their sheep for judging. At three o'clock, the
party gathered under George Washington's massive Revolutionary War camp tent, as they had every year, to dine, make toasts
over American-made wine, and hear Wash speak. But despite
outward appearances, this year's event was different from prior
celebrations: war was imminent. "The cup of reconciliation has
but a drop now lingering on its brink," Wash lamented as clouds
gathered on the horizon. As if to foretell the impending conflict, the skies erupted, and the event came to an early close.[1]

It was a gathering storm rather than a single spark that set
off the War of 1812. In November 1811, the Twelfth Congress
opened its first session with aggressive war hawks taking leadership of the House of Representatives, led by a young Kentuckian
named Henry Clay. Congress began preparing for war, passing
bills to raise an army and prepare the navy, then instituting a
sixty-day embargo in April.[2] Only two days before the sheep
shearing, the *National Intelligencer* had published a piece (anony-

mously authored by James Monroe) stating that "so soon as the physical resources of the nation can be arranged, war will ensue."[3]

Wash clearly had the war—and the stand he would take on it—on his mind as he planned both his guest list and his speech. While he invited local French diplomats, he did not invite British ambassador Augustus Foster.[4] Wash held the sheep shearing on a Federalist holiday, and the party's close ties to the British would normally mean British diplomats would be welcome. But not this year. Foster took the snub personally, recording that he found it "rather singular I was not invited," although he thought Wash was "a strange uncouth Fellow." Far from uncouth, Wash did not want the British ambassador in his audience for the concluding portion of his speech. Addressing a crowd of men lining a long table, shaded by his stepgrandfather's tent, he declared his support for war with Great Britain, "the vast Leviathan of the deep." Hadn't the British learned from losing the American Revolution? "If while the Hercules of Liberty in his cradle, we could strangle a serpent, sure the Hercules of manhood can grapple with the Nemean lion," he contended. "I trust the warlike genius of my country will ascend to any height," he said, in part because he felt that "if united within herself, America has nothing to fear from abroad."[5]

But America was not "united within herself," for even the Custis family could not find common cause. Perhaps Thomas Peter, who with his wife Patty remained a die-hard Federalist and Anglophile, squirmed in his seat as his brother-in-law spoke. Lawrence Lewis, who like Wash was a less ardent Federalist, would have felt more comfortable with this, as likely would his wife Nelly. If Eliza had been there, she might have cheered. Fractures in the nation and the Custis family deepened in a war that was rooted as much in America's sense of hurt pride as it was in policy disputes. Even today, historians debate what really caused this war; was it about commerce? Western expansion? Impressment of sailors? Ideology? The Americans who wanted war were fueled by feeling that all of the disagreements between the two countries tied back to Great Britain's lack of respect for America as an independent nation.[6] In the tumultuous years of war to come, climaxing in the burning of the capital city bearing George Washington's name, the Custis siblings continued to use their ties to their stepgrandfather as an opportunity to enter political debates and the limelight. For the Custises, this war was personal.

President Madison signed the bill declaring war, which had passed narrowly in both chambers of Congress, on June 18, 1812.[7] That day, Wash wrote to a friend in Philadelphia about the fight to come and his fears that the country was not up to the challenge. Gone was the confidence of his speech at the sheep shearing, although he mentioned that day and suggested that his friend read the speech in the newspaper. Were the people in Philadelphia "like the rest of mankind, tired of doing right"? He felt that the people of his region were "persevering as yet" but could be swayed by their desire for luxury goods. "The same sort of people, do not live now, that lived 36 years ago," Wash lamented. "The Lilly Skinned youth, of our Country I am afraid, will not perform their march to Quebec under such privations, as the soldiers of 1775, suffered, in those days." But perhaps "war, by causing privation, & limiting riches, shall restore the vigorous age, of our republic." Wash worried that the Americans of 1812 could not measure up to men like George Washington, and indeed it was Washington's old friend Thomas Pinckney who Wash hoped would take the field as a leading general.[8]

Both George Washington and his family became symbols for both the supporters and opponents of war. One of James Madison's closest advisors, Richard Rush, invoked Washington several times in a lengthy, passionate speech to a "crowd of citizens and strangers" in the House of Representatives. Only weeks after the declaration of war and before any hostilities had begun, Rush took time to address the arguments against the war. He was particularly enraged by the idea that impressment was only happening on a small scale and declared he would share "a fact that shows all the excess of shame that should flush our faces at submission to an outrage so foul." Did his fellow citizens know "that two of the nephews of your immortal Washington have been seized, dragged, made slaves on board of a British ship"?[9]

Some Americans probably did know, as the fact had been noted in a smattering of news stories. One article, published in a Philadelphia newspaper in May, mentioned the circumstance and said "the ghost of Washington must frown indignant at the pusilanimity of his countrymen, for suffering such wrongs to go unrevenged." Rush made a similar point. "How, Americans, can you sit down under such indignities?" he cried. Would they really assert "that those who stand in consanguinity to the illustrious founder of your liberties, are second in all their claims to safety and protection?"[10] It did not matter how many Americans had been impressed, if the blood relatives of George Washington had been. Such an offense to his family was an assault upon the memory of Washington and upon all Americans.

But not all of the public agreed, and some of the first violence of that summer would in fact come in a dispute between Federalists and Democratic-Republicans rather than British and Americans. Less than forty miles north of Washington City in the port city of Baltimore, Maryland, hostilities broke out between the majority Democratic-Republican population and supporters of a local Federalist newspaper. Alexander Contee Hanson's *Federal Republican*, like other Federalist newspapers, had been aggressively critical of the Madison administration. Days after the declaration of war, a mob destroyed the building in which the newspaper was printed. Hanson moved the operation to Georgetown until he could regroup, and Patty Peter reported to a friend in Boston that "Here, in our little village, we have dared, in the very face of the President and all the secretaries, to publish the 'Federal Republican.'" Who, precisely, was this "we"; was Patty directly involved in supporting Hanson? She certainly knew about Hanson's plans; her letter of July 27 accurately reported that the newspaper was returning to Baltimore with "a party of veterans of old times to insure its success."[11] Hanson did indeed return to Baltimore that day and reestablished his newspaper at 45 Charles Street with over fifty Federalists to protect it.

The very next night, a mob arrived to launch fresh attacks, going so far as to aim a cannon at the building. The mayor and the local militia arrived to try to quell the crowds, and they took the Federalist defenders of the paper to jail to keep them safe. The following day, the mob destroyed the newspaper's second home, but they weren't finished yet. That evening, the mob broke into the jail and began violently attacking the Federalists. Some of the Federalists escaped, but eight or nine of them could not and were brutally beaten. These were no ordinary citizens, either: they included several Revolutionary War generals, including "Light Horse" Harry Lee, father of a young boy named Robert E. Lee. Another, General James Lingan, tried to remind the crowd of his patriotism by referring to his Revolutionary War service, but it was to no avail. The attackers beat Lingan, a sixty-one-year-old veteran, to death. The crowd stripped the Federalists of their clothes and, with Lingan dead and several others playing dead, left their bodies in a pile outside.[12]

Federalists were understandably appalled and terrified by the beating and murder of elderly Revolutionary War veterans. Many Federalists in Baltimore feared further attacks and left the city. Before the attack, Patty Peter had felt hopeful, declaring, "I rejoice to find there is still a little of the blood of seventy-six in our veins, and that it can become warm." But news of the attack literally sickened her. When Anna Maria Thornton visited her several days letter, she recorded that Patty was "not well & much affected at the Balt[imo]re business."[13] On August 7, Georgetown's leading men (including Thomas Peter) gathered at the Union Tavern "for the purpose of expressing their sense of the outrage recently committed in Baltimore." They adopted resolutions against mob violence, expressed their support for a free press, criticized the Madison administration, and committed to "wear the accustomed badge of mourning" for thirty days. They also planned to have Francis Scott Key give a speech in Lingan's honor. Thomas Peter was one of three men tasked with carrying out these resolutions. When Wash Custis learned of the planned speech, he offered to lend George Washington's camp tent for the event in honor of defenders of a free press.[14] While Wash and Thomas did not agree on whether to go to war with England, Wash sided firmly with the Federalists in the wake of the Baltimore attack.

In fact, Wash would end up contributing more than his tent to Lingan's memorial event; when Key declined to give the speech, Wash stepped in. He knew a good chance for publicity when he saw it. The Democratic-Republican newspaper in Richmond published an anonymous letter deriding the "Charles-street rioters" who "could pick up nobody else to make use of but that ridiculous creature, Custis, who is the standing laughing-stock of the whole district of Columbia." Wash's supporters believed that the letter was penned by Secretary of State James Monroe's clerk John Colvin, making it a partisan attack from the administration. The Federalists responded in their own paper in defense of Wash, "who for nine years has been extolled in the ministerial prints; for his patriotic exertions, at a great personal expence, in promoting the man[u]facturing interests of the country." They noted that plenty of Democratic-Republicans had supported his sheep schemes; it was only now when he spoke out against "mobocracy and massacre" that the same people made fun of him. As always when Wash came under criticism, his critics had to be reminded of his family connection: the piece concluded with the line "When his illustrious grandfather, Washington, was pronounced a hoary headed traitor by the same men, the grandson must feel flattered by their abuse."[15]

On September 1, 1812, the day chosen for General James Lingan's memorial in Georgetown, the weather was good, but there was unease in the air. Amid worry about further violence, Lingan's body had been buried in a secret location. President Madison had asked the militia not to come out for the event, but they did nonetheless. So did large crowds of mourners, so many that the event had to be moved from St. John's Church to a wooded area at the edge of town, where George Washington's tent was erected. The funeral procession left the Union Hotel and included Lingan's family and several survivors of the mob attack; "a solemn stillness pervaded the streets." A ship on the Potomac River just down the hill fired ceremonial shots as the procession passed storefronts that local merchants had draped with black flags. When the procession reached the woods, the crowds parted, and those in the procession found their seats under Washington's tent. They looked out into a crowd of perhaps 1,500 men and women gathered quietly in the shade of the woods.[16]

After an opening prayer, Wash stood to deliver a lengthy but heartfelt speech that "riveted the attention of the audience" and drew forth tears even from hardened elderly veterans. He spoke without notes and with great power, his words piercing through the quiet woods. Wash had not known Lingan, but as a self-appointed spokesperson for the men and values of the Revolution, he said that he saw the attack as a personal affront and speaking out as his responsibility. "I should indeed disgrace the illustrious name I bear—I should indeed have forgotten the impressions made on my boyhood at Mount Vernon, could I now omit to pay the honors due to virtue, and venerate the Memory of the Brave!" he proclaimed. In addition to emphasizing his ties to Washington, he made a rare mention of his father Jacky Custis. "When my Parent was perishing at York Town, he bequeathed this invaluable legacy to his child," Wash said, "and damned be the man who would relinquish the rights obtained by a parent's sufferings!!" He decried Lingan's murder and the fact that Federalists were now "a persecuted race," emphasizing "the right of opinion, the freedom of speech, the liberty of the press." Lingan's murder, for Wash and many others, was an attack on free speech. Federalists had a right to speak out against the administration and the war, Wash insisted, even if he personally had felt no interest in doing so.

He also proclaimed that despite Federalists' opposition to the administration, they were loyal and valiant members of the military. Indeed, in Wash's impassioned speech, Federalists became the primary protectors of American liberty. "Perhaps at this moment some Fearless Sailor climbs the shattered mast to nail the Flag of my country to its stump," he imagined. *My life on it, that Fellow is a Federalist!* Alternately, imagine "some Gallant Soldier may yet scale the Heights of Abraham," he continued. "I tell you the first foot, which presses the classic ground, *will be a Federalist's.*"

Wash was carried away by his own rhetoric, and the press was not going to let him get away with it. Newspapers around the country published accounts of the speech, with Federalists lauding it in overflowing language and Democratic-Republicans offering acerbic critiques. The *Federal Republican* praised Wash for the "despotic power" he had over his audience, and the editors of the pamphlet edition of his oration compared him to Demosthenes or Cicero.[17] For one newspaper's editors, the fact that Wash was "the Grandson and adopted Child of our beloved WASHINGTON" and had given the speech under Washington's tent was enough to make the speech praiseworthy. "The sentiments," the editors attested, "are worthy of the son of so illustrious a Sire." When news of Captain Isaac Hull's naval victory over the *Guerriere* reached New York just over a week after Wash's speech, the city's *Evening Post* recalled that his speech had declared that the naval victories would be won by Federalists. And? "Mr. Custis was right. Capt. Hull and his brave Officers are federalists."[18] Never mind how the editors knew this to be the case or even whether it was true.

4

On the Democratic-Republican side, the response was quite different. The editors of the *American Watchman* in Wilmington, Delaware, were particularly offended by the assumption that good soldiers and sailors must be Federalists, suggesting that Wash was insinuating that Democratic-Republicans were "cowards and poltroons." The speech was "an absurd effusion" demonstrating "affected pathos and ranting bombast." With presidential elections coming, the editors of the *Virginia Argus* called the whole affair "an electioneering trick" and a "political farce." The paper ran eight short, snippy pieces about the memorial, responding directly to praise of Wash's speech. "O! shades of Demosthenes, Cicero, and lord Chatham...here has arisen an universal orator, 'bred and fattened at Mount Vernon' who can discourse, with equal eloquence, on the morality of man, or the growth of *Merino rams*," the editors sneered. A newspaper in Charleston, South Carolina, also drew on Wash's well-known wool promotion schemes, writing that:

> the head of this gentleman must certainly have been a wool-gathering, for a greater compound and farrago of wash and nonsense was never uttered on any solemn occasion before. Mr. Custis had better attend to the erection of sheep cotes, the shearing of lambs, and breeding of horned cattle, than the delivery of Orations. By the one he may possibly benefit himself and serve his country; by the other he will obtain neither credit for his patriotism nor applause for his talents.[19]

But this critic was to be proven wrong: while Wash's sheep schemes ended with the war, he would be known for his speech in honor of General Lingan for the rest of his life. Whether through joking mentions of "Demosthenes Custis" and "My life on it that fellow is a Federalist" or in words of praise, many Americans did not forget the most important speech he would ever give.[20]

★ ★ ★

Patty was surely in the crowd in the woods when her brother gave his speech, and she began to consider how she might add her own voice as a representative of George Washington's legacy to the political debate over the war. Women's options were limited, but they could and did participate in politics, especially women who were related or married into elite political families. Patty would have observed the political activities of other women in the nation's capital as well.[21] She and her husband Thomas were "of the Boston stamp in politics"—in other words, high Federalists. While the Virginia Federalists had what one historian has called a "fundamental nationalism" that meant they ultimately backed war efforts, the Federalists of Massachusetts felt alienated from the federal government and were virulently against the war.[22] Patty had powerful Massachusetts Federalist friends, including congressmen Timothy Pickering and Josiah Quincy. In the summer of 1812, Quincy became one of the vice presidents of the Boston chapter of the Washington Benevolent Society, a Federalist group. While the Boston branch pledged to provide charity to those in need, this was never their focus; one of the founders said the goal was "to collect together the Gentlemen and separate them from the democrats." They opposed the Madison administration, held parades in honor of Washington's birthday and inauguration, and were demonstrably pro-British, to the extent that Democratic-Republicans accused them of aiding the British during the war.[23] Had there been a chapter of the group in Georgetown, the Peters surely would have joined.

Patty could show her approval for the group from afar, however, and she found a particularly clever way to do so. She carefully selected a Washington relic from her collection of over five hundred objects to send to Boston with Josiah Quincy for him to donate to the Washington Benevolent Society. The chosen relic was Washington's copper gorget (an archaic holdover from suits of armor worn around the neck by officers) from his service in the Virginia colonial militia in 1774. It bore the seal of the Virginia colony with a motto proclaiming it to be one of the king's four domains, and Washington had worn it while serving in the *British* military.[24] It was an ideal object to convey Patty's support for the British in the conflict as well as to associate George Washington himself with the British. Patty arranged for this gift to be presented at the society's April meeting, just as British Admiral Sir George Cockburn's forces were gathering in the Chesapeake Bay.

Patty Peter gave this gorget to the Washington Benevolent Society in Boston in 1813. George Washington wore this piece suspended from his neck when serving as an officer in the colonial Virginia militia in 1774. The gorget bears the coat of arms and motto of the colony of Virginia, En Dat Virginia Quartam, signifying Virginia as one of the four royal dominions.

George Washington's gorget, c. 1774, gilt copper. Boston, Collection of the Massachusetts Historical Society.

When Quincy presented the gorget on April 13, he announced that it had been donated by Patty Peter, "the grand daughter of General Washington...as distinguished by her personal and men-

tal accomplishments, as by her illustrious relation." Patty had told
Quincy "that she had selected the Washington Benevolent Society of Massachusetts as the depository of this precious memorial,
because she knew no place, where the principles of Washington
had been more uniformly cherished, than in the Town of Boston."[25] By "principles of Washington," she had meant Federalist
ideals and policies. In other words, this gift was an opportunity
for her to endorse the anti-war, anti-administration views of
the Boston Federalists. As a woman, she could not simply give
a public speech like her brother; rather, she found an alternative way to voice her views.[26] She knew that this gift and her
words would get press attention, thus amplifying her opinions.

Indeed, several days later, the Federalist newspaper the Boston
Weekly Messenger published an article about the gift. The author
of the piece emphasized Patty's valued place in Washington's
family, giving Patty legitimacy to speak because of her relationship with the first president: "She formed part of the family of
the general, who always discharged towards her every office of
the most affectionate parent." The article repeated Patty's comment about Boston's support for Washington's political ideals
and noted that "If ever, hereafter, we shall be overshadowed by
the shafts of calumny, it will be sufficient to remember that we
received the approbation of the family of Washington."[27] The
Federalists were already feeling "the shafts of calumny"; Wash
had called them a "persecuted race." This mark of support from
Patty Peter was as close as the Boston Federalists could get to
receiving George Washington's own approval.

Newspapers around the country reprinted the story and, of
course, provided fodder for Democratic-Republican ridicule.
The *National Intelligencer* published an article titled "A Gorgeous
Present" that sneered that the Federalists had been "ravished
into extacy on the presentation of an old piece of armor by the
hand of a fair lady." The article also criticized the idea that Patty
Peter's approval "shall be sufficient to justify their conduct."

"We must confess," the writer continued, "our devotion is neither to the relics or the relatives of the deceased WASHINGTON, but to his illustrious civic virtues, and the great leading principles he avowed and endeavored to implant in the breasts of his countrymen."[28] For Democratic-Republicans, less concerned with preserving social hierarchies than the more conservative Federalists, family could not carry the same political power. Patty's and Wash's endorsements of Federalist positions symbolized the antidemocratic impulses of that party, reviving British aristocratic ties between family and power that Democratic-Republicans had long argued against.

Patty, for her part, was untroubled by the *National Intelligencer*'s snub and apparently unconcerned as British warships sailed up the Potomac towards Washington in July 1813. She wrote a breezy letter to Josiah's wife Eliza that month reflecting on both developments. The Democratic-Republican newspaper's story was "too contemptible to excite displeasure"; rather, she felt "that to have *gorged* the editors was a great triumph." She had no interest in having the editors' approval; their dismissal of the "relics and relatives of Washington" was, in Patty's eyes, "rather a compliment." Patty felt far more animosity for the opposition party than the nation with which the United States was at war. She had heard reports that the British were getting close (by July 15 they were within sixty miles of Washington), and rather than feel fearful, she announced that "We are all on the alert here to give the British a warm reception." To her relief, her husband was uninterested in joining the American military; she disliked the idea of his fighting for "so unjust a cause." Fortunately for the residents of the Washington area, the British ships soon retreated, and Washingtonians could breathe a sigh of relief.[29]

That did not mean that the war itself was de-escalating; quite the contrary. While the British left Washington alone for the moment, they launched attacks elsewhere in the Chesapeake

Bay and southern Virginia. But most of Great Britain's attention was focused on the Napoleonic Wars, which were of a scale to dwarf the conflict in America; those wars ultimately spanned over twenty years and caused millions of deaths, while the war with the United States resulted in fewer than four thousand deaths in combat.[30] Americans, too, read the (much-delayed) accounts of European battles with interest. In early 1813, Americans had learned of Napoleon's retreat from Russia. This was a major victory for a key ally of Great Britain as well as a setback for Napoleon, whom Federalists feared as an existential threat to the existence of liberty and republicanism. Thus Federalists were overjoyed at the news, and their leaders in Georgetown (including, of course, Thomas Peter) began planning a celebration in April.[31] This would be the occasion of the second great oration of Wash Custis's career.

On the afternoon of June 5, "a large and brilliant assembly of ladies and gentleman" gathered at Georgetown Presbyterian Church to hear music, speeches, and prayer. Among the crowd were Federalist members of Congress, the Russian ambassador André Dashkoff, and naval officers. Wash rose before the crowd to speak, feeling unwell but nonetheless capable of giving a dramatic, impassioned, and lengthy speech. He lauded the Russian victory, then turned closer to home. He warned his fellow Americans that Napoleon was still a threat to the entire hemisphere, and Wash recognized the difficult situation that the country faced in fending off both Britain and France. He then turned to the war with Great Britain, and without uttering the word *Federalist*, reiterated his point from his earlier speech that it was they who were winning the great battles. It was "the neglected children of our Washington," "the true, legitimate children of our chief," who were winning the war.

After the celebration at the church concluded, some three hundred men gathered at the Union Tavern for dinner and to hear a speech by Maryland Federalist Robert Goodloe Harper.

The dining room was decorated with a bust of the Emperor Alexander (lent by the Russian ambassador) with a painting by Wash hanging above it. Wash's painting depicted a massive black eagle holding a serpent in its talons with the smoldering ruins of Moscow in the background. There was also a large portrait of Washington in military attire, probably lent by Wash, hanging across from the bust of Alexander. It must have been a long evening; in addition to Harper's lengthy speech, there were seventeen official toasts, each followed by a song, plus a further ten toasts by prominent guests.[32]

Wash remained in the news after the speech, receiving as usual both praise and censure. The Russian ambassador sent him a letter of thanks with a medal of Alexander I, and both this letter and Wash's grateful reply were published in the *Federal Republican*. That newspaper also praised the delivery of his oration "in a style of ease and dignity, so peculiar in his oratory." Like his speech at the Lingan memorial, this one, too, would be mentioned even in his obituaries decades later. But Democratic-Republicans were, unsurprisingly, sharply critical, although most of their criticism was directed at Harper's speech; Wash's speech was, in the words of one writer, mere "vapid fustian." They had opposed all Federalist celebrations of the Russian victory as praising a development, in the *National Intelligencer*'s words, "auspicious to the cause of our enemy."[33] Russia was at this same time offering to intercede and host peace negotiations between America and Great Britain, and the United States did not see Russia as an enemy. Still, many Democratic-Republicans saw such celebrations as going too far.[34]

The partisan divisions over the war, both in America and Europe, continued as the war dragged on. When Lawrence Lewis learned of Bonaparte's defeat at the Battle of Leipzig in October 1813, he told his nephew Warner that "The demo[crat]'s are much crestfallen at Bonny's discomforture." He was amazed that there were Americans "rejoicing in Boniparts successes and unhappy at his defeat."[35] Lawrence should not have been surprised; his own sister-in-law Eliza remained an ardent admirer of Napoleon. Perhaps it was better for both Eliza and her siblings that she had moved to Philadelphia to be closer to her daughter.[36] But Napoleon's defeat was no cause for celebration for anybody in America; when he was finally forced to abdicate in April 1814, the end to one conflict meant that Britain could focus its efforts on another. That meant redirecting manpower and resources to the war in America.[37]

By the summer of 1814, as the war entered its third year, it remained unclear which nation would be the victor. The United States had won a number of important battles, particularly naval ones, but it had also suffered defeats. The attempted invasion of Canada had proved a total failure; British sailors had pillaged towns and farms around the Chesapeake Bay; wars with Britain's Native allies had broken out on the western frontier; and the government was running out of funds. With trade severely curtailed, merchants and farmers alike in Virginia were suffering.[38] Wash had had trouble selling produce from his estates, and British sailors had stolen livestock from Smith Island. The prices of basic goods had soared, and he was having trouble affording basic necessities.[39] The same was likely true for the Lewises as well. The Lewises also shared the experience of many planters in the Chesapeake region as at least one of their enslaved people made his way to freedom on a British ship.

The Lewises had forced Michael Lee, the nephew of George Washington's well-known enslaved manservant William Lee, to move to Woodlawn with his mother Lucy and sister Patty in 1802, when he was around seventeen. His father, Frank, had been owned by George Washington and was thus freed in 1801, but Lucy was a Custis bondswoman who served as a cook at Mount Vernon. His elder brother Philip had been separated from the family and sent to Arlington House, where he became a house servant. We know little else about Michael besides these bare facts and that he took the opportunity of seeking refuge on a British ship, where British generals had promised to give enslaved people their freedom. Both on their way to and from the capital in August 1814, British ships on the Potomac River sat for some time just offshore from Mount Vernon, and they had also docked at Alexandria. Michael may have slipped away in the night and walked the short distance to the Potomac while the ships were near Mount Vernon, rowing a small boat to the huge naval vessels. Or perhaps the Lewises had sent him on an errand to Alexandria and he made his way onto a British ship there.

Of course, enslavers like Lawrence were convinced that the British had kidnapped their bondspeople—Lawrence's friend referred to Michael as being "carried away by the British." But just as Americans sought freedom from British tyranny once again, enslaved people like Michael made the same choice as they had in the Revolution. In Michael's case, as in most others, we know little of what became of him. He appeared on a list of Black refugees taken to Halifax, Nova Scotia, one of some 1,600 to arrive in the British Canadian maritime colony. He likely remained in that area the rest of this life; over fifteen years later, Lawrence Lewis and many other enslavers filed claims with the British to be recompensed for their human property. Lawrence received $250 in reparations, while the nephew of perhaps the best-known enslaved man at Mount Vernon likely struggled to eke out a living hundreds of miles away from his family.[40] The opportunities the war offered the Custises versus their enslaved people were different indeed.

In the spring of 1814, the British had returned to the Chesapeake Bay and resumed their raids of coastal towns. Ships continued to arrive over the summer with troops freed by the end of conflict in Europe. The British ships were perilously close to the capital city, and according to Patty Peter, "For some weeks, the citizens have expected a visit from the British, and repeatedly called upon the Secretary of the War Department and the President for protection."[41] But Secretary of War John Armstrong was convinced the British would not attack; Eliza later referred to the "infatuated security" of Armstrong and the rest of the cabinet.[42] Washington was a very small settlement, whereas just up the bay, Baltimore was the country's third-largest city; Armstrong couldn't see why the British would go to Washington, asking, "What the devil will they do here?" Yet Baltimore, while a larger and more important city economically, did not carry the emotional and symbolic weight of the capital city. Finally, in July, the Madison administration recognized the danger (although Armstrong remained in denial) and began organizing local militia.[43] It was to be far too little, too late.

On August 14, 1814, the first British ships arrived at the mouth of the Potomac River. Several days later, a courier arrived in Washington with news from a military observer that he had spotted forty-six ships approaching. Eliza, safely ensconced in Philadelphia, hoped that "the spirit of 76 will be roused in the nation, & every man will draw his sword & throw away the scabbard." With little advance preparation in place, the militia in Washington was ill-supplied and far too small for the task at hand. Meanwhile, the British had unloaded their men and supplies after traveling up the Potomac, and their force of experienced men was marching through Maryland towards Washington on August 22. By then, women and children were packing their things and fleeing the city, and President Madison ordered that the government documents be packed and removed to safety.[44] Patty Peter and her husband decided to stay at Tudor Place; Thomas was suffering from gout, and Patty declared herself "too much of a Tory to run." She wasn't completely unconcerned, though, and she sent her children across the river, presumably to stay with Wash and Molly at Arlington House.[45]

On the morning of August 23, James Madison visited the American troops stationed several miles into Maryland to create a buffer for the nation's capital. He sent a quick note to his wife Dolley to reassure her that the British troops "are not in a condition to strike at Washington."[46] But later the same day, he saw that he was wrong; he wrote Dolley reporting that there were more enemy troops than he had thought and instructing her to be prepared to leave the President's House quickly. The troops who had been protecting the building were gone, leaving Dolley alone with several servants and enslaved people. In the chaos of people fleeing the city, Wash Custis went against the crowds and visited Dolley at the President's House as she was packing the cabinet papers. He wanted to ensure that she saved the full-length Gilbert Stuart portrait of George Washington hanging in the dining room of the President's House.[47]

The following day, the British continued their march towards Washington. Around seven miles short of the city, at the small town of Bladensburg (within sight of the Custises' Uncle and Aunt Calvert's house, Riversdale), a battle erupted between the British and American troops. Madison and his cabinet were there but stayed away from the front lines. Wash, too, was there. He had supposedly contacted Madison and volunteered to fight, but as a *Federal Republican* story reported, he "was repelled." It would not have been personal; the story notes that Wash had rheumatism that so crippled one of his hands that he could not hold a musket. But he was determined to play a part, and he joined the Georgetown Artillery led by Thomas Peter's brother George and helped load one of their six cannons. When Peter was ordered to retreat, he refused, and the editors of the *Federal Republican* were delighted to report "that the last gun [of the battle] was fired by major Peter's corps, and in loading which, Mr. Custis assisted."[48]

While the British suffered greater losses than the Americans, they won the battle, and the American troops made an ignominious retreat as the British proceeded towards the capital city. Nelly immortalized the embarrassing loss in a poem that demonstrated that despite the trials of the previous decade and having given birth to her eighth and final child (a daughter Angela) a year before, she had retained her youthful wit and humor.[49] She began the poem with the disclaimer that if it could "strew one flower in your path, or excite salutary mirth, the design of the Authoress will be fully answer'd."

> …long our Land shall rue that day
> When seized with sad and sore dismay,
> Our valiant bands soon flew the way,
> Cover'd with dust and infamy.
> When first by drum and trumpets sound,
> Our warriors march'd to battle ground,
> Not one in all the ranks was found,
> Who did not strut most manfully.
> Too soon their boasted courage flies,
> Ross, Thornton, Cochburn meet their eyes,
> Trust me, 'twas not with glad surprise
> Our Heroes mark'd their musketry.
> And fainter yet their courage grew,
> When Ross's renegado crew,
> Their hand grenades and rockets threw,
> Dispersing our famed cavalry.
> …On, on, ye chicken hearted knaves,
> Ye're only made for Jemmy's slaves.

The poem closed with a comparison of "Jemmy" (Madison) to her stepgrandfather:

> He only, who his Country saves,
> Shall live, renowned in history.
> Oh Washington! we bless thy name,
> Thine was a race of deathless fame,
> Had'st thou beheld, thy Country's shame,
> Thy Sun had set in misery.[50]

As humiliating as the retreat from Bladensburg was, the worst was yet to come. After the battle, Madison sent a man ahead to Washington City to tell people to leave. Dolley continued packing up the White House, including taking time to make sure the famous portrait of George Washington was taken down and carted away for safekeeping. She knew that Madison and the military leadership were returning to Washington, so she had the table set in the state dining room for an afternoon meal. Dolley left the President's House with the table still set, as Madison, Monroe, Armstrong, and the local military leaders convened in the field to decide their next move. With few men left and those few in poor condition, the leaders moved the ragged troops to the heights above Georgetown. The capital was left unprotected.[51]

In the late evening, the British troops reached the abandoned city. They planned only to burn public buildings and were under instructions not to kill civilians; this was to be a symbolic rather than purely strategic action. Entering the city from the east, they began by setting fire to the Capitol and the Navy Yard. The Peters and several friends (including the Thorntons) who had fled Washington to higher ground at Tudor Place watched as flames licked the skies over the capital city. They were witnessing, in Anna Maria Thornton's words, "the conflagration of our poor undefended & devoted city." Around eleven at night, the British continued on to the President's House, where they helped themselves to the food and wine that Dolley had left out for the American leaders who had never arrived. Patty Peter later heard that they had toasted to "peace with America, & down with Madison." Feeling refreshed, they then set fire to the President's House and the Treasury Building. One British soldier recalled "the destructive majesty of the flames," declaring that "our sailors were artists at the work."[52]

One lone American stood his ground and fought back against the British in a rather foolhardy act of bravado. Remarkably, this one man was John Lewis, Washington's great-nephew who had been impressed by the British. He had intended to fight in a more formal capacity, enlisting in the navy in March 1814, but he was dismissed in July. Perhaps he was dismissed for drunkenness, because he was apparently "in a high state of intoxication" on the night of August 24. Likely emboldened by liquor, he mounted his horse and rode through the occupied streets of Washington, brandishing a sword at the British troops. He was menacing enough that a British soldier raised his gun and fired, mortally wounding him. He rode a few more blocks, likely leaving a trail of blood, before he "fell dead from his horse" onto the street; his body was left there until the next morning.[53]

British troops burned public buildings across the new capital city in August 1814.
J & J Cundee, *Capture of the City of Washington*, 1815. Washington, Library of Congress.

John Lewis, then, was the sole American killed in the burning of his great-uncle's namesake city. While the Democratic-Republican newspaper declared that this was how the British had "shewn their great respect to the memory of Washington," the *Federal Republican* wryly protested that the soldier who fired in self-defense surely "did not stop to enquire whose nephew he was."[54] If the Custises had any particular reactions to John's death—and surely Lawrence and Nelly would have—there is no surviving evidence of it.

By the next morning, most of the citizenry of Washington was unharmed, but almost all of the public buildings in the city were burning to the ground. William Thornton rushed down into Washington from Tudor Place to beseech the British to spare the Patent Office. The mayor of Georgetown, too, went into Washington to speak to the British commanders, pledging that the few men left there would not fight. Patty got a detailed account of the conversation soon after and clearly delighted in it. According to her, General Cockburn told the mayor that "as our President would not protect us, they would." Patty later heard that the troops had spared Georgetown because "the citizens of Georgetown were respectable people." The British were, in Patty's estimation, "a noble enemy." By pure luck, rather than British magnanimity, the fires in Washington City were doused by a severe storm in the afternoon.[55]

She had a chance to see the British troops for herself the next day. Thomas and Patty, who was then several months pregnant, mounted their horses and "rode into the city to see the ruins." Smoke was still rising from the Navy Yard when they arrived. Patty was eager to meet the British officers, who she had heard were "very elegant men." Indeed, she found them to be "very fine looking Men, & perfect gentlemen." She was not the only one to make this observation; a local minister echoed the claim that they were "perfect gentlemen."[56] Patty learned that many of these men had served with the Duke of Wellington in the Peninsular Wars against Napoleon, and "it was painfull to them to be engaged in war against us." While she noted the destruction of the Navy Yard in the two letters she wrote her friends in Boston, she had little to say about the overall state of the city. In fact, the damage was so bad that a visitor who passed through several months later declared, "The appearance of our public buildings is enough to make one cut his throat."[57]

All three Custis women's reflections on the day made pointed comparisons between George Washington and James Madison, who they could not but agree had failed the city. Eliza, as a Democratic-Republican, was the gentlest critic, noting that Madison was "not a military man" and blaming him primarily for trusting Armstrong. She made no direct comparisons between Madison and Washington, but lamented that the British had destroyed "the seat of our national Govt chosen by Washington… Washington is hardly cold in his grave—that hallow'd spot has been trampled on by Ruthless Invaders."[58] Nelly's poem on Bladensburg made clear what she thought of "Jemmy" Madison. Patty, of course, was the most acerbic. Madison was a coward who "fled so swiftly, that he has never been heard of" several days later. According to her, Cockburn emphasized that the British troops' enmity was largely for Madison, who was "under the influence of Bonaparte"; if Washington had been the President, they would never have burned the city.[59]

The British troops did seem to respect their erstwhile enemy General Washington, and they evidenced it in their treatment of Mount Vernon. Its present inhabitant, Bushrod Washington, was at home with his wife as the British squadron passed directly below on the Potomac, but not one boat came close to shore. Bushrod believed that this was because the naval leader Commodore Gordon felt respect for "a place which had once been the residence of my venerable Uncle." Indeed, Gordon told one of the city leaders in Alexandria that he felt "an anxious desire to visit this spot," but decided not to because it might be "peculiarly embarrassing & disagreeable" to Bushrod.[60] Surely Nelly and Lawrence also watched the ships warily from Woodlawn, and perhaps Bushrod sent a messenger to let them know that they would be safe.

Eliza was perfectly secure living on the outskirts of Philadelphia near her daughter's school in 1814, but it was an anxious summer and fall for her. Late that spring, she had become engaged to Francois Denis de Greffe, and he sailed for France in July to try to restore his reputation and his military appointment. Their plan was evidently for de Greffe to return to America and marry Eliza, with James and Dolley Madison as witnesses. If he hadn't recovered his property in France, Eliza would use "my little fortune" to support them both. She would go anywhere in the world with him—even, she said repeatedly, "to Siberian wilds." But in his absence she was ever fearful, as "his ardent feelings might lead him into scenes." She could not bear to lose the "idol of my Soul" and she barely left home, as her "fears for his safety & happiness render me unfit for Gay company."[61]

Eliza launched a campaign to help de Greffe in his mission; President Madison even wrote at her behest to American ambassador Henry Crawford, and Eliza asked Warden to visit Marshall Macdonald of the Council of War for help. "Perhaps if you tell him the destined wife of De Greffe is worthy of his esteem—the adopted daughter of Washington & a devoted friend of the french," Eliza suggested, "he will promote the happiness of De Greffe."[62] In her anxiety to help her fiancé, Eliza wrote Warden lengthy letters every month begging for him to help a man Warden knew to be a scoundrel. Was de Greffe actually in love with Eliza, or was he after her fortune and good name? Given how little money she had and how tarnished her reputation had become, the latter seems unlikely. Nonetheless, she did have Warden advance de Greffe money to purchase items in France to send to her in America. She never received a thing. Was he milking the little fortune she had?[63]

While preoccupied with de Greffe, Eliza also devoted considerable attention to the progress of the war as well as helping Warden's career. She wrote Warden in the wake of the victory at Fort McHenry in Baltimore that "I am as well as I can feel with a mind filled with anxiety for my Country & seperated from De Greffe." Eliza's romantic and political aspirations remained inexorably tied. She could also extend her political advocacy

to friends, and she plied her influence in Washington on Warden's behalf to try to get him reinstated after his removal from
his office as consul general in 1814. "I have written to every
one I thought could serve you," she told him in December. It
was challenging to help him in the midst of a war and living in
Philadelphia, not to mention that she didn't have all the details
of what had happened. He never did regain his post, but she
promised to use her "talents & zeal" to get him another position if there was one he desired. Whether Warden did the same
in promoting de Greffe is unclear; Eliza had no word from her
finacé until the following March.[64]

When Eliza next heard from de Greffe, the war was over; her
own struggles were not. On Christmas Eve 1814, the American and British negotiators signed a treaty ending the war and
returning all to "status quo ante bellum" (as things were before
the war). It was hardly a triumph for America, but with the end
of the Napoleonic Wars, the trade restrictions and impressment
would die down on their own. And Americans felt that they had
won, in part because of Andrew Jackson's great victory at New
Orleans on January 8, 1815—after the treaty had been signed
but before word reached New Orleans.[65] Eliza thought it was
"the most extraordinary event the world ever witness'd"; and
besides, ever thinking of the French, this triumphant end to the
war would signal greater opportunities for trade with France.[66]

Meanwhile, across the Atlantic, de Greffe was still struggling.
Having apparently had some ties to Napoleon, he petitioned
the military to be reinstated soon after Napoleon's escape from
exile in Elba in April 1815. While waiting for an answer, he
also wrote the minister of war asking for permission to marry
Mrs. Custis, the "petite fille du général Washington" (granddaughter of General Washington). He, like Eliza, was trying to
use her connections to his advantage. It is unclear why he had
to apply for permission, but he was refused—as was his military
reinstatement.[67] What he did for the next six or eight months

is unclear, and the next news of him came in early 1816, when he died by suicide by slitting his throat. When Eliza heard, she fell ill. Her grief was layered with anger; she blamed a longtime friend and French expatriate, John Augustus Chevallie, for having persecuted de Greffe and *"thus caused his self murder."* She had "once hoped to have been the cause of happiness to him." Now he was gone.[68]

Even before de Greffe had died, she had lamented that "I stand alone in the world." Now that was truer than ever before. She had no permanent home, she was divorced, and she had lost her best prospect for remarriage. Eliza's three siblings had thriving families and "want nothing from me," leaving her to feel left out. More importantly, they were on different sides of an ugly political divide.[69] She had turned away from them and relied on Warden, whom she referred to as a brother, but who could do little for her from across the Atlantic Ocean. So at odds was she with her siblings that her old friend Elizabeth Powel had to ask whether Eliza's sisters had helped her in the illness caused by her grief. "I well know that you and they on political subjects are too often at varience," she wrote in tasteful understatement, "but a difference in opinion on those topicks, ought not to interrupt family harmony."[70] Nonetheless, the war had divided both the Custis siblings and the country.

One newspaper writer concluded in August 1815 that the tale of the War of 1812 "the future historian" would tell would be of a fight between political parties. As this was a Democratic-Republican paper, the author decried the anti-French, anti-war Federalists who were continually taking credit for victories, such as "how Demosthenes Custis, the peace party Orator, declared 'upon his life' that no man could fight but a federalist."[71] It is fitting that the writer placed Wash Custis in his story of how he imagined historians would remember the war, because Wash and his siblings had indeed played important public roles. During a difficult and fractious period, the Custises seized the opportunity as Washington's heirs to contribute to the national dialogue. The family could never fully forget their role in the war, especially after Patty gave birth to a baby girl in January 1815 whom she named Britannia Wellington—a pointed tribute to those gentlemanly British troops and a partisan statement that lasted a literal lifetime. As one observer noted, "Of her politics you may judge by the names of her daughters."[72]

CHAPTER 7

America's Family:

The First Family Returns to the Spotlight

"I AM ALMOST A VEGETABLE," NELLY DE-
clared in January 1823. She had not left the bounds of the Woodlawn estate in three months.[1] In fact, she had rarely left over the
past decade. Now in her forties, her hair was going gray, and wrin-
kles began to etch her face. "There is a remnant of Nelly Custis"
still there, Louisa Catherine Adams told her husband, and Nelly
attested (speaking of herself in the third person), "although her
form and face are changed, her heart is still the same." Indeed, all
of the Custises and their spouses were now in middle age, getting
older and grayer (Lawrence, according to Louisa, looked more
like George Washington than ever).[2] Many of their friends and
allies were no longer in politics. During the years of the Monroe administration—the so-called "Era of Good Feelings"—the
family partly receded from the public eye and struggled through
numerous devastating losses.

Over the course of 1820 and early 1821, Nelly had lost six
close family members, leaving her feeling "like a shipwreck'd
mariner on a rock in the midst of the Ocean." In the fall of
1820, while away at school in Philadelphia, the Lewises' daughter Agnes had fallen ill. Nelly wanted to bring her home, but
Lawrence also was sick and "would not hear of it"; by the time

Nelly made it to Philadelphia to nurse Agnes, it was too late. Agnes died at just fifteen years old, and Nelly, in her grief, clung closer to her surviving children and could not forgive Lawrence (it appears they even stopped sharing a bed for some time).[3] Only months later, Agnes's cousin (Patty's daughter) Columbia Peter suddenly became unwell and died on a visit to the Lewises at Woodlawn. Patty had not been able to get there in time, and her younger daughter Britannia thought Patty never "recovered from this blow."[4] Then in August 1822, Eliza's daughter and namesake Eliza Law Rogers died suddenly several months after the birth of her fourth child; it was, Nelly saw, "a fatal blow to [Eliza's] peace."[5]

It was a painful time for the family; as Wash wrote in 1822, "Death…has used his scythe with an unsparing hand of late, in my unfortunate family, He has cutt off the young, the gay, the innocent the good & the happy."[6] All four siblings felt the pain of losing daughters and nieces in their prime, a not uncommon but still wrenching experience in this era. It would take some time for them to reemerge onto the Washington City scene and rebuild their image and influence. That rebuilding would serve as excellent preparation for their carefully crafted star turn during the greatest celebrity tour the young country had ever seen: the visit of the Marquis de Lafayette to the United States. His triumphal return and the constant newspaper coverage of it brought a resurgence of the Custis clan, growing their fame again and linking the *first* "first family" to growing nostalgia for the American Revolutionary era.

The Custises had never disappeared entirely from public life during the 1810s; Eliza had made sure of that. While her siblings' Federalist party had collapsed, Democratic-Republican Eliza still had some connections in power. Nelly felt out of the loop and as if she had lost all influence, especially with the fall of the Federalist party. "I no longer care about politics," she told a friend—but not due to lack of interest. "Unless *I held the reins of Government*—and could guide the stubborn thing aright, unless I could lead them to Honor and True Glory, I should think it useless to puzzle my brains about their proceedings."[7] Nelly's vision had echoes of her sister Eliza parading through the city in military garb years earlier.

Only Patty seemed to have decided to cede the field entirely in this new era when her Federalist comrades had lost all power. She clung tenaciously to her pro-British views, causing a stir at the going-away party for the British ambassador and his wife in 1819. It had been four years since the war with England had ended and the United States had reasserted its independence. Imagine the surprise of those assembled, then, when the band suddenly struck up "God Save the King." The managers of the ball had expressly decided that, despite the guest of honor's being English, the anthem should not be played. But Patty privately approached the band and asked them to play it. Afterwards, the furious managers had the band follow it with "Yankee Doodle."[8] There was no longer an audience for Patty's political tune; she would now leave it to her siblings to play politics.

Eliza had her hand in several schemes and continued to believe in the power of her influence, even while away from the capital city and staying with her daughter in Baltimore for long stretches. Her spirited political activism and poised (if self-important) bearing meant she was still a well-known force in Washington political society. Indeed, Eliza made such an impression on the daughter of the attorney general that when the young woman read a Walter Scott novel featuring a spirited but politically controversial countess, her "imagination invested her, throughout, with the person of Mrs. Custis."[9] While Eliza was no longer having love affairs with Frenchmen, she would still have made a fine character in a novel.

In this period, Eliza met and befriended several Irishmen, whose numbers were growing swiftly in America after the War of

1812, and whose cause Wash also regularly supported. A group of Irish Americans were planning to petition Congress for land to set up a colony for Irish emigrants. Congress had acceded to a similar request from a group of Frenchmen, and the Irish Emigrant Association planned to ask for land in Illinois.[10] Eliza thought she knew better; why not go to Alabama or Mississippi, which were flourishing economically and were better connected to rivers and ports? She wrote Thomas Addis Emmet, a highly respected Irish American leader, with the suggestion. He wrote a polite reply and defended the choice of Illinois, then explained what he thought might be a "delicate" objection to her plan, "when I consider that I am addressing a lady born in Virginia."[11] Put simply, he had no interest in establishing a colony in slave country.

Nonetheless, Eliza was hopeful that the petition to Congress would succeed. She told David Bailie Warden of her support for the Irish colony and then, with her usual spark of independence, reminded him that she had told him before "how much I should like to be the foundress of a Colony on some of the fine lands of our Country." Eliza, without a home of her own much less a colony, was bored; being a foundress "would give full occupation to my mind for years, & I should find happiness in making those dependant on me happy." Perhaps this was a dream she had once shared with her ex-husband, who as a land investor himself might have relished establishing a colony. The Irish scheme, too, was a dream unrealized; Congress rejected the request.[12]

Perhaps Eliza's fervor for the Irish around this time is what endeared her to yet another foreign adventurer and swindler, the Irishman John Devereux. She had first met him when he visited Mount Vernon soon after George Washington's death. They were the same age, and they apparently reconnected in Baltimore while she was there helping her daughter and he was working as a merchant. He had delivered arms to Cartagena in 1815 and had become inspired to raise an Irish regiment to support Bolivar's fight for South American independence. He returned to Ireland in the spring of 1818 to raise regiments, although Eliza thought he was simply going home to try to reclaim land that the government had seized from him years before.[13] As with de Greffe, she asked Warden to support her friend, who had "the best heart and most benevolent spirit." This was, as the men he recruited and sent to Venezuela discovered, far from the truth: he sold commissions in the legion using a forged letter from Bolivar and sent the freedom fighters across the ocean unequipped and without resources. He was finally arrested in 1825 and imprisoned, but he escaped to the United States and lived off a pension funded by Venezuela for the rest of his life. Whatever he told Eliza had happened, she maintained her affection for him; in 1828, she declared, "I have ever regarded him as an adopted Brother."[14]

Nelly, too, became more interested in international affairs as she finally reentered Washington society. In 1822, Nelly spent several weeks in Washington City and rediscovered something of the social, political creature she had been as a young woman in Philadelphia. She attended a drawing room at the President's House for the first time since Washington had been president; she had so despised all the presidents after him, not to mention being occupied with small children, that she had chosen not to go there for twenty years. She felt out of place but was gratified by the Monroes' polite attention to her. She befriended Joel Poinsett, a congressman from South Carolina who had formerly served as a diplomat in South America. "I admire him extremely," she declared, and was excited that he had said he would visit her at Woodlawn and teach her Spanish. She also met the son of Irish freedom fighter Theobald Wolfe Tone, the wife of the French ambassador, the Russian ambassador, and the French engineer Simon Bernard. It had been decades since she had spent time in such circles, and she reveled in it. She even began to feel that she might have political influence; she promised Elizabeth Bordley (who had married in 1817 and was now

Mrs. Gibson) that she would try to get a military appointment for her nephew and "felt almost equal to making a direct attack on *King James* [Monroe] himself."[15]

There was another reason even more important to Nelly than politics for going back into Washington society: her daughter Parke needed to meet a husband. That was not going to happen in the isolation of Woodlawn. Parke had seemed yet to fall in love; she had plenty of suitors but had little interest in any of them.[16] She was no coquette and not considered beautiful, although she was elegant, accomplished, and intelligent. Nonetheless, Parke knew that she was seen as a catch on the marriage market; to marry her would be to ally with the Washington family. She was already of a quiet disposition, and this knowledge gave her what one man who met her called "an air of stiffness and sedateness," not to mention "superiority." Of course, as Nelly said, when it came to her daughters' marriages, "never should wealth be my object"; nonetheless, "I trust my Son will be *rich in pocket*, as well as in moral & religious principles, & mental endowments." Nelly also preferred a man from the North (ideally her beloved Philadelphia) so that Parke could live in a place without "the evils attending the *slave* property" and with better schools than were available in the South for her future grandchildren.[17]

Nelly had hoped that a young friend of hers, Christopher Van Deventer, who had retired from the military to a stable job in the war department, or the worldly South Carolina politician Joel Poinsett, would capture Parke's interest.[18] Neither did. But in early 1823, Parke finally fell in love when she met a confident, friendly young army officer named Edward George Washington Butler.[19] Ed Butler's middle name was not merely in homage to Parke's step-great-grandfather, but to commemorate his being born on Washington's birthday, February 22. Ed's close connection to Andrew Jackson initially endeared him to Nelly.

Wash, Nelly, and Eliza were already among Jackson's admirers, but Butler would help them cement those ties. Wash had shown

Jackson around Mount Vernon in 1815, and Eliza and Nelly had admired his military prowess (whether Patty agreed is unclear; after all, he had vanquished her much-admired British soldiers at New Orleans).[20] While it was natural that the descendants of the country's founding military hero would be attracted to other martial figures, it is a bit peculiar that all three overcame their strong partisan commitments to support this "man of the people." He vigorously opposed the kind of government support of agriculture and industry that Wash wanted, supported a strong executive that would have been anathema to the Democratic-Republicans Eliza liked, and despised all the elitism and financial systems of Nelly's Federalists. He was also dogged by accusations, which finally exploded in the 1828 presidential campaign, that his wife Rachel had committed bigamy when they married over thirty years earlier.[21] Still, he remained famous for his 1815 victory at New Orleans—and, perhaps most importantly for Nelly at least, a ward of his was hoping to marry her daughter.[22]

Jackson, like George Washington, never had biological children of his own, but he and his wife Rachel helped to raise several children, including one Ed Butler. While this certainly helped Ed win over Nelly, he was far from her first choice for her daughter: she had hoped for a genteel, well-educated, and wealthy Northerner. Ed was genteel, but he would depend on his army appointments for his limited income, and Nelly admitted that "his mind is not *first* rate."[23] With no fortune, he had to proceed patiently in his courtship, visiting Woodlawn whenever possible. His siblings recognized the prestige of the connection: his sister Eliza reported to their brother Anthony that Ed was visiting "the family of Lawrence Lewis, the adopted nephew of General Washington, who married the celebrated Miss Eleanor Custis, the grand daughter of Mrs Washington."[24] No mention of Parke—it was the family prestige that mattered.

On Nelly's side, it was Ed's connection to Jackson that weighed heavily in his favor. By the end of 1823, Nelly took advantage of this close link. When Ed left Woodlawn that December, she sent him off with a piece of George Washington's china and explained that Washington had used this plate at his birthday celebrations. She also conveyed the request that Jackson dine off of it on the coming anniversary of the Battle of New Orleans. Jackson was flattered by the gift from the woman "adopted by the Genl. as his own daughter," as he explained to his wife.[25]

Wash, likely hearing of Nelly's gift and seeing an opportunity to make his own contribution, selected another Washington relic to give Jackson soon after: Washington's military telescope. Wash's gift made the newspaper, which reported on Wash's remarks in giving the "interesting memorial of our olden time," including his request that Jackson "leave the telescope as Alexander left his kingdom—'to the most worthy.'" Jackson's reply was uncharacteristically humble and grateful, and he told Ed that the gift was "the highest honor that could be paid to me, to be considered worthy, by the representatives of that *immortal man*, the father of his country." More than "all the honours my country has hitherto bestowed on me," Wash's gift particularly touched him. It was not the specific object, but the fact that Wash—a living representative of George Washington— chose to bestow it on him. While fashioning himself as a political outsider of sorts, Jackson valued this tacit endorsement of the Washington family. He planned to call on both Nelly and Wash as soon as he could, which would cement a long friendship between the families.[26]

Nelly clearly valued her growing friendship with Jackson, dismissing the rumors against him and even claiming to take Rachel Jackson under her wing. Nelly reported to Elizabeth Bordley Gibson that Jackson "is not the wretch he is represented" and explained what she had heard about the story behind his marriage to Rachel. She offered Gibson regular updates on her interactions with "Old Hickory," using his famous nickname, and promised to use her friendship with him to try to get an appointment for Gibson's nephew. When she finally met Jackson's wife Rachel in early 1825, she described her as "an excellent plain *motherly* woman, but by no means elegant." Nelly could change that, though; she told Gibson that she would do the good deed of "teach[ing] her the *graces*." Rachel did at least know how to endear herself to Nelly: she told her that Nelly and her family "were very great favorites of Gen'l Jackson."[27] The Custises were back in the news and in Washington City's political maelstrom, and just in time for perhaps their greatest turn in the limelight since their stepgrandfather's presidency.

The Marquis de Lafayette's visit to the United States was cause for exuberant rejoicing and affectionate nostalgia for the entire nation. But perhaps nobody pinned so many hopes and emotions on the visit as the Custis grandchildren. They were surging back into public view, and the publicity of Lafayette's tour offered unparalleled opportunities as newspapers across the country breathlessly followed every move. It is hard to overstate just how ubiquitous newspapers were in America at the time; America had around eight hundred newspapers, based in large cities and small towns, and with the country's postal system, news could easily reach people living in every corner of the country.[28] Celebrities themselves, the public, and the media worked in concert to build a burgeoning celebrity culture in this era that tied personal fame to major issues of the day.[29] Getting newspaper coverage, then, was a vital part of maintaining the family's celebrity. While they knew accompanying Lafayette would get them into the paper, this was not mere opportunism: the Custises genuinely revered and adored Lafayette, whom they had turned to as a surrogate father in correspondence for years. Lafayette's son, too, was close with Nelly and Wash, having lived with them briefly at Mount Vernon. Thus the Lafayettes' return to America was a chance for the Custises to see dear friends. Lafayette and his son visited every state in the young country, but at some of the most important points in their travels, a member of the Custis family was with them. The Custises were not just accessories to the visit; in fact, they played key roles in shaping it.

Lafayette arrived in America during a period of both rising patriotism and sectionalism. There had been an uneasy agreement over the spread of slavery with the Missouri Compromise in 1820, but the debate over slavery would only continue to grow more heated. Partisan tensions also flared as Lafayette arrived just months before the 1824 election. While during James Monroe's two-term presidency there had essentially been only one political party, the race to succeed him was a contentious four-way contest. Lafayette provided a beloved figure that Americans could unite behind. This was also an era of nostalgia for what Americans saw as the heroic figures of the American Revolution. Most of the veterans of that war had passed away, so Lafayette (who had joined the fight at only twenty) was one of the last living ties to the struggle. For Americans who knew how close Lafayette and General Washington had been, it felt like the closest they could get to a second coming of George Washington.

Lafayette received a rapturous welcome, echoing the crowds who greeted George Washington when he arrived in Philadelphia and New York at the beginning of his presidency. Everywhere Lafayette went, crowds greeted him with elaborate visual displays, ranging from military formations to girls in white gowns, from cannon salutes to newly penned songs, from triumphal arches to Washington's own camp tent.[30] It is hard to overstate the level of fanfare that greeted Lafayette at every stop; in Philadelphia, for instance, his welcoming parade was three miles long and included thousands of troops and tradespeople.[31]

Newspapers provided detailed coverage of every step of Lafayette's tour, even before he arrived in the country. There were conflicting reports in July 1824 about when precisely he would land in the United States. When the packet ship carrying Lafayette arrived in New York on August 15, the public learned of it from a thirteen-gun salute from Fort Lafayette. The fleet of boats escorting his ship into New York harbor was, in the words of one reporter, "one of the most splendid spectacles ever witnessed on this part of the globe."[32] While he was met by rapturous crowds, none of the Custises were yet among them. However, Nelly had been vacationing in the Hudson Valley, and as soon as she learned of Lafayette's arrival, she hurried to New York City.

Nelly traveled to New York to be among the first to greet the Marquis de Lafayette and his son at the beginning of their nationwide tour.

Francis Scott King, *Portrait of General Lafayette and a view of his landing in New York in 1824*, 1899. Washington, Library of Congress.

Lafayette spent the last week of August visiting Boston, and when he returned to New York City in early September, he wasted no time in reuniting with Nelly. The *New-York American* reported that he struggled to make his way through crowds of well-wishers as he walked to the house where Nelly was staying. The reporter described her as "mrs. Lewis, or as he himself called her, and she will therefore pardon our repeating it, Nelly Custis, the grand-daughter of Mrs. Washington."[33] Nelly dined with Lafayette and his son the following night, and several nights later they went to see a play at the Park Theatre together—all minutely reported in the newspapers. At the theater, Lafayette sat in a box hung with a banner reading "Friend of Washington," and Nelly and her family sat in the adjoining box. Perhaps Nelly sat at the edge of her box adjoining Lafayette's, with him just across the barrier; the newspaper reported that Lafayette "frequently and affectionately" took her hand.[34] He was "unremitting in his attentions to her," and readers reveled in this reconnection between two people with close ties to George Washington. When Lafayette took a steamboat trip up the Hudson River the next week, Nelly accompanied him— but so did another woman, who would become her nemesis.

The woman was Frances (or Fanny) Wright, a twenty-nine-year-old writer and reformer from England. She had been to America several years earlier and published a book reflecting on both her travels and American politics. The book brought her widespread attention and led to her friendships with both the English philosopher Jeremy Bentham and the Marquis de Lafayette. Accompanied by her sister Camilla, Fanny traveled back and forth between France and England in the early 1820s, often staying at Lafayette's family home, La Grange. Fanny and Lafayette formed an exceptionally close friendship; she wrote him in 1822 that "I am only half alive when away from you." While rumors circulated that she was his mistress, the two had always cast their relationship in terms of father and daughter; in

the same letter as the quote above, she addressed him as "my father" and "my paternal friend." While we cannot know whether
there was a physical component of their relationship, men and
women could have deeply emotional friendships in this era, and
indeed Lafayette had other female friends. To quell the gossip,
Fanny suggested that Lafayette either marry her or adopt her
as his daughter. He refused both, but he was still determined
that she and her sister accompany him on his trip to America.[35]

Lafayette knew that Fanny was a controversial figure, and
he would soon discover the power of Nelly's loathing for his
close friend. When Eliza asked him about Fanny, he explained
that "Miss Wright is enthusiastically beloved by some, admired
by many, envied by others, as is generally the case with distinguished talents and generous souls." Nelly did not take an in-
stant dislike to Fanny, but by the end of a week spent in each
other's company in Philadelphia during Lafayette's visit there,
her enmity was biting. She wrote George Washington Lafayette
of her prayers that he and his father would be "released from
those plagues of Egypt"—in other words, the Wright sisters.
Fanny was like a "Tygress in petticoats," Nelly proclaimed, and
had already made many enemies.

Why did Nelly loathe the Wrights so deeply? Fanny may have
alienated Nelly with her antislavery activism; while in Philadelphia, Fanny tried to introduce Lafayette to an agent of the Hai-
tian government to discuss a scheme to help Black families resettle
there. Fanny's outspoken, forthright manner may have also been
at fault. Certainly there was jealousy at play here as well; Nelly
saw Lafayette as an adopted father and did not want to share him
with another woman, much less a young, socially radical one.
But Nelly planned to use "the privilege of my sex" to make Lafayette see Fanny's faults and to keep Fanny and her sister away
from him. By the time Lafayette reached his next stop in Baltimore, the Wright sisters had been excluded from all but the largest
public gatherings with Lafayette, likely through Nelly's doing.[36]

Despite the Wrights' absence, Lafayette was not disappointed in his visit to Baltimore. He was escorted by some of Maryland's leading citizens to Fort McHenry, where soldiers from the War of 1812 stood arrayed to greet him. Residents of Baltimore, including Revolutionary War veterans, had filled the peninsula connecting the fort to the city. Cannons were fired to announce his arrival. As he proceeded through the lines of troops to the gate of the fort, the troops parted to reveal one of the most treasured relics of George Washington: his Revolutionary War camp tent.[37]

In anticipation of the visit, Wash had written to the leader of Baltimore's welcoming committee and offered to lend his stepgrandfather's well-worn camp tent. The *National Intelligencer* published news of the offer on August 1, and news reports later followed the tent's progress from Alexandria to Baltimore. While Americans drew forth all sorts of Revolutionary relics to present Lafayette, the media attention to the tent showed that it was the most prized relic of all.[38] There would be other valuable Washington relics presented to Lafayette and his son—the Custises saw to that—but the tent was different. It had not just been present during the war; it had sheltered both George Washington and Lafayette. The tent had a large physical presence but was easy to transport, and it followed Lafayette along several stops on his voyage.

Lafayette was clearly moved to see the tent, as well as the people gathered within it. The governor of Maryland emerged from the tent and offered a speech of welcome, then led Lafayette inside to a gathering of the local Society of the Cincinnati, a group of army officers, and Wash Custis himself. Wash had brought more than the tent; he had also set up some of the camp equipage that George had used during the war. On seeing it, Lafayette said quietly, "I remember, I remember! Language cannot express my feelings in meeting my brothers in arms in the tent of Washington." There was a hush inside and tears in the eyes of his old fellow officers.[39]

Lafayette was then escorted into the city of Baltimore in a luxurious carriage by a thousand cavalrymen. He dined at a "sumptuous feast" with military generals, Secretary of State John Quincy Adams, and Wash. While Wash did not have any formal public part in the celebrations, he must have swelled with pride to be included with such major luminaries. He was already thinking ahead to his greater role as Lafayette moved southward. At one of the Baltimore gatherings, he gave the following toast:

> *The tear of LA FAYETTE which soon will moisten the laurels on the grave of Washington the Great*—Long—oh, long, will the votaries of freedom repair to the spot hallowed by the ashes of the father of his country, and the pious pilgrimage of his illustrious son.[40]

Before Wash could take the spotlight at Mount Vernon, however, Lafayette would stay for several days in Washington. There he spent time with Wash, Eliza, and Patty. His entrance to Washington City was, of course, grand and ceremonial. When he reached the city's boundaries, he moved into an "elegant landau provided by the city" and was joined by military leaders, the local organizing committee, and Wash. As the landau and accompanying carriages crested Capitol Hill, they saw over one thousand troops arrayed before them. A group of girls dressed in white welcomed him to the Capitol Building, where the central rotunda had just been completed. Designed by Charles Bulfinch, the round room's tall sandstone walls displayed four large paintings of Revolutionary War scenes by John Trumbull topped by a low wooden dome. The room was filled with men and women there to greet him, perhaps softening the experience of seeing events from his own military career depicted on great canvases. He then exited onto the portico, where he stood under the tent once again along with other veterans of the Revolution.[41]

Lafayette and his entourage next proceeded down Pennsylvania Avenue to the President's House. People lined the streets, and women looked out from the windows of their houses and waved handkerchiefs. At the President's House, he sat down to dinner at a table heaving with dignitaries (and likely Wash as well). After some thirty-four toasts, Lafayette "begged to be permitted to retire, that he might pay his respects to some intimate and respected friends, the connections of the family of the late Gen. Washington, in Georgetown."[42] He left the gathering and rode in a carriage to see Patty and Eliza in Georgetown. As he walked into the parlor at Tudor Place, he approached Patty and gave her an affectionate hug. After sitting with Patty and meeting her children, he stopped to see Eliza at the home she was then renting nearby.[43] Years later, Eliza remembered the comfort she took from his embrace and his tender words: "my dear daughter Custis I am happy to see you again."[44] It had to have been an utterly exhausting day, but it was clearly of great importance to him to see the Custises as soon as he arrived.

Two days later, he visited another of the Custis homes in the evening—Arlington House. Wash had finally decided to build the central section of the house in 1817, despite his financial difficulties in the wake of the War of 1812. The shortcuts in construction necessitated by the tight budget showed; one visitor noted that while from afar it looked like "a superior country residence," up close, he "was woefully disappointed." Another visitor called it "Custis' Folly." The house was covered in a stucco cement scored to look like stones, and the massive columns of the portico were brick around a hollow core, also covered in stucco.[45]

It was dark by the time Lafayette and Wash crossed the Potomac and headed uphill on the winding carriage drive to Arlington House, and the oak and elm trees "obscured what light the twinkling stars afforded." When the carriages emerged from the woods, the house loomed above them like an ancient temple.[46] Some six hundred lights were set around the house and in its windows, sending a warm glow and shadows around the massive white structure. When the party reached the house, Wash escorted them inside, entering the tall doorway into the hall lined with family portraits and lit by a lamp that once hung at Mount Vernon. His ancestors looked on as Wash played host to Arlington House's most famous guest yet.

Wash then took Lafayette and his entourage into the drawing room and introduced his guest to his wife and daughter, as well as his half siblings and two of Patty Peter's children. Molly gave Lafayette a rose that had been picked from Mount Vernon that morning, and the whole family basked in the glow of both the candlelight and their honored guest. Lafayette also noticed a familiar face: that of Wash's enslaved valet Philip Lee. Philip looked enough like his uncle William Lee that Lafayette saw the resemblance, "called Philip to him, and shook him heartily by the hand."[47] While it might seem incredible that Lafayette would recognize the nephew of a man he had last seen decades earlier, throughout his tour he showed a remarkable ability to remember names and faces.[48] William Lee was the most famous enslaved person from George Washington's household, and Wash appeared proud to share the story of Philip and Lafayette with the public; we know of this incident from a letter he sent to the newspaper recounting the story. In Philip we get a rare glimpse of an enslaved person as part of the national story in a form not unlike the Custises, with the key distinction that he was unable to share that story himself.[*]

A great meal awaited the party, but Lafayette was so tired that he only sipped at a cup of coffee. At ten o'clock, he said goodnight to the family and went out to his carriage. To light the way, Wash sent twelve enslaved people holding torches made of lit cedar branches. As the carriage crept along the dark path over the lawn by torchlight, the scattered, sleeping sheep awoke and stood staring at the carriage. When Lafayette turned back to look at the house, he saw the ladies standing on the portico, waving their white handkerchiefs.[49]

---

[*] Several years later, however, a minister helping Philip purchase his wife and children from a local enslaver who intended to sell them invoked Philip's conection to William Lee and George Washington to gain support. It is likely Philip was involved in the strategy behind that effort. See Cassandra Good, "Washington Family Fortune: Lineage and Capital in Nineteenth-Century America," *Early American Studies: An Interdisciplinary Journal* 18, no. 1 (2020): 98.

From Arlington House, the Custises and their visitors enjoyed expansive views over the Potomac River and the nation's capital. The U.S. Capitol building is visible on a hilltop right of center in the image.

Fitz Henry Lane, *View of the city of Washington, the metropolis of the United States of America, taken from Arlington House, the residence of George Washington P. Custis Esq.* 1838. Washington, Library of Congress.

Two days later, Lafayette left Washington City to travel south into Virginia. His carriage, "a superb open coach, drawn by four elegant grays," was followed by another carriage bearing his son and Wash, and finally a cart transporting Washington's camp tent. The entourage entered Alexandria with a military escort and fanfare. The next day brought one of his most important stops on his entire tour: Mount Vernon. Its owner, Bushrod Washington, was away, but several of his relatives along with Wash and Lawrence Lewis were his hosts. Lafayette had come with a number of dignitaries, who joined him for a nostalgic tour of the house—although the Wright women were not part of the group, a "good deed" for which Nelly happily took credit. Only he, his son, and his secretary accompanied the Custises on the short walk down to Washington's tomb. The tomb, at this time, was marked only by a wooden door pressed into a mound of grass topped by cypress trees.[50]

Lafayette entered the tomb alone, emerging with tears staining his face and reentering with his son and secretary. All three knelt in front of Washington's coffin, and when they stood, they all embraced and cried. As they stepped back out of the tomb and into the light, Wash gave Lafayette a ring with Washington's hair inside and delivered a typically dramatic and verbose speech. Lafayette responded with a few brief words of thanks, and there was another series of embraces among the men. Before the group left Mount Vernon, Wash had one more relic to give: the Society of the Cincinnati ribbon on which he had carried the ring was to be cut up and given to the entourage of young men in the party. The group departed by steamboat, and as one newspaper editor declared, "'Tis done! the greatest, the most affecting scene of the grand drama has closed…"[51]

The "grand drama" would in fact continue for another eleven months, but the visit to Mount Vernon had been a high point for both Lafayette and the Custises. With his gift and speech, Wash had ensured that he would take a prominent part in the newspaper accounts of the visit. Wash continued on with Lafayette's party to Yorktown, site of the final battle of the Revolutionary War. As elsewhere, vast numbers of troops met Lafayette; here he was also joined by President Monroe, Chief Justice Marshall, and Virginia state leaders. The local arrangements committee was run by none other than Martha Washington's nephew and Wash's relation Burwell Bassett, with whom Wash probably co-ordinated pitching George Washington's camp tent once again. It stood alongside a massive tent with several wings sent from Richmond, a triumphal arch, and two obelisks, surrounded by the smaller tents of the visiting troops.[52] Conveniently, the next day, October 19, was the anniversary of the British surrender at Yorktown.

The scene must have brought back memories to Lafayette of the battle over forty years earlier, as the land on the shores of the Gloucester River was again carpeted with soldiers and their tents. Washington's camp tent played host to several events, in-cluding a levee for Lafayette to meet local citizens and breakfast with soldiers the next morning. The tent, one reporter noted, "attracted the moving masses, all eager to behold as near as pos-sible the warhouse which had protected" Washington.[53] Wash was likely at Lafayette's side through much of the ceremonies, and he offered a toast to Lafayette at the dinner on the 19th.[54] He appears to have returned home to Arlington after these celebra-tions, while Lafayette continued on to Richmond, Monticello, and Montpelier before returning to Washington for the winter.

In mid-December 1824, it was finally Nelly and Lawrence's turn to host the nation's guest. Lafayette, his son, and his secre-tary spent a quiet four days at Woodlawn, where they met with "the most delicate attentions."[55] The house was far more finely crafted and genteel than Wash's Arlington. A visitor from sev-eral years earlier had described it as "large and magnificent," and noted that guests "were entertained in the most sumptuous manner." The multicourse meal he described may well have been similar to meals served to the Lafayettes: a first course of beef, mutton, oyster, and soup; a second of "puddings pies, tarts, Jellies, Syllabubs, whips, float & Island, sweet Meats &c &c," and finally refreshing glasses of wine along with fruits and nuts. At night, this visitor had slept on a large bed with "linnen sweet & Clean" and had been awakened in the morning by an enslaved person starting the fire and laying out his clothes.[56] Lafayette surely received similar treatment, all made possible by the labor of the many enslaved people on the estate. Perhaps he or his son remembered Nelly's cook Hanson, who had been a distiller at Mount Vernon, or Dolcey, a former Mount Vernon house servant who was Nelly's chief seamstress.

Lawrence and especially Nelly reveled in the visit. Lawrence wrote of it to his brother, sharing the honor but noting with annoyance that the newspapers reported that Lafayette was visiting Mount Vernon rather than Woodlawn. Lafayette did dine at Mount Vernon one evening, but he spent most of his time at Woodlawn. "I felt as if my *own great* adopted Father was in my house," Nelly wrote her friend Elizabeth Bordley Gibson. "It was the first time I had ever received one in *that* character under my roof." Nelly's father and stepgrandfather had died before Woodlawn even existed, so this visit was a particularly special one. "It was a *feast* for me while he staid," she said. Each morning, he kissed Nelly, Parke, and Angela, sharing the fatherly affection that Nelly had craved for so long. She also loved having George Washington Lafayette there; "No one can deserve my regard more than this faithful friend who has loved me so many years, in spite of time, distance, & the changes & chances of life."[57] On the day they left, Nelly gave the younger Lafayette several parting gifts: copies of Martha Washington's recipe for lip balm, her poem on her daughter Agnes's death, a poem in tribute to Mount Vernon, and several other published poems by others. She gave the whole party small gifts of Washington relics as well.[58]

★ ★ ★

Throughout the winter, the Lafayettes and Custises continued visiting one another. It was an exciting time to be in Washington City; the 1824 presidential election had gone to the House of Representatives because none of the candidates had won a majority in the Electoral College. The city was on edge. With the Federalist party essentially gone, the election was a tangle of inchoate ideologies represented by four men: Andrew Jackson, John Quincy Adams, William Crawford, and Henry Clay. Jackson had the largest number of electoral votes and had won the popular vote, but the Twelfth Amendment to the Constitution stipulated that the winner would be decided by a vote of each state delegation in the House of Representatives. Social groups coalesced around their chosen candidates; one resident noted that "Society is now divided into separate batallions."[59] Eliza, Nelly, and Wash were firmly in the Jackson camp. When Congress convened in December 1824, members of the House had to choose among the top three candidates in the Electoral College, pushing Henry Clay out of the race. It soon became clear that it would be a battle between Jackson and Adams.[60]

The candidates and their supporters pressed their cases to House members through January and into early February. Many thought Henry Clay, now out of the race but still a congressman from Kentucky and Speaker of the House, was the key vote to win. While he made it appear his mind was open, he knew from the beginning that he would support Adams—and Lafayette, too, knew this, because he was Clay's longtime friend, and Clay had confided in him.[61] Lafayette likely did not share the secret with the Custises; Nelly, Wash, and Eliza were ardent Jackson supporters, and Nelly disliked the Adams family. Clay met with Adams in early January and let him know of his support, forming an alliance that would later lead to charges of corruption against Clay.

As the February 9 House vote approached, the capital filled

with visitors "attracted to the City by the interest of the approaching crisis," according to the *National Intelligencer*.[62] A snowstorm hit the city on the 9th, but nonetheless spectators trudged through the snow and crowded into the House galleries. While some of the states' votes—including Clay's home state of Kentucky—were already known, there was still considerable uncertainty. Lafayette and other distinguished guests sat on the floor of the House as the votes were being counted.[63] Many expected it would take multiple votes to get a majority, so when the results were announced, it came as a surprise: Adams won easily with thirteen states out of twenty-four. In the galleries above, some cheered and clapped, while others hissed to quiet them. Nelly and Parke were staying in Washington and may well have been among the crowds in the galleries.[64]

That night, President Monroe held a reception at the President's House, and both Jackson and Adams were there—as were Nelly, Parke, and the Lafayettes. Indeed, it seemed that all of the tourists who had come to watch the presidential contest had come; Lafayette's secretary reported that "the crowd was so considerable that it was almost impossible to move."[65] Nelly and Parke, like Jackson's other supporters, were furious at the results; since January, Jackson's camp had attacked Clay for allying with Adams. When Clay was named Secretary of State in March, it fueled the rumors of a so-called "corrupt bargain." No wonder, then, that a fellow guest at the party who chatted with Parke observed that "she was very warm of the result of the election." Like her mother, she was not shy about sharing her political views; she "expressed her opinions with great freedom, and with little regard as to who heard her."[66] Nelly, too, was incensed at the result, telling a friend, "we have more cause to be proud of Andrew Jackson defeated, than the Adams party have of their *Clay* Pres[iden]t." The epithet "*Clay* President" apparently circulated around the room that night, suggesting that

Henry Clay would be able to shape Adams's policies like soft clay in the hands of a potter.[67]

But what all the crowds were waiting for was the inevitable meeting between Jackson and Adams. Jackson, after all, had already expressed considerable anger at the Adams campaign and was known for his fiery temper. When Jackson entered the room, everybody turned towards him, whispered, and moved in his direction. Remarkably, Jackson and Adams both remained gracious and polite. When they spotted one another, they walked across the room and shook hands, with Jackson congratulating his rival. The crowd was delighted, and Adams was "deeply moved" and perhaps a bit embarrassed; Nelly noted that Adams "blushed to the *top of* his *head*."[68] But relations between the two men would not remain cordial; their erstwhile competitor William Crawford was perhaps correct when he called the move "a useless piece of hypocrisy."[69] Jackson's belief in the Adams administration's corruption united his followers behind him as they began to form a new political party and oppose the president. Nelly certainly had no intention of building ties with the new president and his family, declaring that she would not call on the new president's wife Louisa Catherine Adams as "I do not respect her Husband & I despise his Father."[70]

Eliza appears to have remained at home with her grandchildren during the election drama and Lafayette's winter visit, but she still managed to return to the public eye and cement her ties with Jackson. She capitalized on her relationships with both men to give them each gifts with political weight. To Lafayette, Eliza gifted an 1819 biography of Andrew Jackson with the following inscription: "To Marquis de la Fayette, the comrade of Washington whose esteem is precious to his American brethren, this life of Major General Jackson the conqueror of Wellington's Veterans is presented by his affectionate, grateful & devoted friend, Eliza Parke Custis."[71] Perhaps on the same day that she gave him this gift, she gave Lafayette a gold ring with Washington's hair to deliver to Andrew Jackson. It was accompanied by a letter dated February 22—Washington's birthday—declaring that the gift was "a tribute of respect to him, whose glorious achievements place him next to the father of our country." As she often did with such gifts, Eliza concluded the short letter with instructions to use the relic to remember both Washington and "her who gives it to you." Jackson responded on the same day to express his "extreme satisfaction" in the gift.[72]

The story of the gift and the two letters were widely published in newspapers, bringing Eliza public attention that merely handing the gift to Jackson personally never would have. Eliza took the opportunity to assert herself as a representative of George Washington and, as her sister Patty had with the gorget a decade earlier, to attempt to link Washington to her partisan priorities. Eliza's actions were not all about partisanship or the desire for publicity, however; at the same time, she lent her "commodious and easy carriage" to the Lafayettes for their trip southward.[73] She could ill afford to give up such an expensive possession, as she had limited income and no home of her own, but she likely made the sacrifice out of real affection and devotion to Lafayette.

Wash also used Lafayette's visit to hone his political messaging. His time with Lafayette had inspired him to show support for the Latin American independence movements. On the Fourth of July, he held an Independence Day celebration reminiscent of his old sheep shearing festivals, complete with Washington's camp tent as a shelter for the crowd. By moving the date from the Federalist holiday of Washington's inauguration to a day of national celebration—and by removing the focus from a narrow sliver of agricultural interests—he could host a more unifying gathering. Indeed, one of the toasts was "Political parties—We are of none but the party of *our country*." Other toasts showed the crowd's international interests—one toast to Simon Bolivar called him the "second Washington of a second America!" and there was a more general toast to "Our sister Republics of the

South." Simon Bolivar had reached the height of his fame and power around this time, having pushed all of the Spanish forces out of South America. He was so popular in the United States that some Americans even named their children after him.[74] When Wash gave his own speech, he connected the fight for liberty that the tent had witnessed to that of South America, and the crowd responded with enthusiastic applause. Surely he enjoyed the final toast of the night, which was to Wash himself— "a worthy depository of an inestimable treasure."[75]

Wash also made Lafayette the intermediary to deliver a gift to Bolivar, perhaps following Eliza's lead. He arranged for a story to run in the local newspaper the same day as his celebration announcing that he would be giving Bolivar two Washington relics.[76] When the Lafayettes returned to Washington in August, Wash conveyed the letter from the Fourth of July to Lafayette, along with a medal given by the town of Williamsburg to Martha Washington and a miniature by Joseph Field of George Washington. The miniature was a particularly valuable gift, made even more so by being backed with a lock of Washington's hair. Wash introduced himself in his letter to Bolivar as "the adopted child of Washington"; while famous in America, it is unlikely that Bolivar would know who he was.

Wash portrayed himself as offering these "revered reliques" on behalf "of all the Americans who with pure and triumphant acclaim hail you as Bolivar the Deliverer, the Washington of the South." The letter was carefully copied in a neat, formal hand rather than Wash's own loose writing.[77] At a ceremony on September 1, Lafayette gave the gifts, along with a letter of his own, to a representative of the Colombian legation who would take them to Bolivar. Wash then gave the representative his own letter to Bolivar and made a short speech.[78] The affair, as Wash must have intended, was reported in detail in the newspapers. When Bolivar finally received the gifts, he responded to both

Wash and Lafayette, telling them that "The family of Washington honor me beyond my fondest hopes."[79]

The Lafayettes made one final trip to Woodlawn and Mount Vernon in late August. The visit to Woodlawn seemed to have cemented something new for Nelly in her relationship with George Washington Lafayette. If she had kept in touch with him for the decades since he had left America, there is no trace of it; now, she found new and almost urgent value in his affection. It is no wonder: she had been living in relative isolation at Woodlawn with a husband who was no match for her in intellect or temperament. One family friend noted of Lawrence that "as he grew older he became exacting," and Nelly spent her evenings praying with and caring for him as he had essentially become an invalid.[80] Now Nelly's old friend had returned, and as she told him, "No eyes, except Grandmama's, ever regarded me so affectionately as yours do." She wanted a miniature portrait of him so that she could carry those affectionate eyes with her; even without it, she wrote him on the day he left America, "I see you constantly, every word & look are impressed on my memory." Saying goodbye to him had been painful, and she wanted them to keep up a correspondence. She wrote him lengthy letters monthly for the next year, and quite regularly for another year after that. In a telling note early in the correspondence, she told him that nobody but Parke would see his letters to her and, if he wished, not even Parke; in other words, she would not be sharing his letters with her husband. Friendships between men and women were common in this era, but within strict boundaries that Nelly was clearly crossing. While she addressed him as "beloved brother," it is quite possible that the middle-aged mother of three had fallen in love. Still, she knew she would probably never see either Lafayette again.[81]

On September 7, 1825, the marquis and his son finally boarded a ship back to France. The nation's guest could not leave without fanfare. The day began with a ceremony at the President's

House, where President Adams gave a speech. A procession escorted Lafayette to a carriage and the carriage to a dock on the Potomac. Appropriately, a boat called *Mount Vernon* would take him out to the larger ship crossing the ocean, the *Brandywine*. Crowds swarmed the riverbank to watch. Before boarding the boat, the Lafayettes embraced Nelly and Eliza as well as several other friends; only these two eminent women were specifically named in the newspapers at this stage of the farewell journey. Wash, along with local mayors and military officials, traveled with the Lafayettes on the *Mount Vernon* as the ship went down the Potomac and onlookers shouted from the shores. The group went aboard the *Brandywine* with the Lafayettes and had a celebratory meal on the ship, and Wash offered a toast wishing them a safe voyage.[82] When Wash left the Lafayettes behind and sailed back to Washington City on the *Mount Vernon*, he was returning home a man changed by the visit.

In the years following Lafayette's visit, while his sisters largely focused on their families, Wash found new passions and purpose. Lafayette's return had stirred up American interest in the Revolutionary War, and Wash decided to publish records of his conversations with Lafayette about the latter's memories of the war. He likely did so with Lafayette's blessing, as the first story came out while Lafayette was still in Washington City, in February 1825. When he finished this series of articles, he began publishing his "Recollections of Washington" in 1826. The Philadelphia antiquarian John Fanning Watson had asked Wash to share his insights on his famous stepgrandfather, and Wash was more than happy to oblige.[83] The "Recollections" showed the private Washington, the man only accessible to his family. Elizabeth Bordley Gibson had suggested that Nelly write pieces like these several years before, but Nelly had demurred. She said that Wash should be the one to do it: "He has a better memory than I have and he likes to appear in print."[84]

His sheep schemes long over, telling stories about the Revolutionary past gave Wash a new focus as well as a very public forum for maintaining his close connection to George Washington. He would continue to write and publish the pieces sporadically for the rest of his life. Wash also took up Lafayette's support for international struggles for liberty and became a particularly active supporter of the Irish and Greek independence fights. He worked with Irish groups and gave speeches both to them and in support of them. At his Fourth of July celebration in 1826, he urged Americans to support the Irish and Greek fights for liberty. In 1829, the secretary of the Hibernia Society in Alexandria asked rhetorically, "when the biggots of England will hear from the Catholic association of Ireland, that the adopted Son of America's Washington is the willing friend, the Eloquent Orator, and mingling with the proscribed of their Sister Isle, What will be the confusion?"[85] His ties to Washington, as always, made his support invaluable.

Another lifelong preoccupation that seems to have been strengthened by Lafayette's visit was Wash's commitment to colonization of free Black people in Africa. His support for the American Colonization Society and Lafayette's even more expansive antislavery views were growing increasingly controversial by the end of the 1820s. Lafayette had been among a coterie of French intellectuals with ties to British abolitionists who fought for gradual emancipation of enslaved people in the late eighteenth century. By the time of his visit to America, abolitionists were unpopular, and the French government would not abolish slavery until 1848.[86] Surely Wash and Lafayette discussed these developments during their time together. As slavery became an increasingly polarizing issue in America, the Custises would have to pick a side.

CHAPTER 8

The Custises
Confront Slavery

STANDING IN THE CAPITOL BUILDING'S
Supreme Court chamber several months after Lafayette's departure, Wash Custis looked out over an audience of some of the
nation's most prominent men. The leaders and members of the
American Colonization Society sat at mahogany desks while
prominent citizens and politicians crowded onto the surrounding benches for the fledgling society's annual meeting, all beneath a vaulted, semicircular roof buttressed by stone ribs.[1] After
the meeting's business had concluded, Wash rose to give a fiery
speech in support of the society's aim—to settle free African
Americans in Africa. His arguments centered on a claim that
would have been amenable to his stepgrandfather: that slavery
was bad for economic development, whereas free labor would
help enrich the land and the nation.[2] Perhaps Wash's eye caught
the plaster relief across the room depicting winged Fame holding the Constitution as it is showered by rays of sunlight when
he declared that the Constitution had not "sanctioned" slavery.
"I say it would be an insult to those living, and a calumny to
the memory of those who are dead," he boomed, "to say that
one of those illustrious sages ever intended that *slavery* should
be perpetual in this land."[3] It is easy to imagine that his conver-

sations with Lafayette during the Frenchman's recent visit had convinced him of this position.

If Wash Custis was truly convinced that the founders, including George Washington, thought slavery should come to an end, why did he still own over two hundred people? For that matter, if George's desires had been so clear, why did Wash's three sisters fail to free their hundreds more bondspeople?[4] Whatever George's views, slavery had always been part of the Custises' lives, from when enslaved women swaddled and nursed them at birth to when enslaved people prepared their corpses for burial at death. Enslaved people were a constant presence even in the most private spaces and at work in fields to sustain the family's wealth. Was continuing to exploit enslaved labor, particularly with the rise of the abolition movement in the late 1820s and 1830s, betraying George Washington's legacy?

The answer to that question is not a simple yes or no, in part because George's own legacy when it comes to slavery is complex, whether we look at the treatment of enslaved people, the question of emancipation, or engagement with the institution at a broader level. As much as the story of the benign master who heroically freed his enslaved people has dominated America's vision of George Washington the enslaver since the nineteenth century, the reality is uglier.[5] It was that reality that the Custises grew up with, and they each handled their roles in a slave society slightly differently, especially as attitudes towards slavery shifted in the early antebellum era. It is impossible to truly understand the family without a deeper dive into their role as enslavers.

As famous figures who had put themselves forward as the heirs to George Washington's ideals, they knew that the public was watching them. Perhaps when it came to slavery, George Washington left no great legacy to live up to and carry forward. However, the ideals of freedom and equality that Washington and his generation espoused in the founding of the nation were yet to be achieved. It would be up to others—including one man in the Custises' own orbit—to realize those higher ideals.

There is no such thing as a "good master." True, some enslavers forced their bondspeople to do harder work for longer hours; used harsh corporal punishment more often; sold people and split families more often. George Washington did all these things, but to a lesser degree than some other enslavers. With a plantation centered around tobacco and then wheat, the labor was not as backbreaking as that in the cane fields of Louisiana or the cotton fields of the coastal Carolinas. He also preferred not to separate families through sales. But if the Custis children observed George's and Martha's treatment of the enslaved, they would have seen as much cruelty as mercy. Part of what sustained what to us appears such a clearly abhorrent and exploitative system of labor was that white children were brought up with slavery as a normal part of their lives.[6]

At Mount Vernon, there were around three hundred enslaved people by the 1790s. Perhaps the grandchildren saw George lose his formidable temper and strike an enslaved laborer whose work was not up to George's standards; Nelly's husband Lawrence later recalled two stories of George hitting enslaved men on the head, one so hard he "whirled round like a top."[7] George also sometimes punished enslaved people whose behavior he disliked by selling them to the Caribbean, separating them from their families and leaving them to suffer in the far worse conditions of slavery in that region.[8] His stepgrandchildren were probably far more aware of his efforts to get back Ona Judge and Hercules Posey, who had freed themselves in the 1790s, than they were of his abortive efforts at that time to (in his own words) "get quit of negroes" or his engagement with transatlantic writings on gradual emancipation.[9] Martha had, at best, condescending views towards her enslaved people: "The Blacks are so bad—in their nature that they have not the least Gratatude for the kindness that may be shewed to them." Unlike Wash's wife Molly and daughter Mary, who taught their bondspeople to read and gave them religious instruction, Martha appears to have seen enslaved people purely as laborers from whom to extract value.[10]

Patty and Nelly seemed to have followed Martha's example; they and their husbands enslaved large numbers of people on multiple plantations. When Thomas and Patty Peter wed, they sold twenty-three of the sixty people in Patty's dowry. The enslaved inherited by Patty from Mount Vernon in 1802 also had a hard lot, as the Peters sent the majority to their farms, Effingham where Howard University now sits and Oakland in Montgomery County, Maryland, far from any family members who remained in Virginia. The Peters were largely absentee owners, leaving the enslaved at the mercy of whatever manager or overseers were on the property; Patty continued this practice as manager of the family's enslaved people for the two decades between her husband's death and her own. The eighty or so people that the Peters held at Oakland made them one of the largest enslavers in that part of the state, where the median owner held fifteen bondspeople. The Peters probably used Oakland for tobacco farming, and a few decades later, they transferred some enslaved people from fieldwork to quarrying stone.[11]

The enslaved people Nelly inherited from Mount Vernon were initially able to remain closer to home, but their fates worsened in coming decades. At Woodlawn, there were around ninety enslaved people as of 1820, twenty-five of whom worked in agriculture and four in manufacturing. More than half were children, who probably also did fieldwork. They grew wheat, oats, and corn; tended livestock; and kept up orchards and a kitchen garden to feed themselves and the Lewises. Another ten to fifteen people worked in the house, including a large group of enslaved seamstresses under Nelly's command.[12] More bondspeople lived at the Lewises' second farm, Llewellyn, farther northwest in Virginia, which they swapped for the nearby farm of Audley in 1825; it's possible that the Lewises separated families between Woodlawn and the Shenandoah plantations. Given that Nelly believed that "*nine* times out of *ten*, a negro loves those best who are *least* indulgent—*fear* not *principle* governing the *far far* greater part," we can imagine that her treatment of enslaved people relied upon fear of punishment or sale to gain obedience.[13]

The Lewises' enslaved people were under the constant threat of sale; Lawrence regularly discussed selling individuals and families, including with the slave trading firm of Franklin and Armfield in Alexandria. With their finances strapped and Woodlawn running at a loss, in the 1830s the Lewises completely broke up the enslaved community there; they sent twenty-four enslaved people to their daughters in Louisiana and sold another twenty-four to daughter Parke's neighbor, separating them from family in Virginia and consigning them to backbreaking work on sugar plantations.[14]

It is unknown exactly how Eliza treated her enslaved people, since she probably hired out most of the people she inherited to her stepfather, brother, and brothers-in-law. She never had a plantation of her own, so she likely only kept a small number of enslaved domestic laborers with her.[15] In 1803, she either hired out or sold a woman named Rachael and her three young children to the Peters to work on their Oakland plantation.[16] She had inherited three spinners from Mount Vernon—Anna, Alice, and Kitty—at least one of whom she would have found useful for her regular sewing and mending tasks. There is also evidence that she transported small numbers of bondspeople between Virginia and Maryland several times, probably to serve in her household. For instance, she brought Alice's sons, aged fourteen and twelve, to Washington City, perhaps to labor as waiters in her home.[17] Whether her mercurial temper made life more difficult for them we can only imagine; recall, though, that when Ona Judge had learned she would eventually become Eliza's property, Ona was "determined never to be her slave."[18]

We know the most about the treatment of the people enslaved by Wash, although the records there are still spotty. Both Wash's family and later historians described him as a rather disorganized enslaver who never extracted much labor from the enslaved at Arlington House.[19] This was due in part to his personality and lack of focus, but also to his and his wife's qualms about slavery. It appears that the bondspeople (wisely) took advantage of the Custises' lack of close management of their labor, doing the least amount of work possible as a form of resistance. Enslaved people from his Arlington estate recalled long after Wash's death that he readily gave them passes to travel; in fact, he did so often enough that he had sheets with multiple passes printed for his use.[20] Despite the fact that Wash had more laborers than he could employ at Arlington House, the house and grounds were ill-kept; by the 1850s, his niece estimated that "more than half" of the seventy enslaved people there "lived in idleness."[21]

It is hard to know precisely what the enslaved people at Arlington House did, as no records of planting and laborers survive. We know that there was a patch of land by the river where enslaved people grew wheat and corn, crops common for the region and requiring considerably less labor than tobacco had. This meant that Wash was not the only person in Virginia with more laborers than he needed, but the enslaved people on his southern estates were overworked; the issue at Arlington was how little arable land existed. Many plantations in Virginia had shifted to a mix of subsistence and market farming, and that seems to be the case at Arlington. In addition to a small number of field workers, other enslaved people would have tended the kitchen garden, taken produce to local markets, repaired fencing, buildings, and tools, and cared for livestock.[22] It may be that "idleness" was just what labor beyond fieldwork looked like to white observers; it is also possible that enslaved people had enough free time to visit friends and family, tend their own gardens, or simply rest.

Although Wash and his siblings had torn families apart when they divided the dower slaves among themselves, new families built at Arlington appear to have been able to stay together by the mid-nineteenth century. Enslavers rarely recorded the last names of their enslaved people, but records from Arlington often included surnames—suggesting that Molly and Wash recognized family ties and, to some degree, the humanity of the enslaved. Molly's father had done the same, so perhaps it was she who was behind this.[23] Family groups were also able to live together or, if a spouse was on a neighboring plantation, visit. This was an improvement for those who had lived at Mount Vernon, where George Washington had split many families among the five farms that made up his larger estate. It is unclear how often Wash sold enslaved people, as few of his financial records survive, but the persistence of family groups in the last few decades of his life suggests he did not sell people from Arlington.[24] One formerly enslaved man told a newspaper reporter in the 1880s that Wash was "kind to his slaves when he was old, but dey do say he was 'clined to be rude to 'em in his young days."[25] Molly's views on slavery may have influenced Wash over the course of their marriage and encouraged this safeguarding of families.

Molly and later her daughter Mary and her niece Markie had a schoolroom for educating enslaved children and a small log church where the Custis family worshipped with the enslaved on Sunday nights. It was all Molly's doing; Wash admitted that this was "not according to my notions." Yet the education and religious instruction of the enslaved at Arlington was not purely benevolent; the Custis women were imposing their religious views on unfree people, and their end goal was to prepare them to live independently and spread Christianity—thousands of miles away in Africa. Molly hoped that decent treatment (a relative term) and training in literacy and faith would enable the enslaved to support themselves economically and live as good Christians. As Mary wrote of her mother, "the great desire of her soul was that all our slaves should be enabled to emigrate to Africa...not only for their own benefit but that they might aid in the mighty work of carrying light & Christianity to that dark, heathen country."[26] Molly, Mary, and Markie still expected enslaved people to remain subservient and obedient; they were deploying religious instruction in part to make the enslaved content with their place in the social hierarchy. The fact that enslaved people held their own Baptist services, in addition to Molly's evangelical Episcopalian ones, indicates that the Custises' religious instruction did not fulfill their needs or desires.[27]

While Arlington's enslaved population had the unusual opportunity to learn to read, this does not mean that conditions for them were good. Wash did not object to physical punishments, even for people who simply annoyed him; he directed an overseer to deliver "ample correction" (likely a physical beating) to an enslaved man at Arlington House who had been persistent in asking to return to his family at Custis's White House plantation rather than being sold or hired out. When an enslaved man named Merrity resisted his tasks assigned by the woman to whom the Custises had hired him out, Wash advised that the proper response was "to have broken a stick over his head." Even Molly once remarked that beating could improve discipline.[28] Nonetheless, Molly seemed to recognize the humanity of enslaved people. Wash, however, could easily see them as mere property, and he gave a woman named Judy to his granddaughters as "a present from Gampa."[29] "Gampa" Wash apparently demonstrated his love by giving his granddaughters human property.

A watercolor sketch by Wash's daughter Mary of an enslaved girl on the estate provides a rare glimpse of a bondsperson at Arlington House. The girl, perhaps eight or ten years old, stands barefoot on a dirt patch with a field bound by a fence behind her and trees and hills in the far distance. She wears a simple, shapeless, short-sleeved shift covered in an apron that may once have been white, and she balances a wooden piggin (a cropped barrel) on her head, holding it in place with one small but sure hand to balance the weight. The piggin could have held food or water to bring to the field hands, or it might have been for transporting crops from the fields to a wagon or barn. There is a hint of a smile at her lips, but her bare feet and the heavy load on her head show that her life is neither comfortable nor easy.[30] It was not unusual for an enslaved child this age to work, or to go barefoot, but the image is a reminder that the Custises—not just Wash, but all four siblings—built their wealth in part on the backs of enslaved children.

This child, though, was far better off than the bondspeople on Wash's southern plantations, where he and Molly rarely visited and where he relied on distant managers to both supervise and extract labor from enslaved people. When Wash inherited his father's properties in New Kent, King William, and Northampton counties southeast of Richmond, there were well over one hundred fifty people living on the plantations.[31] He knew from the beginning that conditions there were poor, and they never seem to have improved; if anything, they worsened. At the White House plantation, as one enslaved man was beaten, half a dozen of his fellow bondspeople arrived with clubs in hand to rescue him, and a larger crowd looked on and released a "horrid cry." Around 1820, Wash's manager John Walden pushed back against accusations of "cruel, inhuman and barbarous treatment" of Wash's enslaved people in New Kent and King William. Walden admitted that he whipped those who were disobedient or insolent with a switch, not cowhide or sticks (in his view, a more humane punishment), but he denied that his overseers had stabbed or drowned anyone or that he underfed people.[32] For such accusations to circulate, however, neighbors must have observed abhorrent conditions. While Wash directed that his enslaved people should be "well fed, well clothed, [and] treated fairly," he was just as concerned that they be "made to do their duty" and work for him.[33] He did little to ensure that either happened.

Conditions were particularly bad under his longest-serving manager at the large White House plantation, Francis Nelson, who worked there from around 1832 to 1856.[34] Nelson was a poor correspondent, and Wash complained that he "had as well have lived in the Sandwich Islands, for any information that I could receive of my affairs." Wash seems to have rarely visited the southern plantations, and despite Nelson's wife's assurances that the enslaved had "every comfort in eating & clothing," the mistreatment of the 1820s had persisted for decades.[35] The neighbors were concerned enough that they wrote Wash anonymously about how poorly treated and hard-worked his enslaved people were. Wash was "greatly pained, disappointed, & mortified" to learn from his new manager William Winston in early 1857 that the basic needs of his "unfortunate negroes" were not being met. He could not have been entirely surprised, and he readily admitted that his bondspeople were "heavier worked than any slaves in Virginia."[36]

What does this clash between the treatment of people at Arlington and the other plantations, between Wash's expressed wishes and the realities his bondspeople endured, say about Wash as an enslaver? It lends credence to the notion that Molly had some influence over conditions at Arlington, softening treatment where she was present. Wash may also have been less disturbed by exploitation and deprivation he personally did not have to witness. Then again, as a justice of the peace, he regularly enforced slave laws, including a wrenching case of two free Black servants whom a white woman had brought into Virginia without freedom papers and whom he calmly sent to jail, likely to be sold back into slavery.[37] None of his actions—the relative laxness at Arlington, the brutality at the southern plantations, the enforcement of punishing slave codes—were unusual for a Southern gentleman.

George Washington's best-known legacy as an enslaver, however, came not in the treatment of his bondspeople but in the fact that he freed them in his will. Newspapers and pamphlets at the time of George's death widely publicized and lauded this act, and those against slavery took it as a sign that the first president was on their side.[38] But the reality was that George did not free a single person during his lifetime, only one outright at his death, and the rest in his will only at Martha's death.[39] In

doing so, he did not harm the prospects of the stepgrandchildren or his closest nephews; indeed, he knew that his nephews
who would inherit his farms and the Custises had more enslaved
people than they needed to work their lands. For them to have
emancipated all of their enslaved people, however, would have
been an economic sacrifice; human beings were often the most
valuable part of a Southern planter's estate.

The Custises would make no such sacrifice. They chose to
remain enslavers when the Custis girls each inherited around
one hundred enslaved people and Wash around two hundred.[40]
Given that they inherited these bondspeople at the one moment
some Virginians were freeing large numbers of slaves—perhaps
10,000 would be freed in the state between 1782 and 1806—the
siblings' decision to remain enslavers made clear their views on
the institution.[41] That the Custises continued to hold most of their
enslaved people in bondage was not inevitable; it was a choice.

However, not all the siblings were averse to manumission of
small numbers of people. While Patty and Nelly each only emancipated one person, Eliza and Wash both freed larger numbers.[42]
In the District of Columbia, where both Wash and Eliza resided
(until Arlington left DC and returned to Virginia in 1846), the
manumission laws were more flexible than in Virginia.[43] It's worth
noting that many of those who manumitted their own enslaved
people also acted to strengthen the institution of slavery.[44] While
in the years immediately following the American Revolution enslavers explicitly expressed antislavery views and freed people in
response, by the nineteenth century, manumission was not generally about an enslaver's opposition to slavery. The practice became part of the system of slavery in the Upper South rather than
a challenge to it. After all, enslavers could use the possibility of
manumission as an incentive for enslaved laborers to work harder
and be obedient, and in this way, it could even strengthen slavery.[45]

Eliza's attitude towards manumission was likely influenced
by her husband Thomas Law. Thomas had not grown up with
chattel slavery and expressed his wish to gradually emancipate

Eliza's dower slaves in 1797, then constructed a detailed plan of emancipation for the country that he shared with leaders in 1821.[46] While he was the one who filed the deeds of manumission for the people he and his wife owned and freed, it is doubtful he alone decided how to handle the enslaved people that came under his ownership through her. Was the decision to free Nancy Holmes, William Costin, and their extended families Thomas's or Eliza's? Given her personality, it is hard to imagine she was left out of that decision. There is only evidence of Eliza's own involvement in freeing one enslaved person, a boy named David whom she sold to James Madison for $400 with the understanding that David be freed in five years. Near the end of her life, she seems to have turned against manumission, complaining that "the liberation of many negroes within the last twelve or fifteen years, has render'd them generally worthless—utterly corrupted the slaves."[47]

In Wash's case, it appears that manumission was a way of freeing children he had fathered along with their enslaved mothers. While the number of children he fathered would be around ten and the number of grandchildren even higher if we add up all of the children we have manumission records for, that is quite possible; indeed, an anonymous letter to the editor in 1859 attested that Wash had fifteen children with enslaved women, while an 1865 newspaper article claimed it was "a well-known fact" that Wash had *forty* mixed-race children.[48] Perhaps that higher number captured both children and grandchildren. Fathering mixed-race children through the sexual exploitation of enslaved women was not unusual in his family, and it was a recognized and common reality in nineteenth-century Virginia.[49]

It may be that in his lifetime, Wash was only willing to free enslaved people he was related to, suggesting he did not want his own kin to suffer the indignities of slavery. Then again, the 1860 census showed that one half of the enslaved people at Arlington were mixed-race; perhaps he did not free all the children he fathered, or there were other white men (whether overseers, visitors, or even his son-in-law and grandsons) fathering children with enslaved women. As one formerly enslaved person recalled years later, hinting at the horrors of sexual exploitation by white men, "Everyone was so mixed, half-colored and half-white. Those were terrible times."[50] Surviving records of manumissions often reveal very little; we typically have brief entries in court records and only a few surviving sales certificates to go by.

We will probably never know how many children Wash fathered by enslaved women he sexually violated. It's also impossible to know the details of his interactions with these women, who may have included Arianna, Caroline, Rachel, Judith, Eloisa, and Oney.[51] As his property, they had no right to reject his sexual advances, and any relationship he had with them was rooted in exploitation. Sexual violence was but one tool of power for enslavers, and a common one; enslaved women were treated as property incapable of offering consent, and thus under the law, they could not be raped. Perhaps most insidiously, when enslavers' sexual violation of bondswomen resulted in pregnancy, the enslaver was rewarded by gaining property in the form of enslaved children.[52]

What did the women of Arlington House, enslaved and free, make of this? While severely circumscribed, we know that enslaved women could have some modicum of influence in these situations, as for instance when Sally Hemings bargained with Thomas Jefferson for the freedom of the children she bore him (although Wash, unlike Jefferson, did not have one long-term relationship with one enslaved woman; he appears to have sexually violated multiple women).[53] Notably, the only women Wash freed were those emancipated along with children. Did the women at Arlington, like Hemings, extract promises from Wash to free them and their children? If they had, as the scholar Sharon Block points out, their negotiation came with the downside of making what was really coercion look like consent.[54] They could also have approached the more sympathetic Molly to intercede on their behalf. Molly had to live with Wash's grow-

ing brood of mixed-race children, content with her one surviving daughter, and watch that daughter play with her enslaved
half siblings. Although she never spoke of it, Mary Custis must
have known at some point that she was not in fact an only child.

Wash's manumissions began in 1803 with two-year-old
Louisa, daughter of an enslaved woman he inherited from Mount
Vernon named Judith. Louisa may well have been his child; her
mother had been a spinner in the Mount Vernon mansion house
only a few years older than Wash, so he would have known her
and had access to sexually exploit her.[55] Fifteen years later, he
freed another child of Judith's, a fourteen-year-old boy named
John. At the same time, he freed three other children of enslaved women at Arlington. A few years before, during the War
of 1812 (and particularly poor financial conditions at Arlington),
he freed an enslaved woman named Rachel Branham and her
daughters, Marsolina and Almira. While he was then in debt
and could not free enslaved people without the danger of having
them seized as assets, he found—or perhaps his enslaved people
themselves suggested to him—a way around this challenge. (This
work-around would not have survived a legal challenge had any
of his debtors chosen to sue, however.)[56] He sold Rachel and her
daughters to a wealthy Quaker merchant in Alexandria named
Mordecai Miller for $200, and Miller then freed them.[57]

Quakers by this time could not own slaves and remain in the
faith, and Miller, his son Robert, and fellow Quakers Edward
and William Stabler all exercised their antislavery convictions
by quietly purchasing and manumitting enslaved people in Alexandria. In the case of children, they often retained ownership
and trained the child in a trade before freeing him or her (the
law stipulated minors had to be financially supported by those
emancipating them, so the Quakers extracted labor in return),
and the Alexandria Quaker meeting approved this practice.[58]
While $200 was a substantial sum for Rachel and her two daugh-
ters, it was less than their likely monetary value. In later years,
the Millers and Stablers paid only a symbolic amount; several

bills of sale from Wash to Quakers for $1 survive for enslaved people whom the Quakers subsequently freed.[59]

Around 1825, Wash freed an enslaved woman named Maria Carter Syphax—the Maria Carter he had most likely fathered in 1803 or 1804.[60] Maria knew she was Wash's daughter because he had told her so directly and assigned her to a less physically strenuous position as his white daughter Mary's maid.[61] This did not mean that her life was easy. Perhaps as a child, playing along-side young Mary, she did not fully grasp that her father owned her and could do with her what he pleased, including selling her away from her home and family. As she matured and watched Mary get fine clothes, learn Latin and Greek, and attend parties, the reality would have become clearer. In 1821, Maria married another enslaved person on the Arlington estate—a house servant named Charles Syphax, whose father was a free Black man

This daguerreotype shows Maria Carter Syphax,
Wash Custis's daughter with an enslaved woman, when she was in her 60s.

Maria Carter Syphax, c1870. Daguerreotype. Arlington House, The Robert E. Lee Memorial, ARHO 6408.

named William and whose mother must have been enslaved by Wash. According to stories passed down in the Syphax family, the wedding took place in the parlor of Arlington House.[62] When Wash freed Maria and her two young children in 1825, he also gave her seventeen acres of the Arlington estate. There, Maria and Charles established their family, ultimately bearing eight more children as Charles continued to work at Arlington House; he would not be freed until after Wash died, although the rest of his children were born free.[63]

Maria is unusual because she was interviewed by a newspaper reporter as an old woman confined to her bed, a sketch of her wrinkled face appearing in an article on "Lovely Arlington." In rare cases like that of Maria's descendants, there are also family stories. The descendants of Caroline Branham likewise have a family story that she had at least one child by Wash Custis.[64] Caroline, an enslaved house servant who had known Wash from infancy at Mount Vernon, would have been near the upper limit of her childbearing years when Wash inherited her and moved her to Arlington. She had several children fathered by her husband Peter Hardiman. But a girl named Lucy Branham, born in 1806, is identified by both descendants and one nineteenth-century account as her daughter; was Peter the father, or was Wash? Caroline would have been around forty by the time Lucy was born; was Lucy perhaps Caroline's granddaughter, with later stories accidentally skipping a generation?[65]

Mary Gregory Powell, whose father purchased and then freed Lucy, recalled that "it was generally believed" that Lucy was Wash and Caroline's daughter and noted that Lucy "bore a very strong resemblance" to Mary Custis. The first instance of preferential treatment Lucy received was when her three-year-old son Robert (who would later go by the last name Robinson) was sold in 1827 to serve an apprenticeship until he was old enough to be freed. According to Powell, this was specifically to reward his grandmother Caroline Branham for sharing a good account of George Washington's death with writer Jared Sparks. Powell explains that Lucy married "a respectable mulatto named Harrison" and that Powell's father William Gregory also purchased Lucy's other children—daughters Sarah and Eugenia, ages thirteen and eleven, infant Charles, and son Walter—from Wash in order to free them. Until Sarah and Eugenia were old enough to care for themselves, the girls served in the Gregory household as nurses for the children.[66] When Wash freed Caroline's eldest daughter Rachel and her daughters in 1813, was this because he had fathered Rachel's children as well? Another Branham, a girl named Caroline born in 1828 and freed in 1843, could also have been Wash's daughter or granddaughter.[67] While Wash only had one surviving white child, it appears he was the father of many, many more children.

The fact that Wash freed some enslaved women and children did not mean that he opposed slavery wholesale. Wash and his siblings were part of an in-between generation that came of age as sentiments about slavery changed and became much more highly charged. When the Custises were children in the late eighteenth century, Southern enslavers often expressed discomfort with slavery, and Northern states either immediately or gradually ended slavery. By the 1820s, an abolition movement in the North coalesced around the idea of immediate emancipation, widening the gulf between the North and South. But in that decade, there were still those in the Upper South, notably in Virginia, who fell under the broad tent of "antislavery."[68] As opinions shifted, the Custises would still have looked to George Washington's example. What, exactly, was that?

George Washington was wary of public discussions of slavery, and although he privately supported gradual emancipation and owned numerous antislavery texts, publicly he supported fugitive slave laws that enforced bondspeople's status as property. George's opposition to slavery was as much or more about economic efficiency and maintaining his own reputation than it was about morality or recognition of the humanity of unfree people. Having lived in Pennsylvania most of the presidency and having closely observed agricultural methods there, he had concluded that enslaved labor led to less productive farming; this was in keeping with many of his fellow planters at the time. But as historian Bruce Ragsdale notes, George "left the nation no principled statement of opposition to slavery and no practical plan that might have encouraged other planters to end their reliance on enslaved laborers." However, this also left open the question of his position on slavery for succeeding generations; he could be co-opted by both abolitionists and proslavery forces.[69]

In the nineteenth century in the Upper South, slavery posed an even greater economic challenge than it had in George's time. Slavery in Virginia and Maryland had become less profitable, and the siblings were suffering financially; should they join thousands of other families and sell enslaved people to grow cotton and sugar in the Deep South? Some of their neighbors in Virginia supported gradual emancipation; was that the solution? Many who advocated for a gradual end to slavery did not want African Americans to remain in Virginia, or even the United States, and supported setting up a colony for them in Africa.[70] As George Washington's family, the Custises knew that their words and actions were likely to be subjected to public scrutiny, and only Nelly's, Wash's, and Molly's views on the subject survive in writing. But all three had different views on the institution, even as they all expressed qualms with it.

Nelly, who depended on the labor of around ninety enslaved people at Woodlawn, had come to see slavery as an "evil," but more for whites than the enslaved.[71] It is difficult to know what she had thought about slavery prior to this, but in 1817 she explained to Elizabeth Bordley Gibson that she did not want her children to have to stay in a slave society.[72] She went even further in an 1826 letter to George Washington Lafayette, declaring, "I devoutly wish that there was not a slave in the United

States, that there never had been." But—there was a *but*, the follow-up typical of so many Southerners. "But since we have the misfortune to possess them," Nelly continued, Southern whites had to be careful not to "inflame them." Southerners were trying to figure out a solution, but if "persons unacquainted with their natures" (i.e., Northerners) tried to step in, it could be disastrous—in other words, there could be a slave rebellion like the famous one in Saint-Domingue (later Haiti). Here was the crux of Nelly's opposition to slavery—the "evils" were not moral ones, but the constant risk of slave rebellions. "Even my own poor Brother" wasn't cautious enough, she lamented.[73] She may have also been thinking of the "evil" of Wash's sexual exploitation of enslaved women.

Nelly never advocated for any form of emancipation, but Wash and Molly welcomed a new plan that began to circulate around 1816 and 1817: colonization. James Monroe and Thomas Jefferson had secretly corresponded about the idea of sending freed Black people to a colony in Africa in the wake of an attempted slave revolt in Virginia called Gabriel's Rebellion in 1800, and in 1816 a Virginia politician named Charles Fenton Mercer discovered and published those letters. He began working his networks to build support for the cause and establish what became the American Colonization Society (ACS).

The moment was ripe for the idea, especially in Virginia. During the War of 1812, as in the American Revolution, enslaved people had fled to the British for freedom (including one of the Lewises' bondspeople) and fought with British troops against Americans. It was a visible reminder of the violent potential of slave uprisings, one that a rebellion plot uncovered in early 1816 in the Virginia Piedmont reinforced. By this point, white Virginians owned more enslaved laborers than they needed for the farming of wheat to be profitable. They could, of course, have manumitted people—but they would have had to make financial sacrifices, and they were unwilling to do so. Plus, long-standing fears that free Black populations could help foment slave rebellions had led to restrictive laws in the state that made man-umission difficult, and many of those opposed to slavery (like Wash and Molly) did not believe Black people and white people should live together or were equal. Nonetheless, the number of free Black people in Virginia was growing—faster in fact than the white or enslaved populations between 1810 and 1820.[74]

Colonization, as Mercer and its (predominantly Virginian) supporters saw it, solved the thorny problem of this growing free Black population. The ACS would establish a colony in Af-rica and pay to send freed Black people "back" to where they came from (never mind that almost all enslaved people by this time had been born in the United States). While they had no specific site in mind, the British already had a colony for for-merly enslaved people in Sierra Leone. Just south of that colony and with the help of the United States Navy (and a question-able agreement with a local African leader), the ACS acquired a piece of land that it called Liberia. Liberia would serve as an outlet that allowed enslavers to manumit their bondspeople and remove them from the United States, although some supporters saw it primarily as a tool for Black people who had already been freed.[75] The ACS met for the first time in Washington City in 1816, and Molly's brother William Henry Fitzhugh and cousin William Meade were among its founding members and most devoted activists.[76]

Molly was eager to help the ACS from the beginning, tell-ing Meade in 1817 that she hoped to "become an instrument in furnishing the objects of the society." She was ready for Wash to "give freedom to a number of souls," but she knew that he had not yet recognized that this was the right thing to do. Molly's religious convictions told her that slavery was wrong; perhaps as she watched the fair-skinned enslaved children fathered by her husband, she found the idea of their moving across the Atlan-tic attractive. She was also fearful of slave uprisings; she felt it was best that any enslaved people who were freed be "removed from our country before they are permitted to revenge their long indured injuries."[77] Molly ultimately became an important supporter of the organization, advising one of its leaders (Ralph Gurley), raising money, and arranging for the manumission and emigration of some of the enslaved at Arlington. By the 1820s and 1830s, reform organizations were becoming the best path for women to be involved in public affairs, and Molly took advantage of the opportunity through the ACS.[78]

While Molly rarely if ever expressed political views on other subjects, she was truly committed to antislavery. Her support for emancipation had a particular valence for her as a woman; supporting that cause allowed her to enter a contentious political issue. As one scholar says of women's involvement in the movement, "slave emancipation was seen as their own emancipation."[79] Molly never wrote about women's rights, but even if she did not support that movement formally, her actions demonstrated that she saw a role for women in civil society. She was well-educated and taught many of the enslaved at Arlington; she read the writings of British antislavery activist William Wilberforce; and she mentored and trained men to further the work of the ACS.[80] In 1825, when the Supreme Court heard a case on the international slave trade involving the captured slave ship the *Antelope*, she attended oral arguments and brought her daughter Mary with her.[81] In none of her actions, however, did Molly step beyond the bounds of proper female behavior; indeed, her motivation for antislavery activism stemmed from the moral and religious commitments most praised in women of this era, and she never acted with the boldness of her sisters-in-law in other political causes.[82]

Molly likely persuaded Wash to become more involved in the ACS; she was among the first annual subscribers in 1819, while Wash described himself as "a late convert to the cause" in 1824. That year, Wash made a confession that went beyond what many others in the society were willing to say: "He had lived to see, and painfully to feel, the errors of the system of slavery."[83] That he could see and feel this was a credit to Molly, but was also perhaps due to having his own children born into slavery. Perhaps enslaved people themselves influenced his position. Beginning that year, he regularly gave speeches to ACS meetings for a decade.

In October 1825, Wash published a newspaper piece about Lafayette's antislavery views and the Frenchman's interest in the ACS. But this piece was about more than Lafayette; here Wash laid out a plan for the gradual emancipation of his enslaved people over the course of about fifteen years. He said that he would eventually free all his bondspeople and send them to the fledgling colony of Liberia. At the next ACS meeting, he made his strongest antislavery statement yet, calling slavery "the mightiest serpent that ever infested the world."[84] For a man who owned and lived off the labor of hundreds of enslaved people, this was a remarkable statement. It would also turn out to be just a passing phase.

Indeed, just as the colonization scheme began gaining steam, Wash's speeches show a shift that suggests he was no longer as troubled by slavery itself as by the presence of African Americans. He, like many other Americans, had been influenced by a growing race science that codified supposed African American racial inferiority.[85] Given African Americans were inferior, Wash argued, they should not be permitted to live alongside whites in America. At the 1831 annual meeting of the ACS, he asked, "What right, I demand, have the children of Africa to an homestead in the white man's country?"[86] Just over six months later, an event that crystallized racist views—and fears—in the South occurred: Nat Turner's revolt. In the dark of night on August 21, 1831, enslaved preacher Nat Turner and six other enslaved men in Southampton County, Virginia, set in motion a plan to liberate the enslaved by killing white men, women, and children. Turner hoped the killings would spur other free and enslaved Black people to join his crew, until they had sufficient force to fight more like an army. Turner and his men ultimately killed fifty-five whites, but they did not gain compatriots and were defeated the next night. The state of Virginia tried and executed Turner and nineteen others—but that was not enough for many white Southerners, whose longtime fears of a race war were heightened and who were ready to take drastic measures to eliminate any opportunities for the enslaved to gain power.[87]

We do not know just what Wash thought of the rebellion, but his sister Nelly stoutly proclaimed her views in chilling words. She wrote her friend Harrison Gray Otis, the mayor of Boston, an angry letter demanding that he act against abolitionist newspaper editor William Lloyd Garrison. Many believed that Garrison's new paper, *The Liberator*, had spurred Turner on (though there is no evidence of this), and Nelly saw him as "an incendiary of the very worst description" who "merits *Death*." Owning slaves was like sitting on "a smothered volcano—we know not when, or where, the flame will burst forth, but we know that death in the most horrid forms threatens us." White Southerners had "incurred this curse by no act of their own" and were trying, gradually, to be rid of it (which was untrue), and Northerners should leave them alone. If abolitionists continued to interfere, the disquiet caused among enslaved people might "force the whites to *exterminate* them." It is disturbing that Nelly chose to underline the word exterminate, but she was not alone in using this word. Other white Southerners used similar language about both African Americans and Native people.[88]

Still, Nelly's reaction was not the only possible response; her sister-in-law Molly Custis thought quite differently. Nelly likely had discussed her views with Molly, who wrote her daughter Mary decrying the animus against *The Liberator* and hasty conclusions that Northerners were "arrayed against us." Several days later, Molly told Mary that she had lost her train of thought because "there is a conversation going on the subject of Negroes" and "sick, sick, such horrid talks make me."[89] Was it hearing of rebellion that sickened her, or white reactions to it?

And what did Molly think when Wash argued before the ACS several years later that slavery was sanctioned by the Bible, the current problem was Northern pressure on Southerners, and that America was "the *white man's country*"? She might have agreed; as one scholar has noted of Virginia at this time, the "political center of gravity" on the question of slavery was "the idea that a whiter Virginia was a better Virginia." There was a clear current of racism underlying the ACS; indeed, African Americans largely rejected its efforts for this reason. Still, the explicit identification of America as a white man's country went too far for many members. The hall rang out with boos during Wash's speech, and another member rose to respond and call the idea of the white man's country "superlatively ludicrous."[90] It wasn't to Wash, who wanted to make clear that his support for colonization had *nothing* to do with calls for equality—or abolition. If abolitionists thought he was sympathetic to them, he wrote, "it was time I should convince them to the contrary."[91] His support for colonization was about getting African Americans out of the United States.

It was not a big leap from such views to the new tenor of Southern responses to slavery that emerged in this same period: slavery was not an evil to be ended eventually, but a positive good. Wash never seems to have quite reached this conclusion—after all, he continued to manumit people, worked with Molly to send several people she owned to the ACS's new colony of Liberia, and emancipated all of his bondspeople in his will. But he, like his sisters, did subscribe to the paternalistic notion that he was providing for people who could not do so for themselves. This was a defensive response to abolitionist attacks on the morals of enslavers; while earlier critics of slavery had focused on the institution itself, now abolitionists directed their attention to the individuals who held other humans in bondage. Enslaved people, Wash told his niece Markie, were far better off than even

Savage produced this painting from multiple sittings, basing the children on a sitting from 1789–1790 and George and Martha from one in 1795, further widening the age gap between grandparents and grandchildren. The enslaved man in the background probably represented William Lee, but the figure was most likely based on a free Black servant, John Riley. Prints of this painting, often with variations by other artists and engravers, sold well until the 1850s.

Edward Savage, *The Washington Family*, 1789–1796. Andrew W. Mellon Collection. Washington, National Gallery of Art.

This view of Mount Vernon depicts the family at home; George and Martha walk with Nelly toward Wash, one of Washington's aides, and two hounds. Domestic laborers, including an enslaved woman, appear in the background.

Edward Savage, *The West Front of Mount Vernon*, c. 1787–1792. Courtesy of Mount Vernon Ladies' Association.

This miniature shows Jacky Custis at around twenty years old, when he married Eleanor Calvert.

Charles Willson Peale,
John Parke Custis, 1774.
Courtesy of Mount Vernon
Ladies' Association.

Painted a year after Jacky's death and a year before her marriage to David Stuart, this miniature of Eleanor Calvert Custis shows the twenty-four-year-old widow with her hair powdered gray and in a fashionable hedgehog style.

Artist unknown,
Eleanor Calvert Custis Stuart, 1782.
Courtesy of Mount Vernon
Ladies' Association.

British artist Robert Edge Pine painted all four Custis grandchildren on a visit to Mount Vernon in 1785, and the entire set was hung in the Washingtons' bedroom.

Martha and her granddaughters are shown in the balcony as George Washington resigned his military commission in Annapolis, even though they were not present at the event. A larger version of this painting is on display in the Rotunda of the US Capitol.

John Trumbull, *The Resignation of General Washington, December 23, 1783*, 1824–1828. New Haven, Connecticut, Yale University Art Gallery.

Stuart captures Eliza's defiant confidence and wit by depicting her in a quite unusual pose for a woman: arms crossed, gaze piercing at the viewer, and the hint of a raised eyebrow.

Gilbert Stuart, *Elizabeth Parke Custis*, [1795].
Private Collection.

Thomas Law appears fashionably dressed and with his powdered hair tied back in a queue in this portrait by Gilbert Stuart. It was likely painted around the time of his marriage to Eliza Custis in 1796, but the portrait does not make a matching pair with his wife's unusual image.

Gilbert Stuart, *Thomas Law*, c. 1796.
Courtesy of Mount Vernon Ladies' Association.

This pastel portrait of Nelly at around age seventeen, with her windblown hair, shows that she could have a somewhat disheveled appearance.

James Sharples, *Eleanor Parke Custis*, c. 1796.
Courtesy of Mount Vernon Ladies' Association.

The new District of Columbia was anchored by the existing towns of Georgetown and Alexandria, but most of the nation's capital was undeveloped countryside in 1800.

T. Cartwright after George Beck,
*George Town and Federal City,
or City of Washington*, 1801.
Washington, Library of Congress.

The dining room at Mount Vernon, painted a bold green in 1785, was where the Washingtons and their guests ate two main meals a day: breakfast at 7:00 a.m. and dinner at 3:00 p.m.

Dining Room at Mount Vernon.
Courtesy of Mount Vernon Ladies' Association.

This portrait of Nelly shows the young mother looking still youthful but weighed down by recent losses of her grandparents and two young children.

Gilbert Stuart, *Eleanor Parke Custis Lewis* (*Mrs. Lawrence Lewis*), 1804.
Gift of H. H. Walker Lewis in memory of his parents, Mr. and Mrs. Edwin A. S. Lewis. Washington, National Gallery of Art.

The Lewises' home, Woodlawn, was constructed atop Grey's Hill on land gifted to the couple by George Washington. Designed by William Thornton, the house follows a five-part Palladian plan with a main block connected to symmetrical side wings with hyphens.

Carol M. Highsmith, *Woodlawn Plantation overlooking the Potomac River, Alexandria, Virginia*, undated.
Carol M. Highsmith Archive, Library of Congress, Prints and Photographs Division.

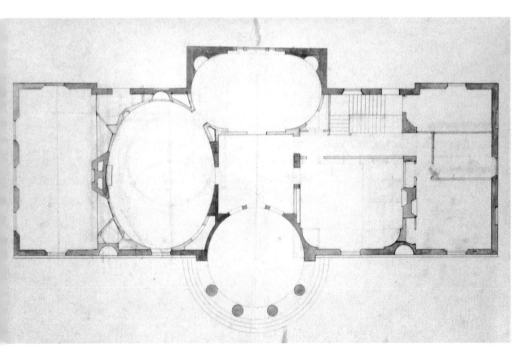

This drawing by William Thornton for Tudor Place shows the existing side wings connected to the new central building he designed. Ultimately the Peters largely discarded Thornton's plans, but they kept the distinctive temple-portico.

William Thornton, *Presentation Drawing*, ca. 1808–1816, MS2_HV.
Washington, DC, Tudor Place Historic House & Garden.

This miniature shows Wash Custis as a young man in the green coat of the cavalry, in which he received an appointment in 1799; the white epaulet signified his status as an officer. He was never called into service.

Robert Field, *George Washington Parke Custis*, [1801]. Richmond, Virginia Museum of History & Culture (1977.26).

This portrait of Molly Custis by a self-taught itinerant artist shows the young mother at around age twenty.

Cephas Thompson (American, 1775–1856)
Portrait of Mrs. George Washington Parke Custis, 1807–1808
Oil on canvas
Virginia Museum of Fine Arts, Richmond.
Gift of Mrs. A. Smith Bowman, 76.21.1
Photo: David Stover
© Virginia Museum of Fine Arts

Eliza's daughter, Eliza Law (later Rogers), gave her portrait to her mother with the inscription "A Trifle for the best of mothers." The younger Eliza is between eight and thirteen years old here.

Artist Unknown, *Eliza Law Rogers*, c. 1805–1810. Courtesy of Mount Vernon Ladies' Association.

George Washington gave Patty Peter this miniature as a gift in 1795, and it was likely one of the miniatures she wore to a party in 1812.

Walter Robertson, *George Washington*, 1794. Washington, DC, Tudor Place Historic House & Garden.

British troops set fire to the President's House on August 24, 1814, leaving it as a burned-out shell. Several days later, Patty and Thomas Peter went to see the damage.

George Munger, *The President's House*, c. 1814–1815. Washington, White House Collection/White House Historical Association.

This watercolor of Arlington House shows an enslaved woman walking near the front of the house, but the artist has left out the slave quarters located immediately behind it. A man in a straw hat, perhaps a visiting tourist, lounges in the grass in the foreground.

Benson Lossing, *Arlington House*, 1853. Arlington House, The Robert E. Lee Memorial, ARHO 123.

This tent, now on display at the Museum of the American Revolution, is one of two tents George Washington used in the American Revolution. There was also a larger dining tent that Wash likely used for big gatherings like his sheep shearings; it is now owned by the Smithsonian Institution.

George Washington's sleeping and office tent, 1779, Linen, Wool, Iron, Oak, Mahogany, Hemp. Courtesy of the Museum of the American Revolution.

This piece, depicting Lafayette visiting George Washington's tomb at Mount Vernon, may be the one that Nelly mentions "young Miller" creating. Miller planned to include Nelly, Lawrence, Wash, Molly, and Eliza in the scene, and that may be who some of the figures are here, although antique dealers Stephen and Carol Huber have identified the group to the right as Washington nieces and nephews.

George Washington's tomb visited by Marquis de Lafayette, Mount Vernon, Virginia (1824).
Painting and silk embroidery on silk. Marta & David Black Americana Collection.

oy Mary Custis Lee — when a girl.

In these two sketches by Mary Anna Randolph Custis, we get a rare glimpse of enslaved people who labored at Arlington. Both are using wooden pails called "piggins." The man, who may be Lawrence Parks, is bringing cabbages to the port to sell at a local market. The unnamed girl (the name "Topsy" was added later) could be delivering food or water to enslaved farm workers or transporting harvested crops.

Opposite Page: Mary Anna Randolph Custis, *Sketch [possibly of Lawrence Parks]*.
Courtesy of George Washington Memorial Parkway.

This Page: Mary Anna Randolph Custis, *Enslaved Girl*, Arlington County, Virginia, 1830,
watercolor, pencil, and ink on wove paper, accession #2007-34. The Colonial Williamsburg Foundation, Museum Purchase.

Wash Custis created this painting of the Battle of Monmouth with historical details also described in his *Recollections*. All the figures in the foreground represent specific individuals, including the Marquis de Lafayette, Alexander Hamilton, and Henry Knox.

George Washington Parke Custis, *Battle of Monmouth*, undated.
Courtesy of the George Washington Memorial Parkway. ARHO 6148.

Wash's daughter Mary Anna Randolph Custis appears here soon before her marriage to Robert E. Lee. Lee family tradition holds that the artist added the parrot to mask his inability to paint hands.

Auguste Hervieu, *Mary Anna Randolph Custis*, 1830. Anonymous Loan and Arlington House. Courtesy of the George Washington Memorial Parkway. ARHO 5840.

As a handsome young man, Robert E. Lee was known for being flirtatious and well-liked by women.

William Edward West, *Robert E. Lee in the Dress Uniform of a Lt. of Engineers*, 1838. Courtesy of Museums at Washington and Lee University, Lexington, Virginia.

This image shows the facilities for visitors available at Arlington Spring on Wash Custis's Arlington House estate. The large pavilion at right was used for dancing.

Elizabeth Moore Reid, *Arlington Spring*, c. 1850. Arlington House, The Robert E. Lee Memorial, ARHO 1883.

This photograph of Patty Peter and one of her granddaughters was taken soon before her death. Patty holds the Walter Robertson miniature portrait of George Washington that he gave her in 1795.

Martha Custis Peter and Martha (Markie) Custis Kennon, c. 1852, A1.2313. Washington, DC, Tudor Place Historic House & Gardens.

"the best class of the poor in Europe." This was a classic tenet of proslavery thought.[92]

Indeed, in subsequent generations of the Custis family, this ideology truly took off, perhaps building on the views of their elders. Markie herself, who had been raised largely by her grandmother Patty and lived for long stretches at Arlington with Wash in the 1850s, wrote an essay addressed to enslaved people on why they should be grateful for their condition. Nelly's son-in-law, certainly sharing information gleaned from her and Lawrence, told a correspondent that the enslaved people George Washington had freed had been a "nuisance" who had now disappeared (far from the truth), but that the Custis enslaved were left to "the enjoyment of health and happiness."[93] Gone was the uneasiness about slavery that troubled George Washington and other enslavers of his generation; a new defensiveness had taken hold among the Custis descendants and more broadly in the South.

Yet for all that the Custises' views were largely in keeping with their times, there was another path—a path that recognized the humanity of African Americans and used every tool possible to help them advance in a society that resisted treating them as equal at every turn. One man whom the Custises knew and respected did just that: William Costin. This was the very William who had grown up enslaved and who may have been the Custises' half brother.

After William's manumission in 1802, the Custis siblings— particularly Eliza and Wash—kept in close touch with him. William worked as a hack driver in the new capital city, using his own carriage and slowly amassing both money and respect in the community. He ran errands for the Custises, conveying family members and making deliveries in his carriage, and he also lent both Eliza and her sister Nelly small sums of money. Nelly addressed a letter to him with "My friend Billy" and closed with "I hope you & your family are well, I will ever be your friend." Eliza referred to him as "my faithful 'tho humble friend Billy—who has evinced his attachment through every change of my destiny." Her trust in William was so deep that she stored her will with him and left him "some bequest for his grateful conduct."[94]

This continuing relationship with the Custis siblings bolsters the case that William was their brother; even more suggestive is the way he named his children. He and his wife Delphy had seven children, five daughters and two sons, all with a particular middle name: Parke.[95] The use of the Parke name came from a Custis family tradition, tied to a clause in ancestor Daniel Parke's early eighteenth-century will, of using Parke as a middle name.[96] Both of Martha Washington's children with her first husband Daniel Parke Custis had this name, as did all four Custis grandchildren. Many but not all the Custis grandchildren's own children had Parke in their names, whereas Costin was entirely consistent. Why would Costin do this unless he believed himself to be a Custis? He even gave his son William the middle name "Custis Parke," and Eliza referred to him as Costin's "Son Custis," suggesting William Custis Parke Costin was known as Custis.[97]

William was able to provide for his large family handsomely because he had worked his way up from hack driver to porter of the Bank of Washington, entrusted with carrying large sums of money. It is possible that Thomas Law, who was a founding stockholder, helped William get hired there in 1818.[98] That same year, William leased part of a lot on A Street in Capitol Hill for ninety-nine years; by 1831, the house he built there and the furniture within it were worth $600. His portrait shows a man with light skin, a prominent nose, and keen eyes behind spectacles, a wisp of brown curly hair peeking out beneath a white top hat. He is well-dressed, with a crisp collared shirt beneath a waistcoat and jacket. William used his wealth and standing in the city to serve the free Black community in Washington, where he became one of its leading figures. He was known as "upright, honorable, and reputable" as well as showing "unflinching integrity."[99]

William took on a leadership role in several new organizations that sprang up to serve African Americans in the city. From the "Resolute Beneficial School" for Black children to the Israel Metropolitan Christian Methodist Episcopal Church to the Columbian Harmony Society (aiming to found a cemetery for free Black people) to the city's first Black Freemasonry organization, William served his community in a variety of ways.[100] While none of this was a direct challenge to slavery, there were few opportunities for him to engage in such work in Washington City. There were nascent antislavery groups farther north, but the primary form of collective resistance in Washington at this time was simply through expanding liberty and opportunity for the city's growing population of free Black people.[101] William wanted to do more. In 1820, he purchased Caroline Branham's twenty-eight-year-old daughter Leanthe from Wash Custis and freed her, then seven years later did the same for two others enslaved by Wash, Eliza Washington and Montgomery Parke. He then raised Montgomery, only four years old, in his own family.[102] Why he freed these particular people is unclear.

William's boldest act on behalf of his community was his resistance to an 1821 law in Washington City requiring all "free persons of colour" to prove their freedom. The law gave them thirty days to show the mayor "evidence of freedom" as well as a certificate signed by three white residents attesting to the freed person's character and financial stability plus payment of a $20 bond. Failure to do so could result in a fine, imprisonment, and even being expelled from the city. William refused. When he was fined for his civil disobedience, he appealed to the US Circuit Court in the District of Columbia. The case came before Judge William Cranch (an enslaver who nonetheless was willing to countenance legal challenges to slavery) in October 1821.[103]

This portrait of William Costin depicts him in gentleman's attire
with his workplace, the Bank of Washington, behind him.

Samuel M. Charles, painter, and Charles Fenderich, lithographer, *William Costin.*
A tribute to worth by his friends [1842]. Washington, Library of Congress.

William likely put careful thought into his choice of a lawyer,
and the man he selected was Elias Boudinot Caldwell. Caldwell
was a founding member of the ACS and served as both clerk of
the Supreme Court and a lawyer for enslaved people suing for
their freedom.[104] Given his involvement in the ACS, it is likely
he knew Wash and Molly Custis, and perhaps they made the

introduction; William could also have known Caldwell directly through his work at the bank. It is hard to imagine that William did not discuss the grounds of his legal defense with Caldwell, particularly given the expansive argument Caldwell ultimately made. According to Cranch's summation, William's lawyer argued that "The constitution knows no distinction of color...all who are not slaves are equally free...[and] equally citizens of the United States."[105] William and Caldwell did not pull this argument out of thin air; during the recent Missouri Compromise debates, Congress had discussed but left unanswered the question of whether free Black people were citizens.[106] That need not have been the argument against the new law; Caldwell could have made a technical argument about the terms of the statute. Apparently he, likely in concert with William, had chosen to use this as an opportunity to make a broader push for liberty and equality. Judge Cranch was not willing to go so far, but he didn't let the city (represented by Thomas Law's son) win entirely. He ruled that it was perfectly constitutional to restrict rights based on race; the problem with this law was that the wording appeared to apply only to new residents, so existing Black residents like William were exempt.

While the case was only a partial victory, William's broader fight for Black political rights was not entirely forgotten. After William's sudden death in his sleep in 1842, Representative John Quincy Adams made a speech in Congress supporting an end to racial restrictions on voting in the District of Columbia. To make his case, Adams invoked William Costin. Could his fellow congressmen explain "why a man whose skin was not white... but who performed all the duties of a good citizen, a good husband, good father, and kind neighbor...should not be entitled to vote, as well as the white man"? Indeed, Adams argued, William "was as much respected as any man in the District" and he could not vote, while "the vilest individuals of the white race" could. The famous Black newspaper in Boston, the *Emancipa-*

tor, took note of the congressman's speech and concluded that the exemplary lives lived by people like William "give lie to the aspersions of slavery and caste."[107]

Perhaps that is all William Costin needed to do to fight slavery and racism: be a decent person. But he chose to do more, at a time when the risks to his livelihood, safety, and family were real. What did the Custises make of it? Here was a man highly respected and, quite frankly, braver than any of them; if they knew or at least guessed he was their brother, were they jealous of the admiration he enjoyed? One thing is certain: William Costin did far more to achieve the Revolutionary ideals of liberty and equality than the Custises themselves. Perhaps it was an unacknowledged stepgrandchild of George Washington who best understood and lived by the principles of the nation's founding.

William Costin's example, whatever the Custis siblings thought of it, does not seem to have changed their views on slavery and race. Indeed, the entire family became more rather than less committed to making America a "white man's country." It was this vision of America, not William Costin's, that would triumph in America in the mid-nineteenth century. Colonization was but one political project in a larger scheme for expanding America's burgeoning empire, and Wash and his sisters were actively engaged in that project on many fronts.[108] They would not squander their return to national prominence in the wake of Lafayette's visit in 1824 and 1825; they would use their fame to further their own vision of America.

CHAPTER 9

The Custis Empire

ON THE NATION'S FIFTIETH BIRTHDAY IN July 1826, crowds filled America's first theater on Chestnut Street in Philadelphia to see the debut of a remarkable new play. *The Indian Prophecy* by "a member of Gen. Washington's family," as the newspapers advertised it, was one of the nation's earliest and most influential plays featuring Native American characters.[1] But its real star was George Washington, about whom the "Indian" would prophesize; it's not surprising, then, that Wash Custis was the play's author.

After a meandering series of conversations between Native people and white settlers set in the Virginia backcountry in the early 1770s, the key moment in the play comes right before the final curtain. The great Menawa, "a chief among chiefs," gathers a group of white men including George Washington to his side to hear his dying words. Pointing at Washington, he declares, "*The Great Spirit protects that man, and guides his destiny. He will be-*come the Chief of Nations, and a people yet unborn, hail him as the Founder of a mighty Empire!" With that, Menawa falls dead, and the curtains close.[2]

The symbolism of Wash's melodrama was too obvious for its patriotic viewers to miss. The Native chief—played by a white man with dark makeup and an elaborate costume—dies as George Washington ascends. Menawa was great, but Washington will become greater. He will not just found a country, but an *empire*. Americans rarely think about the United States in its early years as an empire, but it was a word Washington himself used to describe the new nation.[3] Indeed, the hope of an American empire that stretched across the continent to the Pacific dated to the nation's founding. As Thomas Jefferson saw it, America would be "an empire for liberty" that, rather than dominating rival European powers like Napoleon's French empire, would spread freedom—at least for white people.[4]

It was precisely this "empire for liberty" that Wash Custis imagined when he wrote *The Indian Prophecy* and in his growing number of speeches, published writings, and even artworks. His sisters shared Wash's enthusiasm for helping the American empire not just survive but become stronger and more expansive. In the Custises' eyes, their stepgrandfather had founded a "mighty empire" through conquest, and that empire needed military leaders in Washington's mold in order to grow. While not in the military themselves, the Custises could support military men and marry their daughters off to them, and they could also contribute in a much more personal, tangible way. Once the US military conquered Native lands, they needed to be settled by whites for American power to take root, and the next generation of Custis children were just the people for the task.

Perhaps no man in America was more closely associated with conquest and expanding America's empire in the 1820s and 1830s as the Custises' friend Andrew Jackson. To the Jacksonians, white Americans had a right to enact violence to expand both their liberties and the American empire. Although previous generations of historians extolled Andrew Jackson for representing the "common man," asking who, exactly, the "common man" was makes clear that it meant exclusively white males.[5] While

Nelly, Wash, and Eliza would not have agreed with the populism Jackson espoused, Jackson's expansive—and white—vision of America fit their own.

Andrew Jackson had lost the presidency in the ugly election of 1824, but it was clear in the years following that he was an ascendant power in the nation's capital. After their star turn during Lafayette's visit, the Custises were eager to capitalize on their friendship with Jackson both to boost his power and their own. As Nelly's son-in-law Ed Butler reported to Jackson (his surrogate father), "my good mother [Nelly] makes it a point of duty to defend the General to the last ditch." As representatives of George Washington's legacy, Nelly, Wash, and Eliza hoped to transfer some of Washington's potent political symbolism to Jackson, whom they saw as their stepgrandfather's political heir. When one newspaper published the Democratic-Republican ticket with Andrew Jackson at its head in 1828, it reprinted below that an article from 1824 about Wash's gift of Washington's pocket telescope to Jackson that year (not coincidentally, the year Jackson first ran for president). As the editors noted, this story showed "in what estimation Gen. Jackson is held by the family of Gen. Washington."[6]

Wash could do better than the gift of a relic, though; he used his newfound skills as a playwright to write a drama reminding the public of Jackson's heroism in New Orleans in 1815. Titled *The Eighth of January, or Huzza for the Boys of the West*, the play debuted in New York's Park Theatre in January 1828, when Jackson was already known to be running for president. The play ran in Washington after Jackson's inauguration in March 1829, but it did not succeed in currying favor for Jackson with the city's residents, where he was not as popular as elsewhere in the country. Every time a character mentioned Jackson's name on stage, a man in the audience yelled "CLAY" (Jackson's political foe), and while the rest of the crowd stayed quiet, they failed to cheer for Jackson.[7]

Nelly and Eliza, too, worked to demonstrate the family's support for Jackson. In December 1828, soon after Jackson was elected, both presented him with Washington relics: a piece of Washington china from Nelly, and a locket with George's hair from Eliza. The gifts celebrated the election of a man who was, Eliza told Jackson, "a military Chieftain for such was the father of our Country, whom you made your model." But these were not selfless gifts solely to bolster Jackson and tie him to Washington: that tying together had to go through the Custises themselves. Indeed, Eliza's locket had more than just George's hair: it also had Martha's, Lafayette's, and her own. Americans in this period hungered for relics of Washington, seeing them as tangible manifestations of the father of the country.[8] As custodians of these relics, even women could carve out a public voice and support their chosen politicians.

As usual, the Custises were not entirely united in their political opinions. Patty, who never quite got over the end of the Federalists, could not join her siblings in supporting a president who so regularly attacked elites.[9] A new opposition party, centered in large part around its dislike of Andrew Jackson, was forming: the National Republicans, later called Whigs. In May of 1832, she went to see the National Republican convention in Washington City. Over three hundred representatives gathered, among them Patty's cousin George Calvert and her young half brother Richard Stuart. Patty looked on as the convention ratified Henry Clay's nomination for president and wrote a party platform based on his American System (which advocated for stronger government involvement in finances and infrastructure). While her siblings continued to fawn over Jackson, Patty threw her lot behind his opponent in the 1832 election.[10] Clay lost to the popular incumbent, and Jackson was elected to his second term in 1832.

The year 1832 was also an important year in the new nation's history: it marked one hundred years since George Washington's birth. The commemorations of what would have been Washington's one hundredth birthday in 1832 brought renewed attention to Washington as a political symbol and tool.[11] His farewell address in particular continued to play an important role in debates about the place of the United States in the world.[12] Washington was also a unifying figure at a time when sectional conflict was threatening the nation. As carrier of the Washington family legacy, the Custises felt they had the authority to weigh in on the nation's latest crisis.

In 1832, South Carolina's legislature ratified an Ordinance of Nullification of the tariffs of 1828 and 1832. The state had been protesting the national tariffs on imported goods for several years, arguing that the policy favored the Northern economy and hurt the South. South Carolinians finally declared that if the federal government wouldn't change its stance, the state of South Carolina would simply refuse to recognize the law. While nullification was not an entirely new idea (Jefferson himself had suggested something similar with the Virginia and Kentucky Resolutions in 1798), South Carolinians were essentially challenging the Union itself. President Jackson was no fan of tariffs and believed in states' rights, but he saw nullification as a threat to the country that could lead to civil war.[13]

Jackson's ally and Nelly's friend Joel Poinsett led pro-Union forces in South Carolina, and after Nelly chatted with him on vacation at the springs in Bath, Virginia, in August 1832, she declared, "The Nullifiers vex him very much, & well they may. They are mad to all intents & purposes, & ought to be supplied with straight waistcoats." As Congress debated how to respond to South Carolina's provocation, Nelly and Angela went to Congress to listen to the debates and decry the supporters of nullification, and Poinsett kept her updated by letter. Nelly so disdained supporters of nullification—Nullys—that she declared that Angela would *never* marry a Nully.[14] For both Nelly and Wash, the idea of challenging the Union was an insult to their stepgrandfather; this political question felt very personal to them.

While Nelly still identified as a Southerner and distrusted Northerners, especially on the issue of slavery, Wash proudly embraced his identity as an American rather than a Southerner. In his speech for George Washington's birthday in 1833, as Congress was debating passage of the Force Bill to threaten South Carolina for its actions, he slammed supporters of nullification, "these madmen of the south." The tariffs would promote domestic industry, his long-favored cause, and even Southerners should approve of that. Southerners had to stop "decry[ing] their breathren, the Yankees." Indeed, he cried, "Call me Yankee while I live… The Yankee land…is the very bone and muscle of this empire."[15] While this was a speech commemorating George Washington, like many of his other speeches in this era, Wash's stepgrandfather provided a jumping-off point rather than the focus of his oration. More than ever in these years of increasing nostalgia for the American Revolution, George Washington's legacy granted the Custises their ticket to political relevance.

However, having a friend in the presidency was not enough to revive Eliza's failing health. It's unknown exactly what ailed her; Nelly seemed to think it was emotional rather than physical, saying that her sister "could do better if she chose." It seems likely that the emotional stress and suffering over the prior decade had taken a toll on her health. Her daughter's death in 1822 was a tragic loss from which she never fully recovered, but she had at least found comfort in caring for her grandchildren. Eliza Law Rogers left behind four young children, a son and three daughters, who moved to Georgetown to live with their grandmother. Eliza doted on them but could not save Harriet, who died in May 1825 at age six from what her great-aunt Nelly called a "putrid sore throat." As the losses mounted, Eliza's health sank. She began to accept visitors directly in bed; one old friend reported that she was "astonished" when Eliza invited her to strip to her underclothes, "lie down on the bed, and partake of some refreshment."[16]

From her sickbed, Eliza was starting to organize her Washington relics. The majority would be handed down to her grandchildren with notes pinned to the relics telling their histories. She also saw the relics as a way to cement her own legacy and tie it in people's memory to George Washington's. In a Washington chest, she stored clothes that had been divided all those years ago at Mount Vernon in 1802, among them a pair of her stepgrandfather's black velvet breeches. Taking up her scissors, Eliza carefully snipped out rectangles of velvet an inch or two wide.

 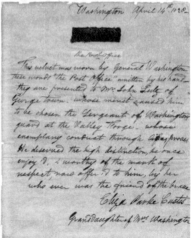

Eliza Custis turned this pair of George Washington's black silk velvet breeches into a source of multiple relics, cutting patches out of them and sending the pieces to friends (including John Lutz, in the letter shown here) as gifts.

Velvet breeches, c. 1789-1799. Courtesy of Mount Vernon Ladies' Association.
Letter, Eliza Parke Custis to John Lutz, 1828 April 14. Courtesy of Mount Vernon Ladies' Association.

These were then glued onto letters, often accompanied by a single word in Washington's hand cut out of one of his letters. She sent these to several people, including to a Polish princess who she had heard was an admirer of Washington. In one of the letters, to her old friends Gideon Snow and his wife, she made clear both her sense of coming death and her hope that Washington's relics would carry both his legacy and her own. "When I am gone & you can see me no more, look upon them," she extolled the Snows, "& when you think of General Washington, remember her who was his best loved child."[17]

Eliza's suffering would only increase. When her son-in-law Lloyd Rogers decided to remarry in 1829 (to James Monroe's granddaughter Hortensia Monroe Hay, twenty years his junior), he wanted his children who had been staying with Eliza in Georgetown to come back home to Baltimore to live with him again. Eliza likely made clear that she did not trust his parenting abilities—as she told Lafayette, "knowing well his peculiar temper & habits, I know better than any one all that awaits them & me"—and vented her frustration that he had "never had that regard for me I deserved."[18] Like John and Edmund Law a few decades earlier, he lost patience and determined to cut off all contact, including barring the children from communicating with their grandmother. As she reported to a friend in 1829, "my heart has been broken by domestic Calamities." She was so ill after Rogers took the last of her grandchildren from her that she told a friend, "I must totter to the grave alone."[19] Tragically, that would not be far from the truth.

That spring, Eliza wrote what sounded like a farewell letter to the Marquis de Lafayette. She was so ill she could not write it herself; a friend took dictation for her. Still alive the next summer, she wanted to secure some outstanding land claims she had inherited from George Washington and sent her beloved Washington portrait by John Trumbull to Wash for safekeeping.[20] Eliza also wrote her grandson Edmund a letter for his thirteenth birthday with her parting advice for him (which his father may or may not have let him read). She explained his direct descent from Martha Washington and that both George and Martha had loved his mother, Eliza Jr. This family lineage was both a blessing and a responsibility: "more will be expected from one, whom it is thought must have heard the virtues of Genl & Mrs. Washington spoken of from his birth, as the model for his study & imitation."[21] These words were her own form of legacy for Edmund.

Eliza's health was not improved by the fact that she had no permanent home. When the two French servants who had been caring for Eliza at a rented house in Georgetown had to leave, she moved into a hotel; why she chose that over living with one of her siblings is unclear, but perhaps their relationships were still too frayed.[22] It is likewise a mystery as to why, suffering from "an incessant cough & fever" in December 1831, she decided to visit her old friend John Augustus Chevallie and his wife in Richmond. The Chevallies sent her to bed and summoned a doctor, but she was "so reduced and so feeble" that they had little hope she would survive.

On New Year's Eve, minutes before the clock struck midnight and without any of her family by her side, Eliza died.[23] The next day, news traveled north to her siblings and ex-husband quickly. According to a family friend, the next morning, Thomas Law's servant was serving breakfast when he told Thomas that his ex-wife had died the previous night. Knowing how long Eliza had been ill and probably believing her to be a hypochondriac, he could not imagine it could be true. "The h—l she did," Thomas supposedly replied. "Hand the potatoes."[24] But it was true: the eldest of the Custis siblings was gone at age fifty-five. Thomas was pained by it; he wrote soon after that "she always loved me" and he still felt a special attachment to her. Nelly saw her sister's passing as an act of mercy; Eliza had had "nothing to live for" after the loss of her grandchildren, and she was "released from severe suffering."[25] Eliza was buried soon after at Mount Vernon, her coffin lying at the feet of George and Martha Washington's own, finally and forever together with those she had most revered.

★ ★ ★

While there was one fewer Custis sibling alive to carry forward the Washington family flame, Wash more than made up for it as he launched into new projects. He had no qualms about throwing himself onto the public stage in support of his vision of a growing American empire for liberty. Even more so than his sisters, Wash took command of George Washington's legacy as a tool for both politicking and building his own career. He joined a cadre of American writers and artists who were carving out new American forms of literature and art in this period. Writers like Peter Force, Jared Sparks, and Benson Lossing (the latter two of whom Wash knew well) gathered historical sources and published histories of the American Revolution, while novelists like James Fenimore Cooper set stories in the Revolutionary era. In the 1830s, writers of both prose and drama were creating a new, American literature that celebrated the new nation's exceptionalism and its great destiny.[26] Wash did not limit himself to one medium. In writings, speeches, and paintings, he would keep the Revolution and especially George Washington's memory alive through a very particular lens—that of the war hero and, as Wash called his stepgrandfather in one poetic ode, "Thou Empire Founder."[27]

It was, in fact, one of Wash's early published recollections that he adapted into his first play, *The Indian Prophecy*. This was to be the first of many historical plays that Wash wrote and paid to produce, all laden with political messages of America's power and promise.[28] In Wash's plays, including *The Indian Prophecy*, *Pocahontas*, and *The Pawnee Chief* (like other similar plays of the era), the United States was a country led by white heroes but peopled with stereotypical noble savages and happy slaves.[29] These two caricatured figures were in fact connected: it was the removal of Native peoples that made way for plantations where white settlers forced enslaved people to labor. These plays are uncomfortable reading for us today, but they appealed to audiences hungry for tales that affirmed the rightfulness of America's expanding though often violent empire.

Comic blackface characters also make their appearance in at least two plays, both about the War of 1812. In his *Eighth of January* play celebrating Andrew Jackson, one of the characters is the stereotyped Black figure of Sambo.[30] Wash has the dubious distinction of being on the cutting edge here: blackface minstrel shows, in which white actors blackened their faces and performed songs and dances with caricatured dialect, were just beginning when he wrote this play in the late 1820s. Wash himself knew a real man named Sambo: one of the formerly enslaved workers at Mount Vernon, Sambo Anderson, still lived near Wash and sold game to local families.[31] In another play, Wash leaned fully into the minstrelsy tradition with the character of Cully, "a Black soldier of the Revolution," in his War of 1812 play *North Point, or Baltimore Defended*. The originator of the dancing Jim Crow minstrel character himself, white actor Thomas D. Rice, played Cully in the play's Baltimore debut. According to Wash, Rice "outdid his Jim Crow all hollow."[32]

Custis did not write only to promote his vision of America; he could also earn decent money as a playwright. It's unclear how much money most of his plays earned him (whatever financial records he kept, and we can only imagine they would not have been particularly neat, have disappeared). However, he reported proudly to his wife in 1833 that *North Point, or Baltimore Defended* had earned him at least $1,000. This was particularly good money considering that he was under deadline to write it and had completed it in nine hours. "You see," he told her, "I should sooner get out of debt by the labour of my brains than of my ploughs, at this rate."[33] While he wrote several more plays, the market for patriotic plays by American authors was waning by 1836, and the financial downturn of 1837 didn't help.[34] Wash would have to find another medium.

Wash was nothing if not creative and resourceful. While he

probably never had any formal artistic training, he turned to painting as a fresh way to document and preserve Washington's legacy.[35] Drawing on some of the same information he had gathered from George himself and other prominent veterans of the American Revolution, Wash began painting scenes of major battles of the American Revolution with as much accuracy as he could. This was a rather unusual choice for any painter in this period. Most American painters were putting forward visions of patriotism through uniquely American landscapes; history paintings were not in vogue at the time and didn't sell. The few paintings of George Washington at this time depicted him in civilian rather than military garb, but Wash made a conscious choice in his art, as in his "Recollections," to focus on his stepgrandfather's martial legacy.[36] Perhaps this shouldn't be surprising; Wash's image of the United States was more focused on a conquering force that spread liberty than its achievements as a democratic republic. He rarely talked about Washington as president but rather as a heroic general.

Indeed, Wash's first great work was a large thirteen-by-eleven-foot portrait of Washington "in the full meridian of life" with the Battle of Princeton in the background. He had completed hasty, allegorical works on large canvases for Washington birthday celebrations in Alexandria years before, but now he devoted more time and focus to his art. Wash turned a small room beyond an unused parlor in the west wing of the house into his studio. The light streamed in and probably made the room too hot for use in the summer, but the rest of the year, he spent hours painting minute details of historical characters and battle scenes onto his canvases. Whenever visitors came to Arlington House, he wanted to be sure they had looked into his studio to see his artwork. A young family friend recalled that often when Wash had been out for the day and heard people had visited the house, he would ask, "Did you show them my pictures?" If yes, he followed up with, "What did they say?" which the young friend admitted was "sometimes rather difficult to answer."[37] Wash's enthusiasm for painting far outstripped his talent.

He was delighted that his painting of Washington at Princeton would be displayed in the Capitol beneath the Rotunda, but this turned into a crushing disappointment. A derisive review of the painting appeared in the April 16 edition of the *United States Telegraph*. The author mockingly lauded Wash, who "can be hailed in the quadruple title of poet, dramatist, orator, and painter! types but of his fame, which shall fill the four quarters of the habitable globe, and shed around his memory the halo of immortal star light." The figure of George Washington, the critic wrote, had a nose "not exactly dumpy," while Nathanael Greene's hair was "of a greenish cast." To George's left were General Knox and Alexander Hamilton, but it was impossible to distinguish whose legs were whose. "This picture is...a sublime effort," the author concluded, "but I would advise [Custis] not to expose it too long to the damps of the Rotunda."[38]

Wash, affronted, wrote the superintendent of public buildings soon after to say that his agent would take the picture down. Defensively, he noted that "some excellent Artists" had seen merit in the painting. Nonetheless, he told his agent to throw the painting into the Potomac River on his way back to Arlington "that it may offend no more." His agent forbore doing this, but the canvas was wrapped into a bundle and stashed away. Years later, Wash ordered two of his enslaved servants to boil the canvas to remove the paint. The grime-covered figures of generals and horses could still be made out before they melted off into the boiling water. The cleaned canvas was cut and made into aprons.[39]

This disappointment did not stop Wash's painting career, however. He continued to paint in his bright tucked-away studio until near the end of his life. His surviving paintings give some sense of what that destroyed Princeton painting must have looked like. The figures are rather angular and look frozen in sometimes awkward motion. It is, as the critic of 1836 observed, sometimes hard to tell which legs belong to whom as the generals crowd together in the foreground and blurry masses of ordinary soldiers fill the middle ground. Yet Wash was clearly paying close attention to detail; the generals all have unique faces and expressions, and even the country house in the backdrop of the Battle of Germantown painting is accurately rendered. Smoke pours from the house's windows as cannons are loaded and the American forces charge forward. While clearly by an amateur hand, the paintings have a sense of drama and action that brought the many battle stories Wash recounted to life.[40] As Wash himself said, "I am an untaught artist, but hope to make up by Zeal of the heart, what I may want in skill & experience."[41]

Wash's zeal often exceeded his skill when it came to his speaking career as well. While he had given occasional speeches in the first two decades of the nineteenth century, by the late 1820s he was regularly addressing audiences at meetings and commemorations. He threw himself into the emotion of his topics, usually patriotic ones, but his verbose, meandering, and often melodramatic orations sometimes provoked criticism. Of an 1831 speech, one listener described Wash's speaking style as "prose run mad cast" with "a great show of action, attitudinizing and gesticulation." When one word would do, Wash used five. Some in the city still critiqued his speeches from the sheep shearing festival days, with one writer derisively calling Wash "the old sheep orator and slave dealer."[42] If Wash was able to brush such criticisms aside, his family wasn't always able to. Nelly winced at the thought of an upcoming speech and the reaction, telling Wash's wife Molly, "my poor dear Brother will enter heart & soul into it—I hope he will avoid everything in speaking or acting which can excite unkind remarks, or admit of being turned into ridicule."[43]

Public speaking was an art in this period, taught in schools as a fundamental skill for citizens of a democratic republic. Speeches were regular features of meetings and festivals and were published in newspapers or pamphlets; these were important venues for working out all sorts of ideas in the new nation, including American politics and identity.[44] At any number of events in Washington City, ranging from political meetings to gatherings of Irishmen to George Washington–related commemorations, Wash gave lengthy and florid speeches. He was such a well-known and regular public orator that in 1839, a publisher (likely at Wash's behest) offered a 250-page compilation of the speeches of "the adopted son of Washington" for sale.[45]

The topics of Wash's speeches varied, but the underlying themes were patriotism, liberty, and the greatness of America's growing empire. In a speech at the Catholic-run Georgetown College, he spoke eloquently to religious liberty. "What matters it to me whether the Catholic citizen erects his altar for the worship of the ever living God in a church or a chapel," he said. "If he is honest, if he is faithful to the Constitution, he is my brother, and under the protection of the laws." Wash was entirely genuine here, and he was a regular guest and orator at Irish Catholic St. Patrick's Day celebrations. Wash told his Irish friends that he celebrated "but few holydays": Washington's birthday, the Fourth of July, and St. Patrick's Day. Even in the twentieth century, Americans with Irish ancestry in the Washington, DC, area gathered at Arlington House to celebrate St. Patrick's Day and pay tribute to their old supporter, Wash Custis.[46]

But when it came to another set of Catholics—Mexicans—Wash believed that they needed to be conquered for the good of American empire and liberty. In a speech he gave to supporters of the war in Texas in 1836, Wash explained that the Mexicans and native Comanche in Texas had lived in "ignorance, bigotry, and barbarism," but as "the Anglo-Saxon" began to arrive, "the savage beast and savage man retire at the pioneers approach."[47] In the 1830s, white Americans saw Mexicans as similar to Native peoples in the United States; both were racially inferior. The racialized identification of white Americans as "Anglo-Saxons" took off in the late 1830s into the 1840s as a catchall term for whites of various European backgrounds who were destined to spread American greatness and liberty.[48] As Wash said, after conquering Texas, "the mightiest Republican Empire that ever enlightened and adored the annals of the world" would conquer the entire hemisphere.[49]

Of course, an American Anglo-Saxon empire in newly acquired territories needed Anglo-Saxon settlers. Men alone would not suffice, or else they would either intermarry with local people of color or fail to have any children, in both cases failing to plant a permanent white population. Both white men *and* women were required for the American empire to stick.[50] You didn't have to look as far as Texas for places that needed peopling; until the War of 1812, lingering British forts and alliances with local Native peoples had restricted white American settlement west of the Appalachians. After the British left, a vast territory from western New York and Ohio down to Alabama and Louisiana lay open to new white settlers who would forcibly conquer or remove the local Native peoples. As it turned out, some of the white families that went west to support America's growing empire were the Custises' children and their own growing broods. George Washington's heirs would people the expanding American empire.

The Custises, like most others of their wealth and status, hoped for their children to find more than love and happiness in their marriages. While the era of parents choosing spouses for their children had long passed, Patty, Nelly, and Wash all had preferences for the sort of people their children might marry— especially their daughters. The ideal husband would be from a well-known and wealthy family, bolstering rather than lowering the Custises' own status and providing households at the level of comfort in which the girls had been raised.

As it turned out, Parke Lewis, America Peter, and Mary Custis all chose men who were far from their parents' first choice. Perhaps unsurprisingly, given their parents' admiration for military figures, all three of their husbands were military men, but the men's faults were in not being rich ones. As the American military had expanded and professionalized, it became a path to education and secure financial standing for many men of limited means.[51] This career did not bring the kind of stability the Custises sought for their daughters; it would mean moving, often to places at the edge of white settlement in the developing West where the US military was helping to move out Native people and prepare the land for white families. In case of war, the men would have to leave their families behind and risk losing their lives. Parke, America, and Mary were all willing to make these sacrifices, leaving their tight-knit families and quiet lives, for the simple reason that they fell in love.

Ed Butler was far from Nelly's vision of an ideal husband for her eldest daughter, but Parke had fallen for him, and Ed was persistent. By the time the marriage approached in 1826, Nelly told a friend that "every one is forcibly struck with his inferiority, & surprised at her choice."[52] It was not only his lack of intellect that was a problem; he had little to no family money and would have to scratch out a living in the military. Ed was assigned to serve under General Edmund P. Gaines in Cincinnati, and he and Parke planned to marry in the spring of 1826 before he departed Washington for Ohio. The morning after their engagement was announced, Ed recalled years later, Nelly's enslaved laundress Dolcey came to Ed's room to congratulate him and said after a polite curtsey, "Pardon me, Major, for obtruding upon you. I merely came to congratulate you on becoming a member of *our* family."[53] To Ed, this showed both the good manners and good treatment of enslaved people, but what might Dolcey have been feeling? Was she worried that she or members of her family would be sent to live with the new couple?

Indeed, Nelly later sent Dolcey's niece Lucinda and daughters Nelly and Sukey far from home to serve the Lewis daughters.[54]

In a small ceremony at Woodlawn with close family and friends, on April 4, 1826, Frances Parke Lewis married Edward George Washington Butler. Not long after, the couple left for Ohio, accompanied (by no choice of her own) by Lucinda, who was given to Parke as a wedding gift and whom Ed later described as "a remarkable woman." Lucinda would help Parke run her tiny new household and became indispensable to the Butlers, later serving as nurse to the Butler children. While Ed later recalled her devotion to Parke, it is hard to fathom what it would have been like for her to be forced to leave the only place she had known and her entire family.[55] The Butlers' new home of Cincinnati had been incorporated less than twenty-five years earlier, but was exploding with growth as its location on the Ohio River made it a strategic trading location. Ed ultimately hoped to retire from the army and move still farther west—and south.

When Ed Butler decided to move his wife and infant son to Louisiana, he was taking advantage of a concerted effort by the American government to bolster the nation's growing empire and raise up families like his.[56] As he told his father-in-law, he had read about "the advantages which Louisiana present to persons of limited means," especially since if he put enslaved people to work growing sugar cane, he could earn back their purchase price in just a year. He knew that the Lewises could not afford to give him and Parke enough enslaved people to run a plantation, so in addition to purchasing land, he would have to purchase more laborers.[57] But his sister and brother-in-law were finding success in the rich soil along the Mississippi River near Baton Rouge, and they eventually helped him find a plantation near them in Iberville Parish in 1831. After a short stint back in Washington, the Butlers moved to their new remote, swampy lands, bringing with them some thirty-eight enslaved people they had purchased from a nearby plantation and then another thirty purchased in Virginia two years later.[58]

While Parke was moving to a place where she was, in Nelly's words, "buried alive" in rural obscurity and unceasing hard work, she could at least correspond with her family and visit them occasionally. The enslaved men and women were being torn from their families with little if any chance of communicating with them, much less seeing them again. They were among the one million enslaved people sent from the Upper South, many from Virginia, to the Lower South to grow cotton and sugar and enrich a new generation of white settlers.[59] In 1835, likely having more enslaved labor than the Lewises needed, Nelly sent her daughter and son-in-law eight enslaved people. We know very little about these men and women, Nelly, Dennis, Tom, George, Jane, Mary, Frances, and John; most seem to have been young, and the Lewises separated them from their parents and siblings.[60] Perhaps they yearned for Nelly and Lawrence's visits to Louisiana so they could inquire after their families, or perhaps the sight of those who had caused them such wrenching pain was unwelcome.

Nelly, Lawrence, and Angela made long visits to Parke, supporting her as she gave birth to one child after another and her husband attempted, fruitlessly, to make a success of their plantation. When Nelly visited in the winter of 1833 to 1834, she watched her daughter and son-in-law eke out a life far from the comforts and gentility of Woodlawn. Still, she found beauty and interest in the place; across the road from the gate of their plantation was the levee above the Mississippi, and Nelly walked there and watched the steamboats pass. The Native people who had likely been forced off these lands still lived close by, struggling to maintain their traditional ways of life. The Native women came to sell baskets, while the men brought venison; they were, in Nelly's condescending eyes, "poor dirty humble & grateful creatures."[61] Never, though, did Nelly or anyone else in the family see themselves as the instrument of the Native people's suffering as they settled on Native lands.

While in Louisiana, Nelly's younger daughter Angela also made a match with a Louisiana man. While Charles Magill Conrad was not a military man, he was no pacifist: less than a year before meeting Angela, he had killed a man in a duel.[62] Given the continuing focus on maintaining honor in this period, this would not have hurt his reputation as a rising lawyer in New Orleans. Indeed, Nelly said the twenty-seven-year-old Charles was "the finest young man in Louisiana—the most popular in New Orleans." In addition to his "irreproachable character" and "affectionate disposition," he was well-educated and spoke both Spanish and French fluently. "In short he is just after *my own heart*," Nelly declared.[63]

Surely part of what attracted Nelly was that she saw in Charles a future public figure: he was far more interested in politics than plantations, unlike Ed Butler. Nelly told him she dreamed of his taking a seat on the Supreme Court.[64] Angela imagined "a glorious destiny" for him as a great orator in the Senate.[65] Charles was worried that she was too ambitious, but she replied that "I hope you have not a *spark less* than myself." Her main goal, she explained, was that he would be known as a star in his profession. She backed off the idea that he should run for office and said that she was happy he had turned down a nomination for the state legislature.[66] Being a lawyer was a powerful position, particularly in a place like New Orleans, as the country had to work out the legal problems of expansion and slavery. For Southern lawyers, even the everyday commercial law cases they handled were often tied up in securing slave property, and Charles was no exception.[67]

Certainly, though, part of their bond was a shared interest in politics, which Angela must have regularly discussed with Nelly. After the Lewises had returned to Woodlawn and Charles remained in New Orleans, Angela wrote her fiancé regular and lengthy letters about the latest political news. As Congress considered military action against the French in early 1835 for refusing to pay old debts for shipping losses during the Napoleonic Wars, Angela supplied Charles with updates. Her knowledge must have come from the newspapers, because she lamented at the end of the congressional session in March that she hadn't gone to hear any of the debates in person.[68] She knew she would soon be moving to Louisiana and would no longer have the chance to attend.

On July 30, 1835, Angela married Charles Magill Conrad. The wedding was held at Woodlawn, probably with a small number of guests.[69] Her parents would not send the new couple off to Louisiana alone; they gave them fifteen enslaved people.[70] In addition, to provide the young couple with cash, Lawrence sold twenty-four people to a Louisiana man for $19,000. The Lewises would again wrench enslaved families apart, forced to new and distant homes in Louisiana.[71] We know that the Conrads kept one enslaved seamstress named Sukey, who had been born at Mount Vernon to Dolcey around 1799. Some of the other enslaved people gifted to Angela may also have been Sukey's young children.[72]

When Angela and her mother arrived at the Conrad home in New Orleans, Angela struggled with "sick & refractory servants," which is not surprising after they had been forced to travel hundreds of miles in poor conditions. Louisiana was not a healthy place for Angela, now pregnant, either; soon after arriving, she had chicken pox, and then measles, which forced her into premature labor. Her daughter, although she went from "small & delicate" to "the finest the healthiest child," died of whooping cough at just a year old.[73] Living on the margins of America's burgeoning empire added another layer of danger to the health risks rampant at the time; it was no wonder the Custises fretted about their children marrying and moving westward.

It was another military officer who probably knew Ed Butler from their shared time at West Point that captured Parke and Angela's cousin America Peter's heart in 1825. William G. Williams had trained as an engineer focused on waterways, particularly the canals and harbors that enabled the movement of goods quickly and efficiently from east to west. America met the young lieutenant after a group of officers from the topographical corps staying in Georgetown came to Tudor Place after a dinner hosted for Lafayette in 1825.[74] She seems to have fallen quickly for the officer with the dark, penetrating eyes and quizzical eyebrows, but as soon as her parents detected her attraction, they expressed their disapproval. William, like Ed, had limited means, but unlike Parke's choice, he could not point to any family members of note. This made him, in Nelly's words, "obnoxious" to Patty and Thomas Peter. They forbade the marriage, but America was so miserable that her brother Washington spoke to them on her behalf and obtained their "reluctant consent."[75]

A month after Parke's marriage to Ed Butler, America wed William in the west parlor of Tudor Place. By August, they were happily settled in Washington, and her parents were finally "reconciled" to the match, as Nelly put it. Despite their tight finances, William did everything he could to spoil his beloved America and their growing family. Her parents supported the couple by giving America two enslaved women as a wedding gift, including an eleven-year-old girl named Stacia and nurse named Elizabeth, both of whom would help America with her future children. Unlike the enslaved people the Lewises gave the Butlers, Stacia and Elizabeth would at least remain in the same town as their families at Tudor Place. However, when William took Elizabeth with him to Cape Cod on a work trip, Elizabeth seized the opportunity for freedom and fled.[76]

In 1838, the Williamses moved to Buffalo for William, now a captain, to do surveying around Lake Erie and for a canal around Niagara Falls. Buffalo was, in William's own words, "very much advanced in everything but painting," a disappointment to the amateur artist whose portraits of his father-in-law, wife, and himself still survive.[77] The young family initially lived in a hotel that William thought was "perhaps the best in the U States." Buffalo had only been incorporated as a city six years before, and it was quickly expanding in population and importance as a hub of trade on the Erie Canal and Lake Erie. While not as far west as Pittsburgh or Cincinnati, Buffalo was still a frontier town whose prospects rose with the country's expansion. In the year the Williamses arrived, Jackson's successor Martin Van Buren signed a law that forced the local Seneca people off their lands in the Buffalo area (including one plot only blocks from the Buffalo harbor) and removed them to Kansas.[78] The timing was no coincidence; William's surveying work would prepare the ground for white settlement as his fellow troops moved Native peoples off the land.

Patty Peter never warmed to William, and despite the drama over America's choice of spouse, she continued to interfere in her children's courtships. In 1839, for instance, she intervened to stop a rising Democratic journalist from courting Britannia. John O'Sullivan had moved to Washington City in 1837 to edit a radical Jacksonian newspaper, and while he hadn't found financial success, he was acknowledged to be a talented writer. He later became known for purportedly coining the term "manifest destiny" to describe the foreordained nature of American expansion.[79] Britannia fell for O'Sullivan, but Patty could not approve of a penniless "poet and eccentric" who was "ardent in his devotion to Locofocoism" (as Molly Custis described him). *Locofocoism* was a derisive term for Democrats, tarring the party with the brush of the radical Locofoco faction that advocated for workingmen's rights and against the fiscal policies that they believed benefited wealthy and conservative people—like Patty Peter. Patty was probably relieved that Britannia eventually settled on an older, wealthy military man, naval captain Beverley Kennon, whom Britannia married in 1841.[80]

America and Britannia's cousin Mary Custis, Wash's daughter, would marry another military engineer whose career also centered on westward expansion. Mary had known her distant cousin Robert E. Lee since they were young children, but while they both came from prominent Virginia families, they faced very different prospects in life. Mary, as Wash's only white child, stood to inherit Arlington House and the other Custis lands and enslaved people, the sole scion of a prominent and respected family with close ties to George Washington. Robert E. Lee, on the other hand, came from a family broken by scandal and financial loss; Thomas Jefferson had described the Lees in 1823 as "these insects."[81]

Robert's father Henry had been a Revolutionary War hero nicknamed "Light-Horse Harry" who knew George Washington and famously eulogized him as "first in war, first in peace, and first in the hearts of his countrymen." But he had fallen on hard times around the time Robert was born in 1807 and was sent to debtor's prison, leaving his wife Ann Carter Lee and children to rely on the charity of cousins. Molly's father William Fitzhugh opened his Alexandria home to his cousin Ann (both were descended from Richard Lee, who immigrated to Virginia in the seventeenth century). The struggling family lived rent-free at Fitzhugh's Alexandria town house at 607 Oronoco Street. It was the same house where Wash had met Molly. Henry Lee made it out of prison only to be gravely injured in the 1812 Baltimore attack on Federalists, then went to the Caribbean, where he died in 1818. Young Robert had hardly known him. Not long after, Robert's half brother Henry IV, ominously known as "Black-Horse Harry," drew the family even deeper into disrepute when he seduced his wife's younger sister (who was his ward), impregnated her, and took her money. Robert was actually living with Henry at Stratford Hall on Virginia's Northern Neck when this happened.[82]

This was not really the sort of family, then, that Wash wanted his sole heir to marry into at a time when economic security and family stability were central to marriage. Wash and Molly had no qualms about associating with the Lees; Robert had known Wash and Molly since childhood and was close with them long before he married their daughter. His brothers Smith and Carter Lee corresponded with Wash, and his sister Mildred was friends with Mary. He had managed, with the extended family's support, to get a good education in Alexandria and later at West Point. And for all his struggles (or perhaps because of them), Robert was intensely careful, patient, and thoughtful; in his earliest portrait in 1838, there is a gentleness to his gaze. With soft brown eyes, delicate brows, and silky brown, slightly wavy hair, he was undeniably handsome. Mary had plenty of suitors, including Robert's elder brothers, but it seems likely that the pair had been attracted to one another since they were teenagers.[83]

Mary was not known as a beauty and cared little for fine or even tidy dress, but she seemed to have a magnetism that drew people to her. She was an amateur artist like her father (although a more skilled one) and better educated than most women of her day; she studied Greek and Latin, which was unusual for a woman, and had grown up surrounded by and conversing with prominent people.[84] Her aunt Nelly referred to her as "charming" as well as "humble & gentle," noting that at the same time Mary had "wit & satire too, when they are required."[85] She was devoted to her parents and to Arlington. She was a prize on the marriage market and likely knew it, but the attachment between Robert and Mary was built on affection and romance rather than practical considerations.

After months of waiting and angling for Wash's approval, the couple finally received his blessing. They were married on June 30, 1831, at Arlington House. It was a rainy night, and the Reverend Reuel Keith arrived so wet that he had to borrow a new set of clothes from Wash. Perhaps Mary's half sister Maria Syphax, married in the house ten years earlier, helped Mary dress; certainly the large party would have generated a great deal of stress and work for the enslaved house servants expected to remain in the shadows during the event. Family tradition recounts that Mary came down the stairs on her father's arm while her aunt Nelly played piano.[86]

Mary and Robert's departure for his latest posting at Old Point on the coast of southern Virginia was painful for her parents. "I have dictated I cannot tell how many letters in the silent hours of night," Molly wrote her daughter soon after. "I will not attempt to tell you how I felt at your departure. I hastened to turn from my own loss to a contemplation of your hapiness." Mary missed home, too, and not long afterwards, she returned to Arlington House while Robert stayed at Old Point. When she rejoined him there, she brought Molly with her, but Arlington House remained Mary and Robert's true home until the Civil War.[87]

Like Mary's cousins' husbands, Robert's military career drew the Lee family westward. Robert, a talented engineer, was sent to Saint Louis in 1837 to work on a project to redirect the Mississippi River. Mary and their three young children accompanied him; a fourth child would be born during the family's stay there. For all his gentleness to white women and children, Robert was ruthless to nonwhite people. Beyond his callous treatment of enslaved people, he called Native Americans "hideous," and when he served in the Mexican-American War, he referred to Mexicans as "weak" and "primitive." As one of his biographers wrote, "much of his military career was spent in subduing anyone who came into conflict with white aspirations."[88] Even more so than Ed Butler or William G. Williams, Robert E. Lee was at the forefront of the expanding white American empire.

The family's exuberant expansion was interrupted by losses. In April 1834, Thomas Peter died after several years of health struggles. The Peters' old friend Anna Maria Thornton came the next day to comfort Patty, and she could already see that Patty would struggle mightily with her grief.[89] The family took the long carriage ride to their farm at Oakland, where they buried Thomas in the family plot. Patty returned to Tudor Place to face the absence of the man she had rarely been apart from her entire adult life. Nearly six months later, Nelly reported that her sister "looks worse than I ever saw her & appears very low spirited."[90] But Nelly would face even more losses by the end of the decade.

In the fall of 1839, a few months after the birth of Angela Lewis Conrad's second son, Angela fell ill. She "did not dread death for herself," but for her husband and parents. She died in her husband's arms at just twenty-six years old. Her widowed husband was despondent. "It seems to me as if one half of my very soul and body had been severed from the other half," he told Nelly. Nelly was gutted that she wasn't with Angela at her death, and even her faith could not reconcile her to it; "I do not murmur at the Almightys will but how can I be at peace with myself."[91]

The always dour Lawrence was "as usual," Nelly noted, "& bears his loss with resignation."[92] Lawrence was himself in poor health; earlier that year he had told his son-in-law, "I feel myself truly old, & my strength fast declining."[93] On November 20, during a visit to Arlington House and as he lay in the bed in which George Washington had died, Lawrence passed away. While Lawrence had kept a lower public profile than his wife and her siblings, he was remembered in his obituary as "the last of Washington's near blood relations," and one newspaper announced his death under the headline "The Last of the Near Ones."[94] Unlike everyone else in the family, no personal account of his death survives; it's not even clear if Nelly was with him at Arlington. There is no mention of his passing—or even of Lawrence himself—in any of Nelly's surviving papers after his death.

This twentieth-century copy of an 1832 portrait of Lawrence Lewis shows him
at age sixty-five, seven years before his death. The glasses resting on his
forehead are a reminder of his decades-long struggle with his eyes.

After John Beale Bordley, *Lawrence Lewis*, probably 20th century.
Courtesy of Mount Vernon Ladies' Association.

After four decades of marriage, many of them apparently
acrimonious, perhaps Nelly saw his death as a sort of escape.
Their marriage seems to have gotten steadily worse over the
years. By the mid-1830s, Lawrence made clear to his children
that he thought Nelly's spending habits were "a course so imprudent" that they were ruining the family. He urged Angela
to speak with her mother, but Angela had no luck; "the habit
had become a disease without a cause."[95] When the couple was
apart, with Nelly in Louisiana and Lawrence in Virginia, she

repeatedly asked him for more funds and defended her spending; "except absolute necessaries I buy nothing for my self," but of course she needed to buy things for her grandchildren. Nelly's letters to him are not strained or angry, nor are they affectionate.[96]

Only weeks after Lawrence's death, Nelly could not sit still. She would have been in Louisiana already to visit the Butlers and to console Charles Conrad if not for Lawrence's ill health, so she determined to set out alone. Wash "said I was mad to come alone"; she trudged through snow and rain in a gloomy December in Washington City to haul her heavy bags onto a stagecoach. She bounced and jostled on the rutted roads for three days, but in a stroke of great luck, a friend from Philadelphia was in the same car. He helped her get safely to Louisville, where she boarded a boat to Louisiana—indeed, on the maiden trip of the Mississippi River's first iron boat. Just over two weeks later, she arrived at the Butlers' plantation, likely rather proud of having made the journey alone at nearly sixty years old.[97] In her longest solo visit to the Butlers, it seems tensions that must have been building for years between her and Ed finally boiled over.

Nelly had likely not hidden her contempt for the life the Butlers led in Louisiana, a life of indebtedness and drudgery even with one hundred enslaved people's labor to exploit. She chafed at Ed's lack of intellectual curiosity from early in the relationship, and a longer acquaintance probably didn't help. Ed had subjected Parke, in Nelly's estimation, to "the most brutal treatment," although nothing in Parke's writings suggested she felt the relationship was abusive. He had a violent passion that reminded Nelly of Andrew Jackson, but it wasn't held in check by the "gentlemanly manner" Jackson had. One day, as Nelly was nursing Parke and her eldest son as they lay ill in bed, that passion exploded. Entering the bedroom in a fury, he told Nelly that "he moved to La. to get as far from me as possible & he would be *damned* if he ever went where I was again." Nelly, he claimed, was widely disliked, and in a particularly low blow, he said that she had made Lawrence so unhappy that he had died prematurely. In the tightly controlled emotional world in which Nelly had been raised, it's hard to overstate how appalling this outburst would have been. As Nelly prepared to leave for the Conrads in New Orleans, likely as quickly as she could after this speech, Ed told her he "hoped I would never come again."[98] She never did.

The new decade in 1840 dawned with a political development that managed to please both Wash and Patty: the election of the Whig candidate William Henry Harrison to the presidency. While Wash's support for Jackson had aligned him with the Democrats, he was not particularly partisan by that time. In Harrison he saw an old military hero rather than a party affiliation. Wash even hit the campaign trail, speaking at a Whig barbecue in Fairfax County, Virginia, for Harrison in September 1840. "There will be something in listening to the adopted son of WASHINGTON speaking in the county in which the Father of his Country lived," the writer announcing the speech gushed. The crowd of three hundred men, women, and children cheered his speech, but Democrats used Wash's presence to tar Harrison as an elitist tied to the old Federalists—Wash, after all, had been a popular speaker for Federalists in the War of 1812, in which Harrison had served. But Wash was undeterred in his support, serving as the orator for a celebration in Alexandria of Harrison's election that November. The week before Harrison's inauguration, Wash gave him a cane made from wood from one of George Washington's carriages, offering a physical stamp of Washington family approval.[99]

Both Wash and Patty were in the crowd when Harrison was welcomed to the nation's capital with a celebratory parade in Georgetown. "He is quite A Genteel good Looking old Man," Patty reported, and had a "much more honest countenance than

Martin." Derisively calling Van Buren by his first name, Patty noted that the departing and incoming presidents dined together at Gadsby's Tavern and sniffed, "*Things* are permitted to dine with *Things* I suppose." Patty herself eschewed going to a party held for the women of Georgetown to meet Harrison, saying that she and Britannia would "pay *our* respects" on inauguration day. She would take her time and meet him on her own terms.[100] As it turned out, Harrison died just a month after his inauguration, and Patty probably never had the chance. He wasn't much older than the Custis siblings, and the new president's sudden death was a reminder that their own lives were entering a final chapter.

CHAPTER 10

"Relicts of a Past Age"

IF ANYONE HAD ASKED THE SURVIVING
Custis siblings what most occupied their time, energy, and attention in the 1840s and 1850s, all three would have agreed:
their grandchildren. By the mid-1840s, Patty, Nelly, and Wash
had just six of the twenty-two children they had held and doted
upon as infants. In Patty's and Nelly's cases, two of their adult
daughters had died and left behind children, and while Wash's
son-in-law Robert E. Lee was fully alive and well, he was often
absent. The fact that the Custis siblings could help raise their
children's children seems to have been more blessing than burden
to them, and they relished their roles as grandparents even as they
struggled against declining health and more devastating losses.

But they were still Custises, and they had not forgotten their
role as carriers of the Washington legacy. Wash was still driven
by patriotism and a desire to preserve the Union, and even as
her health worsened, Nelly stayed fiercely political. Only Patty,
who had never really moved on from the demise of the Federalist party in the 1810s, seemed wholly removed from politics;
as her granddaughter remarked, "dearest Grandmother, with all
her veneration for Washington & all her enthusiastic patriotism,
has still remaining, a little Tory blood in her veins."[1] While Patty

might have denied it, America's empire hit a high point in the late 1840s, but its very growth spelled trouble for the Union that would descend into civil war. At the same time, the Custis siblings' lives too would come to an end. By the dawn of the 1850s, they were in their seventies, long outliving the average life expectancy of the era, but not too old to make a few final marks as the last relics of the first "first family."

A typical day for all three Custis siblings was spent at home caring for their multigenerational families and supervising enslaved people. Living with her son Lorenzo's family at Audley, Nelly settled into a quiet routine as a grandmother: she awoke at sunrise, read prayers before breakfast, and spent most of the day in her room bent over her needlework, making clothing and decorative pieces for her grandchildren and great-nieces and -nephews. As dark fell, she read by candlelight until she felt her eyes drooping closed.[2] She also tended to Angela's boys Charley and Lewis, who had joined Lorenzo and Esther Lewis's growing brood of sons.[3] Nelly's mind remained sharp, but the years had taken a toll on her body. She had become a stout woman with a careworn, plump face, a few curls slipping out from a ruffled bonnet. She still had the wide, round eyes and arched eyebrows of her youth, but they had a wary gaze, and the corners of her lips were turned down.

Southeast of her at Arlington House, Wash too was looking older while still dapper and active. His head was balding, with thin wispy hair remaining on the back of his head. His face was wrinkled and his clothes were from an earlier era, but his eyes still shone.[4] Molly's long face with small gray eyes was framed by light brown hair fading into gray, pulled back in a neat bun; one observer noted that from her eyes came "the soul look," suggesting her deep spirituality.[5] Molly awoke early and began the household's day by leading prayers, followed by breakfast served by Charles Syphax in the dining room, then each family member splitting off to his or her tasks. For Wash, that meant spending the morning in his office in a small log structure by Arlington Spring, where he superintended farm work by en‐slaved people, and the afternoon in his painting room or by the spring, entertaining the visitors he welcomed there. Molly repaired to a room in the north wing to supervise household work, including educating enslaved people and sewing. When Mary and her children (usually the girls Mary, Anne, Agnes, and

This photograph of Nelly was probably taken when she was around seventy years old and in declining health.

Eleanor Parke Custis Lewis, undated.
The Historic New Orleans Collection, Gift of Mr. Richard C. Plater, Jr.

Mildred) were there, Molly may have also helped in their edu‐cation, but much of the day, the Lee children were left to "run wild over the house, gardens & woods."[6]

Left: Wash Custis was in his sixties when he had this photograph taken at the studio of photographer Mathew Brady. He still wears clothes from an earlier era.

Mathew Brady, *George Washington Parke Custis*, c. 1844-1849. Washington, Library of Congress.

Right: This daguerreotype of Molly Custis was likely taken near the end of her life.

Mary Lee Fitzhugh Custis, 19th century, daguerrotype.
Richmond, Virginia Museum of History & Culture (1977.34).

The household across the river and perched above George-town at Tudor Place was likely a quieter and better-ordered one. Patty was a stern figure, whom one niece described as "rather cold & harsh usually." Beneath that reserve were layers of pain and loss, which show vividly in the only surviving image of her. She sits upright, thin and rather fragile, with a heavy brow, firm-set thin lips, and a bonnet tightly secured over her head. Her face reflects the weariness she expressed in a letter to a granddaugh-ter in 1847: "untill long after your age, I scarcely knew what trouble was—the World passed so smoothly on with me—but Oh how changed has been my after years."[7] Britannia did not marry until 1842, so she ran Tudor Place with her mother, and returned again with her daughter Markie Kennon after being widowed in 1846. America Williams's children—especially a second granddaughter named Markie—also spent long periods there. Patty seems to have stayed closed to home, save for visits to church and perhaps to Maryland to see her sons on their farms.

From the controversial annexation of Texas in 1845 onward, the country was in upheaval. Patty might be able to stay clear of politics (although given how few of her letters survive, we can't know for sure), but Nelly and Wash could not. America's most expansionist president to date, James K. Polk, was inaugurated in March 1845, and while he was a protégé of Andrew Jackson, the Custises were not fond of him or his politics. That said, very few were; he was known even within his own party for his blatant dishonesty.[8] Nonetheless, Wash Custis had never missed an inauguration in Washington City, and he likely crossed the Potomac for this one.[9]

As soon as Polk entered the presidency, he started planning to acquire territory from Mexico, no matter what that took. Polk, along with many other Americans, was eager to expand the country's territory beyond the newly acquired territory of Texas. Why not also get California and New Mexico? Polk made a show of diplomacy, but it was clear war was going to be the outcome.[10] While Wash had supported the fight for Texas's independence from Mexico, he never publicly supported Polk's actions in Mexico, which quickly led to war. Army officers like Wash's son-in-law Robert E. Lee eyed Polk and the Democrats' expansion efforts with skepticism. Many Whigs, especially those who rightfully worried that the war was a way to gain new territory to spread slavery, opposed the war, but Polk and the Democrats capitalized on the general public fervor for growing America's empire.[11] Wash certainly shared this fervor, but he also would have known that war with Mexico would mean his army officer son-in-law, nephew William G. Williams, and possibly retired officer Ed Butler would all be put in danger. Nelly and Patty likely shared his concern and gave no sign of eagerness for war.

The family's fears were well-founded. In the winter of 1846, Polk moved troops under Zachary Taylor to territory between the Rio Grande and Nueces River, a region in what is now Texas that Mexico claimed as its own. It was a clear provocation, on top of the recent annexation of Texas, and quickly led to skirmishes between Mexican and American forces. In May, the United States declared war on Mexico. That summer, both Robert E. Lee and William G. Williams traveled to Mexico as army engineers, Lee under Brigadier General Wool's forces and Williams with Taylor.[12] Ed Butler, it seems, was waiting for a commission or felt he could not leave his plantation behind. Both Taylor and the Custises hoped for a speedy end to the war, and Taylor thought his victory in September in the Battle of Monterrey was it: an expanded Texas was now firmly under American control. But that had come at a cost: even Americans who had supported the war were horrified to learn of the mounting casualties, particularly the five hundred at Monterrey.[13] Among those men was Patty's son-in-law William G. Williams, father of five children who had already lost their mother, America, four years earlier.

It took months for the Custises to learn of Williams's death. When Nelly wrote to Molly in December, she was disgusted with how Polk was managing the war but did not yet seem to know about her nephew's death. Already, she thought Polk's prosecution of the war had incurred upon him "more curses loud & deep upon his vile hands than any one else would like to have."[14] Nelly wasn't alone in questioning Polk's strategy, particularly after he shifted most of Taylor's men to a new commanding general, Winfield Scott.[15] The family likely learned about Williams soon after, and in February 1847, Nelly apologized to Williams's eldest daughter Markie for not writing with condolences sooner. She urged Markie to be "a comfort to your aged Grandmother who like myself cannot expect to remain long with her children & you will meet again in Heaven"; had Markie not been deeply religious, this would hardly have been reassuring to a newly orphaned nineteen-year-old. Patty, who had never liked Williams but knew this was a great loss for her grandchildren, counseled Markie to meet the loss with religious resignation.[16]

The danger was not over for the family, however. As the military victories mounted, Polk's ambitions did as well; he wanted all of Mexico's land above the Rio Grande and to invade Mexico itself, so the war continued.[17] Robert E. Lee had shifted to Scott's command and was now one of his most valued officers. He guided the path of troops and gun placements using his skills as an engineer, first finding fame through his careful maneuvering at the Battle of Vera Cruz.[18] As his son-in-law gained national attention, Wash wanted to make sure to link him with the nation's greatest military hero, George Washington. Wash chose a clever way to do this that also drew his own name into the news: he publicized that he was sending Robert a sword George Washington had given to Wash in 1799. Wash was planting the seed of the notion that Robert E. Lee was George Washington's heir in the rising generation.[19]

Nelly was looking towards another man to take up the mantle of George Washington's military legacy. She had become one of Zachary Taylor's many admirers, and she worried about the general left with only a small force against formidable Mexican troops. "A halter for Polk & a scourge for Scott if Taylor is not safe," she proclaimed. In another letter, she acidly referred to the president as "that reptile Polk." She pored over the newspapers seeking information on where Robert was, and she would have come across stories of terrible atrocities American troops committed against Mexican civilians. Could American expansion truly be just and right if this is what it took to accomplish? While the Custises never asked this question in writing, it was one people across the country were confronting.[20]

Still, among some Americans, the war frenzy lived on—including the Butlers, whom Nelly called "Mexico mad" and Ed Butler in particular "deranged." It's unclear why Ed waited so long to join the war effort. But in April 1847, he was appointed a colonel and left Louisiana for Mexico in June, joining American troops who aimed to conquer Mexico City. Parke kept up a regular correspondence with her husband, reporting that their eighteen-year-old son Eddy wanted to be in Mexico with his father and was brandishing a sword, "with which he intended to kill Mexicans—& practices cutting off heads, upon a toy man— until he can obtain more important adversaries."[21] Still, Parke too was reading the newspapers and agreed with her mother; she told her husband that "thousands of our best & bravest, have paid the penalty of our Presidents want of *military* skill."

At home at Arlington with Wash and Molly, Mary Lee was also out of patience with the president. She heard regularly from Robert—although with great delay as mail took time to travel back from Mexico—and learned in the autumn that he was occupying the national palace in Mexico City after the city's fall on September 14. She was grateful for his safety, but she wrote a friend of "the misery this war has occasioned"; even with this latest victory, it was not clear Polk would end the war, because his and his fellow expansionists' desire for more territorial gains kept growing. As she spent time in the city, she regularly heard "the maledictions poured upon the head of our President & his advisers." By this time, there were those who would have been pleased to see Polk dead, including Zachary Taylor, and Nelly thought that if Polk made another misstep, he "should be hung forthwith" from the statue of Thomas Jefferson outside the White House.[22]

But while Polk and some Democrats now had set their sights on conquering all of Mexico, his envoy Nicholas Trist had gone ahead and signed a treaty with the Mexicans at Guadalupe Hidalgo. In July 1848, Polk announced ratification of the treaty, which grew American territory by one third. California, Nevada, Utah, and parts of New Mexico, Arizona, Colorado and Wyoming were now part of the United States; including Texas, this amounted to a staggering half of Mexico's land and was home to around two hundred thousand Native peoples.[23] It was a massive triumph for American expansion, but it had been a controversial war that pitted Whigs and Democrats, anti-war and pro-war

Americans, against one another. Fortunately, both Robert and
Ed returned home safely—Robert having triumphed and made
his name in Mexico. But the upheaval in the Custis family was
not only in a war thousands of miles away; it was happening at
home as well.

The same year war broke out over Mexican territory, there
was a less violent but still passionate fight over the very territory where Wash and Molly lived. For the past decade or so,
residents of Alexandria County—the portion of the District of
Columbia located across the Potomac that had been ceded from
Virginia—had been discussing returning the county to Virginia.
They were tired of not being able to vote for members of Congress or the president (District of Columbia residents could not
vote for president until 1961), and felt they were missing out on
the financial advantages the federal government brought across
the river. They also worried that Northern congressmen would
eventually succeed in their efforts to end slavery in the District.
Alexandria city leaders fought to return to Virginia at both the
national and state level, but not everyone supported the effort;
Wash Custis led the charge of (mostly rural) opponents of retrocession who signed a letter of protest saying the town council
was "disposing of us as so may *swine* in the *market*."[24]

Yet Wash quickly changed his mind. His main point of opposition was whether Virginia would cover Alexandria's debt for
building a canal, and once the state agreed to this, he seems to
have been satisfied. When there were celebrations over retrocession in March 1846, Wash was one of the speakers. He was even
elected as a commissioner to represent the county at the state level
while formal representation arrangements were made. Besides
being one of just two public offices Wash had ever held (he also
served as a justice of the peace for decades), retrocession would
mean that for the first time, Wash could vote in national elections.[25] But for free African Americans in the county—who had

not been allowed to vote in the local retrocession referenda—it meant a shift from the slightly more permissive laws of the District of Columbia to much harsher ones in Virginia.[26]

Just across the river in Washington City, there was growing turmoil over slavery that hit close to home for the Custises. Already there was friction as more and more abolitionist representatives in Congress were horrified to see coffles of enslaved people chained together and marched to market in the city, and the infamous Yellow House slave pens were easily visible just half a mile down the hill from the Capitol.[27] Meanwhile, many representatives from slaveholding states brought enslaved servants with them, including South Carolina congressman John Carter. One of Carter's enslaved servants (and likely also his nephew) Alfred Pope met a fair-skinned enslaved servant owned by Britannia named Hannah Cole. Hannah's mother Barbara was the daughter of one of the enslaved people Patty Peter had inherited from Mount Vernon, and her father was one of Patty Peter's sons. In 1845, Britannia sold Hannah to John Carter so that Hannah and Alfred could be together, and they married in 1847.[28] The Peters, then, had blood ties to the Popes, whether they publicly acknowledged it or not. Just a year later, Alfred Pope would be involved in one of the largest attempted escapes of enslaved people in the country's history.

On April 15, 1848, as residents of Washington City celebrated the triumph of liberty in France's recent revolution, a group of nearly eighty enslaved people quietly left their households and made their way to a ship called the *Pearl* to find freedom. Alfred Pope was among them, but he did not bring Hannah; perhaps Hannah was pregnant or had a newborn, or she simply did not want to leave her mother behind. The *Pearl* was soon captured, and most of the enslavers chose to sell the escaped bondspeople to the Deep South. Alfred Pope was among the lucky few who was able to return home; indeed, he and Hannah were freed at Carter's death two years later. His and his wife's family ties to their enslavers may well have saved them. The city was rocked by the incident, and retribution was swift and drastic. For three nights, from April 18 to 20, proslavery whites vented their fury at the offices of the antislavery newspaper *The National Era*, throwing rocks, giving proslavery speeches, and threatening violence.[29] The whole Custis clan would have been well aware of what was happening from accounts in the local newspapers. The Peters were probably still in touch with Hannah Pope; did they talk to her about what had happened?

For Patty Peter, though, it is unlikely this event made much of an impression; she was again grieving the death of a child. Her son John Parke Custis Peter lived on a plantation he called Montevideo carved out of the Peters' Oakland estate in Montgomery County, Maryland, in a house that looked much like Tudor Place. He owned a quarry that supplied red Seneca sandstone, which was likely quarried by enslaved people and by this time was being shipped down the C&O Canal to Washington City to build the new Smithsonian Institution headquarters. At forty-eight years old and with eight young children, John apparently cut himself on a rusty nail, contracted tetanus, and died. He was buried in the family cemetery on the estate and carried on the family tradition of identifying with George Washington, even in death; his tombstone read, "Great Grandson of Martha, Relict of Washington."[30] Six months later, Patty was grateful that friends had been visiting "to see me in my affliction" and said "the World has lost all Interest to me." Of the ten children she had borne, just two survived: Britannia Peter Kennon and George Washington Peter. Her son—like his sister America—had chosen a spouse Patty disapproved of, so she may have felt that she had lost him in a way, too.[31]

Nelly could sympathize with Patty in her losses. In August 1847, while Nelly was visiting friends, her son Lorenzo fell ill. Nelly rushed home to Audley, where she was "very much shocked" at how sick Lorenzo had suddenly become. Desperate, the family called in five different doctors to treat him, and Mary Custis Lee came to help nurse him, while a minister that was friends with the family came to tend to his soul. But Lorenzo felt he would die, and on August 27, Nelly reported that "he died as an infant sinks to rest."[32] He was just forty-four and left a wife and six sons. Nelly grieved her loss, and she was even more devastated for her grandsons. Unlike her elder sister, though, the world still held great interest—especially when the next presidential election came around.

If the Mexican-American War had taught the Custises one thing, it was this: as Parke said, "I trust never to see any but a *military* man hold the office [of president] again."[33] It's not surprising, then, that when Zachary Taylor became the Whig Party nominee, the Custises were eager to support him. Their enthusiasm wasn't really shared by much of the country; while Taylor was a popular military leader who had seen that his fame on the battlefield might make him electable, he was hardly a politician. As his critics were quick to point out, he had never voted before (this, however, was not a matter of choice but necessity, because he was regularly traveling with the army, and there was no absentee voting available). But Taylor was also curiously silent on policy positions.[34] The choice of someone so apolitical was not entirely unusual at this time; for both parties to keep voters in the North and South happy, they began to run more on leaders' personalities than policy platforms.[35] Wash and Nelly weren't particularly partisan by then (although they aligned more with Whigs than Democrats); they likely would have supported Taylor at the head of either party ticket. Their stepgrandfather and their friend Andrew Jackson were both military men, and they were delighted to have another one to support for president.

Wash stepped up as a regular speaker at Whig campaign events— usually barbecues—in the Washington, DC, area that fall. He gave the same speech over and over: "there was never such demand for a public speaker before, perhaps," one reporter opined. Wash emphasized a startling point: "you will see an old grandfather cast his maiden vote!" He explained why this was—he had wanted to vote, but when Arlington was part of the District of Columbia, he could not. Now that his home was in Virginia, he finally could vote. For his very first vote for president, he considered his choices and looked at what both Taylor and Taylor's opponent Lewis Cass had done for their country. He had chosen "the honest man" and military leader Taylor, and he implied that George Washington would have, too: his vote, he declared, "will hail from the sacred shades of Mount Vernon!"[36]

It had been decades since a particular party or candidate had thoroughly identified itself with George Washington, but Wash pulled it off. One reporter who heard the speech averred, "It seemed as if the immortal George Washington himself was almost speaking to his countrymen." Another reporter noted that Wash "attracted much attention—not for his speaking, but as being a remnant of the Washington family, and a kind of connecting link between the past and present generation." Even those listeners who did not know much about Wash's role in the first "first family" saw in him a relic of the Revolutionary era. His very appearance brought people back in time; the old man's waistcoat and jacket were from an earlier era, and one reporter called him "a hale, fine-looking gentleman of the old time." It was easy to imagine that this old-fashioned gentleman had known George Washington. Accounts of the speech given by the "old man eloquent" were published across the country.[37]

Wash and Nelly were delighted when their chosen candidate won that November, and they saw Taylor as a sort of second coming of George Washington. Nelly said that Zachary Taylor "is to me 'the light of other days,' He is actuated by the same noble principles, the same devoted Patriotism that distinguished The Father of his Country—& he will walk in *his* steps."[38] Wash sent the new president a letter (and probably forwarded a copy to the newspaper, as it appeared in the papers) expressing "his belief that during his administration of the government, he would tread in the footsteps of the immortal Washington."[39] The Custises finally had a friend in the President's House once again, and they were eager to take advantage of it.

Zachary Taylor, for his part, hoped to get to know these fervent supporters with family ties to George Washington. He already knew Parke and Ed Butler from their shared time in Louisiana, and when the Butlers visited him, Taylor wrote a letter to Nelly introducing himself. Wash would first lay eyes on Taylor at his inauguration on March 4, and soon after, Wash visited the White House to introduce himself (an event that, of course, made the newspaper).[40] Before Taylor had even been in office a month, Nelly sent her new friend a patronage request: would he get a commission for Robert E. Lee's son to go to West Point? Mary Custis Lee had asked Polk the year before and gotten nowhere, but with some further prodding from Nelly, Taylor made it happen.[41] Taylor invited Nelly to visit his family at the President's House in late April for a few weeks, and despite her poor health, she was delighted with the opportunity.

In late April, Nelly stayed with Patty for a few days at Tudor Place, then made her temporary home at the President's House. She was so excited at the invitation that she didn't make time to pay a sympathy call on her cousin George Corbin Washington, whose daughter had died just two weeks before and who lived quite close to the Peters. In a rather unusual sympathy letter, she gushed about how delighted she was to visit Taylor— "I can scarcely realize that I am, *indeed* his Guest." She might not make time to visit her grieving cousin, but she did at least pledge to use her influence to try to help George Corbin in his quest to sell the George Washington manuscripts he owned to the government.[42]

Nelly arrived at the White House bearing two baskets of gifts, one with a china bowl (probably a punch bowl) from Mount Vernon and another with items she had sewn for the Taylors, includ-

ing a pair of slippers for the president.[43] She was not disappointed
in her new friend: "his benevolent countenance, his cordial reception, his extreme kindness to me must encrease" the "love
respect & admiration" she already had for Taylor. She also formed
a fast friendship with Taylor's wife, daughter, and son-in-law.[44]
While she had just met the family, she felt she "had known them
all my life." Nelly sat with the president in his office and had
him write and cut out autographs for her, and she may have felt
a swelling of pride when she wrote her old friend George Washington Lafayette with the dateline "President's House." Despite
her celebrity, her time with the Taylors was the first time Nelly
had attended a dinner at the President's House in Washington.
Her time with Taylor brought back memories of her stepgrandfather. "We have, at last, a truly legitimate successor to the Father
of his Country," she wrote, "more truly resembling Washington
in all truly great & noble qualities, than any man on Earth."[45]

Wash also befriended Taylor and continued to build links between Taylor and the first president. He rode with the president
to Richmond for the laying of the cornerstone of the Washington Monument there in February 1850. The following month,
he presented George Washington's portfolio or traveling writing case to Taylor at the President's House on behalf of a cousin.
In typical Wash style, he didn't just stop by and drop off the
relic; he coordinated an event and gave a speech that he knew
would make the newspapers. "May you, sir, with the illustrious
example of the beloved Washington as the polar star to guide
you, grasp with stalwart hand the helm of State," Wash declared.
Taylor replied that he knew that Democratic newspapers had
"ridiculed" his attempts to follow Washington's example, but
he would continue to do so nonetheless.[46]

Taylor's jab at the party press was just one sign that not everybody in Washington, DC, admired "Old Zach" or saw him as
following in George Washington's footsteps. He may have gotten along well with the Custises, but otherwise he wasn't good
at socializing with others in the city. Attendance dropped off at

his levees, and he didn't have the kind of ties with congressmen (or political savvy) that he needed to negotiate the sticky question of handling slavery in the territories gained from Mexico. He opposed Henry Clay's compromise on the issue, which was working its way through the Senate as a package of five laws. Whatever Wash and Nelly thought, Zachary Taylor was no George Washington, and the country was in real peril as several Southern states were starting to consider secession.[47]

A strange turn of fate devastated the Taylors and their new friends the Custises, but it may just have been what kept the country together. On the Fourth of July, over one thousand people attended a ceremony in front of the in-progress Washington Monument on a slight rise of land between the White House and the Capitol. A large stage was set up for dignitaries including the president, his cabinet, members of Congress, and local officials. As the crowd endured the stifling heat of July in DC, Senator Henry Foote gave an hour-long speech, followed by what one commentator derisively called "a tedious supplementary harangue" by Wash Custis. After nearly three hours in the hot sun, Taylor walked back to the White House and tried to cool down by drinking iced water and milk, as well as eating cherries. He was soon crippled by stomach pain, and on July 9, he died of what his doctors concluded was cholera morbus, a general term for intestinal illnesses.[48]

"We were unworthy of him, & the Almighty has removed him from a path strewed with thorns," his friend Nelly concluded. She focused her grief by working on a scrapbook of newspaper articles about "the beloved lamented President."[49] Wash served as a pall bearer at the funeral in Washington, DC, on July 13, which included a hearse drawn by eight white horses and a two-mile-long procession. Around 100,000 grieving citizens turned out to pay their respects.[50] But there was no time to waste when it came to resolving the crisis over the Mexican cession: by late July, Taylor's successor Millard Fillmore and Senator

Stephen Douglas had worked out a plan to get Clay's compromise package through Congress. By the end of September, crisis had been averted and the Compromise of 1850 had passed, setting a tenuous new status quo on slavery. Although Nelly no longer had an ally in the White House, her son-in-law Charles Magill Conrad (who was only a few months into a term in Congress) became Fillmore's Secretary of War.[51] She still had an avenue to influence, but it seems she was ready to leave politics behind.

While Nelly's brief star turn had ended quickly, Wash was still on the rise. He was giving more and more speeches, even as he slowed down physically. With the union of states teetering on the brink of dissolution, Wash devoted much of his focus to national unity (and, of course, George Washington was a potent symbol of that). At a speech at an agricultural fair shortly after the Compromise of 1850 had passed, he asked, "Who dare talk of disunion?... Shall the hateful cry of disunion ring over the grave of Washington?"[52] Despite (or perhaps in some cases because of) such chastisements, his presence as an attendee and/or speaker was in high demand. He was a stand-in for the link between the Revolutionary past and uncertain present. When he attended the annual Washington birthday celebrations, the crowds called for Wash to speak after the main address of the night. His granddaughter Agnes was already exhausted by the time Wash rose to speak at the 1853 celebration. During his speech, she reported, "I counted almost a hundred times they 'Clapped' and finding they never would stop applauding I stopped counting."[53] Wash's speeches continued to be regularly published in newspapers around the country.

Crowds also came to see Wash at Arlington House. Several guidebooks to Washington, DC, included descriptions of it as a site of interest, and multiple newspaper accounts told of visits there. As one writer said, "most persons visiting Washington feel unwilling to leave it until they have seen Arlington." *Harper's Magazine* put a drawing of Arlington House on its cover in 1853, and a cover story by Benson Lossing told of the writer's visit there and included illustrations of the famous

Washington relics in the house.[54] A writer who visited the next year felt that spending time at Arlington with Wash "carries us back to the very life of the times which he eloquently describes."[55] Writers and artists who were creating works about George Washington and his times saw Arlington as a necessary research stop; authors Benjamin Perley Poore, Washington Irving, and Caroline Kirkland as well as artists Thomas Crawford, Junius Brutus Stearns, and Edwin White all visited.[56]

While many visitors came to meet Wash and see the house, plenty never ventured up the steep hill and stayed close to the Potomac River at Arlington Spring. There, a spring bubbled up with cool fresh water at the roots of a large oak tree, and there was a series of wooden buildings to accommodate picnicking and dancing. He regularly sent enslaved servants down to serve guests food and drink, and he often stopped by to chat or even play violin for the visitors, who numbered fifty to two hundred people on warm sunny days.[57] He relished the activity; on the day of a special picnic planned at the spring, Wash's great-niece Markie Williams thought that "never was a girl of sixteen more elated at the prospect of a Ball, than was dear Uncle with this anticipation."[58]

Those who couldn't come to Arlington House often wrote Wash requesting Washington autographs or just clippings of the first president's handwriting. Even Queen Victoria had requested—and of course received—an autograph.[59] He estimated that he received one query every single week. By 1848, he said he was cleaned out of Washington autographs; "The many that I had, are scattered over the face of the civilized globe." He resorted to "cutting up scraps from old accounts" George Washington had kept of the Custis estate. Despite the fact that Markie noted that Wash was "constantly bored with letters from perfect strangers," it's likely that Wash took it in stride as part of the job he had set out for himself as the keeper of Washington's memory.[60]

Wash was also still hard at work recording his memories in writing and paint. In 1852, he declared that he was "now engaged on a magnum opus," an eight-foot-six-inch by six-foot-four-inch canvas of the Surrender of Yorktown. Despite his earlier experience with the public reception of his work, he sent the painting to be displayed in the Rotunda of the Capitol. He said that the work had received praise, but his great-niece Markie marveled at "how deluded he can be, about his pictures." He had stopped writing plays, but he was hoping to have one of his plays produced in New York again in 1854 (he never appears to have succeeded).[61] The "Recollections" that he published in newspapers, usually on Washington's birthday and the Fourth of July, seemed to be his most successful venture. He told his editors in February 1853 that that year's essay would likely be his last, because he was focusing his time on a book compiling the essays.[62] New York–based writer Benson Lossing urged him on, suggesting that Wash set aside his painting and focus on completing the book. "Posterity loves details," Lossing explained, "and in regard to Washington, you, alone, can gratify posterity."[63]

While Wash managed to keep busy gratifying posterity, not everyone in the family was in such hale health. Nelly was entering a steep and uncomfortable decline. In the winter of 1850, she had an "attack of paralysis," and it took two enslaved women to even turn her in her bed. By the following December, she could walk with a cane, but felt "too helpless to be able to enjoy life." She could barely hear, and family members had to speak into a brass ear trumpet to amplify the sound for her. While her mind and memories were still sharp, life had lost its pleasure; she could not even easily write letters to friends and family.[64] But the letters she received, she told her sister-in-law, were "the *cordial drops* in my *existence*." Indeed, letters had become what she lived for; "It appears to me that I only *live* when I receive & read my letters—from letter, to letter, from those I love, my life is really a *blank*."[65]

Yet Nelly was clearly still reading the newspapers and interested in political news, even if it did not animate her as before. She criticized the Whigs for being "so indolent" and letting themselves be pushed around by the Democrats, and she still wanted to be able to help young friends get government appointments—"were my power *equal* to *my will*, *many* should be the better for it." She was intrigued by the visit of Hungarian revolutionary Louis Kossuth, who had come to America to drum up support for Hungarian independence. In Nelly's view, "too many of our Countrymen makes asses of themselves" in their admiration of Kossuth and offers of American aid (none of which came to fruition).[66] Kossuth's argument for American intervention hit a nerve for Nelly because he relied upon a very different understanding of George Washington's farewell address. Suddenly the farewell address was showing up regularly in newspapers and speeches, particularly the section Americans understood to be against intervening in foreign affairs (in actuality, it was against permanent alliances that could draw America into struggles it had no interest in). An Alexandria newspaper published an extract from Wash Custis's "Recollections" under the title "Non Intervention" and the editor noted that the history Wash described "speaks volumes in reference to one of the follies of the present moment."[67]

Like her brother, nothing still stirred Nelly like memories of her stepgrandfather. As he had many years earlier, Alexander Hamilton's son James was now arguing that it was his father who authored the famous farewell address. Nelly was incensed. "Altho, Kossuth may presume to question Washington's policy in regard to intervention &c," she wrote, "He will scarcely turn from the *greater* to the *lesser light*, from Washington to Hamilton to prove *Who* was the *'Master Spirit'* to whom we *owe all we* are, & *all* we may yet become…" She reiterated in multiple letters that she knew for sure her stepgrandfather had authored the address, because she had watched him sew the leaves of paper together before sending it to the printer.[68] She also shared happy memories. On the rare occasions when visitors came to Audley, although she was too ill to eat a meal with them, she offered "a feast of tongue" with stories of the past. When a man whose grandfather had been at the Battle of Princeton visited, "I carried him back 68 years, all that had happen'd since & before, so far as I knew, & shew'd him all the relicks in the house."[69]

After several years of pain and discomfort, however, Nelly's body finally failed in July 1852. Just the month before, she had sensed that she would likely not live much longer, and she wrote her lifelong friend Elizabeth Bordley Gibson of her faith and resignation for what Gibson called "the approaching great change."[70] The decline was sudden. On July 12, something she ate upset her stomach, and within two days she was so weak she could not speak, but she breathed heavily and moaned in pain. Only the sight of her grandsons seemed to bring her relief. One of her half sisters and her daughter-in-law Esther cared for her, and Esther thought "she is resigned, & willing to die, & be at rest, as she told me." That was just as it should have been; in this era, Americans had a specific vision of how to die that emphasized religious resignation and reliance on a better world to come. People generally died with family at their bedside, and Nelly passed with Esther and several grandsons by her side on the night of July 15 at age seventy-four.[71]

The famous Nelly Custis was gone. As she would have wished, her obituary emphasized her relationship to George Washington, noting her fame during his presidency and that her "destinies were of the highest order." Six days later, she was buried in the vault at Mount Vernon next to her daughter Angela. The family erected a gravestone beside the vault with an epitaph Wash had written, noting Nelly's relationship to George Washington and that she was "not more remarkable for the beauty of her person, than the superiority of her mind." Women's tombstones often praised their wifely affection and religious faith, but Wash captured what most distinguished his sister: her intellect. Wash, presumably Molly, Patty, and numerous nieces and nephews traveled by steamboat to Mount Vernon to attend the funeral.[72]

It was likely the last time Molly or Patty ever visited Mount Vernon. Less than a year later, in April 1853, Molly passed after falling suddenly ill. Like Nelly, her family was at her bedside; Patty had rushed to Arlington, Molly's granddaughter Agnes was lying on the bed beside her, and Wash "knelt by her bedside, & implored God to spare her or to make him submissive to His will." Her last words were a softly uttered Lord's Prayer. Several days later, enslaved servants Austin, Lawrence, Daniel, and Ephraim carried her coffin to a grave dug on the Arlington House grounds. Friends and family tossed flowers on the coffin before it was covered in soil.[73]

Wash was despondent; his great-niece Markie Williams moved to Arlington that fall to keep him company, but she found him deeply depressed. "Now... I ought not to be so depressed when I look around me & behold my blessings. There are my children as devoted & kind to me as they can be, my health is being restored,...and my worldly affairs were never so prosperous," he told her, "and yet I am not happy & I feel as if none of these things would make me happy." One day at dinner he even "wished himself dead [and] said he was not fit to live." He did manage to get out to the next Washington's birthday celebration in Alexandria, but he assumed it would be his last and told the crowd that called for him to speak, "I am not what I once was."[74]

But there was still more suffering in store for the family. In mid-June, Markie crossed the Potomac again to Tudor Place, where her grandmother Patty lay dying. Markie, deeply religious herself, prayed at her grandmother's bedside, and Patty's last two words signified her own faithful submission—they were "Prayer" and "Yes." Patty's great-niece Agnes Lee, with the blunt honesty of a thirteen-year-old, recorded of her often severe relation, "We have good reason to believe she went to Heaven for everyone has faults & we could not expect her to be more perfect than the rest of mankind."[75] Patty was buried on the family farm at Oakland and, like Nelly, her obituaries focused on her ties to George Washington. The *Evening Star* published an obituary titled "Nearly the last of the Washington Family," which was reprinted in many papers.[76]

Wash was now truly the "last of the Washington Family," the last person close enough to the first president to have known him so intimately. His health faltered again as he grieved Patty's loss, and at the end of the summer, he was still unsteady. He was unafraid to declare "the days of the Last Relic of Mount Vernon are numbered."[77] Nonetheless, Wash was still in demand and up to satisfying his admirers. President Franklin Pierce, a Democrat from New Hampshire, saw advantage in befriending the famous old man and visited Arlington House several times, as well as inviting Wash to events at the White House. Wash leveraged this connection to again make national news with the gift of another Washington relic: he presented two flags of surrender from Yorktown given to George Washington.[78]

Wash also continued to give speeches, including in the lecture room of the brand-new Smithsonian Institution, for a few events at Mount Vernon, at St. Mary's in Maryland to celebrate the anniversary of the landing of Catholic pilgrims there, and even as far afield as Philadelphia at the United States Agricultural Fair.[79] For all the patriotic triumph of his speeches, focused on the memory and legacy of George Washington, Wash was also deeply concerned about the country's future. When he spoke at an agricultural fair in the fall of 1856—several months after the caning of Charles Sumner on the floor of Congress had escalated the growing rift between North and South—he lamented that "The times…are sadly out of joint." Everyone, he said, should "beware"; "The Constitution, the Union, and the laws, these are the only true ark of safety." At Washington's birthday celebration in February 1857, he again urged loyalty to the Union.[80] But just as the Union was failing, so was Wash's aging body.

In the fall of 1857, Markie reported that Wash "appears more feeble, than I have ever known him." His step was unsteady, and he felt nervous and unable to sleep. When he was invited to speak at the annual US Agricultural Society exhibition in Louisville, he declined, saying, "I am an old relict of a past age, and in the decay of nearly seventy and seven years, I fear for my strength in encountering so long a journey."[81] On September 26, he made it out for one last speech: a dinner hosted by the Mount Vernon Guards for the Continentals.[82] Perhaps the effort was too much;

two weeks later, he fell deeply ill. He resisted going to bed, but the doctor and his family insisted. The doctor diagnosed "a pure case of congestion of the lungs," perhaps meaning pneumonia. His granddaughter Annie wrote her cousin Markie of "her Grandpa's extreme illness," and Markie hurried from Tudor Place to Arlington to be at his bedside. Soon after midnight on October 10, the family was "summoned to take leave of him." He gave them each advice and requested that the family's minister come.

While he had never been deeply religious like his wife, daughter, and great-niece, as he lay dying, he finally had the religious awakening they had all prayed for. Mary seemed relieved that "patient, gentle, humbly as a little child did he implore that mercy which God has promised to the merciful." She "felt that Ministring angels were around him," including her mother Molly "who had so long & so faithfully prayed for him." His granddaughter Agnes's account suggests less complete submission: "when the Doctor poured a little brandy in his mouth 'Don't' he said, 'you know I never liked spirit.'" Nonetheless, she recorded that he went "quietly, peacefully…to his rest."[83] He was seventy-six years old, and he had lived longer than any of his grandparents, parents, or siblings.

Although Wash had passed, he remained in the national spotlight for just a bit longer. His lengthy obituary in the *National Intelligencer* defined Wash's life and career just as he would have liked: as the adopted son of George Washington known "for a more than filial devotion to the memory and character of WASHINGTON." The writer praised Wash for his friendly and welcoming personality and noted that "his departure will awaken universally a profound regret." Popular magazine *Harper's Weekly* published a lengthy illustrated obituary. Both noted his importance as the last surviving member of George Washington's close family. As news of his death spread through newspapers across the country, it seemed that the country was mourning more than the loss of a single person: it was mourning a connection to the Revolutionary past.[84]

Wash's role as a sort of holder of national memory, as much as his personal popularity, accounts for the flood of mourners who poured out of DC across the river to Arlington for his funeral on October 13, 1857. It was a lovely fall day, and "all classes of people" filled every route across the Potomac. There was also an official procession from the city, led by the Washington Light Infantry and followed by "members of the Association of the war of 1812 of the District of Columbia" and the President's Mounted Guard. Mourners filled Arlington House as the family prepared for the burial; Markie escaped outside to gather autumn leaves and flowers to weave into a wreath and place on the coffin. With Reverend Dana of Christ Church in Alexandria officiating, Wash was buried next to his wife Molly.[85]

There was another presence looming over the funeral and Wash's legacy, however. According to William Costin's daughter Harriet, Mary Custis Lee allowed her and one of her sisters to see the man who was likely their uncle in his coffin "when she would permit no one else to see him."[86] Mary did so, Harriet said, because Mary knew about the family relationship, making this the Custises' only recorded recognition of the relationship. Local newspapers also reported that numerous free Black people traveled to Arlington by foot "to be present at the funeral of one who was always to them the kindest of friends," and it may be that many of these people were his mixed-race children, grandchildren, and their communities.[87]

Less than two years after his death, a writer who said he lived just a mile from Arlington House published a letter in the *New York Tribune* claiming that Wash "had fifteen children by his slave women." Frederick Douglass's newspaper noted that while Wash Custis had "no drop of Washington's blood," as the adopted son and representative of "the household of Washington," Wash's sexual exploitation of enslaved women was a "disgrace."[88] Matters were further complicated by the fact that while Wash had freed all of his enslaved people in his will, he had not been as careful as his stepgrandfather in the legal terms, and his executor

Robert E. Lee was in no hurry to emancipate them. His sisters, meanwhile, had emancipated just one enslaved person between them in their wills.[89] But a reckoning was coming, for the Custises and the country.

By the dawn of 1858, then, all the members of the nation's first "first family" were gone. No one still living had dwelled under the same roof with George Washington, sat by his side for tea, watched their children play in his lap. Eliza, Patty, Nelly, and Wash had left behind a large brood of children and grandchildren who had been regaled with their elders' stories of the first president, sat on sofas and ate from dishes from Mount Vernon in their homes, even inherited objects owned by George and Martha Washington. But apart from Robert E. Lee, they were largely private figures, holding on to their ties to the Washington family but not using them to thrust themselves into the spotlight. Who would the extended Custis family be without their matriarchs and patriarch; would they be able to stay united as keepers of the Washington legacy?

At the same time as the Custis descendants might have been questioning their own future, the United States itself was on troubled ground. North and South were pulling farther and farther apart, and it was hard to see how the struggle could be resolved peacefully. A New York newspaper that published its own obituary of Wash noted that the Virginian spoke positively of the North and "insisted on fraternal union" as the key to the nation's continued success.[90] Wash had emphasized this over and over again in the 1850s because that Union was so fragile. George Washington had helped create and worked tirelessly to strengthen that Union, and for the Custises, the Union's failure would be a desecration of their stepgrandfather's memory.[91] As it turned out, the end of the Union would also be the death knell for the Custises' legacies.

Epilogue

SATURDAY, FEBRUARY 21, 1885, WAS BRUTALLY cold and windy, the ground covered in a crust of snow. A large crowd had braved the weather and surrounded the Washington Monument in the District of Columbia. After decades of construction, the monument to the first president was finally ready for its dedication. Under a temporary pavilion at the monument's base, a sea of prominent guests huddled against the cold. Among them were several Washington family members. Not one of them was a Custis.[1]

Indeed, when the coordinator of the dedication ceremony had gone looking for Washington descendants to invite, he had only sought out men and women descended from George Washington's siblings. He was especially interested in finding people with the last name Washington, and he arranged for thirteen men by that name to sit on the floor of the House of Representatives to represent the thirteen colonies and hear the orations that afternoon.[2] Just short of a decade later, a newspaper article titled "The Washington Family To-Day" took a similar approach: to find present-day descendants of Washington, one had to look to his blood relations through his parents' and siblings' lines. In both cases, the Custis descendants are barely a

322 CASSANDRA A. GOOD

footnote: Mary Anna Custis Lee's eldest son was invited to the Washington Monument ceremony but declined, and the later newspaper article names a few Custis descendants briefly in the penultimate paragraph.[3] How had the celebrity of the first family fallen so far?

Much of the responsibility for the Custises' fall lies on the shoulders of the most famous representative of the generation after the grandchildren: Robert E. Lee. Even before he betrayed the United States in the Civil War, public opinion was turning against him and tarnishing the family's reputation. While his wife owned Arlington House after Wash's death, Robert was the executor of the estate, which meant he had to carry out the emancipation of Wash's enslaved people. The will gave Robert five years to do this and stipulated it should only happen after Wash's debts and legacies were paid. This put Robert in a difficult position because Wash had left $10,000 to each of his four granddaughters—as well as nearly $12,000 in unpaid bills. There were ways around this, but Robert was not interested in pursuing them; rather, he went to court to fight the terms of the will so he could raise more money off the enslaved people's labor to enrich his daughters.[4] He did not seem to realize how much public scrutiny he would now be under as the heir to this famous family, and what he did next horrified many members of the public.

Not only did newspapers report that Robert was delaying the emancipation of Wash's enslaved people and holding them in bondage improperly—an assault on the popular perception of George Washington's legacy in itself—but news spread of his mistreatment of the enslaved. Both the enslaved population at Arlington and the public knew that Wash had freed his bondspeople in his will (as George Washington had), and many believed that should happen immediately. Some of the enslaved began to leave Arlington and free themselves, while others simply refused to work. Wash's daughter Mary saw this as "ingratitude & bad conduct" and deplored her father's "injudicious will." Robert would not tolerate this behavior, and he either oversaw or personally administered a brutal whipping and pouring of brine over the backs of several enslaved people who had been caught after attempting to free themselves. This made national news, and the anonymous writer of a letter to the *New York Tribune* on the incident decried it as a desecration of the memories of both Wash Custis and George Washington.[5]

Robert also wanted to make a profit and saw this couldn't happen at Arlington, so he hired out all the able-bodied men and women, some hundreds of miles away. After decades of families being able to stay together at Arlington, by 1860, Lee had split up all but one family.[6] The enslaved people at Arlington, many with deep ties to Mount Vernon and whose parents and grandparents served the first president, were not freed until January 1, 1863. That was the day by which the Virginia court in 1862, interpreting Wash's will, had forced Robert to manumit them. This was (by pure coincidence) the same day the Emancipation Proclamation went into effect, and since Arlington House was controlled by the US Army, historians disagree whether it was this or the court's act that ultimately gave the enslaved people their freedom.[7]

Robert's greatest blow to the family's legacy came with his decision to fight against the nation George Washington had helped to found. While Robert was a Virginian, the choice to join the Confederacy was far from inevitable. President Abraham Lincoln had hoped to make Robert commander of the US forces in the spring of 1861, sending his advisor Francis Preston Blair to extend the offer of the post. Blair "spoke of the looking of the country to him as the representative of the Washington family &c." Robert knew that George Washington and the Constitution itself (not to mention his late father-in-law) would not countenance secession, but he felt a loyalty to Virginia deeper than that of most of his Northern Virginia neighbors and even his family. His wife Mary said she would support him either way, but she took after her father and had made many statements in support of the Union. After learning that Virginia had seceded, Robert resigned from the US Army and accepted a role in the Confederate Army several days later. When he gathered his family together at Arlington to tell them, he said, "I suppose you all think I have done very wrong." Only one person, his daughter Mary Custis Lee, spoke in support of his decision.[8]

Interestingly, the sole personal belonging besides his papers that Robert would keep through the entire war was the sword passed from George Washington to Wash Custis to himself.[9] While the Washington sword might be safe, the "Washington Treasury" of relics long housed at Arlington House was not. Mary Anna Custis Lee resisted leaving her home, declaring in early May 1861, "The zealous patriots who are risking their lives to *preserve* the Union founded by Washington might come & take the granddaughter of his wife from her house & desecrate it... our duty is *plain*, to resist unto death."[10] The risk to her home was shifting her allegiances in the war.

The hilltop site overlooking the capital was too strategic a location for the US Army to leave in the hands of an enemy officer's wife, and Mary soon realized she had no choice but to leave. She packed the Washington relics away in trunks, sending some to Lexington, Virginia, and others to the family home at Ravensworth. The rest, including the collection of canvas and poles that made up Washington's famous Revolutionary War tent, were stored in locked closets, and Mary left the keys with enslaved housekeeper Selina Gray.[11]

Only days after Mary left, the government took over the site and began building fortifications. In December, Selina Gray reported to the general in command that the locked closets had been broken into, and Washington relics were damaged or missing. In response, the government removed them for safekeeping and put them on display at the national museum in the

Patent Office. From the beginning, soldiers described the house as Robert E. Lee's, and while they knew he had married into George Washington's family, there was no mention of Wash.[12] Robert's treachery had erased his father-in-law Wash Custis's name and memory from Arlington.

Practical concerns tinged with vengeance guided the government's next steps. In addition to using Arlington for strategic purposes, the government established a community for bondspeople who had fled slavery to Union lines called Freedman's Village. In the fall of 1863, the US government announced it would sell the estate for unpaid taxes (which was more than a little disingenuous, since the Lees attempted to pay taxes but the tax commissioners insisted Mary had to pay in person, which her health did not allow). The government purchased the property for its own use in January 1864, and Quartermaster General Montgomery Meigs found another use for it: he ordered that fallen US soldiers be buried next to the house on the border of Mary's rose garden. A month later, Arlington officially became a military cemetery. This was doubly useful: it created much-needed burial space because local cemeteries were nearly full, and it ensured the Lees could never return.[13]

However, Robert was not the only Custis descendant to break the family's ties to George Washington's Union. Nelly's son-in-law Charles Magill Conrad represented Louisiana in the Confederate Congress, and both of his sons as well as three sons of Lorenzo's served in the Confederate Army.[14] Parke's sons Edward and Lawrence both joined the Confederate Army, and Edward was killed in November 1861. In the wake of their grief, Parke and her husband worried about their Louisiana home when the US Army entered their neighborhood in late 1862. They asked the commanding officer General Weitzel to protect it, apparently on the grounds of Parke's family connection to George Washington. Weitzel knew "Mrs. Butler was the nearest living relative to the 'Father of his Country,'" and while the troops would not harm the Butlers, he could not promise to spare their house.[15] This was a war, and they were on the wrong side, no matter Parke's ancestry. Many of Patty Peter's descendants also sided with the Confederacy, including Britannia, who preserved Tudor Place by boarding Union officers there under the condition that there was no discussion of the war. Britannia's nephew Orton Williams (Markie's brother) also joined the Confederate Army, and in 1863 he was caught and publicly executed as a spy. The image of his limp body hanging before a crowd of soldiers was on the front page of *Harper's Weekly*.[16]

Even one of George Washington's blood relations, who had so rarely been in the public eye, made news when he died early in the war. The last private owner of Mount Vernon, John Augustine Washington III, had died in September 1861 on a scouting mission while serving under Robert E. Lee. "Our enemies have stamped their attack upon our rights with additional infamy," Robert wrote, "by killing the lineal descendent & representative of him who under the guidance of the Almighty God established them & who by his virtues rendered our republic immortal." Of course George Washington had no direct, lineal descendants; the late Washington III had, however, been the inheritor of Mount Vernon through the traditional lineage of eldest male relations. Northerners, rather than seeing Washington III's death as an attack on the first president's legacy, saw it as just punishment for treason.[17]

Indeed, those loyal to the United States had little sympathy for what the Custis clan had lost after their betrayal of George Washington's legacy. As always, George Washington was a symbol taken up by competing sides, and Southerners, too, had imagined they were following the first president's example by fighting for their independence.[18] But the United States won the war, and it also (at least temporarily) won control of the legacy of George Washington. The Lees would not move back to Arlington, although Mary never gave up trying to regain her home and the Washington relics. She and Robert settled in Lexington, Virginia, where Robert became president of Washington College (now Washington and Lee University). Both his and Mary's health gradually declined, and Robert died in 1870 and Mary three years later.[19] After Robert E. Lee's death in 1870, when one senator suggested moving the thousands of burials from Arlington and returning the estate to the family, there was swift pushback. Someone "allied to the immortal Washington" and "nearly related to the great name," another senator retorted, "should have stood up firmly" and supported the United States. Instead, "he the relative, the immediate connection of the mighty Washington!" had been a leader in the Confederate Army.[20] That stain also followed his wife. Mary Anna Custis Lee, "sole daughter left,/of that stately race," as one poet put it, was an exile from her home; "The blood allied to Washington,/Spurned from the rights *he* gave!" It would be decades before the government compensated Wash Custis's descendants for Arlington and the family regained ownership of the Washington relics.[21]

By the time of the dedication of the Washington Monument in 1885, most of the Custis grandchildren's own children, houses, and relics were gone. Britannia Peter Kennon was Martha Washington's sole surviving great-grandchild, and she remained at Tudor Place, herself a relic of an earlier time and calling herself at the end of her life in 1908 "a Federalist of '76."[22] Tudor Place was the only Custis home still in the family's hands; Woodlawn and Arlington were no longer theirs. The "Washington Treasury" at Arlington had been broken up, and Nelly's grandchildren finally decided to sell their Washington relics. Besides the lure of the cash they could receive, the Lewises thought that "with the separation of the family, the articles will be scattered." Congress appropriated $12,000 for the purchase of the relics, which included various household items from Mount Vernon ranging from dinnerware to mirrors to chairs to the lamp by which (supposedly) George Washington wrote his farewell address.[23] While the relics had been saved, the elderly and retiring Britannia was the only family member with a significant collection of her own. The Custises were no longer the primary keepers of George Washington's legacy.

Perhaps we should not be surprised, then, that the Custises were largely forgotten within a few decades of the grandchildren's deaths. Eliza, Patty, Nelly, and Wash had focused so much on hitching their identities to George Washington that, once that tie was broken, they had left little other personal legacy. Besides, they had never been George Washington's blood relatives; it had been through their own choices and efforts that the nation had known *them*, rather than the many Washington nieces and nephews, as the first president's family. Americans defaulted to a definition of family that they still rely upon today: family was about blood relationships.

That didn't mean that the American public lost interest in Washington's family; to this day, they are interested in presidential descendants. But to be a descendant means being a *blood* descendant, even if your ancestors had little or no personal relationship with the president. In 2008, genealogy company Ancestry.com's chief family historian tracked down the closest male heir to George Washington to answer a question that would have appalled George himself: Who would be king if the first president had become a monarch? This wasn't the first person to go on such a quest; periodicals in 1908, 1951, and 2000 had done the same. The winner this time: Paul Emery Washington, a Texas businessman whose own 2014 obituary noted that he "was the closest descendent of President George Washington."[24] Today, this man's descendants would be able to join the newly formed Society of Presidential Descendants— you can join as direct or collateral descendants, the latter only if you are "related by bloodline, lineage of the president's parents (father and mother)"—but the descendants of the Custis grandchildren could not.[25]

Nor, of course, could the descendants of people Wash Custis fathered in sexually exploitative relationships with enslaved women. A group of these Black descendants has been collaborating with the staff at Arlington House and a small number of white Custis descendants to incorporate their stories into the site's public interpretation. However, Black descendants of Martha Washington do not always want to make those family ties known or pursue DNA research to confirm their relationship with the Custises. Defining who counts as family is a source of agency and power. It's not just opting *into* a family that is a choice—it is also opting *out*. Understandably, some Black descendants do not want to recognize family ties built on sexual violation. Blood descent from the Custises happened by force, and the biological links carry the stains of that pain.[26]

There are many reasons, then, that we lose out when we define our families solely by blood and genes. Not all cultures define their families biologically; Western culture has a particular view of kinship, but not the only one. When we pin family to genetic ties, we exclude not just step-relations like the Custises, but also adoptees, children born through surrogacy, and the many, many people who live and love each other as family but have no blood relationship. In our daily lives, many people experience family as both messier and more expansive than who shares their DNA.[27] But our definitions of family have real consequences, from who can get particular government benefits to who can join prestigious hereditary societies to who shows up in or is erased from family trees. If we imagine families in the past were built only on biology, whose stories are we missing?

The Custises' story is one worth knowing and remembering. We continue to see George Washington as the father of the country, as *our* political father, but few Americans know about the children he raised. From them, we see how family can be built through conscious choices, not just blood. But their unusual saga is not just about family; it is about the United States of

America itself. Their story is America's story in its first century: military triumph and tragedy; democracy and old aristocratic ties; visions of liberty coexisting alongside the horrors of slavery. It is only when we see this fundamentally messy, complex picture of the nation's history that we can understand the work still to be done to achieve America's highest ideals.

Acknowledgments

It is hard to believe that only my name appears on the cover of this book, because it is truly the product of years of collaboration with many, many other people. I have been working on this book since 2011—around a quarter of my life so far—and have been lucky to get to know and even befriend numerous smart and generous scholars in the process.

This book would not have been possible without the support of the staff at Mount Vernon. I am grateful to the Fred W. Smith Library for the Study of George Washington there for two fellowships, where I benefited from the time, space, archives, and expertise of staff. I owe thanks to many at Mount Vernon (some who have moved on to other positions), including James Ambuske, Dawn Bonner, Douglas Bradburn, Kevin Butterfield, Elizabeth Chambers, Susan Doyle, Amanda Isaac, Michele Lee, Stephen McLeod, Sarah Myers, Susan Schoelwer, Dana Stefanelli, and Mary Thompson. And to Adam Erby, Jessie MacLeod, and Samantha Snyder: I cannot thank you enough for answering my constant stream of questions by phone and email over the past several years. Your expertise and friendship have made this project a joy.

This book has been supported by research grants from numerous institutions in addition to Mount Vernon. I also received an Andrew W. Mellon fellowship from the Virginia Museum of History and Culture (VMHC), a Georgian Papers Programme Fellowship from the Omohundro Institute for Early American History & Culture, and a Public Scholar Grant from the National

Endowment for the Humanities (NEH) (any views, findings, conclusions, or recommendations expressed in this publication do not necessarily reflect those of the National Endowment for the Humanities). The NEH funding as well as two course release grants from Marymount University offered essential time to write and revise this manuscript.

The idea for this book started while I was at the University of Pennsylvania, still finishing my dissertation but starting to wonder what had happened to Washington's family. Patrick Spero introduced me to Scott Stephenson, who hired me to do provenance research on several Washington objects in the new Museum of the American Revolution. Hannah Boettcher took over the research from me, and both Scott and Hannah have continued to support my research. At the Library of Congress, a big thank-you to the Manuscript Room staff and Curator of Early American Manuscripts Julie Miller. It has been a pleasure to collaborate with and learn from staff at DC-area historic sites, including Grant Quertermous, Wendy Kail, Rob de Hart, and Haley Wilkinson at Tudor Place; Kimberly Robinson, Erin Coward, Matt Penrod, and Mark Maloy at Arlington House; Susan Berning and Shawn Halifax at Woodlawn; and Callie Stapp at Historic Alexandria.

I offer further thanks to the staff of the many archives and collections I used, especially Jayne Ptolemy at the Clements Library; Jerry Foust at Dumbarton House; Glenn Campbell at Historic Annapolis; Heather Bollinger at the Fairfax County Courthouse; Rebecca Smith at Historic New Orleans; Don Relyea at the Karl C. Harrison Museum of George Washington; Meghan Budinger at Kenmore; Sal Robinson at the Morgan Library; Oliver Walton at the Royal Archives; Lisa Kathleen Graddy, Eleanor Harvey, and Ellen Miles at the Smithsonian Institution; Ellen Clark at the Society of the Cincinnati; John McClure and Frances Pollard at VMHC; and Patricia Hobbs at Washington and Lee. Thanks to Sarah Amundson, Mandy Cooper, Courtney Dalton, Christopher Jones, David McKenzie, Nathan Perl-Rosenthal, and archivists in Special Collections at Louisiana State, Princeton, Tulane, the University of North Carolina, and Yale University for providing digital images of documents. Fellow Washington/Custis family researchers Charlie Clark, Matthew Costello, Chelsea Hansen, John Garrison Marks, David Plater, and Rosemarie Zagarri also shared research materials. Special thanks to David and Rosemarie for many helpful conversations and going above and beyond in sharing archival finds.

I also benefited from receiving materials pre-publication and discussing research questions with documentary editors including Sara Georgini and Sara Martin at the Adams Papers, Michael Woods at the Andrew Jackson Papers, David Hoth and Kathryn Gehred at the Washington Papers, and Michael Cohen at the Zachary Taylor Papers. On a project of this scope, I often relied on the expertise of fellow scholars in areas new to me; thanks to Sari Altschuler, Mark Boonshoft, Scott Casper, Flora Fraser, Janice Hadlow, Michael Hattem, Martha Katz-Hyman, Lindsay Keiter, Wesley Pippinger, Martha Saxton, Marshall Sheetz, Brian Steele, and William G. Thomas.

Many scholars have read and commented on conference papers, articles, and chapter drafts over the years. Thanks to Scott Casper, Michael Cohen, Emily Conroy Krutz, Adam Erby, Lorri Glover, Steve Hammond, Julie Miller, Catherine O'Donnell, Bruce Ragsdale, Brian Rouleau, Honor Sachs, Calvin Schermerhorn, Justin Simard, Mary Thompson, Lisa Wilson, Karin Wulf, Rosemarie Zagarri, the Society for the History of the Early American Republic (SHEAR) Second Book Workshop, the SHEAR Biography Workshop, the Spring 2020 "Early Americanists in Quarantine" crew, my Spring 2021 Omohundro Institute Coffee House group (especially leader Tyson Reeder), and Michael Zuckerman's McNeil Center salon. I was also fortunate to have a great team of reviewers who read and workshopped the entire manuscript for me: Richard Bell, Kathleen Brown,

Richard Godbeer, and Karin Wulf. Their insights helped me to draw out the big-picture arguments and connect with historiography. Special thanks to Rick Bell and Kathy Brown, who line-edited the entire manuscript and made it immeasurably better. Kathy was my PhD advisor and remains a trusted editor, sounding board, and friend.

One of the special pleasures of researching a specific set of people is the chance to work with their descendants. Thanks to Ann Chin, Rob DeButts, Steve Hammond, ZSun-nee Matema, David Plater, and Susan Vogel. Steve is an extraordinary genealogist and activist whose work is truly making change at multiple DC-area historic sites, and I am grateful for the chance to work with him. I also thank Brenda Parker, who has a special gift for understanding ancestors, and the current owner of Eliza Custis's DC "honeymoon house," Mandy Katz, for giving me the chance to see inside.

Numerous friends were part of the research and writing process. A good deal of the work for this book happened while sitting around a table with friends, usually at a coffee shop. Thanks to writing buddies Leigh Johnson, Kate Koppy, Megan McFarlane, Alan Siegel, and Julia Young. Thanks to Erin and Michael McClure and Sarah Meacham in Richmond, Dani Holtz and Craig Franson in Philadelphia, and my aunt Janis Good for hosting me during research trips. Greg Ablavsky and Stephanie Corrigan, Jill Dewitt, Nate and Jane Green, and Beatrice Wayne have talked through ideas and tough questions with me. Also, as I argue in this book, family is not simply a matter of blood relationships, and I am grateful for the love and support of close friends who have come to feel like family.

I wrote this book over the course of a career move, from the Papers of James Monroe at the University of Mary Washington to the history program at Marymount University. I'm indebted to Monroe Papers editor Daniel Preston for teaching me more about early American political history than I ever thought one person could know and making it possible for me to begin my research. At Marymount, thanks to my department chairs and administrators past and present, including Christina Clark, Ariane Economos, Hesham El Rewini, Marnel Niles Goins, Jace Stuckey, and Rita Wong. Because of their support, flexibility, and funding for course releases, I was able to have dedicated time for research and writing over the past several years, and I'm truly grateful. My colleagues in Humanities at Marymount are some of the best people I've met in academia, and I thank them for their support and encouragement. I am particularly grateful to Suzanne Carson for stepping up to cover my classes. Marymount students Noelle Larino and Ashley Swann also provided helpful research assistance.

The move to publishing with a popular press brought in another team of people. Thanks to Rick Bell, Alexis Coe, Doug Egerton, Catherine Kerrison, Tim McGrath, and Megan Kate Nelson for helpful advice, as well as Katie Adams for editing my proposal. My agent Farley Chase instinctively seemed to grasp what I was trying to do with this book and helped find a good home for it. My editor Peter Joseph has given me both the latitude and guidance to write the book I wanted, and his perceptive questions in the editing process helped me know where to flesh out the historical context and where to pull back. Thanks to the whole team at Hanover Square Press, especially editorial assistant Eden Railsback, art director Kathleen Oudit, and copyeditor Jennifer Stimson.

Of course, writing a book about a family brought plenty of chances to reflect on my own relatives and ancestors. I did parallel research on my family's genealogy while writing this book, and it only reinforced how much I am indebted to the wisdom and sacrifices of those who came before me. They were not famous leaders or celebrities, but I carry their imprint nonetheless. My greatest influences, though, have been the family I have grown up with. I am especially indebted to my grandparents

Frieda and Martin Good, who were still alive when I began this book and were always my loving cheerleaders. My parents, Julie and Larry Good, sister Amanda Good and brother-in-law Andrew Chang and now their daughter Emerson, represent all that is best about family: unconditional love, unspoken understanding, and friendship. My gratitude and love for them is boundless.

Key to Notes

People

DBW: David Bailie Warden
EBG: Elizabeth Bordley Gibson
ECC: Eleanor Calvert Custis (later Stuart)
Eliza: Elizabeth "Betsey/Eliza" Parke Custis (Law)
GW: George Washington
GWPC: George Washington "Wash" Parke Custis
JPC: John "Jacky" Parke Custis
MARCL: Mary Anna Randolph Custis Lee
MCP: Martha Custis Peter
MLFC: Mary "Molly" Lee Fitzhugh Custis
MW: Martha Washington
Nelly: Eleanor "Nelly" Parke Custis Lewis
RSC: Rosalie Stier Calvert

Published Papers

Brady: *George Washington's Beautiful Nelly*, ed. Patricia Brady (Columbia, SC: University of South Carolina Press, 1991)

GW Diaries: *The Diaries of George Washington*, ed. Donald Jackson and Dorothy Twohig (Charlottesville, University of Virginia Press, 1976–1979)

GWPC Recollections: George Washington Parke Custis, Mary Randolph Custis Lee, and Benson Lossing, *Recollections and Private Memoirs of Washington* (New York: Deby and Jackson, 1860)

MW Papers: The *Papers of Martha Washington*, ed. The Washington Papers Editors (Charlottesville: University of Virginia Press, 2022)

PGW: The *Papers of George Washington*, ed. W.W. Abbot et al. (Charlottesville: University of Virginia, 1987–)

   RWS: Revolutionary War Series

   CS: Confederation Series

   PS: Presidential Series

   RS: Retirement Series

Archives

AH: Arlington House, National Park Service

DLCCU: Arthur H. and Mary Marden Dean Lafayette Collection, 1520–1973, Cornell University Library, Division of Rare and Manuscript Collections

HNOC: Historic New Orleans Collection

   BFP: Butler Family Papers, MSS 102

LC: Library of Congress

MCHC: Maryland Center for History and Culture

   TLFP: Thomas Law Family Papers

MCWC Diary: Martha "Markie" Custis Williams Carter Diary, AH transcription

MHS: Massachusetts Historical Society

MVLA: Mount Vernon Ladies' Association

   HMC: Historic Manuscript Collection

   PFP: Peter Family Papers

TP: Tudor Place

UVa: University of Virginia, Albert and Shirley Small Special Collections Library

VMHC: Virginia Museum of History and Culture

   MCLP: Mary Custis Lee Papers

Endnotes

Prologue

1. On the Savage portrait and prints, *see* Scott Casper, "First First Family: Seventy Years with Edward Savage's 'The Washington Family,'" *Imprint: Journal of the American Historical Print Collectors Society* 24, no. 2 (October 1999): 2–15; François Furstenberg, *In the Name of the Father: Washington's Legacy, Slavery, and the Making of a Nation* (New York: Penguin Press, 2006), 76–78; Jennifer Van Horn, *Portraits of Resistance: Activating Art During Slavery* (New Haven: Yale University Press, 2022), 76–118; Ellen Miles, *American Paintings of the Eighteenth Century* (Washington, DC: National Gallery of Art, 1995), 146–156; Wendy Wick Reaves, *George Washington, an American Icon: The Eighteenth-Century Graphic Portraits* (Charlottesville: Smithsonian Institution Traveling Exhibition Service and the National Portrait Gallery, 1982), 40–44. On the presidential home on Cherry Street, *see* Henry B. Hoffman, "President Washington's Cherry Street Residence," *The New-York Historical Society Quarterly Bulletin* 23, no. 3 (July 1939): 90–103.

2. Gouverneur Morris, "An Oration," in *Eulogies and Orations on the Life and Death of General George Washington, First President of the United States of America* (Boston: Manning & Loring, 1800).

3. The family tree was compiled by the late John Washington of Bethesda, MD.

4. Patricia Brady, *Martha Washington: An American Life* (New York: Viking, 2005), chap. 2–4; Flora Fraser, *The Washingtons*, chap. 2–4. Technically, Martha had a life interest in, rather than ownership of, one third of her late husband's enslaved people; *see* Mary V. Thompson, *"The Only Unavoidable Subject of Regret,"* 13.

5. On GW's relationship with JPC, *see eg* Fraser, *The Washingtons*, chap. 8; Lorri Glover, *Founders as Fathers: The Private Lives and Politics of the American Revolutionaries* (New Haven: Yale University Press, 2014), passim. Quotes from GW to Jonathan Boucher, 30 May 1768, 16 December 1770; GW to Burwell Bassett, 20 June 1773, *PGW-Colonial Series*, vol. 8: 89, 411; vol. 9: 243.

6. Fraser, *The Washingtons*, 80–83, 89–90; Lisa Wilson, *A History of Step-families in Early America* (Chapel Hill: University of North Carolina Press, 2014).

7. On adoption, *see* Michael Grossberg, *Governing the Hearth: Law and the Family in Nineteenth-Century America* (Chapel Hill: University of North Carolina Press, 1985), 268–276. On definitions of family and the focus on blood relationships, *see* Cassandra Good, "Defining the Family of Washington: Meaning, Blood, and Power in the New American Nation," *Journal of Social History*, 55, no. 4 (June 1, 2022): 899–924. I recognize that descendants of a man named West Ford argue that George Washington was his father, but the currently available historical evidence points to Ford's father as being Bushrod Washington, Bushrod's father, or one of Bushrod's two younger brothers. Most historians believe that George Washington was sterile; he might have sexually exploited enslaved women, but this would not have resulted in children. *See* Jill Abramson, "Did George Washington Have an Enslaved Son?" *The New Yorker*, March 7, 2022, https://www.newyorker.com/magazine/2022/03/14/did-george-washington-have-an-enslaved-son.

8. For the names of the nephews and nieces, *see* Family Trees. On Bushrod Washington, *see* David Leslie Annis, "Mr. Bushrod Washington, Supreme Court Justice on the Marshall Court" (PhD Diss., University of Notre Dame, 1974); Gerard N. Magliocca, *Washington's Heir: The Life of Justice Bushrod Washington* (New York: Oxford University Press, 2022).

9. As Jan Lewis writes, "Every family is two families. First, there are those who are born into it, marry into it, and give birth to its children… Then there are those who think of themselves as the real family—those who write its family story." Jan Ellen Lewis, "The White Jeffersons," in *Family, Slavery, and Love in the Early American Republic: The Essays of Jan Ellen Lewis*, ed. Barry Bienstock, Annette Gordon-Reed, and Peter S. Onuf (Chapel Hill: Omohundro Institute and University of North Carolina Press, 2021), 357–358.

10. For Bushrod Washington's obituary, *see Philadelphia Sentinel*, November 27, 1829. On John Augustine Washington II and III, *see* Carol Borchert Cadou, ed., *Stewards of Memory: The Past, Present, and Future of Historic Preservation at George Washington's Mount Vernon* (Charlottesville: University of Virginia Press, 2018), passim; Scott E. Casper, *Sarah Johnson's Mount Vernon: The Forgotten History of an American Shrine* (New York: Hill and Wang, 2008), passim; John Walter Wayland, *The Washingtons and Their Homes* (Staunton, VA: McClure Printing Company, 1944), chap. 14.

11. On the concepts of fame and celebrity in early America, *see* Leo Braudy, *The Frenzy of Renown: Fame & Its History* (New York: Vintage Books, 1997), part V; Carolyn Eastman, *The Strange Genius of Mr. O: The World*

of the United States' First Forgotten Celebrity (Chapel Hill: University of North Carolina Press, 2021), esp. 129; Páraic Finnerty and Rod Rosenquist, "Transatlantic Celebrity: European Fame in Nineteenth-Century America," *Comparative American Studies An International Journal* 14, no. 1 (January 2, 2016): 1–6; Charlene M. Boyer Lewis, *Elizabeth Patterson Bonaparte: An American Aristocrat in the Early Republic* (Philadelphia: University of Pennsylvania Press, 2012), 121; Sharon Marcus, *The Drama of Celebrity* (Princeton: Princeton University Press, 2020); Bonnie Carr O'Neill, *Literary Celebrity and Public Life in the Nineteenth-Century United States* (Athens: University of Georgia Press, 2017), esp. 3–4; Kenneth T. Walsh, *Celebrity in Chief: A History of the Presidents and the Culture of Stardom* (New York: Routledge, 2015), esp. 13, 18. For the quote, *see* Walsh, 13.

12. Casper, "First First Family," 7; Furstenberg, *In the Name of the Father*, 90–91. While the enslaved man in the background of the original portrait likely represented William Lee, Casper argues that he was modeled on a free Black servant in London, where Savage worked on the painting (Casper, 2).

13. The only joint biography of the siblings is a short book by Elswyth Thane in 1968 titled *The Mount Vernon Family* (New York: Crowell-Collier Press); Thane was not a trained historian, and the book contains no citations. For broader family biographies, *see also* Miriam Anne Bourne, *First Family: George Washington and His Intimate Relations* (New York: Norton, 1982); James B. Lynch (Jr.), *The Custis Chronicles: The Virginia Generations* (Camden, ME: Picton Press, 1997). There have been no scholarly articles or books on Eliza or Patty. Nelly is better known among historians because of the edited volume of her correspondence, Patricia Brady, ed., *George Washington's Beautiful Nelly: The Letters of Eleanor Parke Custis Lewis to Elizabeth Bordley Gibson, 1794–1851* (Columbia, SC: University of South Carolina Press, 1991). There is also a brief biography of her; David L. Ribblett, *Nelly Custis: Child of Mount Vernon* (Mount Vernon, VA: Mount Vernon Ladies' Association, 1993). GWPC features prominently in two works: Murray H. Nelligan, *Arlington House: The Story of the Robert E. Lee Memorial* (Burke, VA: Chatelaine Press, 2002); Elizabeth Brown Pryor, *Reading the Man: A Portrait of Robert E. Lee through His Private Letters* (New York: Penguin Books, 2008). Biographical works on GWPC include Sara Bearss, "The Farmer of Arlington: George W. P. Custis and the Arlington Sheep Shearings," *Virginia Cavalcade* 38, no. 3 (Winter 1989): 124–133; Seth C. Bruggeman, "'More than Ordinary Patriotism': Living History in the Memory Work of George Washington Parke Custis," in *Remembering the Revolution: Memory, History, and Nation Making from Independence to the Civil War*, ed. Michael A. McDonnell et al. (Amherst:

University of Massachusetts Press, 2013), 127–143; Charles S. Clark, *George Washington Parke Custis: A Rarefied Life in America's First Family* (Jefferson, NC: McFarland, 2021). All of these sources have been essential references for this book.

Chapter 1

1. JPC to MW, 21 August 1776, *MW Papers*, 115–116; James Thomas Flexner, *Washington: The Indispensable Man* (Boston: Little, Brown and Company, 1974), 79–80.

2. General Orders, 20 August 1776, *PGW-RWS*, 6: 88. *See* other orders from this time for his activities. On his stay in Richmond Hill, *see* Flora Fraser, *The Washingtons*, 141–142.

3. Patricia Brady, *Martha Washington: An American Life* (New York: Viking, 2005), 111–112.

4. MW to Anna Maria Bassett, 18 Nov 1777; MW to Mercy Otis Warren, 3 March 1778; JPC to MW, 3 April 1778, *MW Papers*, 122, 126.

5. As of late 1771 or early 1772, there were 217 enslaved people on the southeastern Custis estates. "List of Slaves Belonging to George Washington and John Parke Custis, December 1771," *PGW-CS*, 8: 587–592.

6. Eliza to DBW, 20 April 1808, in William Hoyt, "Self-Portrait: Eliza Custis, 1808," *Virginia Magazine of History and Biography* 53, no. 2 (April 1945): 91.

7. GW to JPC, 26 May 1778, JPC to GW, 15 July 1778, GW to JPC, 3 August 1778, in *PGW-RWS*, 15: 225, 16: 77, 230–232. The financial terms are best described in Sara Bearss, "John Parke Custis," *Encyclopedia of Virginia*, https://encyclopediavirginia.org/entries/custis-john-parke-1754-1781/.

8. JPC to MW, 3 April 1778, *MW Papers*, 126. Virginia technically had a residency requirement but, as in other colonies with such a requirement, did not always enforce it. George Washington himself had been living in Fairfax County and elected to the House of Burgesses in Frederick County, where he also owned property. There are also documented cases in several colonies, including Virginia, of men being elected to the legislature from two different counties. *See* Peverill Squire, *The Rise of the Representative* (Ann Arbor: University of Michigan Press, 2017), 38–51; Charles S. Sydnor, *Gentlemen Freeholders: Political Practices in Washington's Virginia* (Chapel Hill: Omohundro Institute and University of North Carolina Press, 1952), 70.

9. Mark Walker et al., "Phase II Archaeological Study: Abingdon Plantation Site, Washington National Airport" (Parsons Management Consultants, 1989), Figure 10; Inventory of John Parke Custis, Fairfax

County Will Book D 1772–1783 p. 274–288; Hoyt, "Self-Portrait: Eliza Custis, 1808," 93–94.

10. MARCL writes in her introduction to her father's recollections that Nelly was nursed by an Englishwoman named "Mrs. Anderson," but Anderson did not arrive at Mount Vernon until the late 1790s (GWPC Recollections, 39). On James Anderson, *see* https://www.mountvernon.org/library/digitalhistory/digital-encyclopedia/article/james-anderson/). Nelly's own account in 1797 is that she was "put out to nurse at the union farm," then called Ferry Farm, just south of Mount Vernon; Eleanor Parke Custis, "History of my birth and parentage addressed to all whom it may concern," [August 1797], DLCCU (hereafter Nelly autobio, 1797, DLCCU). Molly or Moll was a Custis bondswoman whom MW had brought to Mount Vernon in 1759. *See* Hoyt, 96–97; "Appendix C. List of Artisans and Household Slaves in the Estate, c. 1759," entry for "Moll," *PGW-CS*, 6: 282. The annuity of $525/year is recorded in the Custis guardian accounts; *see* JPC Estate Account with David Stuart, Fairfax County Courthouse, Willbook G-1, photostat at MVLA.

11. Alice Coyle Torbert, *Eleanor Calvert and Her Circle* (New York: William-Frederick Press, 1950), 34–35; Hoyt, "Self-Portrait: Eliza Custis, 1808," 93.

12. JPC to GW, 12 December 1779, *PGW-RWS*, 23: 580; Bearss, "John Parke Custis," *Encyclopedia of Virginia*; Hoyt, "Self-Portrait: Eliza Custis, 1808," 95.

13. For a detailed discussion of Costin's ancestry, *see* Cassandra Good, "Ancestry of William Costin," https://www.mountvernon.org/library/digitalhistory/digital-encyclopedia/article/ancestry-of-william-costin/.

14. JPC to MW, 12 October 1781, *MW Papers*, 138; Cassandra Pybus, *Epic Journeys of Freedom: Runaway Slaves of the American Revolution and Their Global Quest for Liberty* (Boston: Beacon Press, 2006), 53; Mary V. Thompson, *"The Only Unavoidable Subject of Regret,"* 278–281.

15. Elizabeth A. Fenn, *Pox Americana: The Great Smallpox Epidemic of 1775–82* (New York: Macmillan, 2002), 269; Fraser, *The Washingtons*, 251–255.

16. Hoyt, "Self-Portrait: Eliza Custis, 1808," 96–97.

17. *See eg* John R. Gillis, *A World of Their Own Making: Myth, Ritual, and the Quest for Family Values* (New York: Basic Books, 1996), 10–15; Daniel Blake Smith, *Inside the Great House: Planter Family Life in Eighteenth-Century Chesapeake Society* (Ithaca: Cornell University Press, 1986), 51, 53; Naomi Tadmor, *Family and Friends in Eighteenth-Century England: Household, Kinship, and Patronage* (New York: Cambridge University Press, 2001), 34–35.

18. Nelly autobio, 1797, DLCCU. It is unclear exactly when the Washingtons made the arrangement to raise the children; while Nelly suggested

that she had been sent to Mount Vernon immediately after her father's death, GW and MW were still away from Mount Vernon part of the year at army headquarters until late 1783.

19.   Hoyt, "Self-Portrait: Eliza Custis, 1808," 96–97.

20.   *See* Dandridge to GW, 7 Jan, 22 Feb, 20 March, 13 May; GW to Dandridge, 20 April, 25 June 1782, Papers of George Washington, LC. The legal guardian served as a trustee for the Custis estates and did not need to be involved in the day-to-day parenting of the children.

21.   ECC to Jacob Read, 31 January 1783, HMC, MVLA; Fanny Bassett Washington to George Augustine Washington, 1 September 1783, HMC, MVLA; Hoyt, "Self-Portrait: Eliza Custis, 1808," 96; Camille Noel, "David Stuart," in *Digital Encyclopedia of George Washington*, n.d., https://www.mountvernon.org/library/digitalhistory/digital-encyclopedia/article/david-stuart-1753-1814/; Ruth P. Rose, "Dr. David Stuart: Friend and Confidant of George Washington," *Northern Virginia Heritage* 10, no. 1 (January 1988): 9.

22.   Lafayette to Adrienne de La Fayette, 20 August 1784, in Idzerda, *Lafayette Papers*, 5: 237–238; GW to William Gordon, 3 November 1784; Jean Le Mayeur to GW, 14 August 1784; GW to Le Mayeur, 30 August 1784, in *PGW-CS*, 2: 38, 65, 116–117.

23.   *GW Diaries*, 4: 72, 206; *PGW-PS*, 5: 310; GW to Mary Washington, 15 Feb 1787, *PGW-CS*, 5: 53; Winslow C. Watson, ed., *Men and Times of the Revolution; or, Memoirs of Elkanah Watson* (New York: Dana and Co., 1856), 243.

24.   1786 list of enslaved people, in *GW Diaries*, 4: 276–283; Dunbar, *Never Caught*, 13, 111.

25.   Robert F. Dalzell Jr. and Lee Baldwin Dalzell, *George Washington's Mount Vernon: At Home In Revolutionary America* (New York: Oxford University Press, 2000), 113–124; Adam Erby, "Designing the Beautiful," in *The General in the Garden: George Washington's Landscape at Mount Vernon*, ed. Susan P. Schoelwer (Charlottesville: University of Virginia Press, 2015).

26.   GW to William Gordon, 8 March 1785; GW to Catharine Macaulay Graham, 10 January 1786; *PGW-CS*, 2: 413, 3: 502. The first tutor, William Shaw, stayed for a year but was not a good fit; *see* Brady, *Martha Washington: An American Life*, 149. On Northern tutors in the South, *see* Elizabeth Brown Pryor, "An Anomalous Person: The Northern Tutor in Plantation Society, 1773–1860," *Journal of Southern History* 47, no. 3 (1981): 363–392.

27.   Nelly to EBG, 16 March 1851, EBG Collection, MVLA; Stuart Accounts with JPC Estates, to John Kelly, 1787 and 1788, MVLA; to John Kelly, 1787 and 1788, George Washington Financial Papers, Ledger B, 1772–1793, pg 248, 275, http://financial.gwpapers.org/.

28. Hoyt, "Self-Portrait: Eliza Custis, 1808," 96–97.

29. Richard Beeman, *Plain, Honest Men: The Making of the American Constitution* (New York: Random House, 2010), eg 56, 401; Douglas Southall Freeman, *George Washington: A Biography*, vol. 6, *Patriot and President* (New York: Charles Scribner's Sons, 1954), 78–85.

30. Freeman, *George Washington*, vol. 6, 110–117, 145–151.

31. John Adams to Thomas Jefferson, 9 October 1787, *Papers of Thomas Jefferson* (hereafter *PTJ*), 12: 220–221; *Massachusetts Centinel*, 26 March 1788; reprinted in *Pennsylvania Journal*, 9 April; *Maryland Journal*, 15 April; *Maryland Gazette*, 15 April; *Virginia Independent Chronicle*, 23 April; *Virginia Centinel*, 30 April. *See also* Cassandra Good, "Defining the Family of Washington: Meaning, Blood, and Power in the New American Nation," *Journal of Social History* 55, no. 4 (June 1, 2022): 899–924.

32. GWPC to Elizabeth Powel, 17 January 1788, HMC, MVLA; Freeman, *George Washington*, vol. 6, 139.

33. *GW Diaries*, 5: 440; Torbert, *Eleanor Calvert and Her Circle*, 55; Freeman, *George Washington*, vol. 6: 157.

34. GW to Henry Knox, 1 April 1789, *PGW-PS*, 2: 2.

35. Address by Charles Thomson; "Washington's Address to Charles Thomson," 14 April 1789, *PGW-PS*, 2: 54–57; *GW Diaries*, 5: 445.

36. Hoyt, "Self-Portrait: Eliza Custis, 1808," 99.

37. ECC to Tobias Lear, 7 February and [September] 1790, PFP, MVLA; 18 April, HMC, MVLA.

38. Dunbar, *Never Caught*, 26–29.

39. Robert Lewis's Journal, 13–20 May 1789, HMC, MVLA; Dunbar, 23–24; Hoyt, "Self-Portrait: Eliza Custis, 1808," 99.

40. MW to Fanny Bassett Washington, 8 June 1789, *MW Papers*, 187.

41. Thomas Edward Vermilye Smith, *The City of New York in the Year of Washington's Inauguration, 1789* (New York: A. D. F. Randolph, 1889), 5, 7, 44.

42. The white servants included "the coachmen, Jacob Jacobus; two footmen, Fides Imhoff and James Howard; porter, James Hurley, houseman, Henry Rhemur; besides the steward, cook, and the 'valet de chambre.' There were also generally two housemaids, two kitchen maids, and two 'washers.'" (Stephen Decatur, *Private Affairs of George Washington, from the Records and Accounts of Tobias Lear* (Boston: Houghton Mifflin Company, 1933), 12–13). The secretaries were David Humphreys, Tobias Lear, William Jackson, Thomas Nelson, and Robert Lewis (*GW Diaries*, 6: 4). On the house, *see* Henry B. Hoffman, "President Washington's Cherry Street Residence," *The New-York Historical Society Quarterly Bulletin* 23, no. 3 (July 1939): 90–103.

43. MW to Fanny Bassett Washington, 8 June 1789, *MW Papers*, 187; Wil-

liam Duer, "New-York in Olden Time," *Home Journal* (New York), 4 August 1849.

44. GWPC would attend Patrick Murdoch's school, while Nelly went to Isabella Graham's, where Graham advertised teaching "reading, english, Spelling and Grammar, Plainwork, Embroidery, Cloathwork, and various works of fancy, Writing, Arithmetic, Geography, Drawing, Painting, Japanning, Philigree, Music, Dancing, and the French language"; *see* Decatur, *Private Affairs of George Washington, from the Records and Accounts of Tobias Lear*, 33, 86, 87, 102.

45. Decatur, 27, 34, 62. George's illness was diagnosed as anthrax, but it may have been a staph infection that caused an abscess; *see* Jeanne E. Abrams, *Revolutionary Medicine: The Founding Fathers and Mothers in Sickness and in Health* (New York: NYU Press, 2015), 63–64.

46. John Fanning Watson, *Annals and Occurrences of New York City and State in the Olden Time* (Philadelphia: Henry F. Anners, 1846), 301.

47. *GW Diaries*, 5: 506; Decatur, *Private Affairs of George Washington, from the Records and Accounts of Tobias Lear*, 12, 101.

48. Fraser, *The Washingtons*, chap. 25; GW to Bushrod Washington, 27 July 1789, *PGW-PS*, 3: 334.

49. Martha Saxton, *The Widow Washington: The Life of Mary Washington* (New York: Farrar, Straus and Giroux, 2019), 284–286; David Stuart to GW, 12 Sept 1789; GW and Martha to David Stuart, 21 Sept 1789, *PGW-PS*, 4: 27, 64–65. The northern tract would later become Arlington House.

50. ECC to Tobias Lear, 8 July, 8 October 1789, HMC, MVLA; 7 February 1790, PFP, MVLA.

51. Elizabeth Bryant Johnston, *George Washington Day by Day* (Washington, DC, 1894), 11, 45.

52. There is very little scholarship on the "first family"; one exception, which does not explore the origin of the term, is Robert P. Watson, ed., *Life in the White House: A Social History of the First Family and the President's House* (Albany: SUNY Press, 2012). Matthew Costello notes that "first lady" came into popular use with Frances Cleveland in 1893; *see* Matthew Costello, "The Origins of the American 'First Lady,'" https://www.whitehousehistory.org/the-origins-of-the-american-first-lady. My search of historical newspapers revealed that "first family" as applying to the president's family appears around the same time, beginning in 1888; it was used previously to denote the most prominent family in a particular area. Costello of the White House Historical Association finds that the term was not widely used until the 1960s with the Kennedy family (email correspondence, July 6, 2022).

53. Historians argue that it was in fact only with George III that the royal family became a subject of popular attention and admiration; *see* Linda

Colley, "The Apotheosis of George III: Loyalty, Royalty and the British Nation 1760–1820," *Past & Present*, no. 102 (1984): 94–129; Virginia McKendry, "Taming the Sovereign: Princess Charlotte of Wales and the Rhetoric of Gender," in *Strategic Imaginations: Women and the Gender of Sovereignty in European Culture*, ed. Anke Gilleir and Aude Defurne (Leuven: Leuven University Press, 2020), 255–290; Marilyn Morris, "The Royal Family and Family Values in Late Eighteenth-Century England," *Journal of Family History* 21, no. 4 (October 1, 1996): 519–532. For examples of colonial American mentions of the royal family, *see eg* Benjamin West, ed., *Mein and Fleeming's Massachusetts Register, with an Almanack for the Year MDCCLXVII: Being the Third after Leap Year, and One of the Julian Period 6480. Calculated for the Meridian of Boston* (Boston: Printed by Mein and Fleeming, and to be sold by Mein at the London Bookstore. North-side of King-Street, 1767); Thomas Pownall, ed., *By His Excellency Thomas Pownall, Esq;... A Proclamation for a General Fast* (Boston: Printed by John Draper, printer to His Excellency the governor and the Honorable His Majesty's Council, 1760).

54. Marcus Cunliffe, "The Two Georges: The President and the King," *American Studies International* 24, no. 2 (1986): 53–73; Eric Nelson, *The Royalist Revolution: Monarchy and the American Founding* (Cambridge: The Belknap Press of Harvard University, 2014), epilogue; Frank Prochaska, *The Eagle and the Crown: Americans and the British Monarchy* (New Haven, CT, London: Yale University Press, 2008), chap. 1–2, quotes p. 19, 20; William E. Scheuerman, "American Kingship? Monarchical Origins of Modern Presidentialism," *Polity* 37, no. 1 (2005): 24–53.

55. Jan Ellen Lewis, "'The Blessings of Domestic Society': Thomas Jefferson's Family and the Transformation of American Politics," in *Family, Slavery, and Love in the Early American Republic*, 331. For a post-Independence almanac with such a listing, *see eg* Samuel Mott, ed., *The Federal Almanac, and Ephemeris...for the Year of Our Lord, 1791* (New Brunswick, NJ: Printed by Abraham Blauvelt, 1790).

56. *Gazette of the United States* (New York), 8 July 1789; MCWC Diary, 7 March 1856.

57. John Adams to Benjamin Rush, 21 June 1811, quoted in Braudy, *The Frenzy of Renown: Fame & Its History*, 457. On GW's self-fashioning and role as a celebrity and a symbol, *see* Paul K. Longmore, *The Invention of George Washington* (Charlottesville: University Press of Virginia, 1999); Barry Schwartz, *George Washington: The Making of an American Symbol* (New York: Free Press, 1987), esp. 188; Kenneth T. Walsh, *Celebrity in Chief*, 18.

58. Decatur, *Private Affairs of George Washington, from the Records and Accounts of Tobias Lear*, 118, 147; Johnston, *George Washington Day by Day*,

45; Smith, *The City of New York in the Year of Washington's Inauguration, 1789*, 24–27.

59. ECC Stuart to Lear, 18 April 1790, HMC, MVLA.

60. Judith Sargent Murray to Winthrop and Judith Sargent, 14 August 1790, in Judith Sargent Murray, *From Gloucester to Philadelphia in 1790: Observations, Anecdotes, and Thoughts from the 18th-Century Letters of Judith Sargent Murray*, ed. Bonnie Hurd Smith (Cambridge: Judith Sargent Murray Society, 1998), 249.

61. On the Residence Act, which settled that the capital would move to Philadelphia for ten years while a new capital was built on the Potomac, *see eg* Kenneth R. Bowling, *The Creation of Washington, D.C.: The Idea and Location of the American Capital* (Fairfax, VA: George Mason University Press, 1991), esp. 6, 8, 164–169, chap. 7; Robert P. Watson, *George Washington's Final Battle: The Epic Struggle to Build a Capital City and a Nation* (Washington, DC: Georgetown University Press, 2021), chap. 10–19.

62. Ellis Paxson Oberholtzer, *Philadelphia: A History of the City and Its People, A Record of 225 Years* (Philadelphia: S.J. Clarke Publishing, 1912), 1: 382, 383, 390–392; François-Alexandre-Frédéric duc de La Rochefoucauld-Liancourt, *Travels through the United States of North America: The Country of the Iroquois, and Upper Canada, in the Years 1795, 1796, and 1797*, Second Edition (London: R. Phillips, 1800), 4: 91–92, 100–101; Henry Wansey, *The Journal of an Excursion to the United States of North America in the Summer of 1794* (Salisbury, UK: J. Easton, 1796), 155, 184.

63. Dunbar, *Never Caught*, 54, 77–79; Gary B. Nash, *Forging Freedom: The Formation of Philadelphia's Black Community, 1720–1840* (Cambridge: Harvard University Press, 1988), chap. 2 and 3. On free Black people in New York City, *see* Leslie M. Harris, *In the Shadow of Slavery: African Americans in New York City, 1626–1863* (University of Chicago Press, 2004), 56.

64. William Parker Cutler and Julia Perkins Cutler, eds., *Life, Journals and Correspondence of Rev. Manasseh Cutler, LL.D.* (Cincinnati: R. Clarke, 1888), 271–272.

65. Dunbar, *Never Caught*, 71.

66. Dunbar, 55–56, chap. 5; Edward Lawler, "The President's House in Philadelphia: The Rediscovery of a Lost Landmark," *Pennsylvania Magazine of History and Biography* 126, no. 1 (January 2002): 44–45. Benjamin Lincoln Lear was born in March 1791 (*PGW-PS*, 9: 25n5).

67. Lawler, "The President's House in Philadelphia." On urban architecture in this period more generally, *see* Bernard L. Herman, *Town House: Architecture and Material Life in the Early American City, 1780–1830* (Chapel Hill: University of North Carolina Press, 2012).

68. Catherine Kerrison, *Jefferson's Daughters: Three Sisters, White and Black, in a Young America* (New York: Random House, 2019), 147.

69. Fraser, *The Washingtons*, 294.

70. Nelly autobio, 1797, DLCCU.

71. Dunbar, *Never Caught*, 57.

72. Tobias Lear to David Humphreys, 12 April 1791, MVLA (copy from the Rosenbach Library). On white children and mastery over the enslaved, *see eg* Lorri Glover, *Southern Sons: Becoming Men in the New Nation* (Baltimore: Johns Hopkins University Press, 2007), 33.

73. Joanne Bailey, *Parenting in England 1760–1830: Emotion, Identity, and Generation* (Oxford: Oxford University Press, 2012), chap. 3; Glover, *Southern Sons*, 23–33; Daniel Blake Smith, "Autonomy and Affection: Parents and Children in Eighteenth-Century Chesapeake Families," in *Growing up in America: Children in Historical Perspective*, ed. N. Ray Hiner and Joseph M. Hawes (Urbana: University of Illinois Press, 1985), 45–60.

74. ECC Stuart to Tobias Lear, September 1790, MVLA; Tobias Lear to David Humphreys, 12 April 1791, MVLA (copies from the Rosenbach Library).

75. Bailey, *Parenting in England 1760–1830*, 202; Glover, *Southern Sons*, 33.

76. MCWC Diary, 1 and 2 April 1854.

77. Tobias Lear to GW, 24 October 1790, 3 April 1791; GW to Lear, 12 and 24 April 1791, *PGW-PS*, 6: 575, 8: 50–52, 84, 129; Benjamin Rush to Julia Stockton Rush, 16 and 17 July 1791, Benjamin and Julia Stockton Rush Papers, David M. Rubenstein Rare Book & Manuscript Library, Duke University.

78. Nelly to EBG, [1796], HMC, MVLA; Brady, 5, 28; Nelly to EBG, 1851, MVLA. Payments to many of her tutors can be found in Washington's Household Account Book, 1793–1797, Historical Society of Pennsylvania (hereafter HSP), transcribed and published in the *Pennsylvania Magazine of History and Biography* 29.4 through 31.3.

79. Fraser, *The Washingtons*, 297, 317.

80. On the political challenges of 1791–1792, *see* Freeman, *George Washington*, vol. 6: chap. 15. On the development (and ugliness) of the first party system during Washington's presidency, *see eg* Lindsay M. Chervinsky, *The Cabinet: George Washington and the Creation of an American Institution* (Cambridge: The Belknap Press of Harvard University Press, 2020); Joanne B. Freeman, *Affairs of Honor: National Politics in the New Republic* (New Haven: Yale University Press, 2001), esp. chap. 1 and 2; Richard Hofstadter, *The Idea of a Party System: The Rise of Legitimate Opposition in the United States, 1780–1840* (Berkeley: University of California Press, 1969), chap. 2 and 3; James Roger Sharp, *American Politics in the Early Republic: The New Nation in Crisis* (New Haven: Yale University Press, 1993), chap. 1.

81. Bob Arnebeck, *Through a Fiery Trial* (Lanham, MD: Madison Books, 1994), 24–35; Watson, *George Washington's Final Battle*, 157–162. On

concerns about personal gain, *see* Bowling, *The Creation of Washington, D.C.*, 213.

82. Freeman, *George Washington*, vol. 6, chap. 6.
83. Powel to GW, 17 November 1792, *PGW-PS*, 11: 395–398; MW to Fanny Basset Washington, 22 October 1789, in *MW Papers*, 193.
84. *PGW-PS*, 12: 264–265.

Chapter 2

1. Nelly autobio, 1797, DLCCU.
2. On Washington's presidency and the attacks on him, *see* Forrest McDonald, *The Presidency of George Washington* (Lawrence: University Press of Kansas, 1974); Nathaniel C. Green, *The Man of the People: Political Dissent and the Making of the American Presidency* (Lawrence: University Press of Kansas, 2020), chap. 2 and 3.
3. Tobias Lear to David Humphreys, 12 April 1791, 8 April 1793, MVLA (copies from Rosenbach).
4. Tobias Lear to David Humphreys, 8 April 1793, MVLA (copies from Rosenbach). The best (albeit still incomplete) source on ECC's many children is Alice Coyle Torbert, *Eleanor Calvert and Her Circle* (William-Frederick Press, 1950).
5. On courtship in this era, *see* Timothy Kenslea, *The Sedgwicks in Love: Courtship, Engagement, and Marriage in the Early Republic* (Northeastern, 2006); Lucia McMahon, *Mere Equals: The Paradox of Educated Women in the Early American Republic* (Ithaca, NY: Cornell University Press, 2012), chap. 5; Ellen K. Rothman, *Hands and Hearts: A History of Courtship in America* (New York: Basic Books, Inc., 1984).
6. Tobias Lear to David Humphreys, 8 April 1793, MVLA (copies from Rosenbach).
7. The conception of adolescence, teenagers, and the particular traits that went with that life phase did not develop until the twentieth century in Western Europe and America; *see eg* Thomas Hine, *The Rise and Fall of the American Teenager* (New York: HarperCollins, 2000), chap. 2.
8. John Alexander Carroll and Mary Wells Ashworth, *George Washington: A Biography*, vol. 7, *First in Peace* (New York: Charles Scribner's Sons, 1957): chap. 2; McDonald, *The Presidency of George Washington*, chap. 6.
9. GW to Samuel and Elizabeth Powel, 24 April 1793, *PGW-PS*, 12: 476–477.
10. Carroll and Ashworth, *George Washington*, 7: 73–76.
11. Thomas Jefferson to James Madison, 9 June 1793; Thomas Jefferson, Notes of Cabinet Meeting on Edmond Charles Genet, *PTJ*, 26: 241, 602.

12. John Adams to Abigail Adams, 15 December 1793, *Adams Family Correspondence* (hereafter *AFC*), 9: 472.

13. William Spohn Baker, *Washington after the Revolution: MDCCLXXXIV-MDCCXCIX* (J.B. Lippincott Company, 1898), 261–262.

14. Robert William Fogel, *The Fourth Great Awakening and the Future of Egalitarianism* (Chicago: University of Chicago Press, 2000), 140–141.

15. Simon Finger, *The Contagious City: The Politics of Public Health in Early Philadelphia* (Ithaca: Cornell University Press, 2012), chap. 8.

16. Baker, *Washington after the Revolution*, 264.

17. Grant Quertermous, ed., *A Georgetown Life: The Reminiscences of Britannia Wellington Peter Kennon of Tudor Place* (Washington, DC: Georgetown University Press, 2020), 136. There is no direct evidence of Martha's and Nelly's presence, but a 7 July 1851 *New York Herald* article mentioned that GWPC was at the ceremony.

18. GW to James Madison, 14 October 1793, *PGW-PS*, 14: 206.

19. On Nelly's illness, *see* John Adams to Abigail Adams, 15 December 1793, *AFC*, 9: 472.

20. The curatorial file for the harpsichord for Mount Vernon cites an import certificate docketed September 30, 1793, on the ship *George Barclay*, sailing from London; the current location of this document is unknown.

21. Winthrop Sargent diary, quotes in GW to James Madison, 14 October 1793, *PGW-PS*, 14: 208–210n3.

22. Judith S. Britt, *Nothing More Agreeable: Music in George Washington's Family* (Mount Vernon, VA: The Mount Vernon Ladies' Association of the Union, 1984), 98, 100.

23. MW to Fanny, 14 January 1794, *MW Papers*, 249.

24. James Thomas Flexner, *George Washington and the New Nation, 1783–1793*, vol. 3, *His George Washington* (Boston: Little, Brown and Company, 1970), 303; Carroll and Ashworth, *George Washington*, 7: 153.

25. GWPC Recollections, 408; on the location of the harpsichord, *see* Edward Lawler, "The President's House in Philadelphia: The Rediscovery of a Lost Landmark," *Pennsylvania Magazine of History and Biography* 126, no. 1 (January 2002): 41.

26. MW to Fanny, 2 March 1794, *MW Papers*, 253; Leslie Buhler, ed., *Tudor Place: America's Story Lives Here* (Washington, DC: White House Historical Association, 2016), 12; Quertermous, *A Georgetown Life*, 131.

27. Nelly to EBG, 21 January 1851, in Brady, 258–259.

28. "To Miss Eleanor Parke Custis on her fifteenth Birthday, March 31st 1794," c. 1851 (likely enclosed in a letter to EBG), HMC, MVLA.

29. MW to Mary Stillson Lear, 24 August 1794, *MW Papers*, 268; GWPC Recollections, 41; Nelly to Jared Sparks, 26 February 1833, in Jared Sparks, *The Life of George Washington* (Boston: F. Andrews, 1839), 522.

30. MW to Fanny Bassett Washington, 15 December 1794, *MW Papers*,

278; Nelly to EBG, 29 January 1831, in Brady, 205; Nelly to Mr. Powers, 21 March 1852, MVLA.

31. Nelly to EBG, 8 September 1794, in Brady, 18. The song, "Pauvre Madelon," was from a 1791 British comic opera titled "The Surrender of Calais," https://www.eighteenthcenturydrama.amdigital.co.uk/Documents/Details/HL_LA_mssLA913.

32. MW to Fanny Bassett Washington, 30 June 1794, *MW Papers*, 263.

33. On the Whiskey Rebellion, *see* William Hogeland, *The Whiskey Rebellion: George Washington, Alexander Hamilton, and the Frontier* (New York: Simon and Schuster, 2015); Thomas P. Slaughter, *The Whiskey Rebellion: Frontier Epilogue to the American Revolution* (New York: Oxford University Press, 1988).

34. *Memoirs of the Long Island Historical Society: George Washington and Mount Vernon* (Brooklyn: Published by the Society, 1889), lxxx.

35. MW to Fanny Bassett Washington, 29 September 1794, *MW Papers*, 272; Carroll and Ashworth, *George Washington*, 7: 197–217.

36. According to GW's diary, he completed his mission and left to go back to Philadelphia on October 20 (*GW Diaries*, 6: 195). Martha's 18 October 1794 letter to Fanny Bassett Washington is dated Philadelphia, so she had already returned there (*MW Papers*, 272).

37. Flexner, *George Washington and the New Nation, 1783–1793*, 321–323; Green, *The Man of the People*, 77.

38. Eliza to GW, 7 September 1794, *PGW-PS*, 16: 650.

39. GW to Eliza, 14 September 1794, *PGW-PS*, 16: 682–683. Historians refer to the marital ideal in this era as "companionate marriage," based on much the same principles as GW lays out; *see eg* Anya Jabour, *Marriage in the Early Republic: Elizabeth and William Wirt and the Companionate Ideal* (Baltimore: Johns Hopkins University Press, 1998); Jan Lewis, "The Republican Wife: Virtue and Seduction in the Early Republic," *The William and Mary Quarterly* 44, no. 4 (October 1987): 689–721; McMahon, *Mere Equals*, chap. 5. On the persistence of financial concerns in the era of companionate marriage, *see* Lindsay Mitchell Keiter, "Uniting Interests: The Economic Functions of Marriage in America, 1750–1860" (PhD Diss., College of William and Mary, 2016).

40. A handwritten note bound with one copy of this letter says the letter had been owned by Betsey's granddaughter (Morgan Library, MA 503). The other copy (both are in GW's hand) is at MVLA.

41. John Adams to Abigail Adams, 29 January 1795, in *AFC*, 10: 363; Quertermous, *A Georgetown Life*, 18. For quote, *see* MCP to Eliza Quincy, 15 February 1812, in Eliza Susan Quincy, *Memoir of the Life of Eliza S.M. Quincy* (Boston: J. Wilson and Son, 1861), 145.

42. JPC Estate Account with David Stuart, Fairfax County Courthouse, Willbook G-1, photostat at MVLA.

43. Dunbar, *Never Caught*, 86.

44. 1796 Peter Slave Accounts, Tudor Place, MS-2. The first person on the list and the only one with a last name listed, Peter Twine, may have been sold to Lawrence Lewis, as a man by that name was later owned by Lawrence Lewis. Another Twine family, Sall and her four children, were dower slaves at Mount Vernon and inherited by the Peters in 1802 (Lawrence Lewis: Public Claim, 27 February 1806, Condemned slaves and free blacks executed or transported records, 1781–1865, Accession APA 756, Box 2, Folder 5, Library of Virginia; "List of the different Drafts of Negroes, [1802]," PFP, MVLA).

45. MW to Fanny Bassett Washington, 25 February 1795, *MW Papers*, 279; John Adams to Abigail Adams, 17 and 29 January 1795; John Adams to John Quincy Adams, 11 February 1795 (*AFC*, 10: 361, 363, 382); MW to Fanny Bassett Washington, 9 March 1795, *MW Papers*, 281.

46. Baker, *Washington after the Revolution*, 302.

47. MW to Fanny Bassett Washington, 6 April and 10 May 1795, *MW Papers*, 284, 286.

48. Lance Mayer and Gay Myers, *American Painters on Technique: The Colonial Period to 1860* (Los Angeles: Getty Publications, 2011), 51; Jane Stuart, "The Stuart Portraits of Washington," *Scribner's Monthly*, June 1876.

49. Charles Henry Hart, *Historical Descriptive and Critical Catalogue of the Works of American Artists in Collection of Herbert L. Pratt, Glen Cove, L.I.* (New York, 1917), 37.

50. The timing of Stuart's earliest painting from life of George Washington has been debated, as some accounts date it to spring and others autumn 1795 (Carrie Rebora Barratt and Ellen G. Miles, *Gilbert Stuart* [New York: Metropolitan Museum of Art, 2004], 133–35). The portrait of Eliza had been dated to 1796, but there is no record that she was in Philadelphia at that time. Thus, both portraits must date from spring of 1795, during her extended visit to the city.

51. The only recent published account of the portrait is Barratt and Miles, 191–194. The painting is in private hands.

52. MW to Fanny Bassett Washington, 10 May 1795, in *MW Papers*, 286.

53. Rosemarie Zagarri, "The Empire Comes Home: Thomas Law's Mixed-Race Family in the Early American Republic," in *India in the American Imaginary, 1780s–1880s*, ed. Anupama Arora and Rajender Kaur (Cham, Switzerland: Palgrave Macmillan, 2017), 78, 84. On wealth in this period, *see* R.D. Hume, "The Value of Money in Eighteenth-Century England: Incomes, Prices, Buying Power—and Some Problems in Cultural Economics," *Huntington Library Quarterly* 77, no. 4 (2014): 373–416.

54. Bob Arnebeck, *Through a Fiery Trial* (Lanham, MD: Madison Books, 1994), 250–253.

55. Robert Morris to Thomas Law, 20 April 1795, Robert Morris Papers, LC.

56. Thomas Law to Charles Rumbold, 10 January 1832, Thomas Law Papers, UVa. No letters from their courtship survive, but there is no other way they could have kept in touch while Betsey was at Hope Park (there is no evidence he visited her). In this same 1832 letter, he wrote that after he told her about his "natural children," "she *wrote* she would be a mother to them" (emphasis added).

57. Claude G. Bowers, *Jefferson and Hamilton* (Boston: Houghton Mifflin, 1925), 273–284; Todd Estes, *The Jay Treaty Debate, Public Opinion, and the Evolution of Early American Political Culture* (Amherst: University of Massachusetts Press, 2006); Green, *The Man of the People*, chap. 3.

58. Carroll and Ashworth, *George Washington*, 7: 320.

59. Chervinsky, *The Cabinet*, 290–301; Flexner, *George Washington and the New Nation, 1783–1793*, 336–337.

60. Nelly to EBG, 13 October and 19 November 1795, in Brady, 20–23.

61. GW to Eliza, 6 January 1796, *PGW-PS*, 19: 339–342.

62. Thomas Law to Charles Rumbold, 10 January 1832, Thomas Law Papers, UVa. *See also* Zagarri, "The Empire Comes Home: Thomas Law's Mixed-Race Family in the Early American Republic."

63. David Stuart to GW, 25 February 1796, *PGW-PS*, 19: 499; Thomas Law to Lloyd N. Rogers [1824], Thomas Law Papers, LC, as cited in Zagarri, 85.

64. GW to David Stuart, 7 February 1796, *PGW-PS*, 19: 441–442.

65. Quoted in Arnebeck, *Through a Fiery Trial*, 347.

66. GW to David Stuart, 7 February 1796; GW to Eliza, 10 February 1796; GW to Thomas Law, 10 February 1796, *PGW-PS*, 19: 441–442, 445–446.

67. Nelly to EBG, 7 February 1796, in Brady, 24–25.

68. GW to Stuart, 7 February 1796; Stuart to GW, 25 February 1796, *PGW-PS*, 19: 441–442, 496–499. Note that Stuart's farm was worked by his wife's dower slaves from her late husband JPC, while the Custis slaves at Mount Vernon were MW's dower slaves from Daniel Parke Custis's estate. While some have interpreted this exchange to mean that GW was trying to purchase or hire out and then free the dower slaves, I have adopted Bruce Ragsdale's persuasive interpretation here. For the former, *see* Philip D. Morgan, "'To Get Quit of Negroes': George Washington and Slavery," *Journal of American Studies* 39, no. 3 (2005): 423–424; Mary V. Thompson, *"The Only Unavoidable Subject of Regret,"* 303–304; Henry Wiencek, *An Imperfect God: George Washington, His Slaves, and the Creation of America* (New York: Farrar, Straus and Giroux, 2004), 229–231, 339–342. For Ragsdale, *see* Bruce A. Ragsdale,

Washington at the Plow: The Founding Farmer and the Question of Slavery (Cambridge: The Belknap Press of Harvard University, 2021), 245–252.

69. Stuart told GW in his February 25 letter, "from what I can learn, it is probable, I may allways have Betsey's for very little: As I am told, Mr Law say's she may do as she pleases with her fortune" (*PGW-PS*, 19: 499). However, by the terms of their marriage settlement, Thomas had control of Betsey's entire dowry valued at $20,000 (District of Columbia Land records, 1792–1886, Book E5, p. 224–227, typescripts, DC Courthouse, available via familysearch.org).

70. Thomas Law to James Madison, 18 October 1797, *Papers of James Madison-Congressional Series*, 17: 52.

71. The supposition that William Costin, his mother Nancy Holmes, and her other children were part of Betsey's dowry is based on what we know about Patty's dowry, the absence of these names on the list of people Betsey inherited from Mount Vernon after Martha Washington's death in 1802, and the fact that Thomas Law later freed the entire Costin/Holmes family (proving that he and his wife owned them). The timing of the emancipation soon after Martha's death makes it highly unlikely that Thomas had purchased them himself. On his views on slavery, *see* Zagarri, "The Empire Comes Home: Thomas Law's Mixed-Race Family in the Early American Republic," 88–89.

72. The manumissions were recorded on July 28, 1802, in District of Columbia Land Records, Book H8, p. 413, typescripts, DC Courthouse, available via familysearch.org; *see* Helen Hoban Rogers, *Freedom & Slavery Documents in the District of Columbia* (Baltimore: Gateway Press, 2007), 20.

73. Quote from *The Granite Freeman* (Concord, NH), 22 May 1845; on Ona's concerns, *see* Dunbar, *Never Caught*, 96–97. It was unclear when Ona would go to the Laws, but it seems it would not be until after Martha's death. Ona says in one interview, "she understood that after the decease of her master and mistress, she was to become the property of a grand-daughter of theirs, by name of Custis" (*Granite Freeman*, above) and in another that she "was given verbally, if not legally, by Mrs. Washington, to Eliza Custis" (Rev. Benjamin Chase. Letter to the editor, *The Liberator*, January 1, 1847. As quoted in *Slave Testimony, Two Centuries of Letters, Speeches, Interviews, and Autobiographies*, ed. John W. Blassingame [Baton Rouge: Louisiana State University Press, 1977], 248–250). Ona was not sent to DC after the wedding to live with the Laws, and when she freed herself in May, it was from Philadelphia; she recalled, "Whilst they were packing up to go to Virginia, I was packing to go, I didn't know where; for I knew that if I went back to Virginia, I should never get my liberty" (*Granite Freeman*, above). It is unclear that, as Dunbar suggests, Ona was a wedding

gift, especially since Martha still needed Ona's services, and Betsey's dowry would have presumably been the same as Martha Custis Peter's: around sixty enslaved people from the southern Custis estates.

74. John Adams to Abigail Adams, 23 February 1796, in *AFC*, 11: 148; Carroll and Ashworth, *George Washington*, 7: 343.

75. *Annals of Congress*, Fourth Congress, First Session, 355.

76. John Adams to Abigail Adams, 23 February 1796; Abigail Adams to John Adams, 5 March 1796; *AFC*, 11: 148, 12: 203.

77. Nelly to EBG, 13 May 1796, in Brady, 28.

78. They signed an agreement called an indenture tripartite with James Barry as trustee on 19 March 1796 (District of Columbia Land records, 1792–1886, DC Archives, Book E5, p. 224–227, typescripts, DC Courthouse, available via familysearch.org). While Law got the dowry, Betsey/Eliza controlled all other assets she might have. On this legal instrument, *see* Amy Louise Erickson, *Women and Property: In Early Modern England* (Routledge, 2002), chap. 6; Keiter, "Uniting Interests," chap. 3; Glenda Riley, "Legislative Divorce in Virginia, 1803–1850," *Journal of the Early Republic* 11, no. 1 (1991): 60; Marylynn Salmon, *Women and the Law of Property in Early America* (Chapel Hill: University of North Carolina Press, 1986), chap. 5.

79. GW and MW to Thomas Law, 28 March 1796, *MW Papers*, 295.

80. On the house, dubbed the "Honeymoon House," *see* the house's nomination form in the National Register of Historic Places, available at https://catalog.archives.gov/id/117692259.

81. Thomas Twining, *Travels in America 100 Years Ago: Being Notes and Reminiscences* (New York: Harper & Brothers, 1894), 94. Nelly to EBG, 30 March 1796, in Brady, 26.

82. GW to Nelly, 21 March 1796, *PGW-PS*, 19: 574–576.

83. Nelly to EBG, 13 May 1796, in Brady, 27–28.

84. Carroll and Ashworth, *George Washington*, 7: 304, 323, 379, 381–382. On the Lafayette family's struggles, *see* David A. Clary, *Adopted Son: Washington, Lafayette, and the Friendship that Saved the Revolution* (New York: Bantam Books, 2007), chap. 15.

85. Dunbar, *Never Caught*, 110–111.

86. Dunbar, 111–112. For the subsequent story of Washington's attempts to recapture Ona Judge, *see* Dunbar, chap. 10–12.

87. Carroll and Ashworth, *George Washington*, 7: 390–399. On the Catawbas' visit, *see* James H. Merrell, *The Indians' New World: Catawbas and Their Neighbors from European Contact through the Era of Removal*, Twentieth Anniversary Edition (Chapel Hill: Omohundro Institute and University of North Carolina Press, 2012), 278–781.

88. Nelly to EBG, 6 September 1796, in Brady, 30.

89. Carroll and Ashworth, *George Washington*, 7: 381–382, 402–403; Nelly

to Lewis Washington, 31 January 1852, PFP, MVLA. Note that Nelly's description of watching him write by the light of a particular lamp in his office at the top of the stairs would be impossible, because this describes his office at the President's House, and she was not there while he was in the spring of 1796. She may well have confused the memory of him at work on the speech during the summer at Mount Vernon with other work she witnessed in the President's House. The lamp is now in the collection of the National Museum of American History.

90. Jeffrey Malanson, *Addressing America: George Washington's Farewell and the Making of National Culture, Politics, and Diplomacy, 1796–1852* (Kent, OH: Kent State University Press, 2015), chap. 1.

91. GW to Samuel Stanhope Smith, 24 May 1797, *PGW-RS*, 1: 153.

92. GW to GWPC, 15 and 28 November 1796, 11 January, 27 February 1797; quote in 28 November and 27 February letters; *PGW-PS*, 21: 224–226, 265–268, 491–493, 753–755.

93. MCP to GW, 18 January 1797, *PGW-PS*, 21: 530–531; Torbert, *Eleanor Calvert and Her Circle*, 65.

94. Benjamin Henry Latrobe, *The Journal of Latrobe*, ed. John H. B. Latrobe (New York: D. Appleton and Company, 1905), 57–58, 61; Unknown to Thomas Law, 21 January 1797, Thomas Law Family Papers (mislabeled in pencil "Miss Custis"), MCHC. On Chevalier, *see PGW-PS*, 6: 261.

95. Sarah McKean to Dolley Madison, 3 August 1797, *Papers of James Madison-Congressional Series*, 17: 37.

96. Carroll and Ashworth, *George Washington*, 7: 342; Baker, *Washington after the Revolution*, 341.

97. GWPC Recollections, 434; Carroll and Ashworth, *George Washington*, 7: 436–437. The account in GWPC Recollections is from Susan B. Echard, daughter of Colonel Read.

98. Carroll and Ashworth, 7: 438–439; Elizabeth Bryant Johnston, *George Washington Day by Day* (Washington, DC, 1894), 37.

Chapter 3

1. GW to Tobias Lear, 9 March 1797, *PGW-RS*, 1: 25; *GW Diaries*, 6: 136; Nelly to EBG, 18 March 1797, in Brady, 30–32.

2. Nelly to EBG, 18 March 1797, in Brady, 31–32; Julian Ursyn Niemcewicz, *Under Their Vine and Fig Tree: Travels through America in 1797–1799, 1805*, ed. Metchie J.E. Budka, *Collections of the New Jersey Historical Society at Newark*, vol. 14 (Elizabeth, NJ: Grassmann Pub. Co., 1965), 95.

3. Nelly to EBG, 18 March 1797, in Brady, 32.

4. GW to GWPC, 3 April 1797, *PGW-RS*, 1: 70; Isaac Weld, *Travels through the States of North America, and the Provinces of Upper and Lower*

Canada, During the Years 1795, 1796, and 1797 (London: J. Stockdale, 1800), 94.

5. The Washingtons had left the chef at Mount Vernon when they returned to Philadelphia in the fall of 1796, probably because they were concerned he would free himself in Philadelphia, where he had a network of free Black people to help him. At Mount Vernon, Hercules's new job working with bricklayers and gardeners may have only fueled his desire to find freedom. Kelly Fanto Deetz, *Bound to the Fire: How Virginia's Enslaved Cooks Helped Invent American Cuisine* (Lexington: University Press of Kentucky, 2017), 83–85; Ramin Ganeshram, "Hercules Posey: George Washington's Unsung Enslaved Chef," February 1, 2022, https://www.bbc.com/travel/article/20220201-hercules-posey-george-washingtons-unsung-enslaved-chef; Mary V. Thompson, *"The Only Unavoidable Subject of Regret,"* 283–285.

6. GW to James McHenry, 3 April 1797, *PGW-RS*, 1: 71.

7. *GW Diaries*, 6: 236–239; for complete accounts of visitors, *see GW Diaries*, volume 6.

8. On the table setting, *see* Carol Borchert Cadou, *The George Washington Collection: Fine and Decorative Arts at Mount Vernon* (Manchester, VT: Hudson Hills, 2006), eg p. 140. On the routine, *see* Nelly to EBG, 23 February 1823, MVLA Binder 25; Niemcewicz, *Under Their Vine and Fig Tree: Travels through America in 1797–1799, 1805*, 103.

9. Lawrence Lewis to GW, 24 July 1797; GW to Lawrence Lewis, 4 August 1797; in *PGW-RS*, 1: 270, 288–289.

10. Flora Fraser, *The Washingtons*, 71–89.

11. GW to GWPC, 15 and 28 November 1796, 27 February 1797, in *PGW-PS*, 21: 224–226, 265–268, 491–493, 753–755; GW to John McDowell, 5 March 1798, *PGW-RS*, 2: 119. On the founders' parental expectations, *see* Glover, *Founders as Fathers*, 108–129.

12. GWPC to GW, 25 March 1797; GW to GWPC, 3 April 1797; *PGW-RS*, 1: 49, 69.

13. Robert Morris to GW, 10 April 1797; Mary White Morris to GW, 9 May 1797; in *PGW-RS*, 1: 93, 135; Nelly to EBG, 24 April 1797, in Brady, 33.

14. GW to Samuel Stanhope Smith, 24 May 1797; GWPC to GW, 29 May 1797, 1 July 1797; GW to GWPC, 10 July 1797; in *PGW-RS*, 1: 153–154, 159, 223–224, 245.

15. Glover, *Southern Sons*, 33, 45, 64, 69–71, 78; Steven J. Novak, *The Rights of Youth: American Colleges and Student Revolt, 1798–1815* (Cambridge: Harvard University Press, 1977).

16. 7 September 1798, entry in Complete and Final Minutes of Faculty Meetings, 1781–1810, p. 132, Office of the Dean of Faculty Records, Series 1A, Seeley G. Mudd Manuscript Library, Princeton University.

17. GW to James McHenry, 29 May 1797; GW to GWPC, 7 January 1798; GW to David Stuart, 22 January 1798, *PGW-RS*, 1: 159–160, 2: 4–5, 37.

18. GW to David Stuart, 22 January 1798; David Stuart to GW, 26 January 1798; GW to David Stuart, 26 February 1798, *PGW-RS*, 2: 37, 49–50, 104–105.

19. GWPC to GW, 12 March 1798, *PGW-RS*, 2: 138. His landlady was Mrs. Frances Bryce/Brice, a widow who operated out of several different houses in Annapolis in the late eighteenth century; Jane W. McWilliams, *Annapolis, City on the Severn: A History* (Baltimore: Johns Hopkins University Press, 2011), 101. The one where GWPC boarded was located at 18 West Street (*Maryland Gazette*, 11 September 1788; 1798 Federal Direct Tax for Annapolis and Middleneck Hundreds, folio 14); HABS survey, https://tile.loc.gov/storage-services/master/pnp/habshaer/md/md0000/md0070/data/md0070data.pdf.

20. GWPC to Lawrence Lewis, 21 May 1798, New York Public Library; John McDowell to GW, 14 and 17 June 1798, *PGW-RS*, 2: 326–328, 335.

21. Edward C. Papenfuse et al., *A Biographical Dictionary of the Maryland Legislature, 1635–1789* (Baltimore: Johns Hopkins University Press, 1985), 2: 488.

22. Fraser, *The Washingtons*, 80–82, 89–90.

23. GW to GWPC, 13 June 1798; GWPC to GW, 17 June 1798, *PGW-RS*, 2: 324, 335–336.

24. Rothman, *Hands and Hearts*, 34.

25. As GWPC put it, "The conditions were not accepted, and my youth being alleged by me as an obstacle to the consummation of my wishes at the present time (which was farthest from my thoughts), I withdrew, and that on fair and honorable terms." GWPC to GW, 17 June 1798, *PGW-RS*, 2: 335–336.

26. GW to Stuart, 13 August 1798; Stuart to GW, 22 August 1798; *PGW-RS*, 2: 525, 557. It is possible that GWPC had also visited home briefly in late June; an Alexandria court record from 25 June 1798 notes that a "George W Custis" had failed to appear in court that day on charges of having stolen two silver spoons from innkeeper John Gadsby. *See* James B. Lynch, *The Custis Chronicles: The Virginia Generations* (Rockland, ME: Picton Press, 1997), 234–235; T. Michael Miller, *Murder and Mayhem: Criminal Conduct in Old Alexandria, Virginia, 1749–1900* (Bowie, MD: Heritage Books, Inc., 2019), 183–184. No further records survive, there is no evidence that GWPC had left Annapolis at this time, and it would be remarkable for Gadsby to have pressed charges for a minor theft against the former president's stepgrandson. There-

fore, I have concluded that it is likely that the accused was a different person from Wash.

27. GW to Stuart, 13 August 1798; Stuart to GW, 22 August 1798; GW to John McDowell, 2 and 16 September 1798, *PGW-RS*, 2: 525, 557, 578, 579n2.

28. Glover, *Southern Sons*, 33.

29. John Adams to Louisa Catherine Adams, August 1822, Adams Papers, MHS.

30. Nelly to Elizabeth Wolcott, 28 December 1797, Thomas Addis Emmet Collection, New York Public Library.

31. Nelly to EBG, 24 April and 30 May 1797, in Brady, 34, 36.

32. GWPC to GW, 2 April 1798; GW to GWPC, 15 April 1798, *PGW-RS*, 2: 219–220, 239–240; Nelly to EBG, 14 May 1798, in Brady, 51.

33. Nelly to EBG, 20 August 1797, in Brady, 39.

34. Mary Louisa Slacum Benham, "Antebellum Reminiscences of Alexandria, Virginia," transcription in Office of Historic Alexandria/Alexandria Archaeology, https://www.alexandriava.gov/uploaded-Files/oha/info/AntibellumMemoirMaryLouisaSlacumBenham.pdf; Nelly to George Washington Lafayette (hereafter GWL), 12 March 1812, DLCCU.

35. Saxton, *The Widow Washington*, 270, 272; 1782 divvy list, MS 734, Historic Kenmore; Richard E. Griffith, *Early Estates of Clarke County*, vol. XI and XII, Proceedings of the Clarke County Historical Association (Boyce, VA: Carr Publishing Co., 1951), chap. 3.

36. Nelly to EBG, 23 Nov 1797, 20 March 1798, in Brady, 41–43, 46–49.

37. Nelly autobio, 1797, DLCCU.

38. Niemcewicz, *Under Their Vine and Fig Tree: Travels through America in 1797–1799, 1805*, 97.

39. Certificate of Proxy: Eleanor Parke Custis to George Washington, 10 January 1798, reproduction, MVLA; GW to William Herbert, 27 October 1797, *PGW-RS*, 1: 433. GW owned twenty-five shares; *see* 1799 "Schedule of Property" enclosed in his will, *PGW-RS*, 4: 519. It is unclear how often women exercised their right to vote for bank boards of directors in America at this time; there is evidence that some women in England did so. *See* Amy M. Froide, *Silent Partners: Women as Public Investors during Britain's Financial Revolution, 1690–1750* (Oxford: Oxford University Press, 2016), 198–200.

40. Nelly to EBG, 23 November 1797, in Brady, 41.

41. Stanley M. Elkins and Eric L. McKitrick, *The Age of Federalism* (New York: Oxford University Press, 1993), chap. 12–14, esp. 583, 593–596, 645–647.

42. Nelly to EBG, 23 November 1797; Nelly to EBG, 14 May 1798, in Brady, 41, 52.

43. John Adams to John Quincy Adams, 26 November 1821, Adams Family Papers, Letterbooks, MHS.

44. Sydnor, *Gentlemen Freeholders*, 18–28.

45. On women's rights in this period, *see* Linda K. Kerber, *Women of the Republic: Intellect and Ideology in Revolutionary America* (New York: Norton, 1986); Mary Beth Norton, *Liberty's Daughters: The Revolutionary Experience of American Women, 1750–1800* (Boston: Little, Brown and Company, 1980); Rosemarie Zagarri, *Revolutionary Backlash: Women and Politics in the Early American Republic* (Philadelphia: University of Pennsylvania Press, 2007). On female voters in New Jersey, *see* Judith Apter Klinghoffer and Lois Elkis, "'The Petticoat Electors': Women's Suffrage in New Jersey, 1776–1807," *Journal of the Early Republic* 12, no. 2 (1992): 159–193; Jan Ellen Lewis, "Rethinking Women's Suffrage in New Jersey, 1776–1807," *Rutgers Law Review* 63, no. 3 (2011): 1017–1035.

46. Nelly to EBG, 1 July 1798, in Brady, 57; GW to John Adams, 13 July 1798, *PGW-RS*, 2: 402–404; Carroll and Ashworth, *George Washington*, 7: 519–520; Elkins and McKitrick, *The Age of Federalism*, 601, 606; Jonathan Horn, *Washington's End: The Final Years and Forgotten Struggle* (New York: Simon and Schuster, 2020), 102–108.

47. Nelly to James McHenry, 26 July 1798, in Bernard Christian Steiner, ed., *The Life and Correspondence of James McHenry: Secretary of War Under Washington and Adams* (Cleveland: Burrows Brothers Company, 1907), 356. For McHenry's reply sending the completed standard, *see* McHenry to Nelly, 12 September 1798, James McHenry Papers, Clements Library, University of Michigan. For Nelly's letter presenting it and the dragoons' reply, *see eg Claypoole's American Advertiser* (Philadelphia), 14 December 1798.

48. On George's organization of the army and time in Philadelphia, *see eg* Horn, *Washington's End*, 116–140, chap. 8.

49. Quertermous, *A Georgetown Life*, 150.

50. GW to James McHenry, 16 February 1799, *PGW-RS*, 3: 384.

51. Nelly to EBG, 3 February 1799, in Brady, 58–59.

52. GW to Bartholomew Dandridge, 25 January 1799, *PGW-RS*, 3: 339; GW to GWL, 25 December 1798, *PGW-RS*, 3: 279; *see* similar language in GW to James McHenry, 16 February 1799 and GW to Charles Cotesworth Pinckney, 31 March 1799, *PGW-RS*, 3: 384, 460.

53. GW to James McHenry, 16 February 1799, *PGW-RS*, 3: 384; Nelly to EBG, 12 February 1826, in Brady, 173; Lawrence Lewis to James Webb, 2 April 1799, HMC, MVLA.

54. Nelly to EBG, 23 February 1823, Binder 25, MVLA.

55. *GW Diaries*, 21 January and 22 February 1799, 6: 331, 335; GWPC Recollections, 450; Agnes Lee, *Growing Up in the 1850s: The Journal*

of Agnes Lee (Chapel Hill: University of North Carolina Press, 1988), 80–81.

56. Thomas Boylston Adams to John Adams, 1 March 1799, *AFC*, 13: 424.

57. Nelly to EBG, 4 November 1799, in Brady, 62–63.

58. GW to Lawrence Lewis, 20 and 28 September 1799, *PGW-RS*, 4: 310–315, 325.

59. Elkins and McKitrick, *The Age of Federalism*, 653–654.

60. Nelly to EBG, 4 November 1799, in Brady, 61.

61. On GW's efforts to get GWPC a military appointment, *see* GW to James McHenry, 14 December 1798; GW to David Stuart, 30 December 1798, *PGW-RS*, 3: 267, 298–299 (quote p. 298). GW later requested that GWPC receive a promotion to lieutenant, but it does not appear that occurred; GW to James McHenry, 25 March 1799, *PGW-RS*, 4: 442. McHenry issued GWPC's commission on 10 January 1799; the original is in Custis Papers, VMHC. The story of the sword is recounted in "A Venerable Present," *Daily National Intelligencer*, 20 March 1848. At his discharge from service, GWPC was made a brevet major. Nelligan, *Arlington House*, 39.

62. Nelly to EBG, 4 November 1799, in Brady, 62–63. GW wrote Patty's husband Thomas Peter congratulating him "on the birth of a 'Manchild'" (3 December 1799, *PGW-RS*, 4: 440). On the deer (the "Washington Stag"), *see* GWPC Recollections, 390–392; Eliza Ambler Carrington, "A Visit to Mount Vernon—A Letter of Mrs. Edward Carrington to Her Sister, Mrs. George Fisher," *William and Mary Quarterly, Second Series* 18, no. 2 (November 22, 1799): 200.

63. On childbirth and lying in, *see eg* Judith Walzer Leavitt, *Brought to Bed: Childbearing in America, 1750–1950* (New York: Oxford University Press, 1988).

64. Interview with Lawrence Lewis, June 1833, John Gadsby Chapman Papers, McGuigan Collection, Harpswell, ME.

65. Tobias Lear's Narrative Accounts of the Death of George Washington, 14 and 15 December 1799, *PGW-RS*, 4: 542–555.

66. Ellen McCallister Clark, "Thomas Law's Description of the Last Illness and Death of George Washington," *MVLA Annual Report* 1972, 28–31; Nelly to Mary Stead Pinckney, 12 January 1800, *MW Papers*, 364. On Martha's move of bedrooms, *see* Carol Borchert-Cadou, "Garret Bedchamber," *George Washington Digital Encyclopedia*, https://www.mountvernon.org/library/digitalhistory/digital-encyclopedia/article/garret-bedchamber/.

67. Henry Lee to GWPC, 16 February 1800, in GWPC Recollections, 57.

68. George Washington's Last Will & Testament, 9 July 1799, *PGW-RS*, 4: 479–511. *See also* Eugene E. Prussing, *The Estate of George Washington, Deceased* (Boston: Little, Brown and Company, 1927). On the

emancipation of his enslaved people, *see* Ragsdale, *Washington at the Plow*, 270–274; Thompson, *"The Only Unavoidable Subject of Regret,"* 293–298, 309–319. Anna Maria Thornton noted on 2 August 1800, "The same order & regularity is observed as when the Genl was living." Worthington Chauncey Ford, ed., "Diary of Mrs. William Thornton, 1800–1863," *Records of the Columbia Historical Society, Washington, D.C.* 10 (1907): 173.

69. ECC to E.C. Lee, 3 April 1800, Ethel Armes Collection of Lee Family Papers, LC; Nelly to Mary Stead Pinckney, 9 November 1800, Custis-Lee Papers, LC.

70. The children were Martha Betty Lewis, George Washington Parke Custis Peter, and Rosalie Eugenia Stuart.

71. Weld, *Travels through the States of North America, and the Provinces of Upper and Lower Canada, during the Years 1795, 1796, and 1797*, 86; Niemcewicz, *Under Their Vine and Fig Tree: Travels through America in 1797–1799, 1805*, 78.

72. On the planning and building of the new capital, *see* Bob Arnebeck, *Through a Fiery Trial* (Lanham, MD: Madison Books, 1994); Adam Costanzo, *George Washington's Washington: Visions for the National Capital in the Early American Republic* (Athens, GA: University of Georgia Press, 2018), part I; Robert P. Watson, *George Washington's Final Battle: The Epic Struggle to Build a Capital City and a Nation* (Georgetown: Georgetown University Press, 2021), parts IV–VI. On the role of enslaved people, *see* Bob Arnebeck, *Slave Labor in the Capital: Building Washington's Iconic Federal Landmarks* (Charleston, SC: History Press, 2014); Chris Myers Asch and George Derek Musgrove, *Chocolate City: A History of Race and Democracy in the Nation's Capital* (Chapel Hill: University of North Carolina Press, 2017), 39; Josephine F. Pacheco, *The Pearl: A Failed Slave Escape on the Potomac* (Chapel Hill: University of North Carolina Press, 2005), 19.

73. Arnebeck, *Through a Fiery Trial*, 374, 403–404.

74. Louis Philippe, *Diary of My Travels in America* (New York: Delacorte Press, 1977), 23.

75. Niemcewicz, *Under Their Vine and Fig Tree: Travels through America in 1797–1799, 1805*, 94.

76. Margaret Bayard Smith to Mrs. Kirkpatrick, 16 November 1800, in Margaret Bayard Smith, *The First Forty Years of Washington Society, Portrayed by the Family Letters of Mrs. Samuel Harrison Smith (Margaret Bayard) from the Collection of Her Grandson, J. Henley Smith*, ed. Gaillard Hunt (New York: Charles Scribner's Sons, 1906), 3; Caroline Dall, "A Centennial 'Posie,'" *Unitarian Review*, 1876, 186.

77. Anna Maria Thornton's careful records of social calls and gatherings indicate the key figures in local society; *see* Ford, "Diary of Mrs. Wil-

liam Thornton, 1800–1863." *See also* Allen C. Clark, "Captain James Barry," *Records of the Columbia Historical Society, Washington, D.C.* 42/43 (1940): 1–16; Gordon S. Brown, *Incidental Architect: William Thornton and the Cultural Life of Early Washington, D.C., 1794–1828* (Athens, OH: Ohio University Press, 2009), 30–33; Kate Kearney Henry, "Richard Forrest and His Times, 1795–1830," *Records of the Columbia Historical Society, Washington, D.C.* 5 (1902): 87–95. On the visit, *see* Ford, "Diary of Mrs. William Thornton, 1800–1863," 94.

78. Margaret Bayard Smith to Mrs. Kirkpatrick, 16 November 1800, in Smith, *The First Forty Years of Washington Society*, 3. Thanks to independent curator Martha Katz-Hyman for explaining the kitchen range to me.

79. Samuel Mitchill to Catharine Mitchill, 21 December 1801, Samuel Latham Mitchill papers 1802–1815, Clements Library, University of Michigan; Eliza to John Law, 21 February 1802, PFP, MVLA.

80. RSC to Charles Calvert, October 1801, in Margaret Law Calcott, ed., *Mistress of Riversdale: The Plantation Letters of Rosalie Stier Calvert, 1795–1821* (Baltimore: Johns Hopkins University Press, 1991), 31.

81. Nelly to Abigail Adams, 20 November 1800, and Abigail Adams to Abigail Adams Smith, 21 November 1800, Adams Papers, MHS; William Cranch to Abigail Adams, 12 March 1798, *AFC*, 12: 445.

82. John Cotton Smith and William Watson Andrews, *The Correspondence and Miscellanies of the Hon. John Cotton Smith* (New York: Harper & Brothers, 1847), 224–225.

83. Nelly to Mary Stead Pinckney, 9 May 1801 and 3 January 1802, Custis-Lee Papers, LC.

84. Josiah Quincy, *Figures of the Past* (Boston: Roberts Brothers, 1896), 275.

85. Nelligan, *Arlington House*, 41–42. For the vote totals, *see Alexandria Advertiser and Commercial Intelligencer*, 29 April 1802; *see also A New Nation Votes*, Virginia 1802 House of Delgates, Fairfax County, https://elections.lib.tufts.edu/catalog/5d86p082k. Wash's letter was published in *Alexandria Advertiser*, 3 May 1802. On Wash's political career, *see* Sara Bearss, "The Federalist Career of George Washington Parke Custis," *Northern Virginia Heritage* 8, no. 1 (February 1986): 15–19.

86. Clark, "Thomas Law's Description of the Last Illness and Death of George Washington," *MVLA Annual Report* 1972, 31.

87. J. David Hacker, "Decennial Life Tables for the White Population of the United States, 1790–1900," *Historical Methods: A Journal of Quantitative and Interdisciplinary History* 43, no. 2 (April 30, 2010): 58.

88. *See* Bushrod Washington to MW, 27 December 1799, *MW Papers*, 349; Abigail Adams to Mary Smith Cranch, 21 December 1800, *AFC*, 14: 493. I am indebted to Bruce Ragsdale for pointing out the uncertainty of the timing and motivations here.

89. Cornelia Lee to Eliza Lee, 14 March 1802, Ethel Armes Collection of Lee Family Papers, LC.

90. Historians have long known that MW had her correspondence with GW destroyed, but a letter from Nelly to Jared Sparks explains "that the letters addressed by Gen'l W, to Mrs MW, were all destroyed by her order during her last illness." It seems most likely that one of the granddaughters was the one to do this, probably by burning them in a fire. *See* Nelly to Sparks, 16 July 1832, MS Sparks 153, Jared Sparks Letterbooks, Harvard University.

91. *Independent Chronicle* (Boston), 15 July 1802.

Chapter 4

1. Samuel Mitchill to Catharine Mitchill, 22 December 1802, Samuel Latham Mitchill Papers, Clements Library, University of Michigan.

2. Cassandra Good, "Washington Family Fortune: Lineage and Capital in Nineteenth-Century America," *Early American Studies* 18, no. 1 (Winter 2020): 105–106.

3. Teresa Barnett, *Sacred Relics: Pieces of the Past in Nineteenth-Century America* (Chicago: University of Chicago Press, 2013), part 1; Jamie L. Brummitt, "Protestant Relics: Religion, Objects, and the Art of Mourning in the American Republic" (PhD Diss., Durham, NC: Duke University, 2018), chap. 2.

4. George Deneale to Joseph May, 21 July 1802, HMC, MVLA; William Thornton to Thomas Jefferson, 28 July 1802, in *PTJ*, 38: 137–138. On the Laws' use of George Washington's clothing, *see* Good, "Washington Family Fortune: Lineage and Capital in Nineteenth-Century America," 105–106.

5. "List of the different Drafts of Negroes, [1802]," PFP, MVLA.

6. Portia Hodgson to Elizabeth Collins Lee, Elizabeth Collins Lee Papers, VMHC.

7. Nelly to GWL, 21 July 1804, DLCCU; Nelly to EBG, 11 January 1805, EBG Collection, MVLA.

8. RSC to Charles Stier, 3 July 1802, Carter transcriptions, MCHC.

9. Nelly to GWL, 21 July 1804, DLCCU. For baptism and death dates, *see* Lewis family record, Martha Washington bible, MVLA.

10. Nelligan, *Arlington House*, 49.

11. Nelly to Mary Stead Pickney, 19 February [1803], Custis-Lee Papers, LC; Lewis family record, Martha Washington bible, MVLA.

12. Hannah Cushing to Abigail Smith Adams, 23 March 1803, Adams Papers, MHS.

13. Nelly to Mary Stead Pinckney, 19 February [1803], Custis-Lee Papers,

LC; Legal Agreement between Lawrence Lewis and Isaac McLain, 15 June 1805, Woodlawn, NT 74.103.247.

14. Cassandra Good, "Report on Slavery at Woodlawn and in the Lives of the Lewis Family," Commissioned by the National Trust for Historic Preservation, 2022, in the National Trust files at Woodlawn.

15. "List of the different Drafts of Negroes, [1802]," PFP, MVLA. These names have been matched against the 1799 slave list and identified by Jessie MacLeod, associate curator, MVLA. On Oakland and Effingham, *see* Wendy Kail, "Oakland: Far from the Madding Crowd," *Tudor Place* (blog), March 2016, https://tudorplace.org/wp-content/uploads/2020/07/Oakland-March-2016_revised.pdf.

16. Examples of this abound, but *see eg* Annette Gordon-Reed, *The Hemingses of Monticello: An American Family* (New York: W.W. Norton & Company, 2009), 105; Brenda E. Stevenson, *Life in Black and White: Family and Community in the Slave South* (New York: Oxford University Press, 1997), 213.

17. Thomas Law to Negro William, 27 July 1802; to Nancy Holmes, 28 July 1802; to Margaret Costin and Others, 5 May 1807; to Delphy Costin and Others, 26 June 1807, in Helen Hoban Rogers, *Freedom & Slavery Documents in the District of Columbia* (Baltimore: Gateway Press, 2007), 1: 20, 75–76; 2: 18, 45, 144, 145n200; Dorothy S Provine, *District of Columbia Free Negro Registers, 1821–1861* (Bowie, MD: Heritage Books, Inc., 1996), 51–52. Delphy Judge is listed among the people Eliza Law inherited in 1802; "List of the different Drafts of Negroes, [1802]," PFP, MVLA. As a married woman, any property Eliza acquired would be owned by her husband.

18. On the rental of ECC's enslaved people and land, *see* 19 August 1802, Arlington County Deed Book, 1801–1865, A-T p. 62; original in Alexandria Deed Book E, p. 127–136.

19. Jennifer Hanna, *Arlington House Cultural Landscape Report* (Washington, DC: Department of Interior, National Park Service, National Capital Region, 2001), 29–30; Nelligan, *Arlington House*, 50, 52–53. GWPC did not undertake this work alone; he soon hired John Ball as farm manager (Nelligan, 52).

20. Hanna, *Arlington House Cultural Landscape Report*, 35; Nelligan, *Arlington House*, 51. The names of the specific plantations seem to have varied over time. White House, where Daniel Parke Custis had lived, in New Kent County, remained consistent. His overseer for his New Kent and King William properties listed White House, Old Quarter, Brick House, Mill New Kent, King William, and Mill King William in an 1806 report that counted one hundred fifty enslaved people on the properties; there would have been others in Northampton (*see* James Anderson to GWPC, 13 March 1806, MCLP, VMHC). His

overseer's reports for tracts in these same two counties from 1818 to 1823 listed White House, Old Quarter, Romancock, Lower Quarter, and New Kent Mill (*see* reports by John P. Walden, MCLP, VMHC).

21. Julia King, *George Hadfield: Architect of the Federal City* (Burlington, VT: Routledge, 2014).

22. Nelligan, *Arlington House*, 58–60.

23. RSC to Mrs. Stier, 29 December 1803, in Calcott, *Mistress of Riversdale*, 70.

24. On the development of GWPC's "memory work," *see* Bruggeman, "'More than Ordinary Patriotism': Living History in the Memory Work of George Washington Parke Custis."

25. *Alexandria Advertiser*, 29 January 1803.

26. Sara Bearss, "The Farmer of Arlington: George W. P. Custis and the Arlington Sheep Shearings," *Virginia Cavalcade* 38, no. 3 (Winter 1989): 124–133; Clark, *George Washington Parke Custis*, 52–55; Nelligan, *Arlington House*, 54–57; Margaret Byrd Adams Rasmussen, "Waging War with Wool: Thomas Jefferson's Campaign for American Commercial Independence from England," *Material Culture* 41, no. 1 (2009): 17–37; Ariel Ron, *Grassroots Leviathan: Agricultural Reform and the Rural North in the Slaveholding Republic* (Baltimore: Johns Hopkins University Press, 2020), chap. 1.

27. *See* 8 March 1803 and 28 March 1803 in *Alexandria Expositor*.

28. William Charles Allen, *History of the United States Capitol: A Chronicle of Design, Construction, and Politics* (Washington, DC: US Government Printing Office, 2001), 21, 46.

29. Howard Gilette Jr., *Between Justice and Beauty: Race, Planning, and the Failure of Urban Policy in Washington, D.C.* (Philadelphia: University of Pennsylvania Press, 2011), 12. For more descriptions of Washington in this era, *see* Constance McLaughlin Green, *Washington*, vol. 1, *Village and Capital, 1800–1878* (Princeton: Princeton University Press, 1962); James Sterling Young, *The Washington Community, 1800–1828* (New York: Columbia University Press, 1966).

30. RSC to Isabelle van Havre, 18 February 1805, in Calcott, *Mistress of Riversdale*, 111; Rosemarie Zagarri, "The Empire Comes Home: Thomas Law's Mixed-Race Family in the Early American Republic," 86.

31. John Law to Thomas Law, 2 September 1802, TLFP, MCHC; Eliza to John Law, 25 December 1802, PFP, MVLA.

32. Eliza to John Law, 25 December 1802, PFP, MVLA. On this controversy, which ultimately led to the Louisiana Purchase, *see eg* James E. Lewis, "A Tornado on the Horizon: The Jefferson Administration, the Retrocession Crisis, and the Louisiana Purchase," in *Empires of the Imagination: Transatlantic Histories of the Louisiana Purchase*, ed. Peter

J. Kastor and Francois Weil (Charlottesville: University of Virginia Press, 2009), 126–129.

33. Samuel Latham Mitchill to Catharine Mitchill, 3 December 1803, Samuel Latham Mitchill Papers, Clements Library, University of Michigan; William Thornton to James Madison, 17 August 1803, *Papers of James Madison-Secretary of State Series*, 5: 319; Sarah (Sally) McKean Maria Theresa Martínez de Yrujo to Dolley Payne Todd Madison, 20 June 1812, Dolley Madison digital edition, https://rotunda.upress.virginia.edu/dmde/. While written later, she was reflecting back on this period.

34. RSC to Charles Stier, 12 September 1803; RSC to M. et Mme. H.J. Stier, 3 August 1803, in Calcott, *Mistress of Riversdale*, 57, 54.

35. On social life in Washington City in this era, and particularly women's role, *see* Catherine Allgor, *Parlor Politics: In Which the Ladies of Washington Help Build a City and a Government* (Charlottesville: University Press of Virginia, 2000); Barbara G. Carson, *Ambitious Appetites: Dining, Behavior, and Patterns of Consumption in Federal Washington* (Washington, DC: AIA Press, 1990); Jan Lewis, "Politics and the Ambivalence of the Private Sphere: Women in Early Washington, D.C." and Fredrika Teute, "Roman Matron on the Banks of Tiber Creek: Margaret Bayard Smith and the Politicization of Spheres in the Nation's Capital," in *A Republic for the Ages: The United States Capitol and the Political Culture of the Early Republic*, ed. Kenneth Bowling (Charlottesville: Published for the United States Capitol Historical Society by the University of Virginia Press, 1999).

36. Eliza to Thomas Law, 10 February 1803, TLFP, MCHC. On retrocession, *see* Mark David Richards, "The Debates over the Retrocession of the District of Columbia, 1801–2004," *Washington History* 16, no. 1 (2004): 54–82.

37. Eliza to Thomas Law, 10 February 1803, TLFP, MCHC; Eliza to John Law, 15 April 1803, 25 September 1803, PFP, MVLA.

38. Green, *Washington*, vol. 1: 45.

39. RSC to Mrs. Stier, November 1804, in Calcott, *Mistress of Riversdale*, 62–63. Based on context, this letter was from the week of November 14. Other than this letter, there is no record of Eleanor Stuart's last child.

40. Margaret Bayard Smith to Mary Ann Smith, 18 November 1803, Margaret Bayard Smith Papers, LC.

41. Eliza to John Law, 15 April 1803, PFP, MVLA; Zagarri, "The Empire Comes Home: Thomas Law's Mixed-Race Family in the Early American Republic," 86, 102n29.

42. There were only a few stray mentions of a French mistress at the time, but Thomas did not explicitly deny the rumors even when confronted. *See* Zagarri, "The Empire Comes Home: Thomas Law's Mixed-Race Family in the Early American Republic," 86. I am indebted to Rosie

Zagarri for many conversations about how and why the marriage fell apart.

43. Thomas Law to George Logan, 10 May 1804, transcript in Alexandria Library file compilation, original in HSP.

44. RSC to Mrs. Stier, 30 July 1804; RSC to Mr. Stier, 15 September 1804; RSC to Isabelle van Havre, 18 February 1805, in Calcott, *Mistress of Riversdale*, 92, 97, 111.

45. Nelly to EBG, 25 August 1811, in Brady, 71.

46. "A Family Picture," Thomas Law Papers, LC.

47. Louisa Catherine Adams to John Quincy Adams, 17 April 1804, Adams Papers, MHS; Dolley Payne Todd Madison to Anna Payne Cutts [c. 8 May 1804], Dolley Madison digital edition, https://rotunda.upress.virginia.edu/dmde/.

48. Thomas Law to John Law, 27 April 1804, TLFP, MCHC.

49. Louisa Catherine Adams to John Quincy Adams, 13 May 1804, Adams Papers, MHS. Two letters reference that the pair stayed "under the same roof": an undated and unsigned letter to Anna Cutts, and Sally McKean Yrujo to Anna Cutts, 28 June 1804, both in Cutts Collection, LC.

50. Norma Basch, *Framing American Divorce* (Berkeley: University of California Press, 2001), chap. 1 and 2; Hendrik Hartog, *Man and Wife in America: A History* (Cambridge: Harvard University Press, 2000), chap. 3; Riley, "Legislative Divorce in Virginia, 1803–1850," 51–67; Salmon, *Women and the Law of Property in Early America*, chap. 4.

51. Thomas Law to George Logan, 10 May 1804, transcript in Alexandria Library file compilation, original in HSP; Thomas Law to John Law, 4 September and 25 September 1804, PFP, MVLA.

52. RSC to Mrs. Stier, 30 July 1804, in Calcott, *Mistress of Riversdale*, 92.

53. Thomas Law to John Law, undated (c. 1810), PFP, MVLA.

54. Sally McKean Yrujo to Anna Cutts, 28 June 1804, Cutts Collection, LC.

55. RSC to Mrs. Stier, 4 December 1804; RSC to Isabelle van Havre, 18 February 1805, in Calcott, *Mistress of Riversdale*, 103, 111.

56. Lee Chambers-Schiller, *Liberty, a Better Husband: Single Women in America: The Generations of 1780–1840* (New Haven: Yale University Press, 1984), 175.

57. It is unlikely that more than a couple of enslaved people accompanied Eliza, as there were many more bondspeople at Riversdale. She may have hired out several people; that October, she hired out an enslaved person named David to Dolley Madison with the agreement that he be freed in five years. *See* Dolley Payne Madison to Eliza, 17 October 1804, *Papers of James Madison-Secretary of State Series*, 8: 185.

58. Michael Grossberg, *Governing the Hearth*, 234–243.

59. The agreement and indentures were witnessed and recorded on 10 August 1804. The originals of the agreement and one of the indentures are in the PFP, MVLA; the official copies are in Liber L No 11 fol. 114, 115, 116, District of Columbia Courthouse.
60. "Baltimore House, 4811 Riverdale Road, Riverdale Park, Prince George's County, MD," HABS Survey, https://www.loc.gov/item/md0567/.
61. RSC to Isabelle van Havre, 4 December 1804, in Calcott, *Mistress of Riversdale*, 103.
62. RSC to Isabelle van Havre, 10 December 1807, in Calcott, 177.
63. Everett Somerville Brown, ed., *William Plumer's Memorandum of Proceedings in the United States Senate, 1803–1807* (New York: The Macmillan Company, 1923), 124; John Quincy Adams, *The Diary of John Quincy Adams, 1794–1845; American Political, Social and Intellectual Life from Washington to Polk*, ed. Allan Nevins (New York: Longmans, Green and Co., 1928), 2: 293; JQA diaries (manuscript), MHS, 27: 66; RSC to Mrs. Stier, 2 March 1804, in Calcott, *Mistress of Riversdale*, 77–79.
64. Josiah Quincy, *Figures of the Past* (Boston: Roberts Brothers, 1896), 275.
65. Potts-Fitzhugh House, National Register of Historic Places Inventory-Nomination Form, https://www.dhr.virginia.gov/VLR_to_transfer/PDFNoms/100-0082_RobtELee_Boyhood_Home_1986_Final_Nomination.pdf.
66. MLFC to GWPC, undated letter, AH.
67. GWPC to MLFC, undated, MCLP, VMHC.
68. GWPC to Thomas Jefferson, 13 February 1804; Jefferson to GWPC, 23 February 1804, in *PTJ*, 42: 460–461, 533.
69. Cornelia Lee to "cousin," 13 April 1804, Ethel Armes Collection of Lee Family Papers, LC.
70. GWPC to James Anderson, 3 June 1804, American Historical Manuscript Collection, New York Historical Society.
71. *Alexandria Advertiser*, 2 July 1804; *Washington Federalist*, 16 July 1804. On GWPC's speaking voice, *see* GWPC Recollections, 72.
72. Nelly to GWL, 21 July 1804, DLCCU.
73. Mr. Herbert to Thomas Law, 9 July 1804, TLFP, MCHC.
74. Aaron Burr to Theodosia Burr Alston, 10 July 1804, in Matthew L. Davis, ed., *Memoirs of Aaron Burr* (New York: Harper, 1837), 2: 324.
75. Given that Burr did save his correspondence with his former mistress Leonora Sansay (he told Theodosia about the letters in the July 10 note), it is unlikely he would have destroyed such letters out of privacy concerns. Eliza mentioned "I see Burr often" to Thomas in a 10 February 1803 letter (TLFP, MCHC).
76. *See* Nancy Isenberg, *Fallen Founder: The Life of Aaron Burr* (New York: Penguin Books, 2008).

77. Brown, *William Plumer's Memorandum of Proceedings in the United States Senate, 1803–1807*, 203–204.

78. Nelly to EBG, 23 March 1806, in Brady, 68.

79. Nelly to EBG, 23 March 1806, in Brady, 68; Nelly to GWL, 21 July 1804, DLCCU.

80. Nelly to Gabriel Lewis, 25 May 1806, HMC, MVLA.

81. Nelly to EBG, 23 March 1806, in Brady, 68; Nelly to Gabriel Lewis, 25 May 1806, HMC, MVLA.

82. National Historic Landmark Nomination Form, Woodlawn, National Park Service, 1998. Lawrence signed a contract in June 1805 with a carpenter and joiner named Isaac McLain to construct a house "Lewis is now about to build" (copy in Woodlawn archives). It is unclear when the work was completed; the nomination form says 1805, but this is highly unlikely based on the date of the contract.

83. RSC to Mr. Stier, 7 October 1805, in Calcott, *Mistress of Riversdale*, 130.

84. "The Episcopal High School Hoxton House" by T. Michael Miller, prepared 8 November 1992, paper on file at MVLA; "Mount Washington: Eliza Custis Law's Farm at Alexandria, Virginia" by Marguerite Carnell Rodney, 12 December 1994, for American Architecture 175 with Richard Longstreth, GWU, in MVLA files; *Alexandria Gazette*, 16 March 1808; Fairfax County Personal Property Tax Lists, Reel 107, 1806B, Library of Virginia. Only enslaved people over sixteen were counted for tax purposes.

85. William C. Allen, "An Architectural History of Tudor Place," in *Tudor Place: America's Story Lives Here*, ed. Leslie Buhler (Washington, DC: White House Historical Association, 2016), 49–93. On the land purchase, *see* Wendy Kail, "Land for Sale: Inquire Within," Tudor Place, 2015, 5, https://tudorplace.org/wp-content/uploads/2020/09/Land-for-Sale-00000002-for-web-pdf.pdf. Thomas Peter later wrote that the money for the purchase came from the sale of land Patty had inherited from GW, but researchers have not yet confirmed this.

86. "Washington's Slave List," June 1799, in *PGW-RS*, 4: 527–542; "List of the Different Drafts of Negroes, [1802]," PFP, MVLA.

87. MLFC to William Meade, December 1807 and 30 January 1810, William Meade Papers, Earl Gregg Swem Library, College of William and Mary.

88. *National Intelligencer*, 15 May 1809; Nelligan, *Arlington House*, 73–74.

89. *Alexandria Daily Advertiser*, 16 October, 8 November, 7 March 1805; Nelligan, 74–75.

90. RSC to Mr. Stier, 9 June 1809, in Calcott, *Mistress of Riversdale*, 206.

91. Nelligan, *Arlington House*, 74, 76–77.

92. Maria Carter Syphax told a reporter, "I am General Custis' daughter... He told me so face to face." *See* "Lovely Arlington," *Morning Star* (Rock-

ford, IL), 4 September 1888. While family histories identify Maria's mother by this name and as having come from Mount Vernon, there is no evidence she was ever there; it is more likely she came from one of the southern Custis estates. Through the advocacy and research of Syphax descendants, the National Park Service (which runs Arlington House) now recognizes Maria as GWPC's daughter. Special thanks to Syphax descendant Stephen Hammond for our many discussions on this topic.

93. Calcott, *Mistress of Riversdale*, 378–384.

94. Mary Boykin Chesnut, *Mary Chesnut's Civil War*, ed. C. Vann Woodward (New Haven: Yale University Press, 1993), 72.

95. Brenda E. Stevenson, "What's Love Got to Do with It? Concubinage and Enslaved Women and Girls in the Antebellum South," *The Journal of African American History* 98, no. 1 (2013): 99–125.

96. Scott E. Casper, *Sarah Johnson's Mount Vernon: The Forgotten History of an American Shrine* (New York: Hill and Wang, 2008), 6, 11–15; Bushrod Washington to Elizabeth Powel, 10 May 1804, HMC, MVLA.

Chapter 5

1. RSC to Isabelle van Havre, 10 December 1807, in Calcott, *Mistress of Riversdale*, 177.

2. On American entanglement in the Napoleonic Wars in the years before the War of 1812, *see* Peter P. Hill, *Napoleon's Troublesome Americans: Franco-American Relations, 1804–1815* (Washington, DC: Potomac Books, Inc., 2011); Bradford Perkins, *Prologue to War: England and the United States, 1805–1812* (Berkeley: University of California Press, 1961); Lawrence S. Kaplan, *Entangling Alliances with None: American Foreign Policy in the Age of Jefferson* (Kent, OH: Kent State University Press, 1987); Reginald Horsman, *The Causes of the War of 1812* (Philadelphia: University of Pennsylvania Press, 1962).

3. Hill, *Napoleon's Troublesome Americans*; Perkins, *Prologue to War*; Kaplan, *Entangling Alliances with None*; Horsman, *The Causes of the War of 1812*.

4. Perkins, *Prologue to War*, 140–142. The most detailed account of the incident is in Spencer C. Tucker and Frank T. Reuter, *Injured Honor: The Chesapeake-Leopard Affair, June 22, 1807* (Annapolis: Naval Institute Press, 1994).

5. Lawrence Lewis to Gabriel Lewis, 22 July 1807, HMC, MVLA.

6. Eliza to John Law, 24 July 1807, PFP, MVLA.

7. Horsman, *The Causes of the War of 1812*, 103–104.

8. Eliza to John Law, 14 July 1807, TLFP, MCHC.

9. GWPC, *An Address to the People of the United States on the Importance of*

Encouraging Agriculture and Domestic Manufactures (Alexandria, VA: S. Snowden, 1808), 7; Nelligan, *Arlington House*, 79.

10. *See* Ragsdale, *Washington at the Plow*.

11. *Alexandria Gazette*, 29 September 1809; Nelligan, *Arlington House*, 91.

12. Nelligan, 92, 96. Purebreds of this breed have long since died out, but it had been bred with other sheep in Virginia, so some of its blood-line persisted in the late nineteenth century; *see* United States Bureau of Animal Industry et al., *Special Report on the History and Present Condition of the Sheep Industry of the United States* (Washington, DC: US Government Printing Office, 1892), 66–67.

13. *Spirit of '76*, 14 February 1810. On newspaper attacks on GWPC, *see* Sara Bearss, "The Federalist Career of George Washington Parke Custis," *Northern Virginia Heritage* 8, no. 1 (February 1986): 16–17.

14. *Spirit of '76*, 30 March and 1 May 1810.

15. *Spirit of '76*, 29 May and 6 July 1810.

16. *Spirit of '76*, 24 July 1810. The last piece was published by Virginian on 19 October 1810.

17. Eliza to John Law, c. 1809 to 1811, TLFP, MCHC.

18. For a good overview and the source of the statistics, *see* Denver Brunsman, "Subjects vs. Citizens: Impressment and Identity in the Anglo-American Atlantic," *Journal of the Early Republic* 30, no. 4 (Winter 2010): 557–586. For a brief summary of the Lewis brothers' case, *see* Nathan Perl-Rosenthal, *Citizen Sailors: Becoming American in the Age of Revolution* (Cambridge: The Belknap Press of Harvard University Press, 2015), 245–247. Thanks to Nathan for sharing scans of the Lewis records from the National Archives with me.

19. Paula S. Felder, *Fielding Lewis and the Washington Family: A Chronicle of 18th Century Fredericksburg* (Fredericksburg, VA: American History Company, 1998), 311. For the quote, *see* Betty Washington Lewis to GW, 25 September 1792, in *PGW-PS*, 11: 155.

20. All of the documents in this case are filed in RG 59, Miscellaneous Correspondence Regarding Impressed Seamen, box #6, entry 928, National Archives and Records Administration (NARA). Charles's tattoos are described in an affidavit dated 12 January 1812 and signed by Lawrence Lewis. John's letters are dated 23 March 1810 and 10 April 1810; these were apparently enclosed in a 16 April 1810 letter from James Maury to Lawrence Lewis, which is not in the file.

21. Lawrence's 1810 letter to Lyman is mentioned in Lyman to Lewis, 30 August 1810. This letter, the affidavits, and Lawrence's 28 January 1812 letter to Daniel Brent are all in NARA.

22. Monroe wrote British ambassador Augustus Foster on 8 February 1812 (RG 59: Notes to Foreign Ministers and Consuls, NARA). Richard Rush's speech published in the *National Intelligencer* on 28 July 1812

says that the two men had both recently been freed. Charles's separation application also indicates he was freed; *see* RG 84, Records of Foreign Service Posts of the Department of State, vol. 499, no. 6919, 19 November 1811, NARA, cited in Perl-Rosenthal, 351n35. On John Lewis's fate, *see* the following chapter.

23. John Lewis to Lawrence Lewis, 10 April 1810, NARA.
24. Tudor Place family tree, research files, TP. On the mortality rate, *see* Susan E. Klepp, *Revolutionary Conceptions: Women, Fertility, and Family Limitation in America, 1760–1820* (Chapel Hill: University of North Carolina Press, 2009), 293.
25. RSC to Isabelle van Havre, 10 December 1807, in Calcott, *Mistress of Riversdale*, 177.
26. MLFC to Nancy [Robinson], 5 October [1807], MCLP, VMHC. Mary's birth year has traditionally been listed as 1808 because the Custis family bible (DeButts-Ely Collection, LC) lists this year. However, Elizabeth Brown Pryor argues that the date has been changed in the bible, and points to two mentions of Mary prior to October 1808 in correspondence (*see* Pryor, *Reading the Man*, 80). The letter cited here, which has no date on it, also mentions the recent death of Sally Peyton, who died on 26 September 1807 (*Enquirer* [Richmond], 10 October 1807).
27. [Anonymous] to MLFC, 31 October 1810, Lee Family Papers, VMHC; Susan Meade to MLFC, 1 November 1810, Custis Family Papers, VMHC. The only mention of Edwa in Molly's or Wash's writings is in MLFC to William Meade, 30 January 1810, William Meade Papers, Earl Gregg Swem Library, College of William and Mary.
28. Eliza to John Law, 29 September 1810, PFP, MVLA; Nelly to GWL, 12 March 1812, DLCCU.
29. MCP to Eliza Quincy, 19 August 1810, in Quincy, *Memoir of the Life of Eliza S.M. Quincy*, 139; Nelly to GWL, 12 March 1812, DLCCU.
30. RSC to Isabelle van Havre, 15 July 1811, in Calcott, *Mistress of Riversdale*, 240; ECC Stuart to Nelly, Monday night [c. summer 1811], HMC, MVLA. On blisters as treatment, *see* Ira Rutkow, *Seeking the Cure: A History of Medicine in America* (New York: Simon and Schuster, 2010), 39.
31. On ECC's death, *see* Eliza to DBW and Eliza to Barlow [c. fall 1811], Custis-Lee Papers, LC; MCP to Eliza Custis Peter, 15 February 1812, in Quincy, *Memoir of the Life of Eliza S.M. Quincy*, 145.
32. John Law to Thomas Law, 7 March 1808, TLFP, MCHC; Eliza to John Law, 25 November 1808, PFP, MVLA.
33. RSC to Isabelle van Havre, 20 January 1809, in Calcott, *Mistress of Riversdale*, 200; John Law to Thomas Law, 27 March 1808, TLFP, MCHC.
34. "The Episcopal High School Hoxton House" by T. Michael Miller, prepared 8 November 1992, paper on file at Mount Vernon; the original deed is in Fairfax Deed Books B3 p. 140, and a typescript is in

the records of the Alexandria Public Library. Miller does not appear to have realized Robinson's relationship with Eliza.

35. John Mifflin to Thomas Law, 9 June 1809, Thomas Law Papers, LC.

36. Thomas Law to John Law, undated [c. 1810], PFP, MVLA.

37. Thomas Law to Lawrence Lewis, 11 May [1811], PFP, MVLA.

38. Thomas Law to John Law, undated [c. 1810], PFP, MVLA.

39. Mary Beth Sievens, *Stray Wives: Marital Conflict in Early National New England* (New York: NYU Press, 2005), 24–25.

40. Thomas Law to John Law, 25 June 1810, PFP, MVLA.

41. Eliza to John Law, [January 1811], PFP, MVLA.

42. Thomas Law to Eliza, 29 March [1811], TLFP, mislabeled under letters from John Law, MCHC; ECC to Nelly, [1811], HMC, MVLA.

43. Thomas Law to John Law, 8 April 1811, PFP, MVLA. The original letter from Nelly to EBG on this subject has not been located, but she discussed the rumors in her 25 August 1811 letter; *see* Brady, 70–71. Nelly denied that she was "influenced by a spirit of malice or revenge" and noted that she and Lawrence had stayed friendly with Thomas after the separation, while the rest of the family wouldn't even talk to him.

44. Edmund Law to Thomas Law, 14 April 1811, TLFP, MCHC.

45. John Law to Thomas Law, 17 April 1811; Edmund Law to Thomas Law, 14 April 1811; Thomas Law to John Law, 26 April 1811; John Law to Thomas Law, 1 August 1811, TLFP, MCHC.

46. GWPC to MLFC, 4 and 18 September 1811, MCLP, VMHC.

47. Nelligan, *Arlington House*, 99–100.

48. *Alexandria Gazette*, 24 December 1811.

49. Samuel Mordecai repeated this story several years later; *see* Mordecai to his sisters, 24 June 1814, transcription in Eliza Custis Law research file at MVLA; original in Mordecai Papers, Southern Historical Collection, University of North Carolina.

50. Dolley Madison to Anna Payne Cutts, 8 June [1811], *DM Digital Edition*.

51. RSC to Isabelle van Havre, 15 July 1811, in Calcott, *Mistress of Riversdale*, 240.

52. Eliza to DBW, 27 July [1811], DBW Papers, MCHC. On Serurier, *see* M. Michel Chevalier, "Le Comte Louis Serurier: Notice Biographique," in *Annuaire diplomatique de l'empire francais*, vol. 4 (Veuve Berges-Levrault, 1863), 163–172.

53. Perkins, *Prologue to War*, 246–254.

54. Eliza to DBW, 3 June 1815, Custis-Lee Papers, LC; Eliza to Ruth Barlow, 15 August 1812, published in Caroline Dall, "A Centennial 'Posie,'" *Unitarian Review* 1876, 187–189.

55. Hoyt, "Self-Portrait: Eliza Custis, 1808." On DBW, *see* Francis C. Haber,

David Bailie Warden, A Bibliographical Sketch of America's Cultural Ambassador in France, 1804–1845 (Washington, DC: Institut Francais de Washington, 1954).

56. On friendships between men and women, including the use of sibling language, *see* Cassandra A. Good, *Founding Friendships: Friendships between Men and Women in the Early American Republic* (New York: Oxford University Press, 2015).

57. Eliza to DBW, 27 July [1811], DBW Papers, MCHC.

58. Eliza to DBW, 27 July [1811], DBW Papers, MCHC.

59. Eliza to Joel Barlow, c. fall 1811; Eliza to DBW, c. fall 1811, Custis-Lee Papers, LC.

60. Foster's journal, 1811–1812, 19 November 1811, in Augustus Foster Papers, LC; Lucy P Washington to Phoebe Morris, 14 December 1811, Morris Papers, Dumbarton House, Washington, DC.

61. Unknown to Anna Cutts, 14 January 1812, Cutts Collection, LC.

62. Samuel Eliot Morison, "The Henry-Crillon Affair of 1812," *Proceedings of the Massachusetts Historical Society* 69 (1947): 207–31; Daniel Preston and Cassandra Good, eds., *The Papers of James Monroe*, vol. 6 (Santa Barbara: ABC-CLIO, 2017), 117; Foster's journal, 1811–1812, 26 January 1812, in Augustus Foster Papers, LC.

63. Jacques Houdaille, "La Mission de Monsieur Greffe, 1810," *Revista de Historia de América* 50 (December 1960): 475–483; Foster's journal, 1811–1812, 24 May 1812, in Augustus Foster Papers, LC.

64. Augustus John Foster, *Jeffersonian America: Notes on the United States of America, Collected in the Years 1805–6–7 and 11–12* (Westport, CT: Greenwood Press, 1980), 82.

65. Eliza to Lafayette, 11 June 1812, Marquis de Lafayette Papers, LC.

66. Eliza to Ruth Barlow, 15 August 1812, published in Caroline Dall, "A Centennial 'Posie,'" *Unitarian Review* 1876, 187–189.

67. Clara Baldwin Bomford to Anna Maria Thornton, 10 November 1812, in Caroline Wells Healey Dall Papers, Clara Baldwin Bomford Letterbook, reel 1, MHS. Clara did not know his name, which is Anglicized as Hughes Lavergne. A letter from DBW on the affair and an affidavit from Lavergne are in the de la Vergne Family Papers, Tulane University Special Collections.

68. Eliza to DBW, 9 November [1813], Custis-Lee Papers, LC.

69. Phoebe Morris to Rebecca Morris, 28 February 1812, Morris Papers, Dumbarton House. *See also* Good, "Washington Family Fortune."

70. Simon Newman, *Parades and the Politics of the Street: Festive Culture in the Early American Republic* (Philadelphia: University of Pennsylvania Press, 1999), chap. 2.

71. Donald R. Hickey, *The War of 1812: A Forgotten Conflict, Bicentennial Edition* (Urbana: University of Illinois Press, 2012), 25, 30–31, 38.

Chapter 6

1. *National Intelligencer*, 7 May 1812; *Palladium of Liberty* (Morristown, NJ), 28 May 1812.
2. Bradford Perkins, *Prologue to War: England and the United States, 1805–1812* (Berkeley: University of California Press, 1961), 343–345; Hickey, *The War of 1812*, 30–31, 36–37.
3. Daniel Preston and Cassandra Good, eds., *The Papers of James Monroe*, vol. 6 (Santa Barbara: ABC-CLIO, 2017), 156–157.
4. *National Intelligencer*, 7 May 1812; Foster's journal, 1811–1812, 29 April 1812, in Augustus Foster Papers, Box 14, folder 4, LC.
5. "Sketches from Mr. Custis's Speech to His Guests at the Arlington Sheep Shearing," *National Intelligencer*, 16 May 1812.
6. Bradford Perkins, author of the classic study on the lead-up to the War of 1812, argues that the war was caused by "irrational and emotional reasons." *See* Perkins, *Prologue to War*, vii, 2. *See also* Cassandra Good, "James Monroe and the Passions of Foreign Policy" (paper presented at the Society for Historians of American Foreign Relations, Washington, DC, 25 June 2015); Hickey, *The War of 1812*, 1–2, 25.
7. Hickey, *The War of 1812*, 43.
8. GWPC to Edmund Logan, 18 June 1812, AH, photocopy of original at HSP.
9. "An Oration Delivered by Richard Rush," *National Intelligencer*, 28 July 1812. On the setting and audience of the speech, *see* "Fourth of July," *Universal Gazette* (Washington, DC), 10 July 1812.
10. *Democratic Press* (Philadelphia), 8 May 1812; "An Oration Delivered by Richard Rush," *National Intelligencer*, 28 July 1812.
11. MCP to Eliza Quincy, 27 July 1812, in Quincy, *Memoir of the Life of Eliza S.M. Quincy*, 164–165.
12. Paul A. Gilje, "The Baltimore Riots of 1812 and the Breakdown of the Anglo-American Mob Tradition," *Journal of Social History* 13, no. 4 (1980): 547–564.
13. MCP to Eliza Quincy, 27 July 1812, in Quincy, *Memoir of the Life of Eliza S.M. Quincy*, 164–165; Anna Maria Thornton Diary, 3 August 1812, Anna Maria Brodeau Thornton Papers, LC.
14. *Spirit of '76*, 11 August 1812; *Federal Republican* (Georgetown), 28 August 1812.
15. *Virginia Argus*, 31 August 1812; *Federal Republican*, 4 September 1812.
16. GWPC, *Oration by Mr. Custis, of Arlington; with an Account of the Funeral Solemnities in Honor of the Lamented Gen. James M. Lingan* (Washington City, 1812). The crowd size estimate and quote are from *Federal Republican*, 2 September 1812.
17. *Federal Republican*, 2 September 1812; Custis, 8. The speech was for

sale as a pamphlet within less than two weeks; *see eg* "Death of Gen. Lingan," *Boston Patriot*, 12 September 1812.

18. *Constitutionalist* (Exeter, NH), 22 September 1812; *Evening Post* (New York), 10 September 1812.

19. *American Watchman* (Wilmington, DE) and *City Gazette* (Charleston, SC), 19 September 1812.

20. *See eg* his obituary in the *National Intelligencer*, 12 October 1857.

21. *See eg* Allgor, *Parlor Politics*; Jan Lewis, "Politics and the Ambivalence of the Private Sphere: Women in Early Washington, D.C."; Rosemarie Zagarri, *Revolutionary Backlash*.

22. Norman K. Risjord, "The Virginia Federalists," *Journal of Southern History* 33, no. 4 (1967): 509; James M. Banner, *To the Hartford Convention: The Federalists and the Origins of Party Politics in Massachusetts, 1789–1815* (New York: Alfred A. Knopf, 1970), 46. On the visible rituals of dissent to the war among New England Federalists, *see* David Waldstreicher, *In the Midst of Perpetual Fetes: The Making of American Nationalism, 1776–1820* (Chapel Hill: University of North Carolina Press, 1997), 257–259. On the Peters' politics, *see* George S. Hillard, ed., *Life, Letters, and Journals of George Ticknor* (Boston: Houghton Mifflin, 1909), 138.

23. Alexander Robinson, "The Washington Benevolent Society in New England: A Phase of Politics during the War of 1812," *Proceedings of the Massachusetts Historical Society* 49 (March 1916): 280, 284.

24. Curatorial file, Washingtoniana 0224.01–.03, MHS; J. Paul Hudson, "George Washington's Military Gorget," *Virginia Cavalcade* 12, no. 3 (Winter 1962): 5–8; Harold Leslie Peterson, *Arms and Armor in Colonial America, 1526–1783* (Harrisburg, PA: Stackpole Books, 1956), 311–312; William M.S. Rasmussen and Robert S. Tilton, *George Washington: The Man Behind the Myths* (Charlottesville: University of Virginia Press, 1999), 40–41. For a complete list of Washington objects in the Peter family, *see* the Tudor Place object inventory in PFP, MVLA.

25. Notes from the quarterly meeting of the Washington Benevolent Society of Massachusetts, Boston, 13 April 1813, enclosed in Washington Benevolent Society to MCP, MS-2, TP.

26. On the societal norms surrounding women and public speaking, *see* Carolyn Eastman, *A Nation of Speechifiers: Making an American Public after the Revolution* (Chicago: University of Chicago Press, 2010), 54–56, chap. 6.

27. "Gen. Washington's Gorget," *Weekly Messenger*, 16 April 1813.

28. "A Gorgeous Present," 30 April 1813, *National Intelligencer*.

29. MCP to Eliza Quincy, 13 July 1813, in Quincy, *Memoir of the Life of Eliza S.M. Quincy*, 174. On the approach of Cockburn's ships, *see* Green, *Washington*, vol. 1: 58–59.

30. Troy Bickham, *The Weight of Vengeance: The United States, the British Empire, and the War of 1812* (New York: Oxford University Press, 2012), 4; Jon Latimer, *1812: War with America* (Cambridge: Harvard University Press, 2009), 4.

31. William E. Nagengast, "Moscow, the Stalingrad of 1812: American Reaction toward Napoleon's Retreat from Russia," *The Russian Review* 8, no. 4 (1949): 302–315.

32. For descriptions of the event, *see Federal Republican*, 6 and 9 June 1813. For Wash's speech, *see Federal Republican*, 16 June 1813.

33. *Alexandria Herald*, 4 August 1813 (*see also National Intelligencer*, 10 September 1813); *National Intelligencer*, 24 April 1813.

34. Nagengast, "Moscow, the Stalingrad of 1812." On the Russian mediation offer, *see* Hickey, *The War of 1812*, 286–287.

35. Lawrence Lewis to Warner Lewis, 6 January 1814, HMC, MVLA.

36. In the summer of 1812, Eliza had moved to Germantown (outside of Philadelphia), where her daughter was in school. *See* Eliza to Ruth Barlow, 15 August 1812, in Caroline Dall, "A Centennial 'Posie,'" *Unitarian Review*, 1876, 187.

37. Hickey, *The War of 1812*, 183–184.

38. Hickey, 228, 237.

39. GWPC to James H. Hooe, 14 June 1813; William Costin to GWPC, MCLP, VMHC; Nelligan, *Arlington House*, 108–109.

40. William Brent to Lawrence Lewis, 2 February 1828; NARA, RG 76, Entry 190 (Case Files, c. 1827–c. 1828), file 727; Gene Allen Smith, *The Slaves' Gamble: Choosing Sides in the War of 1812* (New York: St. Martin's Publishing Group, 2013), chap. 4; Alan Taylor, *The Internal Enemy: Slavery and War in Virginia, 1772–1832* (New York: W.W. Norton & Company, 2013), 162.

41. MCP to Eliza Quincy, 26 August 1814, in Quincy, *Memoir of the Life of Eliza S.M. Quincy*, 175.

42. Eliza to DBW, 18 August 1814, Custis-Lee Papers, LC.

43. Hickey, *The War of 1812*, 203–204; Steve Vogel, *Through the Perilous Fight: Six Weeks that Saved the Nation* (New York: Random House, 2013), 78, 99.

44. Vogel, *Through the Perilous Fight*, 57, 66, 69, 81, 89, 98. For Eliza's quote: Eliza to DBW, 18 August 1814, Custis-Lee Papers, LC.

45. Hillard, *Life, Letters, and Journals of George Ticknor*, 38; Quertermous, *A Georgetown Life*, 134.

46. James Madison to Dolley Madison, 23 August 1814, in *Papers of James Madison-Presidential Series*, 8: 133

47. While the story of Dolley Madison saving the portrait remains well-known, GWPC's role has received little attention. Two sources from people present in Washington at the time recount his role. Charles

Jared Ingersoll published an account including this story, based on an interview with the man who served as chief steward of the President's House in 1814, in a book in 1849; *see* Charles Jared Ingersoll, *Historical Sketch of the Second War between the United States of America and Great Britain* (Philadelphia: Lea and Blanchard, 1849). Anna Maria Thornton also seems to have heard some version of this story; she recorded in her diary for August 24 that "it was supposed that Mr. Custis got some of the soldiers' to take out this picture [of George Washington]." *See* Anna Thornton, "Diary of Mrs. William Thornton. Capture of Washington by the British," *Records of the Columbia Historical Society, Washington, D.C.* 19 (1916): 175.

48. *Federal Republican*, 1 September 1814.
49. Mary Eliza Angela Lewis was born on April 1, 1813.
50. "The Battle of Bladensburg," [1814], Gratz Collection of Washington Papers, HSP.
51. Vogel, *Through the Perilous Fight*, 153–180.
52. Thornton, "Diary of Mrs. William Thornton. Capture of Washington by the British," 175; MCP to Timothy Pickering, 28 August 1814, Pickering Papers, MHS; Vogel, 6, 167, 180.
53. *Federal Republican*, 15 October 1814; Viator, *The Washington Sketch Book* (New York: Mohun, Ebbs & Hough, 1864), 243; Ingersoll, *Historical Sketch of the Second War between the United States of America and Great Britain*, 188.
54. *National Intelligencer*, 14 September 1814; *Federal Republican*, 15 October 1814.
55. MCP to Eliza Quincy, 26 August 1814, in Quincy, *Memoir of the Life of Eliza S.M. Quincy*, 178–179; Vogel, *Through the Perilous Fight*, 189.
56. MCP to Eliza Quincy, 26 August 1814, in Quincy, *Memoir of the Life of Eliza S.M. Quincy*, 177. *See also* James Ewell, *The Medical Companion: Treating, According to the Most Successful Practice* (Philadelphia: Printed for the author, 1817), 670.
57. Frances Walker Gilmer to P.R. Gilmer, quoted in Richard Beale Davis, "The Abbe Correa in America, 1812–1820," *Transactions of the American Philosophical Society*, new series, XLV, pt. 2 (1955), 101.
58. Eliza to DBW, 8 September 1814, Custis-Lee Papers, LC.
59. MCP to Eliza Quincy, 26 August 1814, in Quincy, *Memoir of the Life of Eliza S.M. Quincy*, 177; MCP to Timothy Pickering, 28 August 1814, Pickering Papers, MHS.
60. Bushrod Washington to Saussure, 29 November 1814, MVLA.
61. Eliza to DBW, 28 July, 8 September, and 7 November 1814, Custis-Lee Papers, LC; Eliza to DBW, 14 July 1815, DBW Papers, MCHC.
62. Eliza to DBW, 28 July 1814, Custis-Lee Papers, Warden transcripts, LC. Madison's letter to Crawford has not been located, but Crawford

mentions it in his reply of 14 November 1814 (*Papers of James Madison-Presidential Series*, 8: 355).

63. Eliza to DBW, 29 July 1816, DBW Papers, MCHC.
64. Eliza to DBW, 26 September and 20 December 1814, 14 July 1815, Custis-Lee Papers, LC.
65. Hickey, *The War of 1812*, 316.
66. Eliza to DBW, 8 April 1815, Custis-Lee Papers, LC.
67. Jacques Houdaille, "La Mission de Monsieur Greffe, 1810," *Revista de Historia de América* 50 (December 1960): 478–479.
68. Eliza to DBW, 29 July 1816, DBW Papers, MCHC.
69. Eliza to DBW, 1 July 1814, Custis-Lee Papers, LC.
70. Elizabeth Powel to Eliza, 28 February 1816, Thomas Law Papers, LC.
71. *Centinel of Freedom* (Newark, NJ), 8 August 1815, adapted from a piece in the *Delaware Watchman*.
72. Hillard, *Life, Letters, and Journals of George Ticknor*, 38.

Chapter 7

1. Nelly to EBG, 15 January 1823, in Brady, 130–131.
2. Louisa Catherine Adams to John Quincy Adams, 26 July 1822, Adams Papers, MHS; Nelly to GWL, 9 February 1816, DLCCU.
3. Nelly to EBG, 21 March 1821, 10 (two letters) and 28 October 1820, in Brady, 87–89, 106; Nelly to Betty Carter, 23 November 1820, Tucker Harrison Smith Families, UVa. In her 2 October 1825 letter to EBG, Nelly noted that Angela "sleeps in my bosom always," suggesting she was in a separate bed from her husband; *see* Brady, 167.
4. Nelly to EBG, 4 December 1820, in Brady, 94; MCP to EBG, 14 December 1820, MS-2, TP; Quertermous, *A Georgetown Life*, 76.
5. Nelly to EBG, 14 October 1822, in Brady, 128. Eliza Law had married Lloyd Nicholas Rogers in April 1817 and given birth to daughter Eleanor Agnes Rogers in May 1822.
6. GWPC to MLFC, 26 August 1822, MCLP, VMHC.
7. Nelly to GWL, 9 February 1816, DLCCU.
8. Louisa Catherine Adams to John Adams, 27 February 1819, Adams Papers, MHS; *Commercial Advertiser*, 8 March 1819.
9. Laura H. Wirt to Louisa Cabell Carrington, 9 April 1823, Laura H. Wirt Randall Papers, VMHC. The character she referred to was the Countess of Derby in Sir Walter Scott's *Peveril of the Peak* (1822).
10. Edward Prince Hutchinson, *Legislative History of American Immigration Policy, 1798–1965* (Philadelphia: University of Pennsylvania Press, 1981), 20–21; Kerby A. Miller, *Emigrants and Exiles: Ireland and the Irish Exodus to North America* (New York: Oxford University Press, 1988),

193–194. On Emmet, *see* David A. Wilson, *United Irishmen, United States: Immigrant Radicals in the Early Republic* (Ithaca: Cornell University Press, 2011), 18, 135.

11.   Thomas Addis Emmet to Eliza, 15 December 1817, transcription, Karl C. Harrison Museum of George Washington.

12.   Eliza to DBW, 14 January 1818, Custis-Lee Papers, LC; Hutchinson, *Legislative History of American Immigration Policy, 1798–1965*, 21.

13.   Edmundo Murray, "Devereux, John," in *Ireland and the Americas: Culture, Politics, and History: A Multidisciplinary Encyclopedia*, 2: 250–251. The information on when she met Devereux is from her 8 November 1828 letter to Simon Bolivar, MVLA. On Irish contributions to South American freedom fights, *see* Tim Fanning, *Paisanos: The Irish and the Liberation of America* (Notre Dame, IN: University of Notre Dame Press, 2016).

14.   Eliza to DBW, 3 April 1818, Custis-Lee Papers, LC; Eliza to Simon Bolivar, 8 November 1828, MVLA.

15.   Nelly to EBG, 10 February, 4 March 1822; 15 November 1823, in Brady, 122, 123–124; Nelly to EBG, 19 March 1822, 15 November 1823, EBG Collection, MVLA.

16.   *See above* and Nelly to EBG, 10 November 1822, EBG Collection, MVLA; Nelly to EBG, 3 December 1821 and 10 February 1822, in Brady, 116, 122.

17.   William Turnbull to Edward George Washington Butler (hereafter EGWB), 14 March 1824, BFP, HNOC; Nelly to EBG, 11 Jan 1821, 24 November 1817, in Brady, 100, 84.

18.   Nelly to EBG, 19 March 1822, EBG Collection, MVLA.

19.   Butler first mentioned Parke in a letter to his sister on 10 February 1823; *see* Twiss Collection, HNOC.

20.   "Jackson's Visit to Mount Vernon," November 1815, in John Spencer Bassett, ed., *Correspondence of Andrew Jackson* (Washington, DC: Carnegie Institution, 1927), 2: 219–220; Eliza to DBW, 8 April 1815, Custis-Lee Papers, LC.

21.   Rachel Donelson Robards was in an unhappy marriage to Lewis Robards when Andrew Jackson met her in Nashville, Tennessee. She separated from Robards and lived with Jackson as his wife, but it is unclear when the pair first married and whether they knew that she was not yet legally divorced from Robards. After her divorce was finalized, they legally married in 1794. They were accepted by their community at the time, but the relationship came up occasionally in attacks on Jackson over the years before becoming a major issue in the presidential campaign of 1828. *See* Harriet Chappell Owsley, "The Marriages of Rachel Donelson," *Tennessee Historical Quarterly* 36, no. 4 (1977): 479–492; Robert V. Remini, *Andrew Jackson*, vol. 1, *The Course of American Empire, 1767–1821* (Baltimore: Johns Hopkins University Press,

1977), chap. 5; Robert V. Remini, *Andrew Jackson*, vol. 2, *The Course of American Freedom, 1822–1832* (Baltimore: Johns Hopkins University Press, 1981), 118–121.

22. On Jackson's career, *see eg* Mark R. Cheatham, *Andrew Jackson: Southerner* (Baton Rouge: Louisiana State University Press, 2013); Jon Meacham, *American Lion: Andrew Jackson in the White House* (New York: Random House, 2008); Robert V. Remini, *The Life of Andrew Jackson* (New York: Harper & Row, 1988).

23. Nelly to EBG, 10 August 1824, in Brady, 153. On Butler and his relationship with Jackson, *see* David D. Plater, *The Butlers of Iberville Parish, Louisiana: Dunboyne Plantation in the 1800s* (Baton Rouge: Louisiana State University Press, 2015), chap. 1.

24. Eliza Butler to Anthony Butler, 2 December 1823, Twiss Collection, HNOC.

25. Andrew Jackson to Rachel Jackson, 28 December 1823, in John Spencer Bassett, ed., *Correspondence of Andrew Jackson* (Washington, DC: Carnegie Institution of Washington, 1926), 3: 219–220.

26. *National Intelligencer*, 6 January 1824; Andrew Jackson to EGWB, 20 January 1824, *Papers of Andrew Jackson*, 5: 341.

27. Nelly to EBG, 2 February 1824, 26 January and 2 February 1825, in Brady, 145, 162, 163.

28. Carol Sue Humphrey, *The Press of the Young Republic, 1783–1833* (Westport, CT: Greenwood Publishing Group, 1996), chap. 7; Richard R. John, *Spreading the News: The American Postal System from Franklin to Morse* (Cambridge: Harvard University Press, 2009), 7; David Paul Nord, *Communities of Journalism: A History of American Newspapers and Their Readers* (Urbana: University of Illinois Press, 2001), 88.

29. Sharon Marcus, *The Drama of Celebrity* (Princeton: Princeton University Press, 2020), 4, 10; Bonnie Carr O'Neill, *Literary Celebrity and Public Life in the Nineteenth-Century United States* (Athens, GA: University of Georgia Press, 2017), 3–4.

30. Thomas A. Chambers, *Memories of War: Visiting Battlegrounds and Bonefields in the Early American Republic* (Ithaca: Cornell University Press, 2012), 73–74; Catherine E. Kelly, *Republic of Taste: Art, Politics, and Everyday Life in Early America* (Philadelphia: University of Pennsylvania Press, 2016), 237; Anne C. Loveland, *Emblem of Liberty: The Image of Lafayette in the American Mind* (Baton Rouge: Louisiana State University Press, 1971), 75–77; Sarah J. Purcell, *Sealed with Blood: War, Sacrifice, and Memory in Revolutionary America* (Philadelphia: University of Pennsylvania Press, 2010), chap. 5. For detailed contemporary descriptions of Lafayette's tour, *see* Edgar Ewing Brandon, ed., *Lafayette, Guest of the Nation: A Contemporary Account of the Triumphal Tour of*

General Lafayette through the United States in 1824–1825 (Oxford, OH: Oxford Historical Press, 1950).

31. For a full listing of the parade members, *see* Amos Andrew Parker, *Recollections of General Lafayette on His Visit to the United States, in 1824 and 1825* (Keene, NH: Sentinel Printing Company, Printers, 1870), 112–113.

32. Brandon, *Lafayette, Guest of the Nation*, 33–34, 37.

33. *New-York American*, 8 September 1824.

34. *New York Evening Post*, 9 September 1824.

35. Celia Morris Eckhardt, *Fanny Wright: Rebel in America* (Cambridge: Harvard University Press, 1984); Lloyd Kramer, *Lafayette in Two Worlds* (Chapel Hill: University of North Carolina Press, 1999), chap. 5. For the letter quoted, *see* William Randall Waterman, *Frances Wright* (New York: Columbia University, 1924), 65–66.

36. Eckhardt, *Fanny Wright*, 81. For Nelly's comments, *see* Nelly to GWL, 7 October 1824, DLCCU.

37. Brandon, *Lafayette, Guest of the Nation*, 121–122; Auguste Levasseur, *Lafayette in America in 1824 and 1825: Or, Journal of a Voyage to the United States* (Philadelphia: Carey and Lea, 1829), 1: 163.

38. *National Intelligencer*, 1 August 1824; *Enquirer* (Richmond), 14 September 1824; *Baltimore Patriot*, 16 September 1824; Chambers, *Memories of War*, 74–75.

39. Brandon, *Lafayette, Guest of the Nation*, 122–124; Parker, *Recollections of General Lafayette on His Visit to the United States, in 1824 and 1825*, 117.

40. Brandon, *Lafayette, Guest of the Nation*, 124–132; Parker, *Recollections of General Lafayette on His Visit to the United States, in 1824 and 1825*, 118.

41. Brandon, *Lafayette, Guest of the Nation*, 21–23. On the design of the Capitol in this period, *see* Allen, *History of the United States Capitol*, chap. 4.

42. Brandon, 26–29. There is no mention of GWPC's being at the dinner, but his niece later recorded that he had dined with Lafayette at the President's House three times (MCWC Diary, 22 March 1856).

43. Quertermous, *A Georgetown Life*, 69–70.

44. Eliza to Lafayette, 26 February 1830, DLCCU.

45. Jennifer Hanna, *Arlington House Cultural Landscape Report* (Washington, DC: Department of Interior, National Park Service, National Capital Region, 2001), 46; Nelligan, *Arlington House*, 123–127; Godfrey Thomas Vigne, *Six Months in America* (Philadelphia, T.T. Ash, 1833), 55.

46. Levasseur, *Lafayette in America in 1824 and 1825*, 2: 12.

47. *Eastern Argus*, 9 June 1825, from *The American Farmer*.

48. Chambers, *Memories of War*, 76.

49. This description is a composite of two accounts: "Genl. La Fayette's visit to Arlington House," MS-5, TP, and MCWC Diary, 22 March 1856.

50. Levasseur, *Lafayette in America in 1824 and 1825*, 181–182. The presence of the Custis women is not noted in any of the contemporary accounts, but an undated letter from Nelly to Molly suggests Nelly knew an artist creating a scene in which she, Lawrence, Molly, GWPC, and Eliza were present at the tomb (MCLP, VMHC). A piece of art, combining paint and needlework, does survive and depicts the women; *see* color insert. On Nelly's "good deed," *see* Nelly to EBG, 22 October 1824, in Brady, 154.

51. *National Intelligencer*, 26 October 1824; Levasseur, 181–182; *Niles Register*, 6 November 1824, as printed in Brandon, *Lafayette, Guest of the Nation*, 41–42.

52. *Richmond Enquirer*, 22 October 1824.

53. *National Advocate* (New York), 26 October 1824.

54. Brandon, *Lafayette, Guest of the Nation*, 62.

55. Levasseur, *Lafayette in America in 1824 and 1825*, 2: 11.

56. Thomas H. Hubbard to Phebe Hubbard, 29 December 1817, Thomas H. Hubbard Papers, LC.

57. Lawrence Lewis to Robert Lewis, 14 December 1824, Society of the Cincinnati Archives; Nelly to EBG, 22 December 1824, in Brady, 159.

58. The written gifts are in DLCCU; on the relics, *see* Levasseur, *Lafayette in America in 1824 and 1825*, 2: 11.

59. Margaret Bayard Smith to Mrs. Kirkpatrick, 13 January 1825, in Smith, *The First Forty Years of Washington Society*, 170.

60. This paragraph and the information that follows on the election are from Donald J. Ratcliffe, *The One-Party Presidential Contest: Adams, Jackson, and 1824's Five-Horse Race* (Lawrence: University Press of Kansas, 2015).

61. James C. Klotter, *Henry Clay: The Man Who Would Be President* (New York: Oxford University Press, 2018), 124.

62. *National Intelligencer*, 8 February 1825.

63. Smith, *The First Forty Years of Washington Society*, 187.

64. *National Intelligencer*, 11 February 1825.

65. Levasseur, *Lafayette in America in 1824 and 1825*, 2: 24.

66. R. Lowndes to EGWB, 10 February 1825, BFP, HNOC.

67. Smith, *The First Forty Years of Washington Society*, 183.

68. Levasseur, *Lafayette in America in 1824 and 1825*, 2: 25; Nelly to EBG, 15 February 1825, in Brady, 163.

69. Smith, *The First Forty Years of Washington Society*, 183.

70. Nelly to EBG, 15 February 1825, in Brady, 163.

71. Swann Galleries auction, 16 April 2019, sale 2505, lot 221.

72. *National Gazette*, 6 April 1825.

73. Levasseur, *Lafayette in America in 1824 and 1825*, 2: 30.

74. Caitlin Fitz, *Our Sister Republics: The United States in an Age of American Revolutions* (New York: W.W. Norton & Company, 2016), 128–129.

75. *Daily National Journal*, 7 July 1825.

76. *National Intelligencer*, 4 July 1825.

77. GWPC to Bolivar, 4 July 1825, MVLA.

78. *National Intelligencer*, 3 September 1825.

79. Bolivar to Lafayette, 20 March 1826, translation published in *Washington Times*, 1 May 1821; Bolivar to GWPC, 25 May 1826, MVLA, translation published in *Colombian Review* vol. 1 (July 1921): 179.

80. Mary Gregory (Crawford) Powell, *The History of Old Alexandria, Virginia, from July 13, 1749 to May 24, 1861* (Alexandria, VA: Alexandria Library, 1962), 242; Reminiscences of Eleanor Parke Custis Lewis by EBG, August 1852, HMC, MVLA.

81. Nelly to GWL, 7 August, 7 and 9 September, 5 December 1825, DLCCU.

82. *Columbian Centinel*, 14 September 1825; *National Journal* (DC), 15 September 1825; Nelly to EBG, 2 October 1825, in Brady, 166.

83. Nelligan, *Arlington House*, 147–148.

84. Nelly to EBG, 23 February 1823, Binder 25, MVLA.

85. Nelligan, *Arlington House*, 149; James Berry to GWPC, 18 March 1829, Custis Family Papers, VMHC.

86. François Furstenberg, "Atlantic Slavery, Atlantic Freedom: George Washington, Slavery, and Transatlantic Abolitionist Networks," *The William and Mary Quarterly* 68, no. 2 (2011): 276–279; Lawrence Charles Jennings, *French Anti-Slavery: The Movement for the Abolition of Slavery in France, 1802–1848* (Cambridge: Cambridge University Press, 2000), 3–6, 24.

Chapter 8

1. Rachel A. Shelden, *Washington Brotherhood: Politics, Social Life, and the Coming of the Civil War* (Chapel Hill: University of North Carolina Press, 2013), 57. As Shelden points out, the ACS's annual meeting was held during the annual congressional session so congressmen, some of whom were members and delegates to the ACS, could attend. On the architecture of the room, *see* https://www.aoc.gov/explore-capitol-campus/buildings-grounds/capitol-building/senate-wing/old-supreme-court-chamber.

2. On Washington's views on slavery vs. free labor, *see* Ragsdale, *Washington at the Plow*. James Oakes calls this view "the bourgeois critique of slavery" and argues for its prevalence among late eighteenth-century elites. James Oakes, "The Peculiar Fate of the Bourgeois Critique of Slavery," in *Slavery and the American South: Essays and Commentaries*, ed. Winthrop D. Jordan (Jackson: University Press of Mississippi, 2003), 36.

3. *National Intelligencer*, 13 January 1826.

4. The slave inventory for GWPC's southern plantations from 1823 gave a total of one hundred seventy people; the 1820 census from Arlington listed fifty-eight. At Nelly's Woodlawn, there were ninety-three people (and around eighty more at the Lewises' Audley estate), while MCP and her husband had around one hundred enslaved people. *See* "A Return of Negroes…," 1823, Custis Family Papers, VMHC; 1810 Frederick County, VA, Fairfax, VA, and Montgomery, MD, censuses; 1820 Alexandria, DC, and Georgetown, DC, censuses, NARA.

5. Reliable works on Washington and slavery include Erica Armstrong Dunbar, *Never Caught*; François Furstenberg, *In the Name of the Father*; François Furstenberg, "Atlantic Slavery, Atlantic Freedom"; Jessie MacLeod and Mary V. Thompson, *Lives Bound Together: Slavery at George Washington's Mount Vernon* (Mount Vernon, VA: Mount Vernon Ladies' Association, 2016); Philip D. Morgan, "'To Get Quit of Negroes': George Washington and Slavery," *Journal of American Studies* 39, no. 3 (2005): 403–429; Philip J. Schwarz, ed., *Slavery at the Home of George Washington* (Mount Vernon, VA: University of Virginia Press, 2002); Mary V. Thompson, *"The Only Unavoidable Subject of Regret."*

6. *See eg* Stephanie E. Jones-Rogers, *They Were Her Property: White Women as Slave Owners in the American South* (New Haven: Yale University Press, 2020), chap. 1.

7. June 1833 and undated notes, John Gadsby Chapman Papers, McGuigan Collection, Harpswell, ME.

8. On GW's punishments of enslaved people, *see* Thompson, *"The Only Unavoidable Subject of Regret,"* 247–259.

9. Dunbar, *Never Caught*; Thompson, *"The Only Unavoidable Subject of Regret,"* 283–285. Recent research by Ramin Ganeshram uncovered Hercules's surname, Posey; *see* https://www.bbc.com/travel/article/20220201-hercules-posey-george-washingtons-unsung-enslaved-chef. On GW's engagement with Enlightenment antislavery writings, *see* Furstenberg, "Atlantic Slavery, Atlantic Freedom."

10. MW to Fanny Bassett Washington, 24 May 1795, *MW Papers*, 287; MW's great-granddaughter recorded asking an elderly enslaved woman who had come to GWPC from Mount Vernon whether MW had taught the woman her catechism, to which she responded, "No, oh! No…she never taught any of the servants anything." MCWC Diary, 2 April 1854.

11. 1796 Peter Slave Accounts, MS-2, TP; Wendy Kail, "Oakland: Far from the Madding Crowd," *Tudor Place* (blog), March 2016, https://tudorplace.org/wp-content/uploads/2020/07/Oakland-March-2016_revised.pdf; 1810 census, Montgomery, MD; Mark Auslander, "Enslaved Labor and Building the Smithsonian: Reading the Stones,"

Southern Spaces (blog), accessed January 10, 2022, https://southern-spaces.org/2012/enslaved-labor-and-building-smithsonian-reading-stones/; Barbara Jeanne Fields, *Slavery and Freedom on the Middle Ground: Maryland during the Nineteenth Century* (New Haven: Yale University Press, 1987), 19, 25.

12. Mary Geraghty, "Domestic Management of Woodlawn Plantation: Eleanor Parke Custis Lewis and Her Slaves," (PhD Diss., College of William and Mary, 1993), 20–21, 40, 67; Michael Trinkley, "Archae-ological Survey of Woodlawn Plantation, Fairfax County, Virginia," 2001, 26, https://dc.statelibrary.sc.gov/bitstream/handle/10827/34089/Chicora_Research_Contributions_299_2000-11-13.pdf.

13. Nelly to Harrison Gray Otis, 17 October 1831, *The Life and Letters of Harrison Gray Otis, 1765–1848*, 2: 259–261.

14. On the people the Lewises sent and sold to Louisiana, *see* Lawrence Lewis's will, LVA, Fairfax County will book T, p. 127 (microfilm reel 33); typescript at Woodlawn; Sale to Valerie Hebert, COB R, fol. 258, Iberville Parish Records. Thanks to David Plater for sharing this sale record with me.

15. This conjecture is based on David Stuart's 1796 comment that "I may always have Betsey's [slaves] for very little… I suppose she will exact but a moderate hire from her brother" in addition to the fact that the Laws moved two men from New Kent County (the location of several Custis plantations) to Washington City in 1797. The latter fact suggests the men were from there, forming part of Eliza's dower portion, but stayed on hire to the Custis estate, as many others likely did as well. *See* David Stuart to GW, 25 February 1796, *PGW-PS*, 19: 498; Prince George's County Court (Land Records) JRM 5, p. 0443, Maryland State Archives. The portion of the District of Columbia where the Laws lived was then in Prince George's County, MD.

16. Montgomery County Court (Land Records), 1801–1803, Book K, p. 460, Maryland State Archives.

17. "List of the Different Drafts of Negroes, [1802]," PFP, MVLA; "An Act for the Relief of Eliza P. Custis of Baltimore," *Laws of Maryland*, December Session 1817 (Annapolis: Jonas Green, 1818), 636: 30; Helen Hoban Rogers, *Freedom & Slavery Documents in the District of Columbia* (Baltimore: Gateway Press, 2007), 77n212.

18. *The Granite Freeman* (Concord, NH), 22 May 1845.

19. Deborah Lee, "Ann R. Page and Mary L. Custis from Annfield and Arlington to Africa, with Love," in *Virginia Women: Their Lives and Times*, ed. Cynthia A. Kierner and Sandra Gioia Treadway (Athens, GA: University of Georgia Press, 2015), 256; Doug Pielmeier, "The Evolution of a Virginia Plantation" (National Park Service, 1996), 72–73; Pryor, *Reading the Man*, 128–131.

20. *Evening Star* (Washington), 4 November 1928; Pryor, *Reading the Man*, 128–131. The passes are in Custis Family Papers, VMHC.

21. Marie Tyler-McGraw, *An African Republic: Black & White Virginians in the Making of Liberia* (Chapel Hill: University of North Carolina Press, 2007), 121; MCWC Diary, 18 November 1853.

22. On farm labor in Virginia at this time, *see* Ira Berlin, *Many Thousands Gone: The First Two Centuries of Slavery in North America* (Cambridge: The Belknap Press of Harvard University Press, 1998), 267; Claudia L. Bushman and Richard L. Bushman, *In Old Virginia: Slavery, Farming, and Society in the Journal of John Walker* (Baltimore: Johns Hopkins University Press, 2002), 4–7; Richard S. Dunn, *A Tale of Two Plantations: Slave Life and Labor in Jamaica and Virginia* (Cambridge: Harvard University Press, 2014), 191–194.

23. Herbert George Gutman, *The Black Family in Slavery and Freedom, 1750–1925* (New York: Blackwell, 1976), 230, 237. On Molly's father William Fitzhugh's practice, *see* Gwendolyn White, "William Henry Fitzhugh (1792–1830)," *Encyclopedia Virginia* (blog), accessed March 28, 2022, https://encyclopediavirginia.org/entries/fitzhugh-william-henry-1792-1830/.

24. The only record of a sale of enslaved people by GWPC is in early 1812; he advertised "about 37" people for sale on January 1, 1812, in Centreville, VA ("Negroes," *Alexandria Gazette*, 24 December 1811). It is unclear where these people had lived; it seems likely that they were people he had inherited after his mother's death earlier in 1811. There is also a record around the same time of the sale of an enslaved man named John for $400 to a distant cousin, Charles Lee (Charles Lee Daybook, 31 December 1811 and 31 December 1812, Custis-Lee Papers, LC). On the regular separation of families by selling or hiring out labor in Virginia in this period, *see* Dunn, *A Tale of Two Plantations*, 183; Calvin Schermerhorn, *Money over Mastery, Family over Freedom: Slavery in the Antebellum Upper South* (Baltimore: Johns Hopkins University Press, 2011).

25. "To Arlington," *Harper's Weekly*, 29 May 1886; Pryor, *Reading the Man*, 126–131.

26. Pryor, 133; MCWC Diary, 2 November 1853; MARCL diary, 9 June 1853, Lee Family Papers, VMHC.

27. Pryor, *Reading the Man*, 133–134.

28. GWPC to Anderson, 24 June 1804, Civil War and Slavery Collection, Grand Valley State University; MLFC to MARCL, 20 June 1838, AH; Pryor, 128.

29. GWPC to Robert E. Lee, 14 August 1838, MS-5, TP.

30. Mary Anna Randolph Custis, "Enslaved Girl," 1830 (Colonial Williams-

burg Foundation). My thanks to cooper Marshall Scheetz and Colonial Williamsburg curator Neal Hurst for helping me decipher this image.

31. His overseer for tracts in New Kent and King William counties sent "Returns of Negroes" in 1806 that counted 143 enslaved people. No such count exists for his Northampton properties at this time, but JPC's 1782–1784 estate inventory listed seventeen enslaved people there. *See* James Anderson to GWPC, 13 March 1806, VMHC, MCLP and JPC Inventory, Fairfax County Will Book E1, 11–17; photostat at MVLA.

32. William Parkinson to GWPC, 4 December 1813, MCLP, VMHC; undated [c. 1820] affidavit by John Walden, Custis Family Papers, VMHC.

33. GWPC to William Bromely, 25 May 1824, Custis Family Papers, VMHC, cited in Nelligan, 133.

34. Pielmeier, "The Evolution of a Virginia Plantation," 140.

35. L.R. Nelson to MLFC, 4 May 1853, Lee Family Papers, VHMC. On overseers, their treatment of enslaved people, and their conflicts with plantation owners, *see* William Kauffman Scarborough, *The Overseer: Plantation Management in the Old South* (Baton Rouge: Louisiana State University Press, 1966); William E. Wiethoff, *Crafting the Overseer's Image* (Columbia, SC: University of South Carolina Press, 2006).

36. GWPC to William Winston, 28 January 1857, HMC, MVLA.

37. MCWC Diary, 15 May 1853.

38. Furstenberg, *In the Name of the Father*, 84–85.

39. George Washington's Last Will & Testament, 9 July 1799, *PGW-RS*, 4: 479–511.

40. The estimate for the sisters is based on the assumption that each received around sixty peole for their dowry (MCP received sixty-eight) plus around forty people in 1802. On GWPC, *see* n31.

41. Eva Sheppard Wolf, *Race and Liberty in the New Nation: Emancipation in Virginia from the Revolution to Nat Turner's Rebellion* (Baton Rouge: Louisiana State University Press, 2009), 45.

42. The Peters freed Ralph Anderson in 1830 in return for a $200 payment. Anderson had freed himself in 1810, when he was twenty years old, and the runaway ads suggested he had probably gone to his father Sambo, who had been emancipated and still lived at Mount Vernon. Given that the runaway ads lasted for six months, it is possible that Ralph had essentially been living as a free man for twenty years before the Peters agreed to emancipate him (*Alexandria Gazette*, 12 June and 21 December 1810); Dorothy S. Provine, *District of Columbia Free Negro Registers, 1821–1861* (Bowie, MD: Heritage Books, Inc., 1996), 1: 122. Nelly freed one person, Sam, in her will; John Walter Wayland, *The Washingtons and Their Homes* (Staunton, VA: McClure Printing Company, 1944), 206–207.

43. On DC's more lenient manumission laws pre-1827, *see below note* and

Letitia Woods Brown, *Free Negroes in the District of Columbia, 1790–1846* (New York: Oxford University Press, 1972), 14; Constance McLaughlin Green, *Secret City: A History of Race Relations in the Nation's Capital* (Princeton: Princeton University Press, 2015), 19.

44. There is perhaps no better example than Roger Brooke Taney. Taney manumitted all of his enslaved people in 1818, but later authored the Supreme Court's most proslavery decision in *Dred Scott v. Sanford*; Timothy S. Huebner, "Roger B. Taney and the Slavery Issue: Looking beyond—and before—Dred Scott," *The Journal of American History* 97, no. 1 (2010): 17–38. More broadly, *see* William G. Thomas, *A Question of Freedom: The Families Who Challenged Slavery from the Nation's Founding to the Civil War* (New Haven: Yale University Press, 2020).

45. Wolf, *Race and Liberty in the New Nation*, 44, 47.

46. Zagarri, "The Empire Comes Home: Thomas Law's Mixed-Race Family in the Early American Republic," 89.

47. Dolley Payne Madison to Eliza, 17 October 1804, *Papers of James Madison-Secretary of State Series*, 8: 183; Eliza to Gideon Snow, 24 October 1830, HMC, MVLA.

48. "Some Facts that Should Come to Light," *New York Tribune*, 24 June 1859; "Virginia's F.F's [First Families]," *The Independent*, 12 October 1865.

49. Thelma Jennings, "'Us Colored Women Had to Go Through A Plenty': Sexual Exploitation of African-American Slave Women," *Journal of Women's History* 1, no. 3 (1990): 60–62; Philip D. Morgan, "Interracial Sex in the Chesapeake and Atlantic World, c. 1700–1820," in *Sally Hemings and Thomas Jefferson: History, Memory, and Civic Culture*, ed. Jan Ellen Lewis and Peter S. Onuf (Charlottesville: University of Virginia Press, 1999); Joshua D. Rothman, *Notorious in the Neighborhood: Sex and Families across the Color Line in Virginia, 1787–1861* (Chapel Hill: University of North Carolina Press, 2003), 15, 116.

50. Pryor, *Reading the Man*, 139.

51. Slave Manumissions in Alexandria Land Records, 1790–1863, http://www.freedmenscemetery.org/resources/documents/manumissions.shtml [hereafter Alexandria Manumissions].

52. Alexandra J. Finley, *An Intimate Economy: Enslaved Women, Work, and America's Domestic Slave Trade* (Chapel Hill: University of North Carolina Press, 2020), 31; Saidiya V. Hartman, *Scenes of Subjection: Terror, Slavery, and Self-Making in Nineteenth-Century America* (New York: Oxford University Press, 1997), chap. 3.

53. Gordon-Reed, *The Hemingses of Monticello*, 308–325.

54. Sharon Block, "Lines of Color, Sex, and Service: Comparative Sexual Coercion in Early America," in *Sex, Love, Race: Crossing Boundaries in*

North American History, ed. Martha Hodes (New York: NYU Press, 1999), 143.

55. Louisa was freed on 1 March 1803; *see* Alexandria Manumissions. On Judith, *see* "Washington's Slave List," June 1799, in *PGW-RS,* 4: 527–542; "List of the Different Drafts of Negroes, [1802]," PFP, MVLA.

56. On legal challenges to manumissions by enslavers in debt, *see* Thomas D. Morris, *Southern Slavery and the Law, 1619–1860* (Chapel Hill: University of North Carolina Press, 1996), 388–392.

57. 21 May 1813, Alexandria Manumissions.

58. "Responses to Queries from Unknown Meeting," Box 4, Stabler-Leadbetter Apothecary Archives, Historic Alexandria. On this practice, and the Millers and Stablers in particular, *see* A. Glenn Crothers, *Quakers Living in the Lion's Mouth: The Society of Friends in Northern Virginia, 1730–1865* (Gainesville: University Press of Florida, 2012), 219–220, 266. On the financial support of minors, *see* Wolf, *Race and Liberty in the New Nation,* 155.

59. Bill of Sale from GWPC to Edward Stabler, 8 July 1828, Stabler-Leadbetter Apothecary Archives, Historic Alexandria; Bill of Sale from George Washington Parke Custis to William Stabler, 31 December 1844, AH.

60. As in so many cases of the enslaved, dates are imprecise. Maria's manumission by the family of Edward Stabler is recorded on 2 June 1845 in Records of the Alexandria Circuit Court, Deed Book E-3: 425. That record notes that GWPC sold Maria, her daughter Bertha, and an infant son (William) to Stabler on 6 August 1825 when Maria was "about 20 years of age," clearly as a preliminary step to freeing them. Later records based on her son William's recollections state that she and her eldest two children were freed in 1826, and that this is when GWPC granted her the parcel of his estate (*see* William Syphax to Andrew Johnson, 11 May 1865, in RG 60: Segregated Documents from Letters Received, 1838–1943, Files Relating to Bankruptcy, Arlington Estate, and Ford's Theater; An Act for the Relief of Maria Syphax in *Statutes at Large,* vol. 14, Thirty-Ninth Congress, 1865–67, p. 589, NARA).

61. Based upon recollections Maria shared with a reporter in the 3 September 1888 story "Lovely Arlington," *Morning Star* (Rockford, IL).

62. This story has been accepted and later interpreted by Arlington House staff; it is recorded in Chelsea Hansen's paper "Messages from Behind the Slavery Wall: Syphax Descendant Genealogists and New Directions for Historical Interpretations of Slavery" (American University, 2016). Thanks to Chelsea for sharing this paper with me. While there is no contemporary record of the wedding, records from the 1840s of the wedding the Custises held for the enslaved woman Rose would suggest the Syphax family story is correct. On Rose's wedding, *see* Pryor, 127.

63. E. Delorus Preston, "William Syphax, a Pioneer in Negro Education in the District of Columbia," *The Journal of Negro History* 20, no. 4 (October 1935): 449; 2 June 1845, Alexandria Manumissions.

64. Interview with Zunny Matema, 9 November 2018.

65. Peter Hardiman was a dower slave of ECC whom GW rented at Mount Vernon, but he appears to have ended up at Arlington House; GWPC mentioned that his groom Peter had also been the groom at Mount Vernon, which Peter Hardiman was. Around 1812, GWPC mentioned that Peter had died, so Peter would have been present at the time Caroline purportedly gave birth to Lucy. Caroline had four daughters of childbearing age at this time: Rachel, twenty-one; Jemima, eighteen; Leanthe, seventeen; and Polly, fifteen. *See* Jessie Macleod, "Caroline Branham," George Washington Encyclopedia, https://www.mount-vernon.org/library/digitalhistory/digital-encyclopedia/article/caro-line-branham/; Samuel Wyllys Pomery, "A Dissertation on the Mule," *American Farmer* (Baltimore), 19 August 1825; GWPC to James Hooe, 24 May [1812], George Washington Papers, Washington Family Papers, George Washington Parke Custis Letters and Writings, New York Public Library; "List of the Different Drafts of Negroes, [1802]," PFP, MVLA; Alexandria Manumissions. There is one hint of an unusual connection between Caroline and GWPC in his own words, which he recalled as an old man. Caroline was caring for him when he was ill and suggested "Master Washington lay yr head on my lap," which he did and slept for two hours as she "never moved." It is entirely possible that it was GWPC's own idea to rest his head there against Caroline's wishes, or even as a way of enforcing her bodily submission; might it also hint at what GWPC saw as some deeper connection between them? *See* MCWC Diary, 12 September 1857.

66. Powell, "Scenes of Childhood," 3, 9; Powell, *History of Old Alexandria*, 244. There is no record in Sparks's papers or published writings of an interview with Branham, but the timing lines up; Sparks was in Washington, DC, in 1827 (*see* MS 123, Jared Sparks Personal Papers, Series III, Research, Journal of Three Southern Trips, Houghton Library, Harvard University), and Robert was sold in 1827. GWPC himself wrote in the records of Christ's Church of Alexandria, when recording Caroline's death in 1843, "See account of the death of Washington in Sparks' Life of Washington." *See* Christ Church Burial Register, p. 91, Collection of Christ Church, Alexandria, VA. The manumission for Robert lists him as "the son of Lucy Brannum [Branham]," and he would be apprenticed to Robert Jamieson. The notion that Lucy Branham and Lucy Harrison are the same person comes from both family history and Powell's claim that Lucy Harrison was Caroline Branham's daughter, as well as 1850 census records that show Lucy Harrison living

in the household of a Robert Robertson (likely misspelled) who was an Alexandria baker, and Powell says Robert apprenticed to a baker named Andrew Jamieson. Manumission records for Lucy Harrison and her daughters Sarah and Eugenia line up well with Powell's account.

67. 7 July 1843, Caroline Brannum [Branham], Alexandria Manumissions.

68. Manisha Sinha, *The Slave's Cause: A History of Abolition* (New Haven: Yale University Press, 2016), esp. 95–96.

69. Furstenberg, "Atlantic Slavery, Atlantic Freedom"; Furstenberg, *In the Name of the Father*, 83–84; Oakes, "The Peculiar Fate of the Bourgeois Critique of Slavery"; Ragsdale, *Washington at the Plow*, quote p. 291.

70. On emancipation in Virginia in this period, *see* Wolf, *Race and Liberty in the New Nation*, chap. 5 and 6.

71. Good, "Report on Slavery at Woodlawn and in the Lives of the Lewis Family" (Woodlawn files).

72. Nelly to EBG, 24 November [1817], in Brady, 84.

73. Nelly to GWL, 8 January 1826, DLCCU.

74. Taylor, *The Internal Enemy*, 398–404; Wolf, *Race and Liberty in the New Nation*, 164–67. On the excess number of laborers in Virginia, *see eg* Schermerhorn, *Money over Mastery, Family over Freedom*.

75. *See eg* Eric Burin, *Slavery and the Peculiar Solution: A History of the American Colonization Society* (Gainesville: University Press of Florida, 2008); Nicholas Guyatt, *Bind Us Apart: How Enlightened Americans Invented Racial Segregation* (New York: Oxford University Press, 2016), part 3; Brandon Mills, *The World Colonization Made: The Racial Geography of Early American Empire* (Philadelphia: University of Pennsylvania Press, 2020), 48–52; Paul J. Polgar, *Standard-Bearers of Equality: America's First Abolition Movement* (Chapel Hill: Omohundro Institute and University of North Carolina Press, 2019), chap. 5; Beverly Tomek and Randall M. Miller, eds., *New Directions in the Study of African American Recolonization* (Gainesville: University Press of Florida, 2017).

76. Lee, "Ann R. Page and Mary L. Custis From Annfield and Arlington to Africa, with Love," 267–268.

77. MLFC to William Meade, 14 October 1817, Custis-Lee Family Research Files, AH. Molly may have made a greater impact on her brother, who experimented with having his enslaved people work as tenant farmers to earn their freedom. He ultimately provided for a delayed emancipation for them in his will. *See* White, "William Henry Fitzhugh (1792–1830)."

78. Lee, "Ann R. Page and Mary L. Custis From Annfield and Arlington to Africa, with Love," here quoted p. 271; Tyler-McGraw, *An African Republic*, 118–119.

79. Tyler-McGraw, *An African Republic*, 87.

80. Lee, "Ann R. Page and Mary L. Custis From Annfield and Arlington to Africa, with Love."

81. Henry S. Foote, *Casket of Reminiscences* (Washington, DC: Chronicle Publishing Company, 1874), 16. On the case, *see* John Thomas Noonan, *The Antelope: The Ordeal of the Recaptured Africans in the Administrations of James Monroe and John Quincy Adams* (Berkeley: University of California Press, 1977).

82. This was common of Southern women's views, especially when it came to supporting colonization; *see* Elizabeth R. Varon, *We Mean to Be Counted: White Women & Politics in Antebellum Virginia* (Chapel Hill: University of North Carolina Press, 1998), 44.

83. *The Second Annual Report of the American Society for Colonizing the Free People of Colour of the United States* (Washington, DC: Davis and Force, 1819), 135; *The Seventh Annual Report of the American Society for Colonizing the Free People of Colour of the United States* (Washington, DC: Davis and Force, 1824), 15.

84. *Metropolis* (Georgetown), 12 January 1826.

85. The notion of scientific racism had a long history in both Europe and America, but it took hold in support of proslavery positions by the 1840s. *See eg* Bruce R. Dain, *A Hideous Monster of the Mind: American Race Theory in the Early Republic* (Cambridge: Harvard University Press, 2003), chap. 7; George M. Fredrickson, *The Black Image in the White Mind: The Debate on Afro-American Character and Destiny, 1817–1914* (Middletown, CT: Wesleyan University Press, 1987), chap. 3.

86. *The Fourteenth Annual Report of the American Colonization Society* (Washington, DC: James C. Dunn, 1831), xxi.

87. *See eg* David F. Allmendinger, *Nat Turner and the Rising in Southampton County* (Baltimore: Johns Hopkins University Press, 2014); Patrick H. Breen, *The Land Shall Be Deluged in Blood: A New History of the Nat Turner Revolt* (New York: Oxford University Press, 2015).

88. Nelly to Harrison Gray Otis, 17 October 1831, *The Life and Letters of Harrison Gray Otis, 1765–1848*, 2: 259–261; Kay Wright Lewis, *A Curse upon the Nation: Race, Freedom, and Extermination in America and the Atlantic World* (Athens: University of Georgia Press, 2019), 83, 88; Claudio Saunt, *Unworthy Republic: The Dispossession of Native Americans and the Road to Indian Territory* (New York: W.W. Norton & Company, 2020), esp. section 5.

89. MLFC to MARCL, 8 October 1831, MSS 2c9695 a1, VMHC; MLFC to MARCL, 13 October [1831], MCLP, VMHC.

90. "American Colonization Society," *Christian Advocate and Journal*, 30 January 1835; Lacy K. Ford, *Deliver Us from Evil: The Slavery Question in the Old South* (New York: Oxford University Press, 2009), 378. On racism and the ACS, *see eg* Polgar, *Standard-Bearers of Equality*, chap. 6.

91. Undated letter from GWPC to Ralph Gurley, Gratz Collection, HSP.

92. MCWC Diary, 2 November 1853; on paternalism and evolving pro-slavery ideology, *see eg* Ford, *Deliver Us from Evil*, esp. chap. 17; Peter Kolchin, *American Slavery: 1619–1877* (New York: Hill and Wang, 1993), 184–199.

93. Undated and untitled essay labeled "Views on Slavery," Binder of Transcripts of Journals of Martha Custis Williams, AH; EGWB to Charles Gayarre, 25 April 1853, Charles Gayarre Papers, Louisiana State University.

94. Eliza to John Law, 12 October 1808 and 8 August 1809; Lawrence Lewis to William Costin, 6 October 1813; Nelly to William Costin, 12 June 1816; Thomas Law to Lloyd Rogers, undated (likely early 1832), PFP, MVLA; Eliza to GWPC, 15 July 1830, MCLP, VMHC.

95. The complete names are spelled out in the manumissions and William Costin's will; they are Louisa Parke, Ann Parke, Charlotte Parke, Frances "Fanny" Parke, Harriet Parke, William Custis Parke, and George Calvert Parke. *See* Rogers, 1: 52 and Will of William Costin, Washington, D.C., District and Probate Courts. Wills, Boxes 0014 Quinlin, Tasker C-0018 Degges, John, 1837–1847, accessed on Ancestry.com.

96. "Virginia Gleanings in England," *The Virginia Magazine of History and Biography* 20, no. 4 (1912): 372; Kathryn Gehred, "The Dunbar Lawsuit: How a Decades-Long Scandalous Court Case Threatened George Washington's Estate," 26 February 2018, https://millercenter.org/president/washington/washington-papers/dunbar-lawsuit; Joseph McMillan, "Changes of Arms in Colonial North America: The Strange Case of Custis," *The Coat of Arms*, 11 no. 230 (2015): 130–133.

97. Eliza to GWPC, 15 July 1830, MCLP, VMHC.

98. David O. Stewart, "The Mount Vernon Slave Who Made Good: The Mystery of William Costin," *Journal of the American Revolution*, 22 December 2020, https://allthingsliberty.com/2020/12/the-mount-vernon-slave-who-made-good-the-mystery-of-william-costin/.

99. S.M. Charles, "William Costin: 'A tribute to worth by his friends,'" lithographed by Charles Fenderich (Philadelphia: P.S. Duval's Lith. Press, 1842), Prints and Photographs Division, LC; Robinson, 50–52, 63.

100. *See National Intelligencer*, 29 August 1818; Robinson, 58, 60. *See also* "Masonic History," Most Worshipful Prince Hall Grand Lodge, District of Columbia, https://www.mwphgldc.com/the-early-years. My thanks to James R. Morgan, III, for bringing this to my attention.

101. On the Black community in Washington during this era, *see* Chris Myers Asch and George Derek Musgrove, *Chocolate City: A History of Race and Democracy in the Nation's Capital* (Chapel Hill: University of North Carolina Press, 2017), chap. 2 and 3; Stanley Harrold, *Subversives: Antislavery*

Community in Washington, D.C., 1828–1865 (Baton Rouge: Louisiana State University Press, 2003); Brown, *Free Negroes in the District of Columbia, 1790–1846*; Green, *Secret City*, chap. 2 and 3; Tamika Y. Nunley, *At the Threshold of Liberty: Women, Slavery, and Shifting Identities in Washington, D.C.* (Chapel Hill: University of North Carolina Press, 2021).

102. Provine, *District of Columbia Free Negro Registers, 1821–1861*, 1: 52; Robinson, "Some Aspects of the Free Negro Population of Washington, D.C., 1800–1862," 51.

103. On Cranch, *see* Thomas, *A Question of Freedom*, passim. For the case, *see Costin v. Washington*, 2 Cranch C.C. 254.

104. "O Say Can You See: Early Washington, D.C., Law, and Family," https://earlywashingtondc.org/people/per.000194.

105. *Costin v. Washington*, 2 Cranch C.C. 254. Free Black and enslaved litigants showed considerable knowledge of the law and collaborated with their lawyers; *see eg* Nunley, *At the Threshold of Liberty*, chap. 3; Thomas, *A Question of Freedom*; Anne Twitty, *Before Dred Scott* (New York: Cambridge University Press, 2016), chap. 2.

106. Martha S. Jones, *Birthright Citizens: A History of Race and Rights in Antebellum America* (Cambridge, UK: Cambridge University Press, 2018), 28.

107. *Daily Globe*, 2 June 1842; *Emancipator and Free American*, 9 June 1842.

108. On the connection between the colonization movement and American imperialism, *see* Mills, *The World Colonization Made*.

Chapter 9

1. Murray H. Nelligan, "American Nationalism on the Stage: The Plays of George Washington Parke Custis (1781–1857)," *Virginia Magazine of History and Biography* 58, no. 3 (July 1950): 299–324.

2. GWPC, *The Indian Prophecy* (Georgetown, DC: Thomas, 1828).

3. Soon after the end of the Revolution, GW used the term "rising empire" several times in correspondence; *see eg* GW to Officials of the City of Richmond, 15 November 1784, *PGW-CS*, 2: 135. "Empire" was synonymous with "state" for the founders, although it did encompass hopes of great expansion that would, by necessity, require conquest; *see* Richard H. Immerman, *Empire for Liberty: A History of American Imperialism from Benjamin Franklin to Paul Wolfowitz* (Princeton: Princeton University Press, 2012), 1, 8–9.

4. Fred Anderson and Andrew Cayton, *The Dominion of War: Empire and Liberty in North America, 1500–2000* (New York: Penguin, 2005), chap. 4; Jimmy L. Bryan, "'A Destiny in the Womb of Time': US Expansion and Its Prophets," in *Inventing Destiny: Cultural Explorations of US*

Expansion, ed. Jimmy L. Bryan (Lawrence: University Press of Kansas, 2019), 24; Peter S. Onuf, *Jefferson's Empire: The Language of American Nationhood* (Charlottesville: University of Virginia Press, 2000), 2; William Earl Weeks, *The New Cambridge History of American Foreign Relations*, vol. 1 (New York: Cambridge University Press, 2015), xvii, 121.

5. As historian Daniel Walker Howe bluntly states, "Jacksonian Democracy...was about the extension of white supremacy across the North American continent." *See eg* Anderson and Cayton, *The Dominion of War*, chap. 6; Green, *The Man of the People*, chap. 8; Daniel Walker Howe, *What Hath God Wrought: The Transformation of America, 1815–1848* (Oxford University Press, 2007), eg 4, 330, 510.

6. EGWB to Jackson, 11 January 1827, *Papers of Andrew Jackson*, 6: 260; *United States Telegraph* (Washington, DC), 10 June 1828.

7. *Commercial Advertiser* (New York), 8 January 1828; *National Journal* (Washington), 20 May 1830.

8. Eliza to Andrew Jackson, December 25, 1828, HMC, MVLA. On Washington items as popular relics, *see* Teresa Barnett, *Sacred Relics: Pieces of the Past in Nineteenth-Century America* (Chicago: University of Chicago Press, 2013), part 1; Jamie L. Brummitt, "Protestant Relics: Religion, Objects, and the Art of Mourning in the American Republic" (PhD Diss., Durham, NC: Duke University, 2018), chap. 2; Good, "Washington Family Fortune."

9. MCWC Diary, 7 March 1854.

10. Nelly to Frances Parke Lewis Butler, 13 May 1832, BFP, HNOC; Robert Vincent Remini, *Henry Clay: Statesman for the Union* (W.W. Norton & Company, 1991), 377.

11. *See eg* Michael G. Kammen, *A Season of Youth: The American Revolution and the Historical Imagination* (New York: Knopf, 1978), 48–49.

12. Jeffrey Malanson, *Addressing America*, 117–122.

13. Richard E. Ellis, *The Union at Risk: Jacksonian Democracy, States' Rights and the Nullification Crisis* (New York: Oxford University Press, 1987).

14. Nelly to EBG, 24 August 1832, 10 March 1833, in Brady, 201, 208–209.

15. *Alexandria Gazette*, 14 March 1833.

16. Nelly to Parke, 23 July 1827, BFP, HNOC; Nelly to GWL, 19 May 1825, DLCCU; Caroline Dall, "A Centennial 'Posie,'" *Unitarian Review*, 1876, 187.

17. Eliza to the Snows, 18 October 1828, HMC, MVLA (miscataloged under 1820 on microfilm). Eliza also sent velvet, apparently from the same source, to John Lutz, 14 April 1828, MVLA; Robert Oliver, 26 January 1829, MVLA; Polish Princess Izabela Czartoryska, 26 April 1828, National Museum of Poland in Krakow, copy at MVLA; John Morton, 29 October 1828, Collection of Brian and Barbara Hendelson, on

loan to MVLA. The velvet is likely from a mutilated black silk velvet pair of Washington's breeches in the MVLA collection (W-1918). For more on Eliza's use of relics, *see* Good, "Washington Family Fortune."

18. Eliza to Lafayette, 6 June 1829, Cornell, Lafayette Papers; Eliza to DBW, 6 June 1829, Transcript in LC, Custis-Lee Papers. Rogers's wife, Hortensia, was childhood friends with MARCL, and the pair corresponded occasionally, so not all contact was cut off, and Rogers conveyed "his kindest regards" to MARCL's parents through his wife (*see* Hortensia to MARCL, George Bolling Lee Papers, VMHC; MARCL to Hortensia, 14 October 1830, AH).

19. Eliza to John Trumbull, 30 March 1829, HMC, MVLA; Eliza to Gideon Snow, 22 April 1829, HMC, MVLA.

20. Eliza to Lafayette, 21 May 1829, DLCCU; Eliza to Lawrence Lewis, 13 July 1830, HMC, MVLA; Eliza to GWPC, 15 July 1830, MCLP, VMHC.

21. Eliza to Edmund Law Rogers, 11 January 1831, Karl C. Harrison Museum of George Washington.

22. Eliza to Gideon Snow, 24 October 1830, HMC, MVLA.

23. Fanny Dandridge Lear to MLFC, 31 December 1831, TLFP, MCHC; *Richmond Enquirer*, 3 January 1832.

24. Mary Gregory (Crawford) Powell, *The History of Old Alexandria, Virginia*, 241.

25. Thomas Law to [?] Rumbold, 10 January 1832, in Thomas Law Papers, UVa; Nelly to EBG, 19 February 1832, HMC, MVLA; Nelly to GWL, 1 June 1832, DLCCU.

26. Kammen, *A Season of Youth*.

27. GWPC, "Lines Written for the Centennial Anniversary of the Birth of Washington. Feby 22d. 1832," in a 15 July 1833 letter, AH. On GWPC's "memory work" and creation of "performative pasts," *see* Bruggeman, "'More than Ordinary Patriotism': Living History in the Memory Work of George Washington Parke Custis."

28. Heather Nathans, "Custis, George Washington Parke," in *The Facts on File Companion to American Drama*, ed. Jackson R. Bryer and Mary C. Hartig (New York: Infobase Publishing, 2010), 116; Nelligan, "American Nationalism on the Stage: The Plays of George Washington Parke Custis (1781–1857)."

29. Sarah E. Chinn, *Spectacular Men: Race, Gender, and Nation on the Early American Stage* (New York: Oxford University Press, 2017).

30. *National Intelligencer*, 14 February 1831.

31. On blackface minstrelsy, *see eg* Eric Lott, *Love and Theft: Blackface Minstrelsy and the American Working Class* (New York: Oxford University Press, 1993). The name "Sambo" was only just emerging as a grinning jester character in minstrelsy at this time, but it had been used to de-

note a comic Black servant role as early as the late eighteenth century. Joseph Boskin, *Sambo: The Rise and Demise of an American Jester* (New York: Oxford University Press, 1988), 36–37. On Sambo Anderson, *see* Jessie MacLeod, "Samuel 'Sambo' Anderson," GW Encyclopedia, http://www.mountvernon.org/library/digitalhistory/digital-encyclopedia/article/sambo-anderson.

32. GWPC to J.H. Payne, 18 December 1833, George Washington Papers, Washington Family Papers, George Washington Parke Custis Letters and Writings, New York Public Library.

33. GWPC to MLFC, 12 September 1833, in GWPC Recollections, 59; GWPC to MLFC, 21 September 1833, MCLP, VMHC.

34. Nelligan, "American Nationalism on the Stage: The Plays of George Washington Parke Custis (1781–1857)," 323.

35. It is possible he studied with artist Cephas Thompson in 1807 and 1808, but there is no decisive evidence. *See* James B. Lynch, *The Custis Chronicles: The Virginia Generations* (Rockland, ME: Picton Press, 1997), 256–257.

36. Kent Ahrens, "Nineteenth Century History Painting and the United States Capitol," *Records of the Columbia Historical Society, Washington, D.C.* 50 (1980): 191; Kammen, *A Season of Youth*, 79–85.

37. Elizabeth Randolph Calvert, "Childhood Days at Arlington, mixed with after memories," AH. This document, available in both typescript and handwritten original, is dated 1845, but that is likely when the recollections are from, not when they were written down. It appears to have been written after the Civil War.

38. *United States Telegraph* (Washington, DC), 16 April 1836.

39. GWPC to Major Nowland, 25 April 1836, MVLA; Elizabeth Randolph Calvert, "Childhood Days at Arlington," AH.

40. Only seven known paintings by GWPC survive; four are owned by the Dietrich Foundation and on display at Arlington House. The best source on the paintings is Benson Lossing's 1 September 1853 *Harper's Weekly* story on Arlington House, in which he reproduced rough illustrations of four of the paintings and identified the figures within them. *See also* David Lowe, "A Son's Tribute," *American Heritage* 17, no. 2 (1966): 16–21.

41. GWPC to Mercer, 17 February 1832, Thomas Addis Emmet collection, New York Public Library.

42. "From Our Correspondent," *Rhode Island American*, 28 January 1831; *Cincinnati Daily Gazette*, 20 January 1836.

43. Nelly to MLFC, May 1833, MCLP, VMHC.

44. Eastman, *A Nation of Speechifiers*, 2010.

45. *The Sun* (Baltimore), 10 July 1839.

46. *Alexandria Gazette*, 17 August 1835; *Truth Teller* (New York, NY), 20 April 1839; eg *The Washington Post*, 18 March 1989.

47. "Sketches From the Address of Mr. CUSTIS, of Arlington, delivered in the City Hall, the 24th of May, 1836, at a meeting of the citizens of Washington favorable to the cause of Texas," *Columbian Centinel*, 2 July 1836.

48. Amy S. Greenberg, *A Wicked War: Polk, Clay, Lincoln, and the 1846 U.S. Invasion of Mexico* (New York: Alfred A. Knopf, 2012), 57; Peter Guardino, *The Dead March: A History of the Mexican-American War* (Cambridge: Harvard University Press, 2017), 25–26; Horsman, *Race and Manifest Destiny*, see esp. 1–5, 208–209. There is a vast literature on manifest destiny and American imperialism in the early to mid-nineteenth century; *see eg* Thomas R. Hietala, *Manifest Design: American Exceptionalism and Empire*, Revised Edition (Ithaca: Cornell University Press, 2003); Immerman, *Empire for Liberty*; Daniel Immerwahr, *How to Hide an Empire: A History of the Greater United States* (New York: Farrar, Straus and Giroux, 2019); Weeks, *The New Cambridge History of American Foreign Relations*.

49. *Columbian Centinel*, 2 July 1836.

50. *See eg* Laurel Clark Shire, *The Threshold of Manifest Destiny: Gender and National Expansion in Florida* (Philadelphia: University of Pennsylvania Press, 2016).

51. Jennifer R. Green, *Military Education and the Emerging Middle Class in the Old South* (New York: Cambridge University Press, 2008).

52. Nelly to EBG, 17 January 1826, in Brady, 171.

53. EGWB to Charles Gayarre, 25 April 1853, Charles Gayarre Papers, Louisiana State University.

54. Good, "Report on Slavery at Woodlawn and in the Lives of the Lewis Family," 14–15.

55. On Lucinda, *see* Plater, *The Butlers of Iberville Parish, Louisiana*, 30, 32, 60, 69. *See also* EGWB to Charles Gayarre, 25 April 1853, Charles Gayarre Papers, Louisiana State University.

56. On white settlement and opportunities for wealth in Louisiana built on the government's displacement of Native peoples and permissive attitude towards slavery, *see eg* Maria Angela Diaz, "At the Center of Southern Empire: The Role of Gulf South Communities in Antebellum Territorial Expansion," in *Inventing Destiny: Cultural Explorations of US Expansion*, ed. Jimmy L. Bryan (Lawrence: University Press of Kansas, 2019), 229–245; Walter Johnson, *River of Dark Dreams* (Cambridge: Harvard University Press, 2013), 24–28.

57. EGWB to Lawrence Lewis, 30 August 1827, Lewis Family Papers, UVa. The Lewises did, however, give the Butlers money in a complicated

financial maneuver involving debts owed to Lawrence; *see* Plater, *The Butlers of Iberville Parish, Louisiana*, 38.

58. Plater, 46, 58.

59. *See eg* Steven Deyle, *Carry Me Back: The Domestic Slave Trade in American Life* (New York: Oxford University Press, 2006); Joshua D. Rothman, *The Ledger and the Chain: How Domestic Slave Traders Shaped America* (New York: Basic Books, 2021); Schermerhorn, *Money over Mastery, Family over Freedom*.

60. All are named in Lawrence Lewis's will, Fairfax County Will Book T, p. 127 (microfilm reel 33), LVA; *see also* Mary Geraghty, "Domestic Management of Woodlawn Plantation: Eleanor Parke Custis Lewis and Her Slaves" (2010), Appendix A.

61. Nelly to EBG, 9 February 1834, in Brady, 213. On the Butlers' experience in Louisiana, *see* Plater, *The Butlers of Iberville Parish, Louisiana*.

62. Charles Magill Conrad to Mark Weeks, 16 August 1833, David Weeks & Family Papers, Louisiana State University; James A. Ramage, *John Wesley Hunt: Pioneer Merchant, Manufacturer and Financier* (Lexington: University Press of Kentucky, 1974), 78.

63. Nelly to EBG, 4 July 1834, in Brady, 217.

64. Nelly to Charles Magill Conrad, 19 December 1834, Binder 25, MVLA.

65. Angela to Charles Magill Conrad, 22 February 1835, Binder 25, MLVA.

66. Angela to Charles Magill Conrad, 16 and 22 February, 5 and 14 March, 8 and 17 April 1835, Binder 25, MVLA.

67. On the links between "routine commercial and financial matters" and slavery in American law, *see* Justin Simard, "Slavery's Legalism: Lawyers and the Commercial Routine of Slavery," *Law and History Review* 37, no. 2 (May 2019): 571–603. For example, in 1839, he represented the owners of a steamboat who had been sued by a passenger whose enslaved man Job had died aboard the ship. In another case that year, he represented a local official who supervised the sale of a plantation and the enslaved people living there but never gave the buyer the title (*Lobdell v. Bullitt*, 13 La. 348 [1839]; *Edwards v. Nicholson*, 13 La. 582 [1839]).

68. Transcriptions of extensive correspondence between Angela and Charles Magill Conrad in 1834–1835 are in Binder 25, MVLA. *See esp.* Angela to Charles Magill Conrad, 5 March 1835.

69. Marriages, 4 August 1835, *Daily National Intelligencer*.

70. For the enslaved people given to Angela, *see* Lawrence's will, Fairfax County Will Book T, p. 127 (microfilm reel 33), LVA; typescript at Woodlawn.

71. The Conrads likely sold several enslaved people as well, because the 1840 census shows only eleven enslaved people. It is unclear if Charles

brought any enslaved people to the marriage. On the sale of Wood-lawn slaves, *see* Plater, 72; Deed of sale, 5 January 1837, COB R, Fol. 358, Iberville, LA Court Records.

72. Good, "Report on Slavery at Woodlawn and in the Lives of the Lewis Family," 14–15.

73. Nelly to EBG, 27 July 1836, 20 April 1837, in Brady, 224–225, 227–228.

74. Quertermous, *A Georgetown Life*, 70n27.

75. Nelly to GWL, 5 February and 5 March 1826, DLCCU.

76. Nelly to EBG, 3 August 1826, in Brady, 182; Quertermous, *A Georgetown Life*, 71, 67n12.

77. William G. Williams to GWPC, 14 October 1838, MS-5, TP. The portraits are also in the TP collection.

78. Mark Goldman, *High Hopes: The Rise and Decline of Buffalo, New York* (Albany: SUNY Press, 1984), *see esp.* 32, 47.

79. Robert Sampson, *John L. O'Sullivan and His Times* (Kent, OH: Kent State University Press, 2003); Horsman, *Race and Manifest Destiny*, 219–221. Historian Amy Greenberg argues that a writer working with O'Sullivan, Jane McManus Storm, actually came up with the term. *See* Amy S. Greenberg, *Manifest Manhood and the Antebellum American Empire* (New York: Cambridge University Press, 2005), 20.

80. MLFC to MARCL, 29 January 1839, AH; Quertermous, *A Georgetown Life*, 28.

81. Pryor, *Reading the Man*, 16. For the quote (often misquoted as "those insects"), *see* Jefferson to William Johnson, 4 March 1823, Jefferson Papers, LC.

82. Pryor, 16–37. For a broader history of the Lees, *see* Paul C. Nagel, *The Lees of Virginia: Seven Generations of an American Family* (New York: Oxford University Press, 2006).

83. Robert E.L. deButts, Jr., "Lee in Love: Courtship and Correspondence in Antebellum Virginia," *Virginia Magazine of History and Biography* 115, no. 4 (2007): 488, 489.

84. On Latin and Greek education, *see* Nelly to GWL, 3 Feb 1821, 29 May 1825, DLCCU; for the rest, *see* Pryor, *Reading the Man*, 73–74.

85. Nelly to EBG, 2 December 1823 and 24 June 1827, in Brady, 138, 191.

86. deButts, "Lee in Love," 490–495; Pryor, *Reading the Man*, 77–79, 83.

87. MLFC to MARCL, 10 August 1831, Freeman Collection, Library of Virginia; Pryor, *Reading the Man*, 87.

88. Pryor, chap. 7; 145–150.

89. Anna Maria Thornton Diary, 17 April 1834, Anna Maria Brodeau Thornton Papers, LC.

90. Nelly to MARCL, 12 September 1834, MCLP, VMHC.

91. Hannah Conrad to Nelly, 2 November 1839, HMC, MVLA; Charles

Magill Conrad to Nelly, 8 October 1839, David Weeks & Family Papers, Louisiana State University.

92. Nelly to EBG, 5 November 1839, in Brady, 231–232.

93. Lawrence Lewis to Edward George Washington Butler, 23 June 1839, Twiss Collection, HNOC.

94. *Alexandria Gazette*, 23 November 1839; *Baltimore Sun*, 28 November 1839.

95. Lawrence Lewis to EGWB, 18 January 1837, BFP, HNOC.

96. Nelly to Lawrence Lewis, 26 December 1836, 8 and 26 March, 30 April 1837, Esther Maria Chapin Lewis Collection, MVLA. While in the 1836 letter Nelly signs herself "affect[ionately] yours," the subsequent letters merely offer general blessings to him and the family.

97. Nelly to MLFC, 13 December 1839, MCLP, VMHC.

98. Nelly to EBG, 20 December 1840, in Brady, 233.

99. *Alexandria Gazette*, 15 September, 15 and 23 October, 27 November 1840; *Daily National Intelligencer*, 5 March 1841.

100. MCP to Markie Williams, 13 February 1841, MS-6, TP.

Chapter 10

1. MCWC Diary, 9 September 1853.

2. Nelly to EBG, 17 December 1847, in Brady, 251.

3. Nelly wrote regular updates to the boys' father Charles Magill Conrad; extensive transcriptions from 1839 to 1847 are in Binder 25, MVLA.

4. For images of GWPC in this era, *see* Mathew Brady's photograph from c. 1844–1848, DAG no. 207, LC; Junius Brutus Stearns's 1848 portrait, Washington & Lee University; and an undated portrait by Samuel Lovett Waldo, American University Museum. *See also* the description of him in *Richmond Whig*, 3 November 1848.

5. Elizabeth Randolph Calvert, "Childhood Days at Arlington," AH.

6. Calvert, "Childhood Days at Arlington," AH.

7. Photograph of Martha Custis Peter and granddaughter Markie Kennon, c. 1850, TP; MCP to MCWC, 13 March 1847, MS-6, TP.

8. On Polk, *see* Walter R. Borneman, *Polk: The Man Who Transformed the Presidency and America* (New York: Random House, 2009); Greenberg, *A Wicked War*; Robert W. Merry, *A Country of Vast Designs: James K. Polk, the Mexican War and the Conquest of the American Continent* (New York: Simon and Schuster, 2010).

9. While there is no specific record of Wash's attendance at the inauguration, multiple later news stories noted that he had never missed an inauguration. *See eg Illustrated News*, 25 June 1852.

10. David A. Clary, *Eagles and Empire: The United States, Mexico, and the*

Struggle for a Continent (New York: Bantam Books, 2009), chap. 4; Greenberg, *A Wicked War*, 67–68, 78.

11. Greenberg, *A Wicked War*, 27, 71, 77, 99, 108; Guardino, *The Dead March*, 20–22, 34–35.

12. George W. Cullum, *Biographical Register of the Officers and Graduates of the U.S. Military Academy at West Point, N.Y.* (Boston: Houghton Mifflin, 1891), 1: 331, 420; David A. Clary, *Eagles and Empire: The United States, Mexico, and the Struggle for a Continent*, chap. 5–8; Greenberg, *A Wicked War*, 100–109.

13. K. Jack Bauer, *Zachary Taylor: Soldier, Planter, Statesman of the Old Southwest*, Revised Edition (Baton Rouge: Louisiana State University Press, 1993), 183–185; David A. Clary, *Eagles and Empire*, 191–201; Cullum, *Biographical Register of the Officers*, 1: 331; Greenberg, *A Wicked War*, 128–129.

14. Nelly to MLFC, 1 December 1846, MCLP, VMHC.

15. David A. Clary, *Eagles and Empire*, 251–254; Greenberg, *A Wicked War*, 143–144.

16. Nelly to MCWC, 4 February 1847; MCP to MCWC, 13 March 1847; MS-6, TP.

17. David A. Clary, *Eagles and Empire*, 200, 211–214.

18. For a summary of Robert E. Lee's experiences in the war and what he shared with his family of them, *see* Pryor, *Reading the Man*, chap. 10.

19. Good, "Washington Family Fortune," 117–118.

20. Nelly to EBG, 28 March 1847, in Brady, 249; Nelly to MLFC, 24 May 1847, MCLP, VMHC; Greenberg, *A Wicked War*, 172, 194; Guardino, *The Dead March*, 203–207.

21. Nelly to MLFC, 1 December 1846; Frances Parke Butler to MLFC, 5 June 1847, MCLP, VMHC; Frances Parke Butler to EGWB, 26 July 1847, BFP, HNOC.

22. MARCL to Eliza Mackay Stiles, 1 November 1847, Lee Family Digital Archive, Stratford Hall; Nelly to MLFC, 15 January 1848, MCLP, VMHC; Greenberg, *A Wicked War*, 199, 247; Guardino, *The Dead March*, 323–325.

23. David A. Clary, *Eagles and Empire*, 399–407, 412.

24. "A Proposed Memorial," 4 February 1846, *Alexandria Gazette*; A. Glenn Crothers, "The 1846 Retrocession of Alexandria: Protecting Slavery and the Slave Trade in the District of Columbia," in *In the Shadow of Freedom: The Politics of Slavery in the National Capital*, ed. Paul Finkelman and Donald R. Kennon (Athens: Ohio University Press, 2011), 141–168; Mark David Richards, "The Debates over the Retrocession of the District of Columbia, 1801–2004," *Washington History* 16, no. 1 (2004): 62–67.

25. Richards, "The Debates over the Retrocession of the District of Co-

lumbia, 1801–2004," 67–73. GWPC had served as a justice of the peace since the Madison administration; *see* Clark, *George Washington Parke Custis*, 108. This role involved serving in a court that adjudicated minor infractions.

26. Crothers, "The 1846 Retrocession of Alexandria."

27. Jeff Forret, *Williams' Gang: A Notorious Slave Trader and His Cargo of Black Convicts* (New York: Cambridge University Press, 2020), 47–48; Stanley Harrold, *Subversives: Antislavery Community in Washington, D.C., 1828–1865* (Baton Rouge: Louisiana State University Press, 2003), 20, 61.

28. Quertermous, *A Georgetown Life*, 65n12, 66n13. The latest research at Tudor Place differs slightly from Quertermous's findings and posits that Hannah's mother was Barbara Cole Williams and her grandmother (rather than her mother, as earlier thought) was probably Barbary Twine, inherited from Mount Vernon (Peter Family Tree, TP Files). *See also* Mary Kay Ricks, *Escape on the Pearl: Passage to Freedom from Washington, D.C.* (New York: HarperCollins, 2009), 109, 353.

29. Mark Auslander, "Searching for Three Escapees on The Pearl: The Rosier Men in 1848," 29 December 2020, https://markauslander.com/2020/12/29/searching-for-three-escapees-on-the-pearl-the-rosier-men-in-1848/; Josephine F. Pacheco, *The Pearl: A Failed Slave Escape on the Potomac* (Chapel Hill: University of North Carolina Press, 2005); Ricks, *Escape on the Pearl*.

30. Knight A. Kiplinger, "Montevideo and the Peter Family Cemetery," https://mcatlas.org/filetransfer/HistoricPreservation/Cemeteries/021_Peter_Family_Seneca/research/021_Montevideo_History_2018.pdf; Garrett Peck, *The Smithsonian Castle and The Seneca Quarry* (Charleston: The History Press, 2013), 39.

31. MCP to MCWC, 28 August 1848, MS-6, TP; Quertermous, *A Georgetown Life*, 27.

32. Nelly to Charles Magill Conrad, 28 August 1847, Binder 25, MVLA.

33. Frances Parke Butler to EGWB, 30 September 1847, BFP, HNOC.

34. Bauer, *Zachary Taylor*, chap. 11; Greenberg, *A Wicked War*, 230. On Taylor's lack of voting, *see Nashville Daily Union*, 24 August 1847; Donald S. Inbody, *The Soldier Vote: War, Politics, and the Ballot in America* (New York: Palgrave Macmillan, 2016), chap. 1. Thanks to Michael Cohen for raising this point.

35. David M. Potter, *The Impending Crisis, 1848–1861*, New Edition (New York: Harper Perennial, 2011), 226.

36. *Richmond Whig*, 3 November 1848; *Newark Daily Advertiser*, 9 September 1848. While former president Martin Van Buren was also running for the Free Soil Party, GWPC seems to have been focused only on Cass.

37. *Newark Daily Advertiser*, 9 September 1848; *Daily Union* (DC), 19 October 1848. For coverage *see eg Salem Register*, 21 September 1848; *Times-Picayune*, 28 September 1848; *Wabash Courier*, 7 October 1848.

38. Nelly to EBG, 17 December 1848, in Brady, 251; *Richmond Whig*, 2 February 1849.

39. Zachary Taylor to Nelly [undated; Fall 1848 to January 1849], HMC, MVLA; *Alexandria Gazette*, 8 March 1849.

40. *Richmond Whig*, 2 February 1849.

41. MARCL to James K. Polk, 16 June 1848, in Michael David Cohen, ed., *Correspondence of James K. Polk*, vol. 14, *April 1848–June 1849* (Knoxville: University of Tennessee Press, 2021); Zachary Taylor to Nelly, 12 April 1849, HMC, MVLA; Nelly to MLFC, 1 January 1850, MCLP, VMHC; Cullum, *Biographical Register of the Officers*, 2: 572.

42. Nelly to George Corbin Washington, 26 April 1849, MCHC; George Corbin Washington to H.C. Murphy, 12 February 1849, HMC, MVLA.

43. Eleanor Love Selden Washington to Mary S. Page, 7 May 1849, MVLA; Nelly to MCWC, 25 March 1849, MVLA.

44. Nelly to George Corbin Washington, 26 April 1849, MCHC.

45. Nelly to GWL, 4 March 1849, DLCCU. The autographs are in HMC, MVLA.

46. "The Virginia Washington Monument," *Southern Literary Messenger*, vol. 16.3, March 1850; "Presentation of the Travelling Writing Case of General Washington," *National Intelligencer*, 1 April 1850.

47. Bauer, *Zachary Taylor*, 250, 265, 308; Potter, *The Impending Crisis, 1848–1861*, 106–107; Shelden, *Washington Brotherhood*, 75–76. On Taylor's inability to handle this crisis, *see* Bauer, *Zachary Taylor*, 297–300.

48. Benjamin Perley Poore, *Perley's Reminiscences of Sixty Years in the National Metropolis* (Philadelphia: Hubbard Brothers, 1886), 377–378; Bauer, *Zachary Taylor*, 314–316.

49. Nelly to EBG, 27 July 1850, in Brady, 252. The scrapbook is in the Trist Wood Papers, Southern Historical Collection, University of North Carolina, Chapel Hill.

50. *Daily National Intelligencer*, 12 July 1850; Bauer, *Zachary Taylor*, 317–318.

51. Potter, *The Impending Crisis, 1848–1861*, 111–116. On Conrad's appointment, *see Biographical Dictionary of the United States Congress*.

52. *Alexandria Gazette*, 4 November 1850.

53. *Alexandria Gazette*, 25 February 1852; Lee, *Growing Up in the 1850s*, 10.

54. Casimir Bohn, *Bohn's Hand-Book of Washington: Illustrated with Engravings of the Public Buildings and the Government Statuary* (Washington, DC: C. Bohn, 1856), 125; William Morrison, *Morrison's Stranger's Guide to the City of Washington and Its Vicinity* (Washington, DC: W.M. Morrison, 1852), 120–124. Quote from Mary Eastman, "Arlington," *Lady's*

Home Magazine, March 1857, no. 9. For the *Harper's* article, *see Harper's Weekly*, September 1853.

55. *Salem Register*, 26 June 1854.

56. MCWC Diary, 11 August 1856, 24 February 1857; GWPC to Lossing, 30 December 1852, HMC, MVLA; Clark, *George Washington Parke Custis*, 154.

57. Benson Lossing, "Arlington House," *Harper's Magazine* 7.40, September 1853, 436–437; "Random Recollections of Recent Ramblings—No. XVII," *Daily Herald*, 21 December 1843; John Hill Hewitt, *Shadows on the Wall; or, Glimpses of the Past* (Baltimore: Turnbull Brothers, 1877), 91.

58. MCWC Diary, 3 June 1856.

59. *Boston Evening Transcript*, 21 September 1844. There is no record of GWPC's correspondence with Queen Victoria, but there are two GW autographs in her papers with unknown provenance. Email exchange with Julie Crocker, Senior Archivist, Royal Archives, 10 January 2022.

60. GWPC to Jared Sparks, 12 March 1857, MS Sparks 153, Jared Sparks Letterbooks, Houghton Library, Harvard University; GWPC to G.S. Lyon, 1 January 1848, AH; MCWC Diary, 1 November 1854.

61. MCWC Diary, 26 May 1854; Edmund Law Rogers to GWPC, 7 April 1854, MS-5, TP; GWPC to Edmund Law Rogers, 10 April 1855, HMC, MVLA.

62. GWPC to Gales and Seaton, 20 February 1853, in William Winston Seaton, *A Biographical Sketch* (Boston: James R. Osgood and Company, 1871), 180.

63. Benson Lossing to GWPC, 7 December 1856, MS-5, TP.

64. Nelly to EBG, 27 July and 1 December 1850, 21 January, 4 August, and 14 October 1851, in Brady, 254, 255, 256, 258, 261, 263; Nelly to Markie Williams, 18 May 1851, MS-6, TP. Nelly referred to herself as "deaf" in several letters, including that of 1 December; a brass ear trumpet believed to have been Nelly's is in the collection at Woodlawn (National Trust 61.1).

65. Nelly to MLFC, 13 January 1852, MCLP, VMHC.

66. Nelly to MLFC, 13 January 1852, MCLP, VMHC. On Kossuth and his controversial visit, *see* Timothy Mason Roberts, *Distant Revolutions: 1848 and the Challenge to American Exceptionalism* (Charlottesville: University of Virginia Press, 2009), chap. 7.

67. Jeffrey Malanson, *Addressing America*, chap. 6. For quote, *see Alexandria Gazette*, 27 February 1852.

68. Nelly to Lewis Washington, 31 December 1852, PFP, MVLA; Robert E. Lee to MLFC, 17 March 1852, Lee Family Papers, VMHC.

69. Nelly to MLFC, 18 December 1851, MCLP, VMHC.

70. Reminiscences of Eleanor Parke Custis Lewis by EBG, August 1852, HMC, MVLA.

71. Esther M. Lewis to MLFC, 15 July 1852, MCLP, VMHC. On the "Good Death" in antebellum America, *see* Drew Gilpin Faust, *This Republic of Suffering: Death and the American Civil War* (New York: Alfred A. Knopf, 2008), 6–17.

72. *Alexandria Gazette*, 22 July 1852; Clayton Torrence, ed., "Arlington and Mount Vernon 1856. As Described in a Letter of Augusta Blanche Berard," *Virginia Magazine of History & Biography* 57, no. 2 (April 1949): 156. The draft of the epitaph in GWPC's hand is in the Esther Maria Lewis Chapin Collection, MVLA.

73. Lee, *Growing Up in the 1850s*, 13; "Funeral of Mrs. G. W. P. Custis and Death of General R. E. Lee," *The Virginia Magazine of History and Biography* 35, no. 1 (1927): 23.

74. MCWC Diary, 27 October, 4 and 12 November 1853, 2 April 1854; GWPC to Anna Maria Fitzhugh, 22 February 1854, George Bolling Lee Papers, VMHC; "Washington's Birth Day," *Mercury* (New York, NY), 30 March 1854.

75. MCWC to [MARCL?], 13 June 1854, TP, MS-7; Lee, *Growing Up in the 1850s*, 41.

76. *Evening Star*, 15 July 1854; *Daily True American* (Trenton, NJ), 20 July 1854; *Manufacturers' and Farmers' Journal* (Providence, RI), 20 July 1854; *Salem Register*, 20 July 1854; *Christian Watchman* (Boston), 27 July 1854.

77. GWPC to Benson Lossing, 19 June 1854, Mss2 C9693, VMHC; GWPC to Robert Ball, 27 August 1854, AH; GWPC to Joseph Gales, 7 November 1855, Clinton H. Haskell Civil War Collection, Clements Library, University of Michigan.

78. Franklin Pierce to GWPC, 5 April 1854, MS-5, TP; MCWC Diary, 7 April 1854, 3 June, 21 October 1856; "Revolutionary Trophies," *Daily National Intelligencer*, 23 May 1854. For more, *see* Good, "Washington Family Fortune," 129–130.

79. *National Intelligencer*, 28 February and 19 May 1855, *Alexandria Gazette*, 15 May 1855, *Evening Star*, 19 December 1855, *New York Semi-Weekly Tribune*, 10 October 1856.

80. *Weekly National Intelligencer*, 20 September 1856; *Alexandria Gazette*, 23 February 1857. On the Sumner incident, *see* Joanne B. Freeman, *The Field of Blood: Violence in Congress and the Road to Civil War* (New York: Farrar, Straus and Giroux, 2018), chap. 7; Shelden, *Washington Brotherhood*, chap. 5.

81. MCWC Diary, 27 June and 2 September 1857; *Boston Evening Transcript*, 19 August 1857.

82. *Alexandria Gazette*, 28 September 1857.

83. MCWC Diary, 13 October 1857; MARCL to Benson Lossing, 25 November 1857, AH; Lee, *Growing Up in the 1850s*, 99–100.

84. "Death of Mr Custis," *National Intelligencer*, 12 October 1857; "The Late G.W.P. Custis," *Harper's Weekly*, 24 October 1857. For other printings of the obituary, *see eg Daily Union and American* (Nashville, TN), 13 October 1857; *Charleston Courier* (SC), 14 October 1857; *Evansville Journal* (IN), 17 October 1857; *Daily Crescent* (New Orleans), 19 October 1857; *St. Paul Daily Pioneer* (MN), 20 October 1857.

85. *Evening Star*, 13 October 1857; MCWC Diary, 13 October 1857.

86. Album, 1845–1857, Elizabeth Van Lew Papers, VMHC.

87. *Evening Star*, 13 October 1857.

88. "Some Facts that Should Come to Light," *New York Tribune*, 24 June 1859; "The Custis Slaves," *Douglass' Monthly*, August 1859; *see also* Epilogue.

89. Eleanor Parke Custis Lewis Will, in John Walter Wayland, *The Washingtons and Their Homes* (Staunton, VA: McClure Printing Company, 1944), 207.

90. *Weekly Patriot and Union*, 29 October 1857.

91. Jeffrey Malanson, "The Founding Fathers and the Election of 1864," *Journal of the Abraham Lincoln Association* 36, no. 2 (2015): 1–25; Matthew Mason, "'The Sacred Ashes of the First of Men': Edward Everett, the Mount Vernon Ladies' Association of the Union, and Late Antebellum Unionism," in *Remembering the Revolution: Memory, History, and Nation Making from Independence to the Civil War*, ed. Michael A. McDonnell et al. (Amherst: University of Massachusetts Press, 2013), 265–279.

Epilogue

1. *Chicago Daily News*, 23 February 1885; *Cincinnati Commercial Tribune*, 23 February 1885; *Cleveland Gazette*, 28 February 1885; *The Dedication of the Washington National Monument* (Washington, DC: US Government Printing Office, 1885).

2. *Evening Star*, 9 and 24 February 1885.

3. *Philadelphia Inquirer*, 2 July 1893. For George Washington Custis Lee's decline of the invitation, *see* Ruth Preston Rose, "The Building of the Washington National Monument," *Arlington Historical Magazine* 6 (1980): 49.

4. Jonathan Horn, *The Man Who Would Not Be Washington: Robert E. Lee's Civil War and His Decision that Changed American History* (New York: Simon and Schuster, 2015), 73–74; Micki McElya, *The Politics of Mourning: Death and Honor in Arlington National Cemetery* (Cam-

bridge: Harvard University Press, 2016), 21–22; Pryor, *Reading the Man*, 261–262, 275.

5. MARCL Diary, 1 May 1858, Lee Family Papers, VMHC; Clark, *George Washington Parke Custis*, 174–177; Horn, *The Man Who Would Not Be Washington*, 75–76; McElya, *The Politics of Mourning*, 22–24; Pryor, *Reading the Man*, 264–266. Scholars have debated the veracity of the stories of Robert E. Lee's brutality, but Elizabeth Pryor notes that the stories are entirely credible and line up with other sources; Pryor, 271–274. Lee's most recent biographer, Allen Guelzo, argues that Lee supervised a local constable in the beatings; *see* Allen C. Guelzo, *Robert E. Lee: A Life* (New York: Knopf, 2021), 157–158. For the letter, *see New York Tribune*, 24 June 1859.

6. Pryor, *Reading the Man*, 264.

7. Horn, *The Man Who Would Not Be Washington*, 182–183; Pryor, *Reading the Man*, 274. While Pryor argues the enslaved had a "double liberation," Horn writes that the Emancipation Proclamation was technically what freed them.

8. William Allan, "Memoranda of Conversations with General Robert E. Lee," in Gary Gallagher, ed., *Lee: The Soldier*, 7–24, here p. 10; Guelzo, *Robert E. Lee*, chap. 9; Elizabeth Brown Pryor, "Thou Knowest Not the Time of Thy Visitation," *The Virginia Magazine of History and Biography* 119, no. 3 (2011): 277–296.

9. Richard B. McCaslin, *Lee In the Shadow of Washington* (Baton Rouge: Louisiana State University Press, 2001), 80.

10. MARCL to Mildred Lee, 5 May 1861, Lee Family Papers, VMHC.

11. Horn, *The Man Who Would Not Be Washington*, 120–121; McCaslin, *Lee in the Shadow of Washington*, 78–85; McElya, *The Politics of Mourning*, 26–28, 37, 45; Pryor, *Reading the Man*, 302. On the popularity of the story of Selina Gray as "keeper of the keys," *see* McElya, *The Politics of Mourning*, 43–57.

12. McElya, *The Politics of Mourning*, chap. 1.

13. Horn, *The Man Who Would Not Be Washington*, 204–206, 211, 234–235; McElya, *The Politics of Mourning*, 62–63, chap. 3; Pryor, *Reading the Man*, 306–307, 310–316.

14. On Charles Magill Conrad, *see Biographical Dictionary of the U.S. Congress*. Evidence of Nelly's grandchildren's involvement in the Confederate Army is scattered. For Lawrence Lewis Conrad, *see* Jean L. Cooper, "Lawrence Lewis Conrad (3 Jul 1839–7 Aug. 1883)," *Students of the University of Virginia, 1825–1874* (blog), 19 May 2012, https://uv-astudents.wordpress.com/2012/05/18/lawrence-lewis-conrad-3-jul-1839-7-aug-1883/. For Charles Angelo Conrad, *see* F. Ray Sibley, Jr., *Confederate Artillery Organizations: An Alphabetical Listing of the Officers and Batteries of the Confederacy, 1861–1865* (El Dorado Hills, CA: Savas

Publishing, 2014), 28. For Edward Parke Custis Lewis, *see* James Grant Wilson, *The Presidents of the United States, 1789–1894* (New York: D. Appleton and Company, 1894), 35. For John Redman Coxe Lewis, *see Lexington Gazette* (VA), 14 December 1898. For Henry Llewellyn Daingerfield Lewis, *see* Merrow Egerton Sorley, *Lewis of Warner Hall: The History of a Family* (Baltimore: Genealogical Publishing Co., Inc., 1979), 225.

15. Plater, *The Butlers of Iberville Parish, Louisiana*, chap. 9.

16. Quertermous, *A Georgetown Life*, 42; Frances Scott and Anne C. Webb, *Who Is Markie?: The Life of Martha Custis Williams Carter, Cousin and Confidante of Robert E. Lee* (Westminster, MD: Heritage Books, Inc., 2007), 133, 151–154; *Harper's Weekly*, 4 July 1863.

17. Robert E. Lee to Edward Turner, 14 September 1861, Robert E. Lee Papers, UVa; Horn, *The Man Who Would Not Be Washington*, 142.

18. *See eg* Barbara J. Mitnick, "Parallel Visions: The Literary and Visual Image of George Washington," in *George Washington: American Symbol*, ed. Barbara J. Mitnick (New York: Hudson Hills Press in association with the Museums at Stony Brook and the Museum of Our National Heritage, 1999), 55–70; Anne Sarah Rubin, *A Shattered Nation: The Rise and Fall of the Confederacy, 1861–1868* (Chapel Hill: University of North Carolina Press, 2009), 19–22.

19. Guelzo, *Robert E. Lee*, chap. 18–20; Pryor, *Reading the Man*, chap. 24, 446, 464.

20. *Congressional Globe*, Forty-First Congress, Third Session, p. 79; Horn, *The Man Who Would Not Be Washington*, 245–256.

21. Margaret J. Preston, "Arlington: An Appeal of the Women of the South to the President," 30 May 1866, MCLP, VMHC. On the fight for and later curation of the Washington relics, *see* Hannah Boettcher, "Mary Custis Lee Unpacks the Washington Relics: A Revolutionary Inheritance in Museums, 1901–1918," MA Thesis. University of Delaware, 2016.

22. Quertermous, *A Georgetown Life*, 175.

23. For the quote, *see New York Tribune*, 21 May 1878; for the appropriation, *see U.S. Statutes*, vol. 20, p. 218, Sundry Civil Appropriation Act of June 20, 1878. The objects are now in the National Museum of American History; *see* Registrar's Files and Accession Files for Accession 13152; a list of objects is in accession 13152, Section 3, Exhibit B. They are further described in Theodore T. Belote, "Descriptive Catalogue of the Washington Relics in the United States National Museum," *Proceedings of the United States National Museum* 49, no. 2092 (1915): 1–24.

24. Megan Smolenyak, "The Man (or Woman) Who Would Be King," *Ancestry*, October 2008; Kurt Soller, "America's 'Lost Monarchy': The Man Who Would Be King," *Newsweek*, 7 October 2008,

http://www.newsweek.com/2008/10/07/the-man-who-would-be-king.html; https://www.porterloring.com/obituaries/Paul-Emery-Washington?obId=18154105.

25. https://societyofpresidentialdescendants.org/.

26. This paragraph is based upon conversations I have had in the past several years with multiple Black descendants of the Custises and enslaved women. I have also had the privilege of participating in a series of dialogues between institutional partners and descendants facilitated by Sustainable Equity in 2021 and 2022.

27. There is extensive scholarship on the pitfalls of defining kinship biologically; *see eg* Sarah Franklin and Susan McKinnon, eds., *Relative Values: Reconfiguring Kinship Studies* (Durham: Duke University Press, 2001); Tim Ingold, *The Perception of the Environment* (New York: Routledge, 2011); Sarah McKinnon, "From Blood to Genes?: Rethinking Consanguinity in the Context of Geneticization," in *Blood and Kinship: Matter for Metaphor from Ancient Rome to the Present*, ed. Christopher H. Johnson et al. (New York: Berghahn Books, 2013), 285–306; Francesca Morgan, *A Nation of Descendants: Politics and the Practice of Genealogy in U.S. History* (Chapel Hill: University of North Carolina Press, 2021); David Murray Schneider, *A Critique of the Study of Kinship* (Ann Arbor: University of Michigan Press, 1984); Marilyn Strathern, *After Nature: English Kinship in the Late Twentieth Century* (Cambridge, UK: Cambridge University Press, 1992); Sylvia J. Yanagisako, "Bringing It All Back Home: Kinship Theory in Anthropology," in *Kinship in Europe: Approaches to Long-Term Development (1300–1900)*, ed. David Warren Sabean, Simon Teuscher, and Jon Mathieu (Leiden and Boston: Berghahn Books, 2010).

Index

Page numbers in *italics* refer to images.